THE SCIENCE & PSYCHOLOGY
OF MUSIC PERFORMANCE

THE
SCIENCE & PSYCHOLOGY
OF
MUSIC PERFORMANCE

CREATIVE STRATEGIES FOR TEACHING AND LEARNING

Edited by
Richard Parncutt &
Gary E. McPherson

UNIVERSITY PRESS

2002

OXFORD
UNIVERSITY PRESS

Oxford New York
Auckland Bangkok Buenos Aires Cape Town Chennai
Dar es Salaam Delhi Hong Kong Istanbul Karachi Kolkata
Kuala Lumpur Madrid Melbourne Mexico City Mumbai Nairobi
São Paulo Shanghai Singapore Taipei Tokyo Toronto

and an associated company in Berlin

Published by Oxford University Press, Inc.
198 Madison Avenue, New York, New York 10016

www.oup.com

Library of Congress Cataloging-in-Publication Data
The science and psychology of music performance : creative strategies for teaching and
learning / Richard Parncutt and Gary E. McPherson, eds.
p. cm.
Includes bibliographical references and index.
ISBN 0-19-513810-4   ISBN 978-0-19-513810-8
1. Music—Performance—Psychological aspects. 2. Music—Instruction and study.
I. Parncutt, Richard, 1957– II. McPherson, Gary E.
ML3838 .S385 2002
781.4—dc21   2001036292

Acknowledgments

The first draft of each chapter was independently reviewed by four people: the two editors, another author from the book, and an anonymous external reviewer. Regarding the latter, we are grateful to: Margaret Barrett, Colin Durrant, Jane Ginsborg, Thomas W. Goolsby, Donald Hall, David Hargreaves, Daniel Kohut, Gunter Kreutz, Leopold Mathelitsch, Jeff Pressing, James Renwick, Bruno H. Repp, R. Keith Sawyer, Stanley Schleuter, Emery Schubert, and William Forde Thompson for making their expertise available to us and to the authors.

We take this opportunity to thank the various representatives of Oxford University Press with whom we came in contact during the long process from submission to publication. We especially thank our acquiring editor, Maribeth Payne, and our production editor, Ellen Guerci, for their support and guidance.

Most of all we, the editors, are grateful to the authors for their patience in the face of all those guidelines, bulletins, reviews, comments, recommendations, and deadlines that we sent around by e-mail. At times they must have seemed endless! Now that the authors can see their chapters in the context of the whole book, we hope that they agree with us that it was worth the effort.

December 2001   R. P.

G. E. McP.

Contents

Introduction

How fluently do music psychologists, music educators, and practicing musicians communicate with one another? Circumstances do not always favor an easy interaction. Each group has its own language, and the specialist ways of communicating that exist within each group may not always work across group boundaries. Moreover, cross-disciplinary interactions are not always explicitly encouraged by the institutions within which music researchers and practitioners work. These everyday limitations help to explain why music educators and practicing musicians have not benefited as much as they could from the past few decades of music psychology research and why music psychologists often neglect to cite, and so benefit from, relevant studies published in the mainstream research journals of music education.

In this book, we attempt to bridge the interdisciplinary gaps that currently separate music psychologists, music educators, and practicing musicians by developing new approaches to teaching, learning, and making music that are informed and inspired by the results of recent research in music psychology, music education, and acoustics—whether that research is published in music psychology or in music education journals. In this way, we aim to produce something fresh—a book that is without precedent in either music psychology or music education.

To help achieve this aim, each chapter is coauthored by two internationally recognized scholars: one a scientist (psychologist, acoustician, physiologist, or physician) and the other a performer or music educator. Authors who are well versed in *both* music education and music psychology are coupled with collaborators with relevant complementary expertise in the area of the chapter. These collaborations, many of which are entirely new (some coauthors have not, at the time of writing, met face to face!), have at times been inspirational and at other times frustrating. The artistic authors wondered why the scientific authors sometimes indulged in virtuosic scientific methodology and terminology with little or no meaning for practicing musicians; referred so often to the literature as to give an impression of insecurity; made simplistic generalizations in areas that obviously involved complex cognitive, artistic, and judgmental processes; or stated obvious musical facts as if they had just been discovered. For their part, the scientists wondered why the artists sometimes felt they could develop such complex, impressive-sounding arguments on the basis only of anecdote, intuition, and experience or why they were so ready to rely on their own judgment without taking into account the judgments of their peers. We as editors made similar errors and were not seldom corrected by the authors (for which we thank them).

The book addresses all educational levels, from elementary through to universities and conservatories—although some chapters, depending on their subject matter, are by necessity oriented toward a specific level. The book also strives to be international in its approach and scope by focusing on international commonalities in music education and research and avoiding extended treatment of materials or practices that are specific to a given country. The two authors of each chapter often live and work in different countries; in cases where they do not or where the chapter seemed biased toward a particular country, we had the chapter anonymously reviewed by an expert from another country.

Each chapter begins by surveying relevant psychological and scientific research that may be unfamiliar to many teachers and performers. After that, the chapter authors creatively explore the implications of this research for music performance and education. Of course, considerable caution, creativity, experience, and intuition are required when developing teaching and performance applications on the basis of scientific research results and theories. In some cases the transition is easy, while in others contextual complexities that were neglected by the scientific researchers need to be taken into account and their theories modified accordingly. Likewise, the processes and practices common to music teaching and learning are not always based on developed theoretical models that have been modified and refined as a result of systematic scientific enquiry. One of our jobs as editors was to try to resolve issues of these kinds as they came up in their own special way in each chapter.

The various chapters are organized into three main parts. The first covers the personal and environmental influences that shape the learning and performance of music during a musician's life span, the second surveys the essential subskills of musical performance, and the third looks at specific instruments, techniques, and ensembles. The first and second parts draw mainly on psychologically oriented literature; the third, due to its different subject matter, on a mixture of psychology and acoustics. The music education literature is referred to throughout the book.

The book is broad in its scope but is not intended to be comprehensive. When we first started discussions, we soon realized that it would be impossible to cover all important aspects of music performance in one volume. We especially became aware of deficiencies in various parts of the literature and of the need to focus our efforts on the performance of Western tonal "art music"—mainly because the bulk of research currently available focuses on this genre of performance and also because it currently dictates how music performance is currently taught in most formal institutions around the world. Even within these confines, we have neglected important issues such as gender (Green, 1997; Maidlow & Bruce,

1999; O'Neill, 1997), motor control and technique (Gellrich, 1998; Rosenbaum & Collyer, 1998; Schmidt & Lee, 1999), music technology (Berz & Bowman, 1994; Webster, 2002; Williams & Webster, 1999), and percussion instruments (Fletcher & Rossing, 1998); and within each chapter, the authors have had to select what they perceive to be the most important scientific and artistic material that corresponds to their topic. This book cannot even be regarded as a general exposition of *scientific* aspects of music performance—although of course many such aspects are covered. Instead, it is primarily about *applying* scientific findings. In this sense it is more exploratory than encyclopedic.

The book is intended for a range of different groups of readers. We are writing first for music educators with a specific interest or expertise in music psychology. The second target group comprises practicing musicians who are interested in the practical implications of scientific and psychological research for music performance. The third group consists of advanced undergraduate and postgraduate students of music education and music psychology—especially those whose instructors recognize the potential of music psychology to inform music education and vice versa. Fourth, we are writing for researchers in the area of music performance who consider it important for the results of their research to be practically useful for music educators and musicians. Almost every chapter poses questions, either directly or between the lines, that have not yet been adequately answered in the empirical literature and could be the topic of future research projects. In that sense, music psychologists may benefit at least as much as music educators from the book.

As in any interdisciplinary effort, problems of terminology arise (cf. Clarke, 1989). We have aimed for a linguistic style that can be understood across the various subdisciplines of music psychology, music education, and music performance and have tried to avoid terms that are not understood in all the main disciplines of each chapter. In some cases, we felt that one discipline could benefit from adopting the terminology of another or from adopting a more clearly defined terminology than that currently in general use. In any case, we have tried to be consistent. For example, we consistently use the word *note* to refer to dots on a page and *tone* to refer to the physical sound that is produced. Following standard practice in auditory psychophysics (psychoacoustics, music perception), we distinguish physical measurements of musical tones (frequency, SPL, spectrum) from corresponding perceptual attributes (pitch, loudness, or timbre). We have adopted the metric system and its standard abbreviations, including, for example, *ms* for milliseconds and *Hz* for hertz (cycles per second). When referring to octave register, we follow the American Standards Association (1960): C_4 = middle C (261 Hz), A_4 = 440 Hz, and so on. We follow U.S. usage for note values (quarter notes rather than crotchets, etc.). Interval sizes are expressed in either equally tempered semitones or cents (hundredths of a semitone).

References

American Standards Association. (1960). *USA standard acoustical terminology.* New York: American Standards Association.

Berz, W. L., & Bowman, J. (1994). *Applications of research in music technology.* Reston, VA: Music Educators National Conference.

Clarke, E. F. (1989). Mind the gap: Formal structures and psychological processes in music. *Contemporary Music Review*, *3*, 1–15.

Fletcher, N. H., & Rossing, T. D. (1998). *The physics of musical instruments* (2nd ed.) New York: Springer.

Gellrich, M. (1998). Über den Aufbau stabil-flexibler Fertigkeiten beim Instrumentalspiel. In G. Mantel (Ed.), *Ungenutzte Potentiale—Wege zu konstrukitvem Üben* (pp. 131–151). Mainz: Schott.

Green, L. (1997) *Music, gender, education.* Cambridge: Cambridge University Press.

Maidlow, S., & Bruce, R. (1999). The role of psychology research in understanding the sex/gender paradox in music–plus ça change. *Psychology of Music*, *27*, 147–158.

O'Neill, S. A. (1997). Sex and gender. In D. J. Hargreaves & A. C. North (Eds.), *The social psychology of music* (pp. 46–63). Oxford: Oxford University Press.

Rosenbaum, D. A., & Collyer, C. E. (Eds.) (1998). *Timing of behavior: Neural, computational, and psychological perspectives.* Cambridge, MA: MIT Press.

Schmidt, R. A., & Lee, T. D. (1999). *Motor control and learning: A behavioral emphasis* (3rd ed.). Champaign, IL: Human Kinetics.

Webster, P. (2002). Computer-based technology and music teaching and learning. In R. Colwell and C. Richardson (Eds.), *New handbook of research on music teaching and learning* (pp. 416–439). New York: Oxford University Press.

Williams. D., & Webster, P. (1999). *Experiencing music technology* (2nd ed.). New York: Schirmer.

PART I

THE DEVELOPING MUSICIAN

1

Musical Potential

ANTHONY E. KEMP & JANET MILLS

This chapter discusses the identification of musical potential in childhood and considers the impact of an environment that is nurturing and stimulating. It addresses the place of musical ability tests as well as personality assessment and suggests that while these are areas for the teacher's consideration, they may prove to be of minor significance in any formal selection processes. The chapter describes the manner in which parents and teachers might consider musical potential, not as something finite but as something that may gradually emerge during childhood. The question of children's potential to play various instruments is considered as well as the existence of certain stereotypes prevalent in musical circles. Suggestions are offered to parents and teachers so they may become aware of a child's potential as soon as it becomes observable and nurture it in a facilitating environment.

"This child is musical, you know." How often have we heard an adult—a proud parent, an elderly relation, a friend of the family—say something like that! What do they mean? And are they right?

The chances are that the adult is trying to say something positive about the child, something that marks him or her out as more special than other children in a manner that is wholesome or at least harmless. Being a *musical* child is, in the eyes of an interested adult, normally good. The adult thinks that something has been spotted in the child that destines him or her for greatness as some kind of musician or at least indicates that it is worth giving the child opportunities that may be denied to other children, for example, lessons on a musical instrument. In other words, the adult is suggesting that the child has what we shall describe in this book as *musical potential*: a latent, but as yet unrealized, capacity to do something musical—for example, play the flute.

But is the adult right? Is it possible to spot that one child has more potential than another to play flute or piano or trombone before either has been given a chance to try doing any of these things? The biographies of musicians sometimes give an impression that verges on that of a baby emerging from the womb with the musical skills of a very competent adult. But clearly that cannot be the case.

Research into the Identification of Musical Potential

Some children who seem much like other children nevertheless turn out to be gifted musicians. No child is a blank sheet with respect to music, but the experiences that children have of music vary widely with respect to quantity and quality. The signs of musical potential that adults think they spot are manifestations of *musical achievement*. These are the results of musical experience and learning, formal or informal, that some children have had, but others lack. And there has to be someone there to spot these signs.

A child may move in time to music, play large numbers of pieces of Bach from memory, sing along with a parent, or become engrossed when an older sibling plays the viola. However, a child cannot sing along with a parent if the parent does not sing. Neither can a child play Bach on the piano if there is no access to a piano or the child has never heard any Bach. Nor can a child be seen moving in time to music if no one has time to spot this happening. It is likely that virtually all children have the potential to do all manner of things musical that they never have the chance to do.

Musical potential is something that all children have, although arguably some may have more of it than others, and musical potential may come in different shapes and forms. Musical behavior such as joining in singing means that a child has responded favorably to an opportunity to learn in music but does not necessarily mean that a child has more potential for music than any other child. Neither does it necessarily mean that the child will show more *aptitude* if offered the chance to learn an instrument, that is, that he or she will realize the potential to develop the *ability* to play it effectively more speedily than any other child.

This chapter encourages the reader to take a broad view concerning the identification of musical potential. Howe (1990a) argued that high achievement in any field is fuelled by nonintellectual qualities. He cites Shuter-Dyson's (1985) account of how, in selecting pupils for places in a specialist music school, a headmaster placed principal emphasis on the pupil's insatiable appetite for music that was so strong that without it he or she would have felt deprived. Howe (1990b) went on to identify these personal qualities of the high achiever:

> What are these qualities? They seem to be ones that are only weakly governed by abilities as such. They appear to depend more on motivation and on temperament and personality. Gaining an all-important sense of direc-tion or purpose seems to involve the combination of particular abilities and these other attributes. (p. 68)

Despite the more psychometric focus of his work, Seashore (1938) made much the same claim. He maintained that in considering the "musical mind" we should view it as "a total personality . . . functioning in a total situation" and emphasized the possession of essential capacities in the hearing, feeling, understanding, and expressing of music that result in a "drive or urge toward music" (pp. 1–2).

Like Howe, Cattell (1971) also maintained that the close analysis of any ability is impossible without an understanding of three "modalities": *ability, personality,* and *motivation.* While he claimed that these were conceptually distinct, nevertheless they were intertwined in reality. Each of these areas will be discussed later in this chapter.

Musical Ability Tests

Some research into the musical abilities of very young children provides insights into the extent to which many people may ultimately underachieve in music. Bridger (1961) noticed that some babies less than five days old moved when the pitch of a note that had been playing for a long time was changed by only a major third. It is, of course, possible that they spotted changes of pitch even smaller than a major third—they just did not move. Chang and Trehub (1977b) found that babies aged five months noticed simple rhythmic changes, for example, ** **** instead of **** **. They also found that the babies appeared to have grasped the concept of melodic shape. When a six-note melody to which they had been listening repeatedly was transposed to another key, their heart rate remained constant: when the order of the six notes was changed, their heart rate decreased (Chang & Trehub, 1977a).

Over the last century there have been a number of attempts to find a scientific way of determining children's musical potential that saves the expense of giving them some lessons to see how they get on. In 1919 Carl Seashore published the first version of his Measures of Musical Talents. These were based on the psychometric techniques of the time and tried to establish the limits of a person's hearing, for example, the highest note that he or she could perceive or the smallest pitch interval that could be recognized. The theory behind these tests was that better hearing implied higher levels of musical talent.

The limitations of such tests were highlighted by Seashore (1938) himself in a case of a professional musician and his apparently nonmusical brother. It transpired that the brother performed significantly better than the musician on the battery of tests of musical capacity, causing Seashore to ponder whether the brother was musical or not. The fact that the brother had not shown any interest in pursuing music rather suggests that he possessed all the necessary auditory skills but that he lacked the motivation and temperament to mobilize these in any musical activity.

Nevertheless, subsequent researchers have continued to devise test batteries. Over the last 35 years Edwin Gordon (1965, 1971, 1982) has developed tests that are used mainly in the United States, and range from Audie, a game for children aged 3–4 years, through the Music Aptitude Profile, which is intended for children aged 11–18 years, to the Advanced Measures of Music Audiation, which are designed to be used as college entrance tests. Arnold Bentley developed his Measures of Musical Abilities (1966) that were issued on LP records and used for a number of years in many schools in the United Kingdom. Many teachers find it very helpful to have access to test results that they can use when deciding which children might be offered special provision, for example, instrumental lessons. However, these tests still make demands that children can meet more easily if they have had prior musical experience. In addition, Bentley's tests were too demanding of the recording technology that was available at the time. For example, in two of his questions one is intended to notice that two tones are of identical pitch, rather than going *down* or *up*. However, on listening to the recording it is clear to many teachers or pupils with a good ear that the second tone is slightly lower than the first, a fact that was subsequently verified using later computer technology (Mills, 1983). Yet children who wrote *down* instead of *same* for these questions lost two marks.

Another danger with tests of this type was that teachers sometimes used them outside the context for which they were intended. For example, the manual that accompanied Mills's *Group Tests of Musical Abilities* (1988) stated clearly that their main purpose was that of providing additional positive information relating to a child about whom a teacher knew very little. They were never to be used to say no to a child who wanted to do something musical. However, almost every question that was received about them once they were published related to their being used to do precisely that.

Biographical Data

Research that has pursued young musicians' biographical details encourages us to consider the importance of environmental factors as being far more significant than inborn talent. Bloom (1985), Sosniak (1990), and Sloboda and Howe (1991) suggest that the most important factor in developing a child's musical talent is providing a stimulating environment from infancy onward, encouraging his or her first musical responses if and when they occur. Coupled with this is the necessity for appropriate musical opportunities and support from parents and teachers who are caring and encouraging (see chapter 2).

Research that attempted to identify early manifestations of "natural" talent by interviewing the parents of talented young musicians failed to provide much in the way of specific indicators. Howe et al. (1995) questioned parents about musical behaviors in the early years of talented musicians in comparison to a less talented group and found that the only behavior that emerged was singing from an early age. These children may have been fortunate enough to grow up in an environment in which singing was tolerated or possibly encouraged. Other factors such as moving to music, showing a liking for music, being attentive to music, and requesting musical involvement did not occur at higher levels in the more talented.

Sloboda, Davidson, and Howe (1994) carried out research with a group of adult musicians who were asked about their early musical experiences. It emerged that many recalled "deeply felt and intensely positive early experiences to the 'internal' aspect of musical events, which seemed to lift them outside the normal state of awareness" (p. 353). We shall return to this again later in a discussion that concerns children's musical motivation. Here we should note that such powerful experiences will tend to occur in those homes that provide an appropriate kind of stimulating environment in the form of either recorded music or music performed live by parents and older siblings.

Personality

Enough has been said earlier to suggest that the identification of musical potential may involve a much broader profile of personal factors than merely auditory skills and musical precocity. This raises the question of whether certain personal attributes might somehow sustain musical development and motivation, and certainly personality studies of musicians tend to support this notion. However, it must not be overlooked that some aspects of personality may be the result of musical engagement. Research has not, as yet, disentangled the causal direction, but it is generally accepted that both effects may be operative (see Kemp, 1996).

Research into the personalities of talented musicians suggests that they have a distinct pattern all their own and that this pattern, if not fully in place in young musicians, is well on the way to being developed. Kemp (1996, 2000) has shown, for example, that young musicians as an overall group display significant levels of introversion that remain in place through childhood and into adulthood. However, it must be emphasized that the musician's form of introversion takes a slightly different nature from that normally found in general populations, simply because it does not involve the usual element of shyness. The most prevalent aspect of the young musician's introversion is a significant level of self-sufficiency coupled with an element of aloofness or detachment particularly located in the very talented.

One might ask what purpose these traits might have in the development of musical potential. An answer to this question relates to the demands that music increasingly makes upon the young child in terms of the amount of time spent practicing in seclusion. More extroverted children will find periods of separation from their friends more difficult to deal with and may well drop out of instrumental tuition during the early stages, preferring activities that are more social and group-oriented. Clearly, some instruments make more demands in terms of practice hours than others before an acceptable sound is produced. One might, therefore, expect an interrelationship to occur between instrument and level of introversion (see Kemp, 1996). We will return to this later in a discussion that concerns instrumental choice.

In passing, another point needs to be made that concerns the nature of introversion. The introverted child is one who tends to engage in considerable private and imaginative activity, developing an internal world of ideas and symbolic thought (Kemp, 1996). This was certainly Jung's (1923) view: introverts tend to direct their energies inward toward a more personal and subjective response to what goes on around them. This can take the form of painting, writing stories, making up rhymes, or improvising. Such a child may respond naturally to musical activity, engaging readily in all its emotional nuances. These tendencies toward creative thinking and activity blend well with another very significant aspect of the musician's personality, which involves a special form of sensitivity. The musician's sensitivity tends to incorporate a level of feeling and intuition that the musician needs in the performance of music if it is to become personal and cherished. The point must not be overlooked, however, that the more a child engages in activities of this kind, the more likely it is that levels of introversion and sensitivity will be developed. This notion is borne out by the buildup of these traits in adult musicians (Kemp, 1996).

One additional feature of the adult musician's temperament should be mentioned at this point. Although most young musicians do not display the anxiety found in music undergraduates and professionals, it has been located in the very talented who attend special music schools (Kemp, 1996). Much has been written about the performance anxiety suffered by adult musicians, and one is led to consider that this is acquired during the maturational process. Musicians find themselves increasingly investing much of themselves in their music, very often finding it difficult to separate their personal identity from that of being a successful musician. When self-esteem is so closely intertwined with the musician's persona, any kind of setback, be it a substandard performance rating, criticism, or examination failure, is perceived as a direct attack on the person him- or herself.

Identifying and Developing Musical Potential

The issues briefly discussed earlier raise several questions about the upbringing of young musicians that need considering by both parents and teachers. It has to be said at this point that there can sometimes be conflict between parents and teachers about what is in the very best interests of the child. This is especially true when parents and teachers invest too much of themselves in the vision that they have for the child's musical future.

Environment Versus Innate Talent Controversy

The point was made earlier that certain influential researchers have stressed the environmental factors that they maintain are of paramount importance in the realization of a child's musical potential. However, the question of the existence of innate talent also needs to be addressed. In reviewing the literature, during which they adopt a pro-environment position, Howe, Davidson, and Sloboda (1998) maintained that there was little evidence for the early emergence of musical talent. What evidence that existed was in the main anecdotal and retrospective and thus, in their view, inadequate. In summing up they did not claim to have full or precise answers to the question and conceded that individual differences in some special abilities might have genetic origins.

The peer commentary concluded the paper of Howe et al. demonstrated the degree of controversy that surrounds the issue, particularly on the part of those who wish to take up polarized position. In his criticism of these researchers Csikszentmihalyi (1998) maintained that it is doubtful whether talent can be explained exclusively by either position. Cattell (1973) would have supported this view from his perspective of personality development. Those personality characteristics that, it is claimed, in part influence musical development, are themselves inherited to some degree. Cattell (1973) maintained that, roughly speaking, personality development is fairly equally influenced by genetic and environmental factors. In other words, a child who is perceived as having inherited a parent's introversion may be more predisposed to be comfortable in a potentially solitary pursuit such as practicing a difficult instrument. However, the more extroverted child may find the more social setting that singing provides more suitable.

That point, having been made, does not in any way negate the onus placed on parents and teachers to provide the right kind of environment for a child's interest in music to develop. This, as suggested earlier, is dependent upon parents being vigilant in noticing the child's earliest musical responses. Engaging with these at a playful level will ensure that the child sees that he or she is valued.

The playful element, so often overlooked by parents and by many teachers of young children, was stressed in research carried out by Sosniak (1990) that describes in some detail the early stages of learning an instrument. Initially, lessons should be fun and engaged in with a teacher who is both warm and enthusiastic. The teacher should provide safe and contained environment in which musical play takes place. Sosniak (1990) describes the process in this way:

> For relatively little effort, the learner got more than might be expected. The effect of the early years of playful, almost romantic involvement . . . seemed . . . to get the learner involved, captivated, "hooked"—motivated to pursue the matter further. (p. 155)

The question that arises, of course, is whether there are a sufficient number of teachers who are prepared to teach beginners in this fashion and also whether those parents who are ambitious for their child's musical progress are prepared to pay the fees for such a permissive kind of teaching!

However, once "hooked" in the way described by Sosniak, the child will proceed naturally and gently to the next stage, in which the teaching becomes more focused and systematic. Although playfulness is not totally left behind, objectives become more narrowly defined and there is a gradual expectation that appropriate skills and knowledge will be acquired.

Developing Motivation

The process described earlier assumes that the first manifestations of a child's musical responses are internally motivated—they are, one might suggest, manifestations of the child's first musical needs. In small infants these can develop into a repertoire of enjoyable activities in which carers can engage and of which the child will learn to request more. These behavioral indications of the child's motivation toward music belong to the child and must not be commandeered by the parent. Any effort on the part of a parent to pressurize development will tend to destroy the child's sense of motivation.

In a sense, this should remain true throughout all music learning. The child's intrinsic motivation for music can so easily be swamped by a parent's and, later, a teacher's driving efforts toward the achievement of further skills and knowledge. In other words, inappropriate forms of extrinsic motivation may have the effect of reducing the child's sense of commitment and internal drive (see chapter 3).

Let us briefly return to the research of Sloboda et al. (1994) in which they suggested that many musicians have had childhood experiences at very deep levels in which the sound of an instrument or a particular piece of music exerted a powerful and lasting response. Jacqueline du Pré experienced such an event before her fifth birthday that she later recalled with clarity:

> I remember being in the kitchen at home, looking up at the old-fashioned wireless. I climbed onto the ironing board, switched it on, and heard the introduction to the instruments of the orchestra. . . . It didn't make much of an impression on me until they got to the cello, and then . . . I fell in love with it straightaway. Something within the instrument spoke to me, and it's been my friend ever since. (In Easton, 1989, p. 26)

This, albeit anecdotal, evidence, represents a not uncommon experience reported by adult musicians. Walters and Gardner (1992) have described these as *crystallizing experiences* and attempt to explain them as overt reactions to a quality or feature of an occurrence that yields an immediate change in individuals' concept formation, their performance within it, and self-concept. Such powerfully charged experiences appear to have a lasting impact upon the individual, leaving him or her in a highly motivated state that may last a lifetime. As in the case of Jacqueline du Pré, this may take the form of an insatiable attraction to an instrument's qualities. Clearly, the environment that is rich with all manner of musical experiences is more likely to stimulate such responses than one that is bereft of cultural stimuli. Once an experience of this kind has occurred, parents and teachers need to recognize, harness, and develop this form of personal commitment and take care not to swamp it with invasively close monitoring and unnecessary forms of extrinsic motivation.

Choosing an Instrument

Common sense tells us that the best way of seeing whether someone has potential to play an instrument or sing is to offer tuition and see how the young person progresses. Common sense tells us also that if he or she does not progress this may be the fault of the teacher rather than the student or, simply, the instrument is not the most suitable one. Few pupils could make a success of absolutely any instrument, and so it makes sense to give serious consideration to the question of what instrument a child might learn. Gordon (1991) claims that when his instrument Timbre Preference Test is used with children, they have a 75% better chance of continuing on the instrument of their choice. However, the basis on which children are steered toward a particular instrument is frequently far less scientific, and not informed by research.

In cases like that cited in the previous section, where the pupil arrives with a clear motivation to pursue a particular instrument or sing, little consultation may be necessary. If the drive is very strong toward a particular instrument, parents and teachers may be advised not to attempt to redirect the child toward an alternative, even in a case where the choice appears to be inappropriate. For other children certain general aspects of their personality and abilities might be kept in mind (see Kemp, 1981, 1996) but should not, in any circumstances, be allowed to dictate the choice of instrument. For example, string playing may frequently attract the quieter, more introverted and studious child, whereas brass playing may appeal to the more socially outgoing and extroverted. Singers also tend to be more extroverted, sensitive, and imaginative types. Keyboard players tend to be more extroverted but not as extroverted as the brass players and singers. Clearly, the kinds of demands that instruments make on the learner, particularly in terms of the relative ease with which reasonably pleasing sounds can be produced in the early stages, will help determine whether the beginner will persevere or, in time, discontinue instruction.

Quite apart from personality, another aspect that we might consider is a young person's physique. As long ago as 1935, Charles Lamp and Noel Keys, a teacher and a university lecturer both working in San Francisco, wrote of the selection methods of instrumental teachers as follows: "In the absence of scientifically validated conclusions, music instructors have been forced to resort to *a priori* reasoning and uncontrolled observation" (p. 587). They went on to show that some of the popular theories of the day about the physical characteristics that suited particular instruments were of very little value. These included theories that are still heard today, for example, that long, slender fingers are needed for string instruments, even teeth are required for woodwind and brass instruments, and thin lips are better suited to brass instruments with small mouthpieces and vice versa. The statistical correlations that Lamp and Keys found between the supposedly favorable characteristics and the progress that pupils made on instruments were positive but small. In other words, pupils with thin lips were slightly more likely to make a success of the French horn, but there were plenty of examples of pupils with thick lips who succeeded at the French horn and pupils with thin lips who did not. The length and slenderness of pupils' fingers predicted their success on the violin only very slightly more effectively than the evenness of their teeth!

Fifty years later, Mills (1983) obtained some very similar findings. Seventy-four instrumental teachers completed checklists of the physical characteristics of a total of 299 instrumental pupils aged 7–18, and these were compared with ratings of their instrumental performance. Again, the correlations were positive but small. There were many high-achieving pupils with supposedly undesirable physical attributes, for example, buck-teethed bassoonists, clumsy percussionists, and thin-lipped tuba players. Some of these pupils have gone on to make careers as instrumentalists.

Mills (1995) identified a physical characteristic that predicted instrumental achievement better than any other criterion. This related to the comparative length of the ring and index fingers of the left hand. She found that violinists and viola players frequently possessed left hands where the ring finger was longer than the index finger (in common with 70% of the general population). However, other instrumentalists generally possessed the less common left hand shape.

So does this mean that pupils should be screened for a digital formula and steered toward an instrument accordingly? Not at all; a few pupils with the less desirable digital formula do succeed, and others could as well. What it means is that teachers may need to be more alert to the need to adapt their teaching of technique to suit the shape of the pupils, perhaps particularly if a pupil has a different shape from his or her teacher. Wagner (1988) has devised a "biomechanical hand profile" that can help piano teachers with this, because the hand shape of an adult student may be compared with that of a professional reference group and also that of his or her teacher.

However, it is stressed here that there are many exceptions to the generalized findings described earlier that raise serious questions about their predictive power. The music profession abounds with forms of folklore that stereotype different kinds of instrumentalists, and these have found their way into general parlance. For example, research has shown that some instruments like the violin and flute are perceived as being feminine in character, while others such as the brass are gendered as masculine (see, for example, Abeles & Porter, 1978). These perceptions concerning instruments may well result in playground ridicule, leading to high dropout rates for some instruments, particularly among boys (O'Neill, 1997). However, none of the preceding issues should be adopted by parents and teachers in selecting or rejecting children for particular instruments. The only exception to this might be where a child is not strong enough to hold an instrument or where hand span will not allow a comfortable position on an instrument's keys. Clearly, the maturational process will remedy this in time.

Teaching Methods and Pupils' Individual Differences

The research carried out by Sosniak (1990) and Manturzewska (1990) clearly suggests modes of approach for young beginners, who, it has been seen, require a warm, nurturing, and playful climate in the early months. From then on, the sensitive and imaginative teacher will modify his or her teaching according to the individuality of the child. Pupils who do not receive this kind of teaching and who instead are met with formal approaches and teaching methods may not respond and may wish to discontinue lessons after a short period. These kinds of teachers may well consider the child to be unmusical and feel justified in rejecting him or her without realizing that the fault lies in the approach.

The research that suggests that young musicians tend to be introverted and sensitive should not be overlooked. "Still waters run deep" is a saying that can often be applied to the child who keeps his or her musical enthusiasms hidden. Sometimes these can be ignored by the rigid teacher as lying outside the "requirements" of tuition. For example, a child with a particular enthusiasm such as improvising, jazz playing, or scat singing may be rejected as unsuitable for tuition. In other words, the process of identifying musical talent is a much more complex task than is often realized. Talent is often left unrecognized because a teacher's perception of what constitutes talent is too narrowly or poorly defined.

Unlike classroom learning, individual tuition with a sensitive and responsive teacher—a kind of mother figure—can be a haven in which the introverted child may feel listened to and valued in a way not experienced anywhere else. The converse may also be true: the extroverted child may well respond to the kind of group teaching that prevails in the early stages, particularly in brass tuition and, of course, in choirs. Such individuals may also be encouraged to undertake some of their practice together.

Research also suggests that young musicians as an overall group tend to be dependent types, depending upon their parents and teachers in the early stages. However, this research also indicates that those individuals who make most headway and who are likely to emerge as professional musicians are very much more inclined to be independent (Kemp, 1995). There is a lesson here for parents and teachers who, while exercising an important role of encouragement in the early stages of musical development, need to be able to let go of talented pupils and allow them to assume more responsibility for personal decision-making. The biographies of many young musicians report personal problems that occurred in later adult life and were caused by parents and teachers who had overprotected them, projecting too much of their own ambitions onto young, talented musicians, in some cases living through their accomplishments in a vicarious fashion. Strong-minded children who have a clear idea about how they want to learn and what pieces they wish to play, while perhaps being less comfortable for the teacher to deal with, may well be the very ones who succeed in the long term. Roe (1967) once remarked that too much loving and too little neglect does not produce a creative child. While this may overstate the case, it might be said that a child's creativity requires a certain degree of personal space if it is to thrive.

Finally, the research referred to earlier that suggests very talented young musicians as well as more mature performers display anxiety needs to be addressed in passing. Whereas certain levels of anxiety may well be of significance for all performing artists in order to facilitate performance at optimal levels, its etiology is clearly more complex than that. Many professional musicians suffer levels of acute debilitating anxiety before and during performance, and one is forced to consider whether this is a learned response (see chapter 4). One possible explanation relates to instrumental teaching that makes undue demands upon the pupil in terms of the kind of graded performance examinations offered in many parts of the world. Parents wish to see their children making swift progress, and sometimes there can be a competitive element involved as parents draw their offspring into a grade race. Such parents will sometimes place the teacher under pressure to enter pupils for examinations prematurely, proceeding to the next immediately after the completion of the last. This clearly has a narrowing effect on the amount and variety of repertoire being learned. Perhaps more important, however, it may cause pupils to be entered for examinations before pieces have been adequately prepared or before the pupils have developed an acceptable margin of safety, thus reducing the examination to an anxiety-inducing event rather than what could be a pleasurable and aesthetic experience. Such regular encounters with performance anxiety may result in what was initially a temporary form of anxiety (*state anxiety*) taking on the more permanent manifestation of anxiety (*trait anxiety*) of the kind found in more mature musicians.

Conclusion

Based on a broad range of literature, this chapter has argued that the identification of musical potential in young children needs to occur in the child's natural surroundings as an ongoing process. It has been suggested that identifying musical potential should not be a unique occurrence in which ready-made musical aptitude tests are applied. Such a practice will sometimes overlook other important factors. This chapter has suggested that musical potential is a much more complex phenomenon that involves a number of factors besides abilities. While aural capacities are no doubt of some significance in musicianship, they are not of themselves a reliable indicator of musical potential.

This chapter has emphasized additional factors that may assist parents and teachers in developing a more comprehensive view of what constitutes musical potential. Among these a child's natural inner motivation is clearly of paramount importance. After all, there is little musical future for a child who possesses all the necessary aural skills yet lacks the personal interest in harnessing them in musical activity. A similar point can be made concerning personality. Certain personality traits appear to support musical involvement and, it is claimed, without these musical progress, particularly for some instruments, may be more problematic, although not impossible.

Motivation and personality are phenomena that are best assessed over time, and it is therefore emphasized here that the identification of potential is an ongoing process that will occur in the home from birth onward and during the early years of any more formal tuition. Because musical potential takes many forms and will occur at different levels, each individual child requires individual consideration. For this reason, a parent or teacher may occasionally find it helpful to use a published test to identify a child's relative strengths or weaknesses in some aspect of musicianship. However, it is the quality of the nurturing environment that is critical, and the onus for this is placed firmly on parents and teachers, by not pushing this process but allowing the child to manifest the form and direction that development might take. It is these people who need to provide not only a musically stimulating environment but also one in which the child's enthusiasms are noticed, listened to, and responded to with sensitivity and imagination.

References

Abeles, H. F., & Porter, S. Y. (1978). The sex-stereotyping of musical instruments. *Journal of Research in Music Education, 26*(2), 65–75.

Bentley, A. (1966). *Measures of musical abilities.* London: Harrap.

Bloom, B. S. (Ed.) (1985). *Developing talent in young people.* New York: Ballantine.

Bridger, W. H. (1961). Sensory habituation and discrimination in the human neonate. *American Journal of Psychiatry, 117,* 991–996.

Cattell, R. B. (1971). *Abilities: Their structure, growth, and action.* Boston: Houghton Mifflin.

Cattell, R. B. (1973). *Personality and mood by questionnaire: A handbook of interpretive theory, psychometrics, and practical procedures.* San Francisco, CA: Jossey-Bass.

Chang, H. W., & Trehub, S. E. (1977a). Auditory processing of relational information by young infants. *Journal of Experimental Child Psychology, 24,* 324–331.

Chang, H. W., & Trehub, S. E. (1977b). Infants' perception of temporal grouping in auditory patterns. *Child Development, 48,* 1666–1670.

Csikszentmihalyi, M (1998). Fruitless polarities. *Behavioral and Brain Sciences, 21,* 411.

Easton, C. (1989). *Jacqueline du Pré: A biography.* London: Hodder & Stoughton.

Gordon. E. (1965). *Music aptitude profile.* Boston: Houghton Mifflin.

Gordon. E. (1971). *Iowa tests of music literacy.* Iowa City: Bureau of Educational Research and Service, University of Iowa.

Gordon. E. (1982). *Intermediate measures of music audiation.* Chicago: GIA.

Gordon. E. (1991). A study of the characteristics of the Instrument Timbre Preference Test. *Bulletin of the Council for Research in Music Education, 110,* 33–51.

Howe, M. J. A. (1990a). *The origins of exceptional abilities.* Oxford: Blackwell.

Howe, M. J. A. (1990b). *Sense and nonsense about hothouse children: A practical guide for parents and teachers.* Leicester: British Psychological Society.

Howe, M. J. A., Davidson, J. W., Moore, D. M., & Sloboda, J. A. (1995). Are there early childhood signs of musical ability? *Psychology of Music, 23*(2), 162–176.

Howe, M. J. A., Davidson, J. W., & Sloboda, J. A. (1998). Innate talents: Reality or myth? *Behavioral and Brain Sciences, 21,* 399–407.

Jung, C. G. (1923). *Psychological types* (H. G. Baynes, Trans.). London: Routledge & Kegan Paul.

Kemp, A. E. (1981). Personality differences between players of string, woodwind, brass and keyboard instruments, and singers. *Council for Research in Music Education Bulletin, 66–67,* 33–38.

Kemp, A. E. (1995). Aspects of upbringing as revealed in the personalities of musicians, *Quarterly Journal of Music Teaching and Learning, 5*(4), 34–41.

Kemp, A. E. (1996). *The musical temperament: Psychology and personality of musicians.* Oxford: Oxford University Press.

Kemp, A. E. (2000). The education of the professional musician: Its psychological demands and outcomes. *Musical Performance, 2*(3), 93–110.

Lamp, C. J., & Keys. N. (1935). Can aptitude for specific instruments be predicted? *American Journal of Educational Psychology, 26,* 587–596.

Manturzewska, M. (1990). A biographical study of the life-span development of professional musicians. *Psychology of Music, 18*(2), 112–139.

Mills. J. (1983). *Identifying potential orchestral musicians.* Unpublished doctoral thesis, University of Oxford.

Mills. J. (1988). *Group tests of musical abilities.* Slough: NFER-Nelson.

Mills. J. (1995). *Music in the primary school.* Cambridge: Cambridge University Press.

O'Neill, S. A. (1997). Sex and gender. In D. J. Hargreaves and A. C. North (Eds.), *The social psychology of music* (pp. 46–63). Oxford: Oxford University Press.

Roe, A. (1967). *Parent–child relations and creativity*. Paper prepared for conference on child-rearing practices for developing creativity. Macalester College: St. Paul, MN, November 2–4.

Seashore, C. E. (1919). *Manual of instructions and interpretations of measures of musical talent*. Chicago: Stoelting.

Seashore, C. E. (1938). *The psychology of music*. New York: McGraw-Hill.

Shuter-Dyson, R. (1985). Musical giftedness. In J. Freeman (Ed.), *The psychology of gifted children* (pp. 159–83). Chichester, UK: Wiley.

Sloboda, J. A., Davidson, J. W., & Howe, M. J. A. (1994). Is everyone musical? *Psychologist*, *7*(8), 349–355.

Sloboda, J. A., & Howe, M. J. A. (1991). Biographical precursors of musical excellence: An interview study. *Psychology of Music*, *19*(1), 3–21.

Sosniak, L. A. (1990). The tortoise, the hare, and the development of talent. In M. J. A. Howe (Ed.), *Encouraging the development of exceptional skills and talents* (pp. 149–64). Leicester: British Psychological Society.

Wagner. C. (1988). The pianist's hand: Anthropometry and biomechanics. *Ergonomics*, *31*, 97–132.

Walters, J., & Gardner, H. (1992). The crystallizing experience: Discovering an intellectual gift. In R. S. Albert (Ed.), *Genius and eminence* (2nd ed.) (pp. 135–155). Oxford: Pergamon.

2

Environmental Influences

HEINER GEMBRIS & JANE W. DAVIDSON

Environmental and genetic factors affect individual development from fetus to adult, both generally and in the case of music. We consider the difference between shared and nonshared environmental influences, and different types of interaction between the individual and environment. Parents, teachers, and peers strongly influence this development. Early nonverbal interactions between child and mother or caretaker, and parental support for music activities in childhood, seem to be of particular importance. These and other influences (e.g., exposure to music through the media) occur in the more general framework of the societal, historical, and generational context. Environmental conditions for musical development may be optimized by paying more attention to shared music experiences between child and parents (e.g., parent-baby singing), and exposing the child to a wide variety of music.

The origin of human abilities has been discussed since antiquity, and the possession and development of musical skills in Western culture has intrigued educationalists and psychologists for well over a century. Theories and beliefs about the relative influence of nature and nurture have dominated the discussion. When we assess the literature on the topic, it appears that dominant cultural ideologies have had a strong influence on the development and persistence of ideas about musical ability. For instance, it appears that the notion of genius that emerged in the eighteenth and nineteenth centuries is responsible for the fact that up to the present day in public opinion musical ability is often still considered to be a special gift that is relatively independent from environmental influences and learning processes. Biological evidence indicates that genetic factors influence general development in three broad ways: maturational staged development, physical capacity, and mental capacity (Bee, 1992; Plomin & DeFries, 1999). Clear examples of each can be found in musical contexts. For example, there is a gradual development of hand and eye dexterity as a child grows, so an eight-year-old child is better able to coordinate bow and string in violin playing than a three-year-old. People with wide hand spans have a physical advantage to develop as pianists over those with small hand spans. Generally, some people can perform mental tasks such as problem solving more readily than others. They may be able, therefore, to identify musical patterns quickly and thus carry out aural discrimination tasks more rapidly.

Thus an innate component is clearly featured in musical ability. Most researchers (e.g., Gordon, 1986) agree that the development of musical abilities is based on the interaction between innate capacities and environment. Depending on environmental conditions, the relative importance of innate differences changes. It would seem that in domains where culture exerts a relatively homogeneous influence on development innate differences would be especially visible. If someone grows up in a society that attempts successfully to develop musical abilities of all its members comprehensively and effectively with the same type of training, emerging individual differences in musical abilities should be attributed to innate factors. Conversely, in nonhomogeneous surroundings (e.g., with greatly varying musical training) the relative importance of the environment for causing individual differences in musical abilities increases, and the relative contribution of innate predispositions declines (e.g., Bouchard et al., 1990).

The current chapter will focus upon environmental influences, since these are the ones that we understand more fully at the present time. In addition, as Davies (1994) has argued, in light of the psychological evidence to date, there is an accompanying moral incentive to try to optimize the environmental circumstances that may aid maturity, development, and learning processes in as many people as possible, and this is something important for teachers to explore.

Nature and Nurture

Definitions

The broadest range of environmental factors that influence musical development are the sum of all external conditions that bear on musical experiences and activities. These include: (1) sociocultural systems such as the music culture and technological culture, (2) institutions such as the home and school, and (3) groups such as classes and peers. In a more narrow sense, and borrowing from the psychology of personality (cf. Asendorpf, 1999, p. 249), the (musically) relevant environment can be construed as all the regularly recurring situations that impact on musical experience and activities. Those regularly recurring situations, to which the individual is exposed, constitute the current environmental conditions of the individual. Important characteristics of a person's environment are the frequency and duration with which the person is exposed to a particular situation (*situational exposition*), for example, the frequency and duration with which he or she listens to music, watches video clips, or sings in a choir. The environment and its characteristics provide the framework in which musical socialization takes place. No unified definition exists for the term *socialization* in social psychology or in sociology. However, in this context we assume that musical socialization is the learning process through which the individual grows into a musical culture, developing and adjusting his or her musical abilities, activities, ways of experiencing, and values in interrelation with the social, cultural, and material environment (cf. Gembris, 1998, p. 190).

Shared and Nonshared Environmental Influences

Based on twin studies and adoption studies, population genetics has demonstrated that environmental influences contribute primarily to the *dissimilarity* of children growing up in the same family, while genetic influences contribute to the similarity (cf. Plomin et al., 1997). The influence of environmental influences consists of two different parts. On the one hand, there are such environmental influences as social strata, education, and parents' musical interests, which are shared by all siblings of the same family (shared environmental influences). On the other hand, there are environmental influences that are not the same for all children of one family, for example, the position of siblings in the family, the varying behavior of parents and teachers to the siblings, different friendship groups, and divergent musical experiences (nonshared environmental influences). So we can say that the environmental influences on siblings do vary not only between different families but also within the same family. There is clear evidence that, with the exception of the IQ in childhood, the nonshared environmental influences are more important for the development of personality characteristics (IQ, extroversion, neuroticism, etc.) than the shared environmental influences (see Reiss et al., 1994; Plomin et al., 1997).

It seems possible that these findings also apply to musical development. Casual observations show that the musical development of siblings may take distinctly different ways despite the children's being exposed seemingly to the same family situations. Take, for instance, the fact that the siblings of the famous cellist Jacqueline du Pré grew up in the same home and also received musical training, but in contrast to their renowned sister they did not attain international careers. Such differences need not necessarily be attributed to the effects of a different genome but may also be explained by the effects of the nonshared environment. The differentiation of shared and nonshared environmental influences is a new and promising way to explain differences in musical interests, motivation, and development.

Interaction of Environment and Individual

The impact of the environment on the individual and his or her development is by no means unidirectional in the sense that the individual passively endures the influence of the environment. Instead, the individual interacts with his or her surroundings in three different ways (Plomin, DeFries & Loehlin, 1977). There is first a so-called passive covariation between an individual's genetic material and environment via the shared genes of parents and children, because parents and other relatives create a certain way of life and family environment (including professional status and education, interests, musical activities), which in turn provides influential circumstances for the child (e.g., presence of musical instruments and parental music listening and performance). The interaction of this environmental configuration with the child's innate potential causes musical children to grow up in a stimulating atmosphere simply due to their parents' own musical potential. A second, so-called reactive or evocative nature–nurture covariation arises from the correspondence between the social environment and the genetically influenced personality or temperament and needs of the child. A child who is eager to learn will thus evoke more learning opportunities from his or her environment than a less eager one, and a musically interested child will provoke more musical offers than a musically less interested one. For instance, if parents realize that their child is interested in music, they may buy instruments for the child or provide opportunities to hear music. The third, so-called active nature–nurture covariation exists if the child actively selects offers from his or her environment or tries to shape the environment consistent to his or her genome (e.g., the child may ask for music lessons or choose for friends peers who are also interested in music).

The relative importance of those three genotype-environments does not remain the same throughout life but modulates. The passive nature–nurture relationship is relatively most important during childhood, and then the importance of this type of nature–nurture relationship diminishes. At the same time, the evocative and active nature–nurture relationship increases with chronological age, because children and adults evocatively and actively take charge in shaping their surroundings (cf. Plomin et al., 1997).

Home Environment and the Family

Beginnings of Environmental Influences

The environment starts to influence the individual before birth. Recent studies demonstrate that the conditions under which the fetus develops in the womb can already affect a fetal programming that may have lasting impact on the health and susceptibility to illnesses of the adult individual. A major factor in this is the stress hormones, growth hormones, and nutrients that are absorbed by the child through the placenta (Seckl, 1998). Infants are able to hear music and speech several weeks prior to their birth and can recognize these after birth (e.g., Satt, 1984; DeCaspar & Spence, 1991; Hepper, 1991; Lecanuet, 1996). Trevarthen (1999–2000) has argued that the fetal experience is musical in the sense that the fetus feels the rhythms of the mother's body and hears the inflections—the melodic contours—of external noises, including speech and music. At the present time, it is somewhat difficult to assess the importance of this kind of musical stimulation on later development. The commercial music market offers pregnant women a variety of special music programs that are supposed to have a positive effect on the state of health of the mother and unborn child. However, there is a lack of decisive evidence about these programs' influence on the fetus.

In early infancy, parents and the family provide the most important influences for the musical development. During the infant phase, the nonverbal communication (mother–infant cooing or *motherese*) between child and mother or caretaker is crucial for communication. The expressive communicative content of the parent–child interaction (e.g., emotions, needs, mental states) is mediated primarily by musical parameters such as pitch, melody, rhythm, tempo, and dynamics (Noy, 1968; Papoušek, 1996). This "communicative musicality" (Malloch, 1999–2000, p. 31) enables the attunement and sharing of mental states, emotions, and meanings. By use of preverbal, quasi-musical interaction between parents and child in the course of child care, musical competencies are almost incidentally developed, and as a result and without being aware of it parents provide their infants with a type of elementary music education that stops with the acquisition of language (Papoušek & Papoušek, 1995). This kind of musical communication is presumably the most important environmental influence on musical development in early childhood (see Noy, 1968).

Family and Musical Development

Although there is clear evidence from everyday experience and from empirical data that the family environment exerts an important influence on musical development, there is a lack of comprehensive theories that connect the results of the existing studies. Badur (1999) examined the results of studies that dealt with the relationship between the family environment on the one hand and music abilities, skills, attitudes, and preferences, as well as musical careers and excellence, on the other. The result of the analysis shows that music-related activities of the family support the musical development of children in many ways. Such activities are primarily singing and making music together. Additional activities such as attending concerts with the family, talking about music, and practicing in the presence of parents may also be useful. Other characteristics of the family such as the music abilities and attitudes of the parents or other family members or the presence of musical instruments only seem of importance if they lead to musical activities in which the child is involved.

In an extensive biographical study on the careers of outstanding Polish musicians, Manturzewska (1995) also examined the characteristics of the family backgrounds. She concluded that the family background constitutes the most influential factor for a musical career in the realm of classical music. Among the characteristics of the outstanding musician's home environment (apart from the aforementioned features) Manturzewska (1995, p. 15) mentions:

- Child-centered attitude of the parents with emphasis on the musical education of the child
- Deliberate organization and channeling of child's interests, time, and activities
- At least one person in the family believing in the potential of the future musician and encouraging the child

- Music being a genuine value in family life
- Emphasis not being placed on a musical career but on enjoying making music
- Praise and rewards even for small successes
- A positive emotional atmosphere for musical activity
- Careful selection of teachers and monitoring of musical development
- Conscious and active organization of a supportive and understanding network for the child, including personal contacts to professional musicians and music teachers
- Willingness to invest considerable time and effort in musical activities

Similar findings have emerged from the studies of other authors (e.g., Bastian, 1989; Sloane, 1985; Sosniak, 1985). Since the parental behavior serves as a model for children, parental musical involvement (instrumental or vocal) may be motivating for children.

The importance of parental support is also evident in the study by Davidson, Sloboda, and Howe (1995/1996; see also Sloboda & Davidson, 1996; Zdzinski, 1996). The authors interviewed 257 children between the ages of 8 and 18 who had instrumental lessons and performed to varying levels of achievement with regard to the role that parents and teachers played. However, the findings indicated that children in the highest achieving group were supported the most and most consistently by their parents, up to the age of 11. Thereafter the parents' support diminished while the children were increasingly driven by intrinsic motives to practice regularly by themselves. Conversely, for the children in the groups with lower levels of achievement and the dropouts, parental support was initially weak and set in forcefully during the teenage years in order to motivate the children. The authors interpreted this result as the parents' last (and often unsuccessful) attempt to keep their children playing. Note that the active parents were not necessarily professional musicians but rather interested amateurs and music buffs. The least musically interested were the parents of those children who had stopped playing and taking lessons. In sum, the results underscore the decisive importance of early and continuous parental support. According to the authors, high levels of musical achievement are most likely unattainable without such supportive parental involvement.

Although the influence of family environment may be crucial, there are examples of successful musicians, such as the jazz trumpeter Louis Armstrong, who received very little parental care and almost no formal education. However, a detailed reading of Armstrong's biography (see Collier, 1983) shows five critically important factors in his musical development:

1. Early frequent and casual exposure to musical stimuli
2. Opportunities over an extended period of time to explore the jazz musical medium
3. Early opportunities in music to experience intense positive emotional or aesthetic states
4. An opportunity to amass large numbers of hours of practice
5. A number of externally motivating factors such as role model performers whom Armstrong used to watch to gain "informal tuition"

These environmental factors have been fairly systematically studied by music psychologists and have now been identified as the key factors in musical development (see Sloboda & Davidson, 1996). This example suggests that a successful career in music without noteworthy support of the family background is possible but exceptional.

The Role of the Teacher

Teachers are perhaps the most important early influence besides the parents, not only because teachers transmit musical abilities but also because they more or less influence musical tastes and values and are role models and hold a key position with regard to motivation—for good or for bad. Results of a study by Davidson et al. (1998) suggest that the first teacher is of special and critical benefit. Professional qualifications, along with personality characteristics and interpersonal skills, come into play (e.g., Davidson, Howe & Sloboda, 1997; Olsson, 1997). In the study by Davidson et al. (1995/1996), the first teacher was perceived very differently by the young learners they interviewed. The students with the highest achievements found their teachers to be entertaining, friendly, and proficient musicians, whereas the lowest-achieving students remembered their teachers as unfriendly and incompetent. With increasing age this combination of teacher characteristics did not change for the lowest group, but the higher-achieving students started to distinguish between their teachers' personality (e.g., friendly, encouraging) and the professional qualities. As the good and best students become older and more self-motivated, it is the professional quality that becomes most relevant. Children who had dropped out of their lessons did not make this distinction. When the teacher was personally pleasant, he or she was also perceived as professionally satisfactory. We can see here how crucial the personal aspects are in addition to the professional ones; especially at young ages, they may motivate students to play. This highlights the importance of the emotional climate that surrounds musical experiences. Children who develop outstanding instrumental achievements tend to have learned in a positive emotional atmosphere that was enjoyable and free of anxiety. The learning context of children who drop out tends to be negative and characterized by anxiety. Other influences of socialization in terms of personality are discussed by Kemp and Mills in chapter 1 and O'Neill and McPherson in chapter 3.

Societal Influences

Historical and Generational Influences

The general (including musical) education system of a country and its cultural institutions and traditions are essential determinants of the musical development of its people. A comprehensive overview and description of these factors in different countries is provided by Hargreaves and North (2001). The importance of the sociocultural framework as an environmental factor that influences musical development becomes more evident if we look at these factors from a historic point of view. In a transhistorical time-series analysis that covers several centuries, Simonton (1975, 1977) found that political circumstances such as political instability affected the creative development of composers.

In a biographical study, Gembris (1997) explored the influence of time- and generation-specific factors in musical biographies. The interviewees were professional musicians, music teachers, music amateurs, and nonmusicians born between 1903 and 1975 who lived in (the former West) Germany. The analysis of biographies showed that the development of musical experiences, attitudes, preferences, careers, and so forth, was more or less influenced by time- and generation-specific factors such as World War I, National Socialism, World War II, the spreading of rock-and-roll and pop music, and the spreading of portable radios and cassettes players and videos.

For example, during the period of the Nazi government, between 1933 and 1945, in Germany, Jewish musicians were persecuted. They could not practice their trade, and their lives and careers changed dramatically. The political system controlled and restricted the musical experiences and activities of virtually all people living at that time. Similarly, in the former socialist Eastern Bloc countries the freedom to produce music and to develop musical activities was constrained and regulated by the state. People who were considered politically unreliable due to their beliefs were excluded from music academies and universities. A quite different kind of generation-specific influence in the Western nations has led to considerable differences in the musical experiences, attitudes, and preferences between those generations who grew up with rock and pop music and those who grew up in the decades before the emergence of rock and pop music in the 1950s–1960s. Today we cannot predict the effect of the spreading of music videos, portable music players, computer technology, and the constant background of music in everyday life on the musical development of young people.

Mass Media and Peer-Group Influences

According to a representative study (*KidsVerbraucherAnalyse 99*, 1999), 93% of 6- to-9-year-old children hear music in their leisure time and this proportion grows to 98% among 10- to-13-year-olds. Brown, Campbell, and Fischer (1986) estimated that 12- to-14-year-old American adolescents listen to music more than seven hours a day on average. If the trend for the continuous spreading of media such as music videos, CDs, MiniDiscs, MP3-players, and so on, continues, young people will be exposed to more and more music. It is certain that young people hear much more music outside their music lessons than in them. This, together with other factors (e.g., the strongly emotional nature of music listening, influences of the peer group on music preferences), makes it probable that the development of listening behaviors and preferences will be far more influenced by such environmental factors outside the school than by music lessons. But because of methodological issues, it is very difficult to assess these environmental factors with any accuracy and to calculate the extent of their possible effects. For instance, the validity of assessment may be problematic and depends on the precise definition of the meaning of *music listening*. Concerning music listening, Lull (1987) differentiates among *exposure* (simply being exposed to music), *consumption* (what is learned and remembered because of the contact with music), and *use* of music (conscious listening to and use of music). Most investigations do not take these differences into consideration. Furthermore, there are extreme interindividual differences as well as large variations in the amount of time children watch and listen to music (Huston & Wright, 1998). Musical development and musical biographies cannot be explained without consideration of these kinds of influences. Unfortunately, there is far too little research on these important topics.

Educational Implications

From the literature discussed earlier, it is obvious that environmental factors take effect from very early in the developmental process. Certainly in the United States and increasingly throughout the Western world, efforts are being made to capitalize on opportunities that environmental stimulation might provide for individual development and advancement in a number of domains. There are clear advantages of such concern, for as Radford (1991) points out, children placed in highly enriching environments will progress faster than the traditionally understood stages of cognitive development like those proposed by Piaget. This suggests that children can only move to higher levels of conceptual assimilation after having worked with specific experiences allied to their maturational state (see Gardner, 1982, for a useful discussion of Piagetian approaches to understanding mental development).

However, in agreement with Radford (1991), we are cautious about recent ideas that might be interpreted as attempts to create exceptional musical achievers. It is possible to suggest ideal social and emotional environmental circumstances that have emerged from the research literature, but we are reluctant to say that these will have broad-ranging consequences. In fact, it is fairly well established (see Sloboda, Davidson & Howe, 1994, for a detailed discussion of these issues) that *hothouse environments* give young music learners no significant advantage over their peers when they reach adulthood. Indeed, Burland and Davidson (submitted) worked with the young adults who presented themselves as outstanding young musicians in the original study of young musicians in specialist musical education (see Howe et al., 1995; Davidson et al., 1996). These students were initially interviewed in 1991; now, one decade later, many of them are teachers, lawyers, and administrators, as well as outstanding musicians. So early indications of advancement and success do not necessarily mean there will be adulthood advantages.

The results of available studies suggest that the following environmental factors influence musical development.

Fetus. The research of Hepper (1991) suggests it could be worth playing music to the fetus during pregnancy. A range of CDs are now available for pregnant women—some to assist the mother to relax and some to relax and stimulate the fetus. But any other music may be suitable if the mother likes it.

Infant and Toddler.   Surely one of the most important things is the intensive non-verbal, quasi-musical communication between the mother or other caretakers and the child. This communication, together with holding, rocking, and singing to the child, connects the loving care of the parents to the experience and the active use of musical parameters and their meaning. Because many parents have forgotten how to sing, some music schools and music teachers offer special parent–baby singing courses in which parents can learn how to sing with their child. This is a relatively new but very important approach of music education for several reasons: First, the emotional communication between parents and child is supported. Second, skills in the use of musical elements and song singing are improved. Third, this may be an opportunity for the parents to become interested in their own musical activity and development, which in turn may produce a greater attention to the musical development of their child.

Any kind of music exposure and musical enrichment of the environment can be for the good of the child. Gordon (1990) suggests playing a great variety of music (e.g., different styles, instrumentation, etc.) to provide as rich sources of musical stimulation as possible. Early exposure to music helps the child to naturally assimilate the rules of the prevailing harmonic and tonal language.

For instrumental learning, the Suzuki approach (see Suzuki, 1969, 1981; chapter 7 in this volume) and the Pace Method (see Pace, 1999) are excellent ways to promote very early engagement and to encourage practice and creativity—but it seems important to begin before the age of 5 years. These programs provide the children with the key adult support necessary to engage and sustain their interest in music. In both cases, teachers take on roles of a parental nature, gently coaxing the child, but within a structured framework.

Parents.   In the aforementioned programs parents are encouraged to attend lessons and learn themselves or, alternatively, to take note of what has been done and what should be done in home practice. This teacher–parent interaction was found to be of critical importance in all the studies undertaken by Davidson, Sloboda, Howe and Moore throughout the 1990s. The parent should be prepared to sit with his or her child in the early stages of practice and attend lessons to find out what needs to be done at home. Then, as the child's skills begin to develop, a more autonomous practicing strategy can be promoted, but regular encouragement of and listening to practice activities can help enormously.

Teacher.   From what is known of teachers and their strategies, it seems that a warm and friendly first teacher is essential. Then as the child advances a more demanding taskmaster can be sought. Here it seems that parents should take note of how their children feel about their music teachers. The one-to-one traditional learning situation can be highly rewarding, but it can also be very intimidating, so the child needs to feel safe with the teacher.

Diversity.   It seems that teachers, parents, and others engaged in promoting musical activities for young people should be prepared to provide opportunities for experimentation, a broad range of creating and participating experiences. Here the critical task seems to be to ask questions in order to stimulate the imagination and general motivation of the child as well as to provide technical expertise and ideas about expression and musicality (Hallam, 1998). Of course, children will often perform to a standard of behavior expected of them (Rosenthal & Jacobsen, 1968; Blatchford et al., 1989). It is for this reason that in very large classroom contexts children often underachieve, as the pace is set for the average child in the group, not the individual.

Challenge.   It is important for the child to always be sufficiently challenged and stretched without being overwhelmed or threatened. Because of the individuality of every child it is not possible to give general statements that concern the optimal challenge; finding this out is one of the most subtle tasks of the teacher.

All of the preceding assumes the availability of sufficient time and money to develop these skills. Unfortunately, in Western culture music is an expensive pursuit, and we are aware that much of what we have said points toward the middle and upper classes. Consider again the case of Louis Armstrong, who developed into one of the world's leading jazz trumpeters without money or formal lessons or, for that matter, a supportive mother. But his environmental conditions did conspire to provide him with many of the necessary ingredients that the middle-class Western child who is learning classical music requires in order to develop musically.

By following the preceding points, parents and teachers can create a positive and stimulating environment that systematically nurtures musical skill acquisition. However, the research domain itself is far from complete, with many questions left unanswered. The following need more research:

- Nonshared environmental influences
- Musical development outside the arena of so-called classical music—
  for example, the careers of rock, pop, and folk musicians
- The real impact of leisure time factors such as youth and fan cultures
  and the media on musical development

Finally, methodologies could still be explored, improved, and developed. For practical reasons, we cannot trace all aspects of the musical involvement and development of every individual in an experimental sample. However, the methodological problem of measuring the influence of the environment on musical development needs to be tackled if we are to understand more fully the implications of environmental influences on how people develop musical skills.

References

Asendorpf, J. B. (1999). *Psychologie der Persönlichkeit* (2nd ed.). Berlin: Springer.
Badur, I.-M. (1999). Musikalische Sozialisation in der Familie. Ein Forschungsüberblick. In C. Bullerjahn, H. J. Erwe, and R. Weber (Eds.), *Kinder–Kultur.*

Ästhetische Erfahrungen–Ästhetische Bedürfnisse (pp. 131–158). Opladen: Leske + Budrich.

Bastian, H. G. (1989). *Leben für Musik: Eine Biographie-Studie über musikalische (Hoch-)Begabungen.* Mainz: Schott.

Bee, H. (1992). *The developing child* (6th ed.). New York: Harper Collins.

Blatchford, P., Burke, J., Farquhar, C., Plewis, I., & Tizard, B. (1989). Teacher expectations in infant school: Associations with attainment and progress, curriculum coverage and classroom interaction. *British Journal of Educational Psychology, 59*(1), 19–30.

Bouchard, T. J., Lykken, D. T., McGue, M., Segal, N., & Tellegen, A. (1990, October). Sources of human psychological differences: The Minnesota study of twins reared apart. *Science, 250,* 223–228.

Brown, E. F., Campbell, K., & Fischer, L. (1986). American adolescents and music videos: Why do they watch? *Gazette, 37,* 19–32.

Burland, K., & Davidson, J. W. (submitted). Training the talented.

Collier, J. L. (1983). *Louis Armstrong: An American genius.* New York: Oxford University Press.

Davidson, J. W., Howe, M. J. A., Moore, D. M., & Sloboda, J. A. (1996). The role of parental influences in the development of musical ability. *British Journal of Developmental Psychology, 14*(4), 399–412.

Davidson, J. W., Howe, M. J. A., Moore, D. M., & Sloboda, J. A. (1998). The role of teachers in the development of musical ability. *Journal of Research in Music Education, 46*(1), 141–160.

Davidson, J. W., Howe, M. J. A., & Sloboda, J. A. (1997). Environmental factors in the development of musical performance skill over the life span. In D. J. Hargreaves and A. C. North (Eds.), *The social psychology of music* (pp. 188–206). Oxford: Oxford University Press.

Davidson, J. W., Sloboda, J. A., & Howe, M. J. A. (1995/1996, Winter). The role of parents and teachers in the success and failure of instrumental learners. *Bulletin of the Council for Research in Music Education, 127,* Special Issue: The 15th ISME International Research Seminar, 40–44.

Davies, J. B. (1994). Seeds of a false consciousness. *Psychologist, 7*(7), 355–357.

DeCasper, A. J., & Spence, M. J. (1991). Auditorily mediated behaviour during the perinatal period: A cognitive view. In M. J. S. Weiss and P. R. Zelazo (Eds.), *Newborn attention: Biological constraints and the influence of experience* (pp. 142–176). Norwood, NJ: Ablex.

Gardner, H. (1982), *Human development* (2nd ed.). Boston: Little, Brown.

Gembris, H. (1997). Time specific and cohort specific influences on musical development. *Polish Quarterly of Developmental Psychology, 3*(1), 77–89.

Gembris, H. (1998). *Grundlagen musikalischer Begabung und Entwicklung.* Augsburg: Wissner.

Gordon, E. E. (1986). *The nature, description, measurement, and evaluation of music aptitudes.* Chicago: GIA.

Gordon, E. E. (1990). *A music learning theory for newborn and young children.* Chicago: GIA.

Hallam, S. (1998). *Instrumental teaching.* Oxford: Heinemann.

Hargreaves, D. J., & North, A. C. (Eds.) (2001). *Musical development and learning: The international perspective.* London: Cassel.

Hepper, P. G. (1991). An examination of foetal learning before and after birth. *Irish Journal of Psychology, 12,* 95–107.

Howe, M. J. A., Davidson, J. W., Moore, D. M., & Sloboda, J. A. (1995). Are there early childhood signs of musical ability? *Psychology of Music, 23*(2), 162–176.

Huston, A. C., & Wright, J. C. (1998). Mass media and children's development. In W. Damon, I. E. Sigel, and K. A. Renninger (Eds.), *Handbook of child psychology*: Vol. 4. *Child psychology in practice* (5th ed., pp. 999–1058). New York: Wiley.

KidsVerbraucherAnalyse 99 (1999). Bergisch-Gladbach: Bastei-Verlag, Gustav H. Lübbe GmbH, Axel Springer Verlag, & Verlagsgruppe Bauer.

Lecanuet, J.-P. (1996). Prenatal auditory experience. In I. Deliège and J. A. Sloboda (Eds.), *Musical beginnings: Origins and development of musical competence* (pp. 3–34). Oxford: Oxford University Press.

Lull, J. (1987). Listeners' communicative uses of popular music. In J. Lull (Ed.), *Popular music and communication* (pp. 140–174), Newbury Park, CA: Sage.

Malloch, S. N. (1999–2000). Mothers and infants' communicative musicality. *Musicae Scientiae*, Special Issue: Rhythm, Musical Narrative, and Origins of Human Communication, 29–57.

Manturzewska, M. (1995). Das elterliche Umfeld herausragender Musiker. In H. Gembris, R.-D. Kraemer, and G. Maas (Eds.), *Musikpädagogische Forschungsberichte 1994* (pp. 11–22). Augsburg: Wissner.

Noy, P. (1968). The development of musical ability. *Psychoanalytic Study of the Child, 23*, 332–347.

Olsson, B. (1997). The social psychology of music education. In D. J. Hargreaves and A. C. North (Eds.), *The social psychology of music* (pp. 290–305). Oxford: Oxford University Press.

Pace, R. (1999). *The essentials of keyboard pedagogy: I. Sight-reading and musical literacy.* Chatham, NY: Lee Robert's Music.

Papoušek, H., & Papoušek, M. (1995). Beginning of human musicality. In R. Steinberg (Ed.), *Music and the mind machine: The psychophysiology and psychopathology of the sense of music* (pp. 27–34). Berlin: Springer.

Papoušek, M. (1996). Intuitive parenting: A hidden source of musical stimulation in infancy. In I. Deliège and J. A. Sloboda (Eds.), *Musical beginnings: Origins and development of musical competence* (pp. 88–112). Oxford: Oxford University Press.

Plomin, R., & DeFries, J. C. (1999). The genetics of cognitive abilities and disabilities. In S. J. Ceci and W. M. Williams (Eds.), *The nature-nurture debate* (pp. 178–196). Oxford: Blackwell.

Plomin, R., DeFries, J. C., & Loehlin, J. C. (1977). Genotype–environment interaction and correlation in the analysis of human behavior. *Psychological Bulletin, 84*, 309–322.

Plomin, R., DeFries, J. C., McClearn, G. E., & Rutter, M. (1997). *Behavioral genetics* (3rd ed.). New York: Freeman.

Radford, J. (Ed.). (1991). *Talent, teaching and achievement.* London: Jessica Kingsley.

Reiss, D., Plomin, R., Hetherington, E. M., Howe, G., Rovine, M., Tyron, A., & Stanley, M. (1994). The separate worlds of teenage siblings: An introduction to the study of the nonshared environment and adolescent development. In E. M. Hetherington, D. Reiss, and R. Plomin (Eds.), *Separate worlds of siblings* (pp. 63–109). Hillsdale, NJ: Erlbaum.

Rosenthal, R., & Jacobson, L. (1968). *Pygmalion in the classroom.* New York: Holt, Rinehart & Winston.

Satt, B. J. (1984). *An investigation into the acoustical induction of intrauterine learning*. Doctoral dissertation, California School of Professional Psychology, Los Angeles.

Seckl, J. R. (1998). Physiologic programming of the fetus. *Clinical Perinatology, 25*(4), 939–962.

Simonton, K. D. (1975). Sociocultural context of individual creativity: A transhistorical time-series analysis. *Journal of Personality and Social Psychology, 32*(6), 1119–1133.

Simonton, K. D. (1977). Creative productivity, age, and stress: A biographical time-series analysis of 10 classical composers. *Journal of Personality and Social Psychology, 35*(11), 791–804.

Sloane, K. D. (1985). Home influences on talent development. In B. S. Bloom (Ed.), *Developing talent in young people* (pp. 439–476). New York: Ballantine.

Sloboda, J. A., Davidson, J. W., & Howe, M. J. A (1994). Is everyone musical? *Psychologist, 7*(8), 349–355.

Sloboda, J., & Davidson, J. (1996). The young performing musician. In I. Deliège and J. A. Sloboda (Eds.), *Musical beginnings: Origins and development of musical competence* (pp. 171–190). Oxford: Oxford University Press.

Sloboda, J. A., Davidson, J. W., Howe, M. J. A., & Moore, D. M. (1996). The role of practice in the development of expert musical performance. *British Journal of Psychology, 87*(2), 287–309.

Sosniak, L. A. (1985). Learning to be a concert pianist. In B. S. Bloom (Ed.), *Developing talent in young people* (pp. 19–67). New York: Ballantine.

Suzuki, S. (1969). *Nurtured by love*. New York: Exposition.

Suzuki, S. (1981). *Ability development from age zero*. Athens, OH: Ability Development Associates.

Trevarthen, C. (1999–2000). Musicality and the intrinsic motive pulse: Evidence from human psychobiology and infant communication. *Musicae Scientiae*, Special Issue: Rhythm, Musical Narrative, and Origins of Human Communication, 155–215.

Zdzinski, S. F. (1996). Parental involvement, selected student attributes, and learning outcomes in instrumental music. *Journal of Research in Music Education, 44*(1), 34–48.

3

Motivation

SUSAN A. O'NEILL & GARY E. McPHERSON

Research on motivation in music seeks to understand how children develop the desire to pursue the study of a musical instrument, how they come to value learning to play an instrument, why they vary in the degree of persistence and the intensity they display in achieving their musical goals, and how they evaluate and attribute their success and failure in different achievement contexts. Current theories view motivation as an integral part of learning that assists students in acquiring the range of adaptive behaviors that will provide them with the best chance of achieving their own personal goals. We review the literature on these topics and provide a framework for understanding the complex range of thoughts, feelings, and actions that either sustain or hinder musicians through the many years that it takes to develop musical skills.

Why do some children seek the challenges of learning and persist in the face of difficulty, while others, with seemingly equal ability and potential, avoid challenges and withdraw when faced with obstacles or difficulties? Over the past 20 years, this fundamental question has underpinned an enormous body of educational and psychological research. The findings have contributed to our understanding of motivation by clarifying what initiates a desire to pursue certain goals, by explaining why certain goals are valued over others, by describing how students vary in the degree of persistence and intensity they display in achieving their own goals, and by specifying how children evaluate and attribute causes for their success and failure in different achievement contexts (see Pintrich & Schunk, 1996, for a comprehensive overview). An important outcome of this research is that motivation is no longer viewed as a distinct set of psychological processes but as an integral part of learning that assists students to acquire the range of behaviors that will provide them with the best chance of reaching their full potential.

With this in mind, our chapter begins with a review of key theories and research that can help musicians understand the complex nature of motivation as it applies to music performance achievement. This is followed by a discussion of teaching strategies that can be used to help music students establish and sustain positive motivation as they work toward achieving their goals.

Motivation Theories

Expectancy-Value Theory: Why Do I Want to Play an Instrument?

Expectancy-value theory, one of the most important strands of motivation research, seeks to provide a framework for understanding why individuals are interested in or care about an activity to a sufficient degree that they believe it might be important to them in the future (Pintrich & Schunk, 1996). The model describes four components relevant to students' expectations and valuing of an activity. The first, *attainment value*, refers to how important a student believes it is to do well on a task. For example, playing well at a music recital will be important for a student whose self-concept involves a strong sense of identity in terms of being a capable musician. Second, the feeling of enjoyment an instrumentalist has when performing for the sheer pleasure of making music is defined as *intrinsic motivation*. Third, students form perceptions of the *extrinsic utility value* of learning their instrument according to its usefulness to their future goals, including career choices. A student who plays an instrument exclusively for the pleasure of performing with an ensemble will value music performance differently from a student whose intention is to become a professional musician. Fourth, the perceived negative aspects of learning an instrument, such as the amount of practice needed to continue improving, are defined as the *perceived cost* of engaging in the activity. Children may decide that the cost of practicing each day is not worth the effort, because it does not leave sufficient time for other things in their life, such as sports or social activities (Eccles, Wigfield & Schiefele, 1998).

Using this framework, researchers who studied academic achievement in subjects like mathematics and reading have found that even very young children are able to distinguish between what they like or think is important for them and perceptions of their own personal competence in a particular field (Wigfield, 1994; Wigfield & Eccles, 1992) and that these beliefs predict how much effort they will exert on the task, their subsequent performance, and their feelings of self-worth, even after previous performance has been taken into account (see also Eccles & Wigfield, 1995; Eccles et al., 1998; Wigfield et al., 1997). There is also evidence that individuals' subjective task values (i.e., the degree of importance and interest a particular activity has to an individual) are important predictors of activity choices in adolescent years (Eccles et al., 1983).

Research in music is consistent with findings in academic disciplines and provides important clues to our understanding of how young people come to value musical learning and view it as important to themselves and their goals.

For example, in Britain approximately 48% of 5- and 6-year-old children express an interest in learning to play an instrument, but by age 7 this desire has halved to about 25%, where it remains constant until the age of 11, when it declines to only 4% of nonplaying 14-year-olds (Cooke & Morris, 1996). In the United States, opportunities to learn an instrument in a school instrumental program typically become available at a time when children's interest in learning music and beliefs about its usefulness and importance are rapidly declining (Eccles et al., 1983, 1993). Eccles et al. (1993) found that even children who have had very little experience with instrumental music appear to have just as reliable and differentiated self-beliefs about their ability and the importance they place on this activity as for activities (such as reading and sports) with which they have considerably more experience. Not surprisingly, children who devalue instrumental instruction and consider themselves lacking in musical ability will be more likely to engage in it for a short time and then stop (Wigfield et al., 1997; Wigfield, O'Neill & Eccles, 1999).

McPherson (2000) studied 133 young beginning instrumentalists between the ages of seven and nine and found that children bring to their music instruction expectations and values that potentially shape and influence their subsequent development. For example, interviews with the children before they began instruction show that they were able to make clear statements about their valuing of and expectations for music learning without a great deal of previous experience. They could differentiate among their interest in learning a musical instrument, the importance of being good at music, whether they believed their learning would be useful to their short- and long-term goals, and the cost of participation, in terms of the effort needed to continue improving. For many, learning an instrument was no different from participating in a team sport, taking up a hobby, or pursuing other recreational activities. Most of the children were intrinsically interested in learning an instrument but did not see it as important to their long-term future careers. Others were less intrinsically motivated but recognized the importance or utility value of learning in terms of their overall education. For the majority of children, learning an instrument was something useful to do while they were in school but of far less value in later life. Only a handful viewed their involvement as something that could possibly lead to a future career. Even before commencing, many children were also able to provide a definite view of their own potential compared to those of their peers.

One of the more interesting findings from the McPherson study was the relationship between the children's commitment to learning their instrument before they started lessons and their achievement nine months later. Students who predicted that they would play their instrument for only a few years progressed the slowest, irrespective of the amount of practice they did at home. Students who predicted that they would play their instrument until the end of their schooling achieved higher performance levels, which increased according to the amount of their practice during the period studied. The highest achieving students were those who expressed a long-term commitment to playing, coupled with high levels of practice. These students, who indicated that they planned to play their instrument for most of their lives, were typically more inclined to express intrinsic reasons (e.g., "I've always liked music for as long as I can remember") rather than extrinsic reasons (e.g., "I wanted to learn because all my friends were joining the band") for wanting to play.

Self-Efficacy: How Well Can I Perform?

Related to children's valuing of an activity is their sense of competence or *self-efficacy*. Competence beliefs have been described as evaluations of how good one is at an activity (e.g., Eccles et al., 1983; Nicholls, 1984, 1990), expectancy beliefs about how good one's performance will be in the future (e.g., Eccles et al., 1983), or self-efficacy beliefs that one can produce the desired outcome (e.g., Bandura, 1997). In other words, self-efficacy is associated with the degree to which a musician believes in his or her own ability and capacity to achieve certain goals (Stipek, 1998). According to Pajares (1996), "Self-efficacy beliefs act as determinants of behavior by influencing the choices that individuals make, the effort they expend, the perseverance they exert in the face of difficulties, and the thought patterns and emotional reactions they experience" (p. 325). Perceptions of personal competence are so powerful that they are theorized to influence a student's motivation and future decision to continue developing his or her skill in an area (Hackett, 1995).

Research in music supports these assertions. McPherson and McCormick (1999) studied 190 pianists aged between 9 and 18 who completed a questionnaire immediately before undertaking an externally graded performance examination. Results indicated that the level of the pianists' self-efficacy before they entered their performance examination helped to predict their subsequent examination result. This finding is consistent with educational research that suggests that students who display high self-efficacy will tend to perform at a more advanced level in examinations than their peers who display the same level of skill but lower personal expectations (Pintrich & Schunk, 1996). This is because high levels of self-efficacy strengthen confidence and ensure persistence, often in spite of difficulties (Pajares, 1996).

According to Eccles, Wigfield, and Schiefele (1998), more work is needed on the links between competence beliefs and values and whether they relate differently to performance and choice. In music, for example, it is important to establish whether these beliefs are associated with the amount of time students spend practicing and the choice of easy or difficult musical tasks. Yoon (1997) studied 849 children between the ages of 8 and 11 to investigate the extent to which competence and values predicted activity choice (sports versus music) and frequency of practice. Results indicated that self-perceptions of competence (i.e., "How good are you at playing a musical instrument?") and subjective task values (i.e., "How important is learning to play an instrument?") played a key role in predicting both activity choice and amount of practice. In other words, the findings suggest that children are more likely to engage in musical activities when they feel capable in music and value it.

However, findings from a recent study by O'Neill (1999b) suggest that valuing a musical activity may be even more important in sustaining motivation for practice than believing in one's ability to succeed. O'Neill found that the extent to which 60 young musicians aged between 12 and 16 valued their practice sessions (i.e., "Was this practice important to you?"; "How important was this practice in relation to your overall goals?") was a significant predictor of the amount of time they spent practicing. Interestingly, frequency of practice was not predicted by the students' beliefs about how competent they were (i.e., "Were you succeeding at what you were doing?") and whether they were living up to their own and others' expectations. One interpretation is that the young musicians who valued their practice highly did so because it provided them with the opportunity to demonstrate aspects of their competence, which in turn reinforced the value they placed on learning to play an instrument and motivated them to achieve their goals. According to Eccles and her colleagues (e.g., Eccles, 1987; Eccles & Harold, 1992), values are linked to more stable beliefs about the characteristics of one's overall self-concept and sense of identity, whereas competence beliefs are more unstable and likely to fluctuate in different situations and with the demands of different tasks. In addition, it is possible the young musicians were not interpreting the notion of importance in the same way (e.g., they may have been more or less concerned with intrinsic or extrinsic reasons for doing the task), and this may have contributed to differences in amount of practice. It would be useful if future research examined the extent to which self-perceptions of competence and values might vary in relation to different practice activities (e.g., formal, deliberate practice versus informal, fun practice; easy tasks versus demanding tasks) and how this might relate to the amount of time spent practicing different tasks.

Flow Theory: Matching Challenge to Skill

Researchers have also conceptualized motivation in terms of the changes that take place within the person when a student is actually involved in learning music. From this perspective, researchers study the types of activities that students find intrinsically motivating and compare these with the types of activities that result in less efficient learning. This is the essential ingredient of Csikszentmihalyi's (1990) *flow theory*, which suggests that optimal experience requires a balance between roughly equal levels of perceived challenge and skill in a situation that involves intense concentration. According to this explanation, activities are seen as pleasurable when the challenge is matched to the person's skill levels. If an activity is too easy and skill levels are high, boredom will develop; if an activity is too difficult and skill levels are low, anxiety will result; if both challenge and skill levels are low, students feel apathy. To remain in flow, the complexity of the activity must increase by developing new skills and taking on new challenges. Flow experience is characterized by the presence of clear goals and unambiguous feedback, focused concentration, a sense of outcomes under the person's own control, a distorted sense of time (e.g., an hour of practice seems to go by quickly), losing a sense of self-awareness, and experiencing the activity as intrinsically rewarding (see also Csikszentmihalyi, Rathunde & Whalen, 1993).

O'Neill (1999a) examined the extent to which flow experiences accounted for differences in the amount of time spent practicing among 60 young musicians between ages 12 and 16 who varied in their levels of performance achievement. The moderate achievers from a specialist music school reported fewer flow experiences when practicing than their higher-achieving peers at the same school and the musically active young people attending a nonspecialist state school. Although further research is needed, the results suggest that the evaluative context of a specialist music school contributed to the reduced flow experiences of the students who were considered less musically able than their peers. During individual interviews, the moderate achievers at the music school tended to regard the high-achieving students as competitive and criticized the lack of opportunity the school provided for them to engage in nonmusical activities such as sports and other arts programs. However, both the high achievers at the specialist music school and the musically active young people at the state school were more likely to describe their peers as supportive and encouraging and that they valued the social opportunities afforded by their school to engage in music making with other like-minded peers. An implication of these findings is that music educators need to consider different ways of fostering the motivation of music students who are considered less competent in order to ensure that the quality of their musical experiences remains intrinsically rewarding.

Attribution Theory: Why Did I Succeed or Fail?

Beliefs about the causes of success and failure can influence a variety of future achievement behaviors, expectancies, self-perceptions, and other emotional responses (Austin & Vispoel, 1998). Expectations are central to continuing motivation, so understanding how students attribute the causes of their success or failure, particularly in a stressful environment such as a music performance, is an important part of understanding variation in students' performance. In attribution research, theorists explore the impact of these beliefs on expectations for future success and individuals' perceptions of both their own abilities and the difficulty of the various tasks. Weiner (1986, 1992), the researcher who has made the greatest contribution to this area, believes that it is not success or failure per se but the causal attributions made for these outcomes that influence students' expectations of whether they think they will continue doing well or poorly.

Attribution researchers have focused on the perceived relationship between children's achievement and the types of reasons they give to explain their performance. According to Stipek (1998), the most common attributions are ability ("I did well because I'm a good musician") and effort ("I did well because I practiced hard"). Less common attributions include luck ("I had a lucky day"), task difficulty ("The examiner asked me the easiest scales"), and strategy ("I practiced the hard part in small sections"). Weiner (1986, 1992) identified three dimensions of causal attributions: (1) whether the cause is internal or external to the student, (2) the extent to which the cause remains the same or changes, and (3) the extent to which the individual can control the cause. For example, there is an important distinction between how children view ability and how they view effort. Ability is viewed as something internal, stable, and beyond a student's control ("I can't do this because I'm not a good musician"), whereas effort is seen as internal, unstable, and controllable ("If I do more practice I'll be able to play this piece"). In addition, students who perceive their success as being due to internal reasons such as effort are more likely to have a higher sense of self-worth (self-esteem) than students who believe their success was due to external reasons, such as luck.

A detailed review of available evidence by Eccles et al. (1998) shows that young children view ability and effort as complementary and are not always able to distinguish between these two constructs, but that their understanding changes over time. By the age of 11 or 12, children have come to understand these processes more deeply and begin to realize that instrumentalists with less ability need to try harder and practice more in order to achieve similar results to those of students with greater ability. The realization that you need to do more practice than someone who shows greater ability means that you will come to view yourself as a less capable musician.

In music, Vispoel and Austin (1993) found that junior high school students who attributed the failure of a fictitious music student to insufficient effort or poor learning strategies were more likely to anticipate improved future performance than students who attributed failure to a lack of ability. McPherson and McCormick (2000) conducted a study of 349 instrumentalists between the ages of 9 and 18 who were completing graded performance examinations. The results demonstrated that over 50% perceived their performance examination result to be a consequence of how much effort they had given to preparing for the examination or how hard they tried during the examination. The majority of students went into their examination reporting healthy attributions. If they did well, then they could attribute their success to having prepared thoroughly. If they did poorly, then they could blame their result on not having done enough preparation or not trying hard enough during the examination.

However, the findings also revealed that 12.4% of the beginners, 9.9% of the intermediate-level players, and 19.5% of the advanced musicians attributed their result to either luck, how hard the exam might turn out to be (i.e., task difficulty), or their overall ability. Other research suggests that students who believe that their success or failure is a result of ability tend to approach a task differently from their peers who associate success and failure with effort and that low achievers often make maladaptive or unhelpful attributions in comparison with high achievers (Arnold, 1997; Pintrich & Schunk, 1996). The latter students are more likely to attribute success to luck and their inability to complete a task successfully to such factors as ability. They are also less likely to feel that an increase in effort will have any positive benefits for their development or capacity to achieve at a higher level.

Mastery Motivation: How Confident Do I Feel?

Weiner's work on attribution theory helped pave the way for research focusing on specific learning styles, such as the differences between adaptive and maladaptive student motivational patterns. Research by Dweck and her colleagues

(Dweck, 1986, 2000; Dweck & Leggett, 1988; Henderson & Dweck, 1990) demonstrated that children's motivational patterns influence their behavior and performance when they encounter difficulty or failure. For example, students who display adaptive *mastery-oriented* patterns tend to remain high in their persistence following failure and appear to enjoy exerting effort in the pursuit of task mastery. In short, students of this type remain focused on trying to achieve in spite of difficulties that may interfere with their progress. Conversely, maladaptive *helpless* patterns are associated with failure to establish reasonable valued goals or to attain goals that are within one's reach. Because helpless students feel that the situation is out of their control and that nothing can be done about it, they tend to avoid further challenges, lower their expectations, experience negative emotions, give up, and perform more poorly in the future. What is especially interesting about these two motivational patterns is that helpless children are often initially equal in ability to mastery-oriented children. Indeed, some of the brightest, most skilled children exhibit helpless behavior (Dweck, 2000).

O'Neill (1997) investigated the influence of these motivational patterns on the development of children's musical performance achievement after the first year of learning to play an instrument. The findings indicated that children who displayed mastery-oriented behavior after experiencing failure on a problem-solving task prior to beginning instrumental music instruction made more progress after one year of instrumental lessons than the children who initially displayed helpless behavior. However, when the amount of time spent practicing of those children who had demonstrated mastery and helpless behavior was compared, the results indicated that helpless children were practicing roughly twice as much as mastery children to reach the same level of moderate performance achievement. This suggests that although some helpless children were spending large amounts of time practicing, they appeared to be using their time less efficiently. For example, helpless children may avoid practicing pieces that pose particular difficulties, spend more time practicing items they can already play well, and use strategies that are unlikely to improve their performance. However, mastery children tend to seek challenges and adapt their practicing strategies in order to increase competence and improve their performance.

It is possible that motivational patterns may influence children's skill development much sooner in instrumental music learning than in other subject areas. During the initial stages of learning to play a musical instrument there are many challenges to overcome (e.g., posture, position, rhythm, tone, notation). As a result, many children experience confusion, difficulty, and failure very early in their instrumental training. In addition, unlike academic school subjects where children are rarely given the choice of not pursuing an activity, learning to play a musical instrument requires a great deal of autonomy, because it is often up to the child to decide when and where to practice and also whether new or difficult material is practiced or avoided. As O'Neill's (1997) study suggests, it is in these circumstances that helpless children may differ quite markedly from mastery-oriented children in their use of practice time.

Implications for Teaching

What can music teachers do in order to provide a teaching environment that maximizes student motivation? As we suggested in the opening of this chapter, one of the most important elements is viewing motivation as an integral part of all teaching and learning. On the one hand, students who lack motivation will not expend the necessary effort to learn. On the other hand, highly motivated students are eager to come to music lessons and learn. In a review of instructional strategies and achievement motivation, Ames (1992) examined how different approaches to teaching and evaluating performance can influence students' motivational patterns in areas such as intrinsic motivation, attributions that involve effort-based strategies, and active engagement. In the following section, we explore these ideas further. Based on the research already discussed in the chapter, our aim is to highlight what we consider to be some of the most important dimensions of music teaching that can help foster students' confidence and commitment.

Potential

As explained in chapter 1 by Kemp and Mills, one of the most widely debated issues in music is the notion of talent. Folklore would have us believe that those who are talented are more likely to achieve and therefore display more adaptive motivation. However, this is not always the case. As discussed earlier, research has demonstrated that some of the most skilled individuals who display high levels of initial competence exhibit helpless behavior, which can result in failure to reach their full potential (Dweck, 2000). Beliefs about ability influence both the goals students choose to pursue and their achievement behavior. Dweck (2000) distinguishes between two different self-theory beliefs: *entity* beliefs, where ability is viewed as a fixed trait (e.g., musical talent is something you are born with), and *incremental* beliefs, where ability is viewed as something malleable that can be increased through effort. Students who hold entity beliefs are more likely to develop an overconcern with proving their competence, avoid challenges, and show an inability to cope with failure or difficulty. One can imagine how difficult it would be to teach strategies for improving a poor performance to students who believe they simply do not have the potential to do it (i.e., "It either comes naturally or it doesn't"). In contrast, students who possess incremental beliefs thrive on challenges and view performance opportunities as providing chances to learn new things rather than merely display their ability. For students who consider performance achievement to be the end point of a learning process, a poor performance can be viewed as a problem that needs to be solved. They are therefore more receptive to learning new strategies for improving their performance.

Stipek (1996) provides the following strategies to improve students' self-efficacy (i.e., the belief that they can master a situation and produce positive outcomes) by emphasizing incremental beliefs and mastery motivation:

1. Teach students specific strategies (such as dividing a difficult section or piece into smaller parts) that can improve their ability to focus on their tasks.
2. Guide students in setting their own long-term goals and the short-term goals that will help achieve them.
3. Communicate your expectations that your students have the potential to achieve and provide them with supportive statements such as "You can do this," "You will improve this with practice," and "Keep going; you will get there". However, know your students well enough to understand how much skill support they need and get them to stretch their abilities realistically. It is important for teachers to encourage students who feel less able to take personal responsibility for their behavior, including setting appropriate goals in which they are challenged and perceive themselves as having the necessary skills to cope with the demands of the task.
4. Ensure that students are not overly anxious about their performance achievement. Although researchers have found that many successful students show moderate levels of anxiety (e.g., Bandura, 1997), some students have consistently high levels of anxiety, which can undermine their ability to succeed. Some of children's high anxiety is related to unrealistic achievement expectations and pressure by parents, teachers, or peers. Many students experience higher levels of anxiety as they reach higher skill levels where they face more frequent evaluation, social comparison, and, for some, experiences of failure (Eccles, Wigfield & Schiefele, 1998).
5. Provide students with positive adult and peer models. For example, students who observe teachers and peers coping effectively and mastering challenges often adopt the role models' behaviors. Modeling is especially effective in promoting self-efficacy when students observe success by peers who are similar in ability to themselves (see Schunk & Zimmerman, 1996).

Success and Failure

Findings of attribution research reinforce the need for teachers to help their students develop adaptive attributional responses so that they can motivate their students for both short-term musical development and long-term musical involvement. To do this teachers need to monitor their students' attributions by spending time talking with them about what they have achieved and where they can improve and helping them to map out strategies that ensure that their musical practice is well organized and efficient (see chapter 10). Of vital importance is the need to encourage students to attribute any failure to controllable causes such as a lack of effort. Students who report effort attributions tend to display greater persistence and stronger emotional reactions, such as a feeling of pride for a high result or shame following failure (Austin & Vispoel, 1998). Thus stressing the importance of effort, in contrast to ability, is one way of diminishing the effects of counterproductive attributions with which students often explain their own achievement.

Enjoyment

Research has begun to clarify important motivational differences when children practice repertoire assigned by their teacher rather than pieces they have chosen themselves. In a study of 257 students drawn from various levels of music training, Sloboda and Davidson (1996) found that high-achieving musicians tend to do significantly greater amounts of formal practice, such as scales, pieces, and technical exercises, than their less successful peers. Interestingly, they are also likely to report more informal practice, such as playing their favorite pieces by ear, "messing about," or improvising. Sloboda and Davidson conclude that these informal ways of practicing contribute to musical success because the highest achieving students are able to find the right balance between freedom and discipline in their practice.

In a detailed case study of a young beginning clarinettist, Renwick and McPherson (2000) discovered an elevenfold increase in the time spent practicing a piece that she chose to learn herself, as compared to repertoire assigned by the teacher. In addition to this remarkable difference there were also major differences in the quality of the girl's practice. When practicing the teacher-assigned pieces, the girl almost exclusively used a play-through approach, playing her pieces from beginning to end with little attention to correcting mistakes. With the piece she wanted to learn herself, there was a marked increase in the way she monitored and controlled her performance, as evidenced in greater use of silent fingering, silent thinking, singing, and more varied strategies for correcting wrong notes. Other useful techniques that teachers can explore to encourage students to vary their practice are concentrating on different repertoire on selected days, maintaining a log book to identify aspects that need revision and refinement, and continually varying habits, all of which help alleviate the daily grind of practicing.

Engagement

Intrinsic motivation is maximized when students are given repertoire that requires a reasonable amount of effort to be learned. Repertoire that is completed with little effort or that causes confusion or frustration can result in low engagement during practice. Students will be more intellectually involved when practicing repertoire that requires higher order or divergent thinking and active problem solving than when practicing mundane drill and practice exercises. Encouraging students to come to the next lesson with five different ways of playing an exercise or to devise a set of similar exercises to overcome a technical problem will be more intrinsically motivating than merely telling them to practice an exercise until it has been mastered. McPherson and McCormick (1999) showed that a distinguishing feature of musicians who do greater amounts of practice is the level of their cognitive engagement while they practice. In their study, students who reported higher levels of practice tended to be more inclined to rehearse music in their minds (mental practice) and to make critical ongoing judgments on the success or otherwise of their efforts. They were also more capable of organizing their practice in ways that provided for efficient learning, such as practicing the pieces that needed most work and isolating difficult sections of a piece that required further refinement. Anything that a teacher can do to encourage more active cognitive engagement as a student learns independently will have positive benefits for the pace of their improvement and subsequent intrinsic desire to continue learning.

Goals

According to Covington and Omelich (1979), maintaining one's sense of competence is critical for maintaining a positive sense of self-worth. However, evaluations of performance, competitions, and social comparisons can make it difficult for some children to maintain such positive competence beliefs. Stipek, a leading educational psychologist, believes that stressing evaluation "focuses attention on performance goals, engenders a feeling of being controlled, and destroys whatever intrinsic interest students might have in a task" (1998, p. 172).

In British Commonwealth countries, North America, and other regions where music competitions and/or graded performance examinations flourish, music educators disagree about the real worth of evaluations that are based on some sort of ranking or assessment. Austin (1991), for example, believes that competitions curtail achievement, especially in situations where repeated failure will tend to diminish self-efficacy and self-determination: musicians "would derive greater pleasure and benefit from performing more frequently and in settings that (a) balance emotional risk with support from teachers, family, and peers, and (b) provide for detailed instructional feedback beyond numerical indicators of *musical greatness*" (p. 156). Massie (1992), however, argues that competitions encourage skill development (see further, Asmus, 1994).

Since formal evaluation of solo and group music performance is so common in schools and community music programs, there can be no simple answer to the question of whether it hinders or curtails motivation. Obviously, the context and nature of a music evaluation will vary considerably among different learning settings. However, success in any form of music evaluation is likely to depend not only on the amount of time students devote to practicing but also on the way they feel about the examination and the degree to which they believe in themselves and feel confident enough in their own ability to give the performance evaluation their best effort. Above all, students need to feel that they are participating in the evaluation because they want to, rather than because their teacher or parents want them to (see, for example, Davidson & Scutt, 1999).

Music examinations and competitions can provide opportunities for structuring the learning environment, especially when teachers use the requirements to make their own short- and long-term goals clear to the student. But it is also important to encourage students to identify their own goals and aspirations by allowing them some choice in the works they are to learn and the pieces they are to prepare for their performance. Any evaluation of a child's progress can be valued as an independent form of assessment, which can be used to define future goals. Information obtained from music evaluations therefore needs to be seen by students as helpful and suggestive, not definitive and critical. Many students thrive in an environment that includes the completion of grade examinations or participation in competitions in their instrument or voice. However, equally valid is the claim that not all students are suited to this type of stressful environment and that a good teacher will be perceptive enough to realize when a student is not ready or emotionally capable of being formally assessed and compared with his or her peers.

Conclusion

In this chapter we have outlined research according to five theoretical perspectives. First, expectancy-value theory informs us about ways that children can value learning an instrument, as well as beliefs that concern what they think they might gain from their learning. Second, self-efficacy constructs allow us to understand how confident learners feel about their ability to perform on an instrument, especially when faced with a stressful situation such as a public music performance. According to the third perspective, flow theory, activities are more pleasurable when the challenge of the task and the musician's skill are optimally balanced. Fourth, attribution theory addresses the different reasons a musician will give to explain a good or poor performance. Fifth, mastery motivational patterns tell us about what occurs during the event and how some learners, despite their ability, give up when faced with difficulties.

Much work has been carried out on the role of socializing agents in assisting students to maintain sufficient motivation to practice and achieve (chapters 1 and 12 in this volume; McPherson & Davidson, in press). Indeed, there is little doubt that motivation to continue instrumental training is inextricably linked to the social and cultural environment, and so it is also important to consider how motivation for playing an instrument might be influenced by external factors such as parents and teachers. Important as these factors may be, no amount of parental support is likely to make a child without some intrinsic interest engage in the long-term effort required to succeed at even modest levels of musical competence. Consequently, understanding how students think about themselves, the task, and their performance is important if teachers are to establish and sustain a stimulating and challenging learning environment. Students need to feel that their involvement in learning to play an instrument provides them with a sense of personal choice and responsibility for reaching the goals that they set themselves. With this in mind, the challenge for teachers is to be receptive to each child's perspective on his or her own learning and to develop an understanding of the complex range of thoughts, feelings, and actions that either sustain or hinder the children through the many years that it takes to develop their musical skills.

References

Ames, C. (1992). Classrooms: Goals, structures, and student motivation. *Journal of Educational Psychology, 84*, 261–271.

Arnold, J. A. (1997). A comparison of attributions for success and failure in instrumental teaching among sixth-, eighth-, and tenth-grade students. *Update: Applications of Research in Music Education, 15*(2), 19–23.

Asmus, E. (1994). Motivation in music teaching and learning. *Quarterly Journal of Music Teaching and Learning, 5*(4), 5–32.

Austin, J. (1991). Competitive and non-competitive goal structures: An analysis of motivation and achievement among elementary band students. *Psychology of Music, 19*(2), 142–158.

Austin, J. R., & Vispoel, W. P. (1998). How American adolescents interpret success and failure in classroom music: Relationships among attributional beliefs, self-concept and achievement. *Psychology of Music, 26*(1), 26–45.

Bandura, A. (1997). *Self-efficacy: The exercise of control.* New York: Freeman.

Cooke, M., & Morris, R. (1996). Making music in Great Britain. *Journal of the Market Research Society, 28*(2), 123–134.

Covington, M. V., & Omelich, C. L. (1979). Effort: The double-edged sword in school achievement. *Journal of Educational Psychology, 71*(2), 169–182.

Csikszentmihalyi, M. (1990). *Flow.* New York: Harper & Row.

Csikszentmihalyi, M., Rathunde, K., & Whalen, S. (1993). *Talented teenagers: The roots of success and failure.* Cambridge: Cambridge University Press.

Davidson, J. W., & Scutt, S. (1999). Instrumental learning with exams in mind: A case study investigating teacher, student and parent interactions before, during and after a music examination. *British Journal of Music Education, 16*(1), 79–95.

Dweck, C. S. (1986). Motivational processes affecting learning. *American Psychologist, 41*, 1040–1048.

Dweck, C. S. (2000). *Self-theories: Their role in motivation, personality and development.* Philadelphia: Psychology Press.

Dweck, C. S., & Leggett, E. (1988). A social-cognitive approach to motivation and personality. *Psychological Review, 95*(2), 256–273.

Eccles, J. S. (1987). Gender roles and women's achievement related decisions. *Psychology of Women Quarterly, 11*, 135–172.

Eccles, J. S., Adler, T. F., Futterman, R., Goff, S. B., Kaczala, C. M., Meece, J., & Midgley, C. (1983). Expectances, values and academic behaviors. In J. T. Spence (Ed.), *Achievement and achievement motives* (pp. 75–146). San Francisco, CA: Freeman.

Eccles, J. S., & Harold, R. D. (1992). Gender differences in educational and occupational patterns among the gifted. In N. Colangelo, S. G. Assouline, and D. L. Amronson (Eds.), *Talent development: Proceedings from the 1991 Henry B. and Jocelyn Wallace National Research Symposium on Talent Development* (pp. 3–29). Unionville, NY: Trillium Press.

Eccles, J. S., & Wigfield, A. (1995). In the mind of the achiever: The structure of adolescents' academic achievement related beliefs and self-perceptions. *Personality and Social Psychology Bulletin, 21*, 215–225.

Eccles, J., Wigfield, A., Harold, R. D., & Blumenfeld, P. (1993). Age and gender differences in children's self and task perceptions during elementary school. *Child Development, 64*, 830–847.

Eccles, J. S., Wigfield, A., & Schiefele, U. (1998). Motivation to succeed. In W. Damon (Series Ed.) and N. Eisenberg (Vol. Ed.), *Handbook of child psychology: Vol. 3. Social, emotional and personality development* (5th ed., pp. 1017–1095). New York: Wiley.

Hackett, G. (1995). Self-efficacy in career choice and development.. In A. Bandura (Ed.), *Self-efficacy in changing societies* (pp. 232–258). New York: Cambridge University Press.

Henderson, V. L., & Dweck, C. S. (1990). Motivation and achievement. In S. S. Feldman and G. R. Elliott (Eds.), *At the threshold: The developing adolescent* (pp. 308–329). Cambridge, MA: Harvard University Press.

Massie, D. L. (1992). Band olympics: Musical muscle. *Music Educators Journal, 79*(4), 48–49.

McPherson, G. E. (2000). Commitment and practice: Key ingredients for achievement during the early stages of learning a musical instrument. *Proceedings of the XXIV International Society for Music Education Research Commission, Salt Lake City, USA, July 10–15, 2000.* (To be published in a forthcoming issue of *Bulletin of the Council for Research in Music Education.*)

McPherson, G. E., & Davidson, J. W. (in press). Musical practice: Mother and child interactions during the first nine months of learning a musical instrument. *Music Education Research.*

McPherson, G. E., & McCormick, J. (1999). Motivational and self-regulated learning components of musical practice. *Bulletin of the Council for Research in Music Education, 141*, 98–102.

McPherson, G. E., & McCormick, J. (2000). The contribution of motivational factors to instrumental performance in a music examination. *Research Studies in Music Education, 15*, 31–39.

Nicholls, J. (1984). Achievement motivation: Conceptions of ability, subjective experience, task choice, and performance. *Psychological Review, 91*, 328–346.

Nicholls, J. (1990). What is ability and why are we mindful of it? A developmental perspective. In R. J. Sternberg and J. Kolligian (Eds.), *Competence considered* (pp. 11–40). New Haven, CT: Yale University Press.

O'Neill, S. A. (1997). The role of practice in children's early musical performance achievement. In H. Jørgensen and A. C. Lehmann (Eds.), *Does practice make perfect? Current theory and research on instrumental practice* (pp. 53–70). Oslo: Norges Musikhøgskole.

O'Neill, S. A. (1999a). Flow theory and the development of musical performance skills. *Bulletin of the Council for Research in Music Education, 141*, 129–134.

O'Neill, S. A. (1999b). The role of motivation in the practice and achievement of young musicians. In S. W. Yi (Ed.), *Music, mind and science* (pp. 420–433). Seoul: Seoul National University Press.

Pajares, F. (1996). Self-efficacy beliefs and mathematical problem-solving of gifted students. *Contemporary Educational Psychology, 21*, 325–344.

Pintrich, P. R., & Schunk, D. H. (1996). *Motivation in education: Theory, research and applications.* Englewood Cliffs, NJ: Prentice-Hall.

Renwick, J., & McPherson, G. E. (2000). "I've got to do my scale first!": A case study of a novice's clarinet practice. In C. Woods, G. B. Luck, R. Brochard, F. Seddon, and J. A. Sloboda (Eds.), *Proceedings of the Sixth International Conference on Music Perception and Cognition.* Keele, UK: Keele University, Department of Psychology. CD-ROM.

Schunk, D. H., & Zimmerman, B. J. (1996). Modeling and self-efficacy influences on children's development of self-regulation. In J. Juvonen and K. R. Wentzel (Eds.), *Social motivation* (pp. 154–180). Cambridge: Cambridge University Press.

Sloboda, J. A., & Davidson, J. W. (1996). The young performing musician. In I. Deliège and J. A. Sloboda (Eds.), *Musical beginnings: The origins and development of musical competence* (pp. 171–190). Oxford: Oxford University Press.

Stipek, D. J. (1996). Motivation and instruction. In D. C. Berliner and R. C. Calfee (Eds.), *Handbook of educational psychology* (pp. 85–113). New York: Macmillan.

Stipek, D. J. (1998). *Motivation to learn: From theory to practice* (3rd ed.). Boston: Allyn & Bacon.

Vispoel, W. P., & Austin, J. R. (1993). Constructive response to failure in music: The role of attribution feedback and classroom goal structure. *British Journal of Educational Psychology, 63,* 110–129.

Weiner, B. (1986). *An attributional theory of motivation and emotion.* New York: Springer.

Weiner, B. (1992). *Human motivation: Metaphors, theories, and research.* Newbury Park, CA: Sage.

Wigfield, A. (1994). Expectancy-value theory of achievement motivation: A developmental perspective. *Educational Psychology Review, 6,* 49–78.

Wigfield, A., & Eccles, J. S. (1992). The development of achievement task values: A theoretical analysis. *Developmental Review, 12,* 265–310.

Wigfield, A., Eccles, J. S., Suk Yoon, K., Harold, R. D., Arbreton, A. J. A., Freedman-Doan, C., & Blumenfeld, P. C. (1997). Change in children's competence beliefs and subjective task values across the elementary school years: A 3-year study. *Journal of Educational Psychology, 89,* 451–469.

Wigfield, A., O'Neill, S. A., & Eccles, J. S. (1999, April). *Children's achievement values in different domains: Developmental and cultural differences.* Paper presented at the Biennial Meeting of the Society for Research in Child Development, Albuquerque, NM.

Yoon, K. S. (1997, April). *Exploring children's motivation for instrumental music.* Paper presented at the Biennial Meeting of the Society for Research in Child Development, Washington, DC.

4

Performance Anxiety

GLENN D. WILSON & DAVID ROLAND

Performance anxiety is a common problem among both amateur and professional musicians. It afflicts individuals who are generally prone to anxiety, particularly in situations of high public exposure and competitive scrutiny, and so is best understood as a form of social phobia (a fear of humiliation). Some degree of tension adds electricity to a performance, but pessimistic self-talk and feelings of panic can seriously affect it. The most effective psychological treatments seem to be those that combine relaxation training with anxiety inoculation (developing realistic expectations of what will be felt during performance) and cognitive restructuring (modifying habitual thoughts and attitudes that are self-handicapping, regardless of their origins). Preliminary research with hypnotherapy and the Alexander Technique suggests that these might also be effective in reducing performance anxiety.

Performance anxiety, sometimes called stage fright, is an exaggerated, often incapacitating, fear of performing in public. As in any other kind of phobia, the symptoms are those produced by activation of the body's emergency system, the sympathetic branch of the autonomic nervous system, including all the well-known effects of increases of adrenaline in the bloodstream (Fredrikson & Gunnarsson, 1992). The changes observed would have an adaptive function in relation to a physical threat, preparing us for an athletic response (fighting or fleeing). Unfortunately, running from or attacking an audience is seldom appropriate and the aftereffects of the alarm system can interfere with musical performance. For example, the increased heart pumping intended to supply additional oxygen to the muscles is felt as distressing palpitations. The increased activity of the lungs and widening of airways produces a feeling of breathlessness. The sharpening of vision has an aftermath in visual disturbances such as blurring. The diversion of resources away from digestion produces "butterflies" in the stomach. The redirection of body fluids such as saliva into the bloodstream produces a dry mouth sensation, and the activation of the body's cooling system produces sweaty palms and forehead.

These alarm reactions would enhance our survival if we were confronted with a tiger in a jungle, but they are less useful when we are faced with an audience who is expecting us to entertain them. Of course, we do not really fear physical attack if our performance is substandard, but human pride is apparently such a powerful motive that the fear of humiliation or disgrace can produce a similar degree of emotional panic. This is bound to be counterproductive to finely tuned vocal or instrumental performance, which requires a clear head and steady hand and voice.

Incidence

The incidence of performance anxiety is considerable. Wesner, Noyes and Davis (1990) found 21% of the students and faculty at an American University School of Music reported "marked distress" that arose out of anxiety, while another 40% experienced "moderate distress." "Marked impairment" of performance was reported by 17% and "moderate impairment" by another 30%. The most troublesome symptoms were specified as poor concentration (63% of those claiming impairment), rapid heart rate (57%), trembling (46%), dry mouth (43%), sweating (43%), and shortness of breath (40%). Other commonly reported symptoms were flushing, quavering voice, nausea, and dizziness. Nine percent said they often avoided performance opportunities because of anxiety, and 13% had interrupted an actual performance on at least one occasion.

Many other studies support such high incidences. Van Kemanade, Van Son, and Van Heesch (1995) polled all the members of professional orchestras in the Netherlands and found that 91 out of 155 respondents, 59%, had been affected professionally or personally by stage fright and 10% suffered anticipatory anxiety for weeks before significant performances. In a comparative study of different types of performers, Marchant-Haycox and Wilson (1992) found musicians to be most affected by anxiety (47%), followed by singers (38%), dancers (35%), and actors (33%). Performance anxiety is clearly a problem of some magnitude, and it is not restricted to the inexperienced amateur.

Associated Factors

Given that performance anxiety represents a fear of negative evaluation by others, it is not surprising that it relates closely to other forms of social phobia (Steptoe & Fidler, 1987; Cox & Kenardy, 1993). To some extent it also relates to personality traits that create anxiety. Perfectionism relates to having an unrealistically high expectation of yourself and others. It also relates to an overconcern with small flaws and mistakes, with a tendency to focus on what's wrong and discount what's right (Bourne, 1995). Perfectionists tend to be very self-critical and as a consequence suffer low self-esteem. Another personality trait leading to anxiety is the need to have excessive personal control (Bourne, 1995). This tendency leads the person to being uncomfortable and feeling unable to succeed in unpredictable circumstances.

Mor, Day and Flett (1995) have studied the interaction of perfectionism, personal control, and performance anxiety in professional musicians, actors, and dancers. They distinguished between self-oriented perfectionism (self-imposed high standards) and socially prescribed perfectionism (high standards imposed by others). Their findings suggest that high personal and social standards together with low personal control were most strongly associated with debilitating performance anxiety. Socially prescribed perfectionism was more strongly associated with debilitating performance anxiety than self-oriented perfectionism. Those performers who exhibited higher levels of perfectionism overall and lower personal control also experienced less satisfaction with their performances. Mor et al. (1995) conclude that cognitive-behavioral interventions designed to reduce perfectionist attitudes and to improve a sense of personal control may be effective in reducing severe performance anxiety.

There is some reduction of performance anxiety with age and experience, but many professional musicians battle with it throughout their career. Evidence that concerns sex differences is equivocal; some researchers (e.g., Wesner et al., 1990) find a female prevalence in performance anxiety, consistent with higher levels of anxiety and phobias in general, while others (e.g., Van Kemanade, Van Son & Van Heesch, 1995) find an equal incidence in males and females.

In their discussion of social anxiety Beck and Emery (1985) state that the anxious person's perception of a threat to him or her is the trigger for their anxiety response. This perception of a threatening event is created by:

1. Overestimating the probability of a feared event
2. Overestimating the severity of the feared event
3. Underestimating coping resources (what you can do about it)
4. Underestimating rescue factors (what other people can do to help you)

Any situation that increases the performer's sense of threat will increase his or her level of performance anxiety (Wilson, 2002; Roland, 1994b; Hamann, 1982; Abel & Larkin, 1990; Cox & Kenardy 1993). For this reason solo performance is usually much more stressful than performing a duet, which is in turn more stressful than playing in a trio, and so on; the relationship between stage fright and number of coperformers is that of a steeply declining curve. (Beyond a certain number of coperformers, adding more makes little difference.) Public performance is more anxiety-evoking than private performance, though the degree of anxiety does not have such a simple relationship to the size of the audience as it does to the number of coperformers. While it might be supposed that performing on TV to an audience of 10 million would be far more frightening than performing in a small auditorium, this is not necessarily the case. The actual proximity of an audience (e.g., being able to see the expressions on their faces) may be more significant than their numbers, and the status relationships between performer and audience are critical.

Nearly all performers report that auditions are the most stressful performance situations because they combine scrutiny and evaluation on the one hand with a socially inferior situation on the other. The evaluation of the audition panel will have a direct effect upon career progress. Other competitive (judged) situations are also more stressful than performances given for entertainment, again depending on the relative status of performer and listener. Competitors for a top international prize are typically less susceptible than students being graded at early levels of music education. There is also an interaction between the performer's personality and the effect that an audience will have on him or her; those most susceptible to stage fright (people who are inclined to be anxious and introverted—i.e., shy and withdrawn) tend to perform worse under scrutiny, whereas the presence of an audience may actually extract the best from those who are more sociable and confident, stable extroverts (Graydon & Murphy, 1995).

Optimal Arousal

A certain degree of arousal actually helps the quality of performance as judged by an audience, and this applies to a level that is experienced by the performer as unpleasant, stressful, and presumed to be detrimental (Gellrich, 1991; Wilson, 1994). In other words, performers themselves are not always good judges as to how anxiety is influencing their performances and awareness of this fact may itself be helpful.

It is widely accepted that the quality of performance is related to arousal with an inverted-U (rainbow-shaped) curve. That is, very low levels of arousal are insufficiently motivating and give rise to lackluster performances, while excessive arousal interferes with performance because concentration is disrupted, memory blocks occur, and there is a loss of steadiness in hands and voice. This rainbow-shaped function is called the Yerkes-Dodson Law after the researchers who first described it. This law further states that the peak of the curve will be reached earlier for difficult than for easy tasks. In other words, more complex tasks deteriorate more easily under stress than simple ones. Although this effect was first established in laboratory rats, there is ample evidence that it applies to human subjects and within the context of musical performance (Anderson, 1994; Hamann & Sobaje, 1983).

Wilson (2002) proposed a three-dimensional extension of the Yerkes-Dodson Law, grouping sources of stress into three major categories:

1. *Trait anxiety:* any personality characteristics, constitutional or learned, that mediate susceptibility to stress
2. *Situational stress:* environmental pressures such as public performance, audition, or competition
3. *Task mastery:* ranging from performances of simple, well-rehearsed works to those of complex, underprepared material

These three sources of stress vary independently; hence whether anxiety is beneficial or detrimental to performance depends upon their interplay. This model accounts for a great many research findings and has practical implications for the performer. For example, highly anxious individuals perform best when the work is well mastered and the situation relaxed, whereas low-anxiety individuals rise to a challenge and perform better with a more demanding audience. Anxiety-prone musicians should pick easy, familiar works to perform, especially for auditions or important public performances. However, hard preparation may turn a difficult work into a relatively easy one, thus reducing performance anxiety.

Hardy and Parfitt (1991) have suggested that a *catastrophe model* is more appropriate than the Yerkes-Dodson rainbow function in describing the sudden plunge in performance quality once arousal has passed a certain stress point. They note that excessive arousal can lead to a precipitous crash in performance rather than a gentle tailing off and small reductions in anxiety at this point are not capable of pulling the performer back to the optimal point on the curve. According to Hardy and Parfitt, it is necessary to distinguish cognitive (mental) anxiety from somatic (bodily) agitation. It is primarily the mental component that is likely to show the catastrophic decrement in performance.

This viewpoint is consistent with research that seeks to clarify what is going on in the heads of performers who are most susceptible to stage fright. Steptoe and Fidler (1987) identified various types of self-talk that were common among performers, and the type most associated with stage fright they called catastrophizing. This refers to an imaginary or anticipated disastrous outcome (e.g., "I think I am going to faint" or "I'm almost sure to make a dreadful mistake and that will ruin everything"). The most healthy cognitive strategy, called realistic self-appraisal, consisted of self-comments such as "I'm bound to make a few mistakes, but so does everyone" and "The audience wants me to play well and will make allowance for a few slips." The first type of statement would render a performer panic-prone, while the latter is generally optimistic and incorporates some inoculation against errors.

Treatment Approaches

Drugs

Many performers attempt self-treatment with anxiety-reducing drugs such as alcohol, Valium, and cannabis (Wills & Cooper, 1988). These may get a performer through a performance but are ultimately destructive in that they create dependence and the fine edge of the performance is lost. Two controlled studies of the effects of tranquilizers on performance have been reported: one found buspirone to be largely ineffective (Clark & Agras, 1991) and the other found benzodiazepines to be detrimental (James & Savage, 1984).

Beta-adrenergic blockers, which act specifically to inhibit peripheral autonomic symptoms, are more promising in that they supposedly leave the head clear while at the same time eliminating problems such as tremor and butterflies. Evidence is mixed as to whether they improve musical performance as judged by the outside observer. In any case, they seem less than ideal because of possible side effects such as loss of sexual potency, nausea, tiredness, and blunting of affect. In asthmatics the blockers are particularly dangerous and occasionally precipitate heart failure. Although many musicians take them regularly (some estimates suggest about one-quarter), in the United States and some other countries, their use for performance anxiety is not sanctioned by medical authorities. They may be helpful in breaking strongly conditioned anxiety cycles and getting performers back onstage when they have been frightened off, but psychological procedures aimed at restoring self-control to the performer would seem preferable, because performers are then relying on their own resources.

Psychoanalysis

Various psychoanalytic interpretations of performance anxiety have been offered (e.g., Nagel, 1993; Gabbard, 1979). These attribute the development of performance anxiety to early childhood experiences such as conflicts associated with genital exhibition and fear of parental punishment for masturbation. Such notions are difficult to verify, and although analysts sometimes provide descriptions of successfully treated case studies, these do not satisfy scientific criteria of evaluation. While early experiences may well contribute to performance anxiety, it is not clear that these need to be revisited as part of the treatment procedure; methods that focus on the here and now (notably the behavioral and cognitive methods to be discussed next) show more evidence of effectiveness.

Behavioral Therapy

Some standard behavioral approaches for the treatment of phobias have been applied to musical performance anxiety. The best known is *systematic desensitization*, which involves training in muscular relaxation followed by having the client imagine increasingly sensitive scenes that relate to the conditions that typically evoke anxiety (progressive exposure to a *fear hierarchy*). For example, an anxious pianist may begin by imagining playing an easy piece to relatives on a friendly family occasion. Once comfortable with that image, the pianist can move on to a scenario that includes some strangers, and so on, until a major concert is imagined. The theory is that phobias are maintained by the relief one obtains by avoiding the phobic object; hence what is necessary is a method for persuading the client to encounter that object (in this case a critical audience) in gradual, stepwise stages. Some studies suggest that classic desensitization does help with performance anxiety and speech anxiety (Wardle, 1975; Appel, 1976; Allen, Hunter & Donahue, 1989). However, exposure by itself does not necessarily extinguish performance anxiety, since many musicians perform for years without ever conquering their fears spontaneously (Steptoe & Fidler, 1987; Wesner et al., 1990).

Cognitive-Behavioral Therapy

Targeting a phobic person's behavior is sometimes insufficient for treating the underlying anxiety because the way a person thinks about his or her situation is critical to the onset of the anxiety. Since negative self-talk often mediates performance anxiety (Lloyd-Elliott, 1991; Steptoe & Fidler, 1987), it follows that some form of cognitive restructuring, such as reorganizing the individual's habitual ways of thinking during performance, might be helpful.

An important target for most cognitive procedures is the performer's focus of attention. Kendrick et al. (1982) showed the effectiveness of a procedure called attention training with a group of 53 pianists who sought help for performance anxiety. This consisted of the identification of negative and task-irrelevant thoughts during piano playing and training in substituting for them optimistic, task-oriented self-talk. Improvement was compared against behavior rehearsal (playing repeatedly before friendly, supportive audiences) and a wait-list control. Both treatments were clearly superior to the wait-list control, but on some assessment criteria attention training was superior to behavior rehearsal. The authors admitted that their treatment included many elements, such as verbal persuasion, modeling, instruction, performance accomplishments, group influence, and homework assignments, but nevertheless felt that the key element to their treatment was the modification of maladaptive thoughts.

Subsequent research provides some backing for this conclusion. In a trial of cognitive therapy versus antianxiety drugs, Clark and Agras (1991) found that the beta-blocker buspirone did no better than placebo, but cognitive restructuring was clearly superior to both. Sweeney and Horan (1982) reported that both cognitive therapy and cue-controlled relaxation training were individually superior to a control condition that consisted of musical analysis training, but the combination of cognitive therapy and relaxation was best of all.

A particular form of cognitive restructuring that shows promise is that called stress inoculation (Meichenbaum, 1985; Salmon, 1991). The idea is that it is important to implant realistic expectations about what will be experienced during performance as well as promoting optimistic self-comments. Performers are taught to anticipate the symptoms of anxiety that are bound to arise before important public appearances and to befriend them, that is, reframe them as less threatening, even desirable, reactions. For example, the adrenaline effects (e.g., pounding heart, faster breathing) are reappraised as normal emotional responses that are not conspicuous to an audience and can provide energy, thus contributing to a more lively, exciting musical performance.

In an interview study with successful professional performers, Roland (1994a) found that they viewed anxiety or nervousness before a performance as a normal and even a beneficial part of performance preparation. They described experiencing a hyped-up, excited feeling before performing, an increase in mental focus, and sometimes inspiration. Similarly, Hanton and Jones (1999) found that elite swimmers viewed precompetition anxiety as helpful to a far greater extent than nonelite swimmers. Clearly, perceiving preperformance anxiety as a normal and helpful aspect of performing can be an important cognitive strategy.

In an attempt to improve upon the standard cognitive-behavioral treatment for musicians with performance anxiety, Roland (1994a) developed some modifications. He compared two treatment groups with a wait-list control group. The standard cognitive-behavioral treatment incorporated relaxation techniques (breathing awareness, progressive muscle relaxation, and mental suggestions and imagery to produce a relaxed state) and cognitive techniques (normalizing the experience of anxiety and developing positive self-talk). The modified cognitive-behavioral treatment group incorporated the same relaxation techniques, normalizing the experience of anxiety but without training in positive self-talk. It also included training in task-oriented thinking, setting performance goals, mental rehearsal, and developing a preperformance routine. The training sessions were conducted over four two-hour weekly sessions. The modified treatment showed no superiority over the standard procedure (though both were effective relative to controls).

Hypnotherapy

If confident self-talk is the key to alleviating performance anxiety, then verbal suggestions delivered under hypnosis might also be an effective treatment. Stanton (1993) describes a two-session hypnotherapy procedure that combines success imagery with rational-emotive therapy (overriding crippling myths such as the idea that anything short of perfection is a disaster); three cases were apparently successfully treated in this way. In a more controlled study, Stanton (1994) paired music students according to their scores on a performance anxiety questionnaire and assigned one of each pair to hypnotherapy and control groups. Hypnotherapy consisted of two 50-minute sessions, one week apart, which included relaxation suggestions, induction of slow breathing, pleasant visual imagery (clouds and a lake), and verbal suggestions that linked these images to increased mental control. The control group met twice at the same interval for similar-length discussion sessions. The hypnotherapy group (but not controls) showed a significant reduction of performance anxiety immediately after treatment and further gains six months later.

Although hypnotherapy appeared effective in Stanton's studies, there are reasons that these results should be treated as preliminary. First, his procedure included relaxation and it may be that this would be equally effective without trance induction. Second, doing better than nothing is not a great achievement. What is needed is a comparison of the cost-effectiveness of hypnotherapy and that of standard practice (currently cognitive-behavior therapy).

Alexander Technique

Although not specifically developed as a treatment for performance anxiety, the Alexander Technique (AT) deserves mention because it is widely used by musicians for this purpose. For example, Watson and Valentine (1987) found that more than half of British orchestral musicians used some form of complementary medicine for anxiety reduction and of these AT was the most common (43%).

Named after the Australian actor Fred Alexander, who devised it, AT is characterized as a form of kinesthetic reeducation that uses a mixture of verbal instructions and hands-on demonstration to correct postural misuse. AT has become very popular among performers and others, though it is only recently that scientific evaluation has been attempted.

Valentine et al. (1995) assigned 25 musicians to either 15 sessions of AT or a no-treatment control, assessing them at audition, in class before and after treatment, and at a final recital. Measures included physiological and self-report indices of anxiety and ratings of videotaped musical performance by judges who were blind to the treatment assignment. The AT group showed more improvement in musical skill, a more positive attitude to performance, and lower levels of anxiety than the controls. However, the benefits were confined to the low-stress (classroom) situation and did not transfer to recital. Furthermore, the improvements were not related to positive changes in postural habits as rated by the AT teachers, suggesting that, such as they were, they must have been due to some other mechanism. A likely candidate would be some kind of cognitive restructuring (e.g., distraction from anxiety cues or destructive self-talk). This preliminary research suggests that AT has some beneficial effect but perhaps not for the reasons its proponents believe. Again, a comparison of its efficacy with that of cognitive therapy would be useful.

Implications and Strategies

The research described earlier suggests that a cognitive-behavioral approach is the treatment of choice for performance anxiety. There are a number of strategies that can be employed at a cognitive and behavioral level.

Cognitive Strategies

Cognitive strategies include normalizing the experience of preperformance anxiety, increasing positive self-talk, mental rehearsal of the performance, and goal setting.

Viewing Anxiety as Positive.   The first step is for performers to view the experience of some preperformance anxiety as a normal and even helpful part of performing. However, this view is not one that performers or athletes automatically or easily arrive at. Both Roland (1994b) and Hanton and Jones (1999) found that performers and athletes usually go through some unpleasant performance and competition experiences before arriving at a more positive view of performance anxiety. It can be concluded from this that there is no easy way for the beginning performer to become acclimatized to live performing other than by actually doing it repeatedly and in many different types of performance situations.

Positive Self-Talk.   In the interview study with successful professional performers, Roland (1994b) found that 69% used positive self-talk prior to performing. The earlier literature review referred to studies that have attempted to train performers in the use of realistic, positive self-talk. In this approach, unrealistic negative self-statements are challenged and analyzed for their veracity. Typically overanxious performers will catastrophize about their chances of failure. The aim is to help performers realistically appraise their perception of a performance and adopt more positive and helpful self-statements. Doing this reduces the sense of threat the performers feel and increases their sense of self-control. An example of this reappraisal process would be asking the musician, "What's the worst thing that can really happen to you in this performance?" Often the process of answering this question, assessing the actual likelihood and implications of its outcome, will be sufficient to provide the performer with a more realistic appraisal of the situation. This will in turn reduce the sense of threat and fear experienced by performers (see further Bourne; 1995, Seligman, 1995; Meichenbaum, 1985).

Mental Rehearsal and Imagery.   Mental rehearsal is another strategy for preparing for performance (Roland, 1994a; Murphy & Jowdy, 1992). Hanton and Jones (1999) and Orlick (1990) found a similar use of mental rehearsal strategies in elite athletes. Taylor and Taylor (1995) have developed imagery techniques for dancers. Mental rehearsal requires performers to imagine as vividly as they can, going through their performance in the ideal way they would like it to go. In imagining this they can draw on all senses—sound, sight, touch, taste, smell, and kinesthetic. They can include in their rehearsal the positive self-talk they wish to experience. By doing this performers can imagine themselves watching their own performance as an audience member might (external focus) or watching their performance as if they were actually performing (internal focus). The effect of mental rehearsal appears to be that it provides a form of neuromuscular programming so that the performer is more likely to automatically behave in the preferred way during the actual performance (Roland, 1997). This process is similar in nature to self-hypnosis.

Goal Setting.   Goal setting has become a standard cognitive strategy in sports and in work environments but appears to have been little applied in musical settings (Burton, 1992; Roland, 1997). Research in these settings indicates that working out short- and long-term goals improves the quality of performance of the goal setter. Goals can be broken into process goals and outcome goals. Process goals include the aspects of the performance that the performer wishes to achieve to create a good performance; for example, these could relate to technique or the interpretation of a piece. Outcome goals relate to more observable achievements such as securing a position in an orchestra and learning a certain repertoire. In the case of children, the type of goals parents set for their children can be a major influence on the child's attitude to performing. On the one hand, parents who set learning- or process-oriented goals are more likely to encourage their children to enjoy the process of performing. On the other hand, parents who set performance outcome goals are more likely to encourage perfectionist tendencies in their children, thus encouraging performance anxiety (Ablard & Parker, 1997). This suggests that it is healthier to place an emphasis on process-oriented goals most of the time.

Behavioral Strategies

Behavioral strategies include relaxation, adopting a preperformance routine, following an anxiety hierarchy, and adopting supportive lifestyle habits.

Relaxation. Training in relaxation skills has become a standard approach in anxiety management in general (e.g. Bourne, 1995) and in the treatment of performance anxiety in particular (Nagel, Himle, & Papsdorf, 1989). The regular practice of relaxation helps to reduce the physiological response to stress, prevent the cumulative effect of stress, improve memory and concentration, increase energy and productivity levels, and reduce muscle tension (Bourne, 1995). Roland (1994b) found that 71% of the professional performers he interviewed used breathing relaxation prior to performing and some performers used other forms of relaxation activity prior to performing. Hanton and Jones (1999) found a high use of precompetition relaxation strategies in elite swimmers.

There are two main ways in which relaxation strategies can be applied. One is on a regular basis, while the other is as part of a preperformance routine. Roland (1997) has suggested that performers need to practice relaxation training outside of performance conditions before they can successfully practice it prior to a performance. Relaxation strategies can include progressive muscle relaxation, mental suggestions and imagery to produce a relaxed state, meditation, breathing awareness, yoga, tai chi, stretching, and AT.

Preperformance Routines. A preperformance routine appears to be an important element in helping performers to achieve an optimal mental and physical state for their performance (Roland, 1994b). A preperformance routine might include a warm-up on the instrument, the use of positive self-talk, a focus on performance goals, the use of a relaxation strategy, controlling the type and amount of interaction with others, a nap earlier in the day, and monitoring food and fluid intake. Ultimately, all performers need to work out through experimentation a standard routine that helps them to achieve a state of readiness for performing.

Anxiety Hierarchies. For performers who have had a bad experience of performing that has greatly undermined their confidence or for the new performers who are just starting out, the use of an anxiety hierarchy can be very useful. The performer is helped to work out a hierarchy of performance situations that range from the situation that induces the least amount of anxiety to the situation that induces extreme anxiety. These can be rated from 0 (no anxiety) to 100 (extreme anxiety). Performers then commence carrying out the performances that have a low rating until they become comfortable. They then work progressively up the hierarchy, becoming comfortable with each stage before moving on to the next. This structured approach provides an indication of the stage of performance the performer is ready for; thus the likelihood of the performer being overwhelmed by a performance situation is greatly reduced. As performers progress through the hierarchy they practice their anxiety management skills such as relaxation and positive self-talk so that these become an integral part of the approach.

Supportive Lifestyle.   There are standard lifestyle habits that are valuable for general stress management. These include regular physical exercise, adequate sleep, and a healthy diet. Regular exercise is likely to help prevent the buildup of stress-related chemicals in the body. Avoiding high-caffeine, high-sugar, and spicy foods prior to performing and instead eating easily digestible complex carbohydrates, fruits, and vegetables is likely to produce a sustained release of energy during the performance. This will reduce the chance of fluctuations in concentration (Stanton, 1988; Robson, Davidson, & Snell, 1995). Other factors sometimes outside of the performers' control can affect their response to the stress of performing. These can include family, financial, and health difficulties. A first step is acknowledgment by the performers of the effect these may be having on their performance.

Flow State.   As a final consideration in examining performance anxiety, performers can aim for the experience of *flow* in performing. Flow is the state in which performers perform to their optimum, the experience of which is usually described by the performer as exhilarating (Csikszentmihalyi, 1992; see chapter 3). Csikszentmihalyi and other researchers such as Jackson (1995) have attempted to determine the conditions that are likely to precipitate the flow experience. It is these conditions that music educators and performers can be mindful of in their approach to performance. One of the critical conditions for flow is that there needs to be a skill-challenge balance such that the performers are being challenged during practice or performance but not too far beyond their skills at that time. A second condition is that performers need to have a clear goal or purpose. A third condition for the repeated occurrence of flow experiences is that the performers look for feedback before, during, and after performing. This allows performers to assess their progress and to make corrective adjustments to their future performances.

Conclusion

This chapter has provided an overview of the incidence and nature of performance anxiety in music, an issue that is clearly of importance to every musician and music educator. In our opinion, the best approach for the treatment of debilitating performance anxiety is cognitive-behavior therapy, although drug therapy, clinical hypnosis, and the Alexander Technique also appear to be beneficial to some degree. A key implication of our review is that there are a number of positive strategies that can be employed by every performer, no matter how experienced or inexperienced he or she may be, in order to overcome the types of anxiety problems that all musicians face as they learn how to perform confidently.

References

Abel, J. L., & Larkin, K. T. (1990). Anticipation of performance among musicians: Physiological arousal, confidence and state anxiety. *Psychology of Music, 18*(2), 171–182.

Ablard, K., & Parker, W. (1997). Parents' achievement goals and perfectionism in their academically talented children. *Journal of Youth and Adolescence, 26*(6), 651–667.

Allen, M., Hunter, J. E., & Donahue, W. A. (1989). Meta-analysis of self-report data on the effectiveness of public speaking anxiety treatment techniques. *Communication Education, 38,* 54–76.

Anderson, K. J. (1994). Impulsivity, caffeine and task difficulty: A within subjects test of the Yerkes-Dodson Law. *Personality and Individual Differences, 16,* 813–829.

Appel, S. S. (1976). Modifying solo performance anxiety in adult pianists. *Journal of Music Therapy, 13,* 2–16.

Beck, A., & Emery, G. (1985). *Anxiety disorders and phobias: A cognitive perspective.* New York: Basic Books.

Bourne, E. (1995). *The anxiety and phobia workbook.* Oakland, CA: New Harbinger.

Burton, D. (1992). The Jekyll/Hyde nature of goals: Reconceptualising goal setting in sport. In T. Horn (Ed.), *Advances in sport psychology* (pp. 221–250). Champaign, IL: Human Kinetic.

Clark, D. B., & Agras, W. S. (1991). The assessment and treatment of performance anxiety in musicians. *American Journal of Psychiatry, 148,* 598–605.

Cox, W. J., & Kenardy, J. (1993). Performance anxiety, social phobia and setting effects in instrumental music students. *Journal of Anxiety Disorders, 7,* 49–60.

Csikszentmihalyi, M. (1992). *Flow: The psychology of happiness.* London: Rider.

Fredrikson, M., & Gunnarsson, R. (1992). Psychobiology of stage fright. *Biological Psychology, 33,* 51–61.

Gabbard, G. O. (1979). Stage fright. *International Journal of Psychoanalysis, 60,* 383–392.

Gellrich, M. (1991). Concentration and tension. *British Journal of Music Education, 8*(2), 167–179.

Graydon, J., & Murphy, T. (1995). The effect of personality on social facilitation whilst performing a sports related task. *Personality and Individual Differences, 19,* 265–267.

Hamann, D. L. (1982). An assessment of anxiety in instrumental and vocal performers. *Journal of Research in Music Education, 30*(2), 77–90.

Hamann, D. L., & Sobaje, M. (1983). Anxiety and the college musician: A study of performance conditions and subject variables. *Psychology of Music, 11*(1), 37–50.

Hanton, S., & Jones, G. (1999). The acquisition and development of cognitive skills and strategies: 1. Making the butterflies fly in formation. *Sport Psychologist, 13,* 1–21.

Hanton, S., & Jones, G. (1999). The effects of a multimodal intervention program on performers: 11. Making the butterflies fly in formation. *Sport Psychologist, 13,* 22–41.

Hardy, L., & Parfitt, G. (1991). A catastrophe model of anxiety and performance. *British Journal of Psychology, 82*(2), 163–178.

Jackson, S. (1995). Factors influencing the occurrence of flow state in elite athletes. *Journal of Applied Sport Psychology, 7,* 138–166.

James, I., & Savage, I. (1984). Beneficial effects of nadolol on anxiety-induced disturbances of performance in musicians. *American Heart Journal, 108*(4.2), 1150–1155.

Kendrick, M. J., Craig, K. D., Lawson, D. M., & Davidson, P. O. (1982). Cognitive and behavior therapy for musical performance anxiety. *Journal of Consulting and Clinical Psychology, 50*, 353–362.

Lloyd-Elliot, M. (1991). Witches, demons and devils: The enemies of auditions and how performing artists make friends with these saboteurs. In G. D. Wilson (Ed.), *Psychology and performing arts* (pp. 211–218). Amsterdam: Swets & Zeitlinger.

Marchant-Haycox, S. E., & Wilson, G. D. (1992). Personality and stress in performing artists. *Personality and Individual Differences, 13*, 1061–1068.

Meichenbaum, D. (1985). *Stress inoculation training.* New York: Pergamon.

Mor, S., Day, H., & Flett, G. (1995). Perfectionism, control, and components of performance anxiety in professional artists. *Cognitive Therapy and Research, 19*(2), 207–225.

Murphy, S., & Jowdy, D. (1992). Imagery and mental practice. In T. Horn (Ed), *Advances in sport psychology* (pp. 221–250). Champaign, IL: Human Kinetic.

Nagel, J., Himle, D., & Papsdorf, J. (1989). Cognitive-behavioural treatment of musical performance anxiety. *Psychology of Music, 17*(1), 12–21.

Nagel, J. J. (1993). Stage fright in musicians: A psychodynamic perspective. *Bulletin of the Menninger Clinic, 57*, 492–503.

Orlick, T. (1990). *In pursuit of excellence: How to win in sport and life through mental training* (2nd ed.). Champaign, IL: Leisure.

Robson, B., Davidson, J., & Snell, E. (1995). "But I'm not ready yet." *Medical Problems of Performing Artists, 10*(1), 32–37.

Roland, D. (1994a). The development and evaluation of a modified cognitive-behavioural treatment for musical performance anxiety (Doctoral dissertation, University of Wollongong, Australia). *Dissertion Abstracts International* (University Microfilms No. 9424349), UMI, Ann Arbor, MI.

Roland, D. (1994b). How professional performers manage performance anxiety. *Research Studies in Music Education, 2*, 25–35.

Roland, D. (1997). *The confident performer.* Sydney: Currency.

Salmon, P. (1991). Stress inoculation techniques and musical performance anxiety. In G. D. Wilson (Ed.), *Psychology and performing arts* (pp. 219–229). Amsterdam: Swets & Zeitlinger.

Seligman, M. (1995). *The optimistic child.* Sydney: Random House.

Stanton, H. E. (1993). Alleviation of performance anxiety through hypnotherapy. *Psychology of Music, 21*(1), 78–82.

Stanton, H. E. (1994). Reduction of performance anxiety in music students. *Australian Psychologist, 29*, 124–127.

Stanton, R. (1988). *Eating for peak performance.* Sydney: Allen & Unwin.

Steptoe, A., & Fidler, H. (1987). Stage fright in orchestral musicians: A study of cognitive and behavioral strategies in performance anxiety. *British Journal of Psychology, 78*(2), 241–249.

Sweeney, G. A., & Horan, J. J. (1982). Separate and combined effects of cue-controlled relaxation and cognitive restructuring in the treatment of musical performance anxiety. *Journal of Counselling Psychology, 29*(5), 486–497.

Taylor, J., & Taylor, C. (1995). *Psychology of dance.* Champaign, IL: Human Kinetic.

Valentine, E. R., Fitzgerald, D. F. P., Gorton, T. L., Hudson, J. A., & Symonds, E. R. C. (1995). The effect of lessons in the Alexander Technique on music performance in high and low stress situations. *Psychology of Music, 23*(2), 129–141.

Van Kemanade, J. F., Van Son, M. J., & Van Heesch, N. C. (1995). Performance anxiety among professional musicians in symphonic orchestras: A self-report study. *Psychological Reports, 77,* 555–562.

Wardle, A. (1975). Behavior modification by reciprocal inhibition of instrumental music performance anxiety. In C. K. Madsen, R. D. Greer, and C. H. Madsen Jr. (Eds.), *Research in music behavior: Modifying basic behavior in the classroom* (pp. 191–205). New York: Teachers College.

Watson, P., & Valentine, E. (1987). The practice of complementary medicine and anxiety levels in a population of musicians. *Journal of the International Society for the Study of Tensions in Performance (ISSTIP), 4,* 26–30.

Wesner, R. B., Noyes, R., & Davis, T. L. (1990). The occurrence of performance anxiety among musicians. *Journal of Affective Disorders, 18,* 177–185.

Wills, G. D., & Cooper, C. L. (1988). *Pressure sensitive: Popular musicians under stress.* London: Sage.

Wilson, G. D. (2002). *Psychology for performing artists* (2nd ed.). London: Whurr.

5

Brain Mechanisms

ECKART ALTENMÜLLER & WILFRIED GRUHN

Neurological foundations of music perception, performance, and learning rely on individually variable, widely distributed neuronal networks in both hemispheres. Music performance is a complex voluntary sensorimotor behavior that becomes automated during extensive practice with auditory feedback. It involves all motor, somatosensory, and auditory areas of the brain. Practicing a musical instrument results first in a temporary and later in a stable increase in the amount of nerve tissue devoted to the various component tasks. Overuse of movement patterns may degrade motor memory and voluntary control of movements (musician's cramp). Neuronal networks established during music learning may depend on teaching strategies. Brain regions corresponding to specific subtasks of music performance are larger in musicians with early training, which may account for their superior capacity to acquire complex musical sensory-motor and auditory skills.

Music performance at a professional level is one of the most demanding tasks for the human central nervous system. It involves the precise execution of very fast and, in many instances, extremely complex physical movements under continuous auditory feedback. A further aspect of music performance—although not specifically addressed in this chapter—is the involvement of emotional experiences.

Extensive practice is required to develop new skills and carry out these complex tasks. Motor skills, on the one hand, can only be automated by countless repetitions; aural skills, on the other hand, are developed through a broad variety of listening experiences. These skills are not represented in isolated brain areas but rather depend on the multiple connections and interactions established during training within and among the different regions of the brain. The general ability of our central nervous system to adapt to both changing environmental conditions and newly imposed tasks during its entire life span is referred to as *plasticity:* in music, learning through experience and training is accompanied by development and changes that not only take place in the brain's neuronal networks, for example as a strengthening of neurons' connections, but also occur in its overall gross structure.

The aim of this chapter is to give a short review of current knowledge about the brain mechanisms involved in music perception, music production, and music learning. We believe that a basic understanding of the enormously complex neurobiological processes that underlie the musician's training and performance will eventually stimulate new insights into the practice and theory of music education. So far, the results of laboratory experiments have been, by necessity, restricted to very limited aspects of music making. Consequently, the brain mechanisms that underlie the rich universe of accomplished musicianship are mostly still inaccessible to brain research.

To understand neural substrates of music performance it is first necessary to understand some basic neuroanatomy and neurophysiology. In the next section we introduce essential general information for musical readers.

Neurophysiological Background

Brain-Imaging Methods

During the last decade, rapid improvements in brain-imaging methods have enabled researchers to carry out substantial new investigations into the biological foundations of music performance. The general term *functional brain imaging* covers the various methods of objectively monitoring neuronal activity during music perception, musical reasoning, and music production. These methods allow documentation of the dynamics of developing brain circuitry during the acquisition of new mental representations. They show our brain at work.

There are two principal approaches that can be used to assess brain activity. The first of these involves methods such as *electroencephalography* (*EEG*) and *magnetoencephalography* (*MEG*), which make it possible to directly measure the electrical activity of the neurons in the cerebral cortex. The second enables the assessment of brain metabolism, cerebral blood flow, and oxygen consumption of nerve cells and allows for indirect analysis of neuronal activity based on the close links between oxygen consumption and the firing activities of nerve cells. The need for oxygen is reflected in local increases of blood flow in the nervous tissue, which can, in turn, be assessed by measuring the local concentration of radioactively labeled marker substances in the blood such as oxygen or glucose. While *positron emission tomography* (*PET*) uses this kind of data collection, certain inconveniences arise with the use of this method due to the application of low dosages of radioactivity. Much safer is the method of *functional magnetic resonance imaging* (*fMRI*), which uses the magnetic properties of oxygen in blood cells in order to calculate oxygen consumption.

The main advantages of EEG and MEG are their excellent temporal resolution, which enables the monitoring of rapid processes and changes. These methods also allow communication flows among different areas of the brain to be analyzed through the calculation of so-called *coherence* between activated neuronal cell assemblies. In contrast, the main advantages of PET and fMRI are their excellent *spatial resolution*, which allows particular tasks to be related to specific brain structures. Nevertheless, the temporal resolutions of PET and fMRI are still relatively poor (ranging from six seconds to one minute), meaning that more rapid cognitive processes cannot be tracked. A further factor is cost: MEG, PET, and fMRI rely on extremely complex and expensive technologies. Only EEG is affordable enough to be used outside specialized brain-imaging centers.

General Structure of the Brain

The human brain can be subdivided into three parts: the *hindbrain*, the *midbrain*, and the *forebrain* (see Figure 5.1). The hindbrain consists of the *medulla*, *pons*, and *cerebellum*. The hindbrain and the midbrain together constitute the *brain stem*, which is phylogenetically (i.e., in terms of evolution) the oldest part of the brain. The brain stem regulates all vital functions such as breathing, heartbeat, arousal, body temperature, and equilibrium. Furthermore, the brain stem controls many sensory and motor functions such as eye movements and the coordination of visual and auditory reflexes. The cerebellum lies behind the pons and mainly processes body equilibrium and the accurate timing of movements. It is involved in the learning of motor skills and is particularly relevant to the learning skills required in musical performance. The midbrain lies above the pons and contains two structures. The first of these—the *thalamus*—transmits incoming information from all sensory systems to the cerebral cortex and so acts as a gateway to the cortex. The latter—the *hypothalamus*—regulates *autonomic* and *endocrine* functions. Finally, the forebrain consists of the two outer cerebral hemispheres and three deep-lying structures: the *basal ganglia*, the *hippocampus*, and the *amygdaloid nucleus*. The last two structures lie at the inner border of the temporal lobe and are not shown in Figure 5.1. The basal ganglia participate in regulating motor performance, the hippocampus is involved with aspects of memory storage, and the amygdaloid nucleus coordinates autonomic and endocrine responses in conjunction with emotional states.

All cognitive functions are governed by the cerebral cortex—the outer part of the brain—which is the most complex organ in the human body. According to recent estimates, the cerebral cortex consists of about 100 billion neurons, which are interconnected by a dense web of nerve fibers. Each nerve cell can communicate with approximately ten thousand other cells. Small, prominent buttons (*synapses*) in the nerve fibers form these connections. The cerebral cortex is divided into two hemispheres that are interconnected by a large fiber bundle that contains about 100 million fibers. This is known as the *corpus callosum*.

Four important features characterize the organization of the cortex. First of all, each hemisphere is concerned primarily with sensory and motor processes on the opposite (*contralateral*) side of the body. Second, although appearing to be similar, these hemispheres are neither completely symmetrical in structure nor equivalent in function. Third, the cortex is hierarchically organized, with distinct primary, secondary, and tertiary (or associative) sensory or motor re-

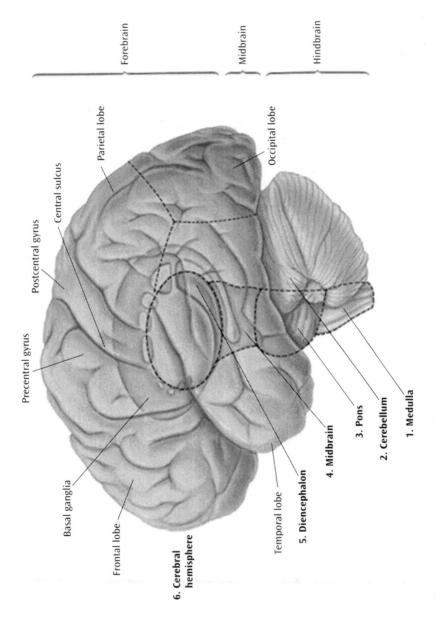

Figure 5.1. Overview of the anatomical structures of the brain. Left hemisphere is shown.

gions. *Primary sensory regions* (or *areas*) are directly linked to the sensory organs via the thalamus. *Primary motor regions* are directly linked to the spinal chord. *Secondary* and *tertiary* sensory and motor areas are adjacent to the primary areas and process more complex stimulus features. Fourth, early intense training processes, starting before the age of about ten years, may lead to enlargement of the cortical areas involved in the trained faculty.

Each hemisphere is divided into four anatomically distinct cortical lobes called the frontal (front), temporal (side), parietal (upper back), and occipital (back) lobes (Figures 5.1 and 5.2). The frontal lobes are largely concerned with the planning of future action and the control of movement. The parietal lobes, which are located behind the frontal lobe and separated by a deep fissure known as the *central sulcus*, are mainly concerned with the processing of somatic sensation and body image. The occipital lobes, which are responsible for processing vision, lie behind the parietal lobes at the back of the brain. The temporal lobes are separated from the frontal and the parietal lobes by a further deep fissure—the *lateral sulcus*. These temporal lobes deal not only with hearing but also with other aspects such as cross-modal learning, memory, and emotion.

Functional Neuroanatomy of Music

Perception

Music perception involves the *primary* and *secondary auditory areas* (A1, A2) and the *auditory association areas* (AA) in the two temporal lobes (Figure 5.2). The primary auditory area, localized in the upper portion of the temporal lobes just above the ears, receives its main input from the ears via the thalamus and can be regarded as the first station of cortical auditory processing. It is mainly involved in basic auditory processing such as pitch and loudness perception, perception of time structures, and spectral decomposition. The left side of the primary auditory cortex is specialized in the rapid analysis of time structures, such as differences in voice onset times when articulating *da* or *ta*. The right deals primarily with the spectral decomposition of sounds. The secondary auditory areas surround the primary area in a beltlike formation. Here more complex auditory patterns such as timbre are processed. Finally, in the auditory association areas, auditory *gestalt* perception takes place. Auditory gestalt can be understood, for example, as pitch-time patterns like melodies and words. In right-handers and in about 95% of all left-handers, the *Wernicke region* in the back portion of the upper part of the temporal lobe in the left hemisphere (above and behind the left ear) is specialized in language decoding.

In contrast to the *early auditory processing* of simple acoustic structures, listening to music is a far more complex task. Music is experienced not only as an acoustic structure in time but also as patterns, associations, emotions, expectations, and so on. Such experiences are not based on a uniform mental capacity but on a complex set of perceptive and cognitive operations represented in the central nervous system. In some parts, these operations act interdependently;

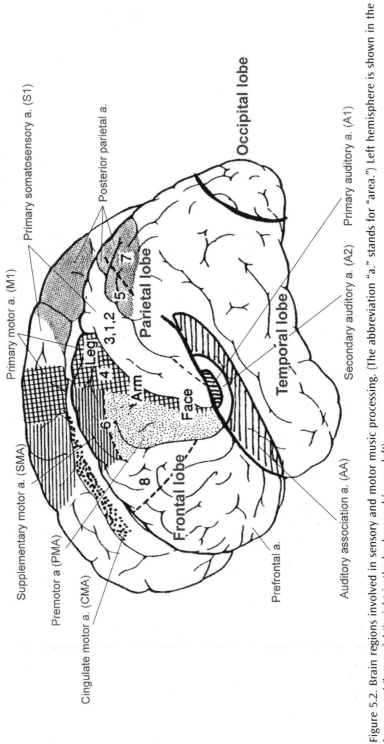

Figure 5.2. Brain regions involved in sensory and motor music processing. (The abbreviation "a." stands for "area.") Left hemisphere is shown in the foreground (lower right), right in the background (upper left).

Primary motor a. (M1)

Primary somatosensory a. (S1)

Posterior parietal a.

Supplementary motor a. (SMA)

Premotor a (PMA)

Cingulate motor a. (CMA)

Prefrontal a.

Auditory association a. (AA)

Secondary auditory a. (A2)

Primary auditory a. (A1)

Occipital lobe

Parietal lobe

Temporal lobe

Frontal lobe

Leg

3,1,2

5

7

4

Arm

6

Face

8

in others, they function independently. Integrated in time and linked to previous experiences through the aid of memory systems, they enable us to experience music as meaningful. This feeling of meaning takes place on a nonverbal level and is closely linked to emotions.

The neuronal basis of the respective operations may be compared to modules working partly as isolated neuronal processing units. Time and pitch structures, for example, seem to be processed, at least in part, by separate modules, since they can be selectively impaired following brain lesions. Generally speaking, musical time structures are largely processed in the left temporal lobe, whereas pitch structures are processed primarily through networks in the right temporal lobe.

The situation becomes more complicated when considering that the perception of music may occur at different hierarchical levels. With respect to melodic structures, interval-based listening through step-by-step analysis of a melody must be distinguished from contour-based listening in which the more general features of a melody are analyzed. The first type of listening is regarded as a *local* mode of cognitive processing; the latter, as a *global* or *holistic* mode. By analogy, note-by-note rhythm processing may be considered as a local task, in contrast to meter processing, which is a more global task. From studies of brain lesions and functional imaging studies we have learned that local processing relies, to a great extent, on structures in the brain's left hemisphere. Global processing, in contrast, is reliant upon those structures in the right hemisphere (e.g., Peretz, 1990). Since music listeners may switch from one mode to another, it is evident that the neuronal networks involved in music processing are adaptive, rapidly changing, and not fixed in definite music centers. It should be emphasized that as soon as music is processed extended neuronal networks are activated that reflect the individual's way of listening and processing. These include not only the temporal but also the frontal, parietal, and occipital lobes of both hemispheres of the brain (Schuppert et al., 2000). Some factors that determine the generation of such networks will be discussed later.

Performance

Music performance on a professional level requires extremely refined motor skills that are acquired over many years of extensive training and that have to be stored and maintained through further regular practice. Auditory feedback is needed to improve and perfect performance. Music making, therefore, relies primarily on a highly developed auditory-motor integration capacity, which can be compared to the oral-aural loop in speech production. In addition, somatosensory feedback constitutes another basis of high-level performance. Here the kinesthetic sense, which allows for control and feedback of muscle and tendon tension as well as joint positions and which enables continuous monitoring of finger, hand, and lip position in the frames of body and instrument coordinates (for example, the keyboard, the mouthpiece, etc.), is especially important. In a more general context, the motor system of music performance can be understood as a subspecialty of the motor systems for planned and skilled voluntary limb movements.

Voluntary skilled limb movements involve four cortical regions in both hemispheres (Figure 5.2): the *primary motor area* (M1) located in the *precentral gyrus* directly in front of the central sulcus; the *supplementary motor area* (SMA) located anterior to the M1 of the frontal lobe and the inner (medial) side of the cortex; the *cingulate motor area* (CMA) below the SMA and above the corpus callosum on the inner (medial) side of the hemisphere; and the *premotor area* (PMA), which is located adjacent to the lateral aspect of the primary motor area. SMA, CMA, and PMA can be described as *secondary motor areas*, processing movement patterns rather than simple movements. In addition to the cortical regions, the motor system includes the cerebellum and the subcortical structures of the basal ganglia. The sensory areas are necessary in order to maintain the control of movements. Their steady kinesthetic feedback information is required for any guided motor action. The sensory areas are located in the *primary somatosensory area* (S1) behind the central sulcus in the parietal lobe. The parietal lobe is involved in many aspects of movement processing. It is an area where information from multiple sensory regions converges. In the posterior parietal area, the body coordinates in space are monitored and calculated and visual information is transferred into body coordinates. As far as musicians are concerned, this area is prominently activated during sight-reading and the playing of a complex piece of music (Sergent, 1993).

The *primary motor area* (M1) represents the movements of body parts in a separate but systematic order. The representation of the leg is located on the top and the inner side of the hemisphere, the arm in the upper portion, and the hand and mouth in the lower portion of M1. This representation of distinct body parts in corresponding brain regions is called somatotopic or homuncular order. Just as the *motor homunculus* is represented upside down, so, too, is the *sensory homunculus* on the other side of the central sulcus. The proportions of both the motor and the sensory homunculus are markedly distorted since they are determined by the density of motor and sensory innervation of the respective body parts. For example, control of fine movements of the tongue requires many more nerve fibers that transmit the information to this muscle, as compared to muscles of the back. Therefore, the hand, the lips, and the tongue require almost two-thirds of the neurons in this area. However, as will be pointed out later, the representation of body parts may be modified by usage. Moreover, the primary motor area does not simply represent individual muscles: multiple muscular representations are arranged in a complex way so as to allow the execution of simple types of movements rather than the activation of a specific muscle. This is a consequence of the fact that a two-dimensional array of neurons in M1 has to code for three-dimensional movements in space (for a review see Rouiller, 1996). Put simply, our brain represents movements, not muscles.

The *supplementary motor area* (SMA) is mainly involved in the coordination of the two hands, in the sequencing of complex movements and in the triggering of movements based on internal cues. It is particularly engaged when the execution of a sequential movement depends on internally stored and memorized information. The SMA can be subdivided into two distinct functional areas. In the anterior SMA, it would seem that the planning of complex movement patterns is processed. The posterior SMA seems to be predominantly engaged in two-handed movements and, in particular, in the synchronization of both hands during complex movement patterns. Electrical stimulation of this area during open-brain surgery can produce an interruption of two-handed piano playing (for a brief review see Marsden, Deecke, & Freund, 1996).

The function of the *cingulate motor area* (*CMA*) is still under debate. Electrical stimulation and brain-imaging studies demonstrate its involvement in movement selection based on reward, with reference to the close links between the cingulate gyrus and the emotion-processing limbic system. It seems clear that the CMA plays an important role in mediating cortical cognitive functions and limbic-emotional functions.

The *premotor area* (*PMA*) is primarily engaged when externally stimulated behavior is being planned and prepared. It is involved in the learning, execution, and recognition of limb movements and seems to be particularly concerned with the visual information necessary for movement planning.

The *basal ganglia*, located deep inside the cerebral hemispheres, are interconnected reciprocally via the thalamus to the motor and sensory cortices, thus constituting a loop of information flow between the cortex and the basal ganglia. They are indispensable for any kind of voluntary actions that are not highly automated. Their special role consists in the control of voluntary action by selecting appropriate motor actions and by comparing the goal and course of those actions with previous experience. In the basal ganglia, the flow of information between the cortex and the limbic emotion system, in particular the amygdala, converges. It is, therefore, assumed that the basal ganglia process and control the emotional evaluation of motor behavior in terms of expected reward or punishment.

Finally, the *cerebellum* contributes essentially to the timing and accuracy of fine-tuned movements.

Musicians' Brains are Different

The organization of motor systems described earlier can be applied to skilled movements in general. However, in the following section we expand this to include literature that focuses on the unique qualities of the musicians' brain.

Comparison of the brain anatomy of skilled musicians with that of nonmusicians shows that prolonged instrumental practice leads to an enlargement of the hand area in the motor cortex (Amunts et al., 1997). This enlargement appears to be particularly prominent in all instrumentalists who have started to play prior to the age of 10 years. Furthermore, in professional musicians the normal anatomic difference between the larger, dominant (mostly right) hand area and the smaller, nondominant (mostly left) hand area is less pronounced than that in nonmusicians. These results suggest that functional adaptation of the gross structure of the brain occurs during training at an early age.

Similar effects of specialization have been found with respect to the size of the corpus callosum (Schlaug et al., 1995a). Professional pianists and violinists tend to have a larger anterior (front) portion of this structure, especially those who have started prior to the age of 7. Since this part of the corpus callosum contains fibers from the motor and supplementary motor areas, it seems plausible to assume that the high demands on coordination between the two hands and the rapid exchange of information may either stimulate the nerve fiber growth—the *myelination* of nerve fibers that determines the velocity of nerve conduction—or prevent the physiological loss of nerve tissue during aging.

However, it is not only motor areas that are subject to anatomical adaptation. By means of MEG, the number of nerve cells involved in the processing of sensory stimulation in individual fingers can be monitored. Using this technique, professional violinists have been shown to posses enlarged sensory areas that correspond to the index through to the small (second to fifth) fingers of the left hand (Elbert et al., 1995). Their left thumb representation is not different from that of nonmusicians. Again, these effects were most pronounced in violinists who started their instrumental training prior to the age of 10.

A further example of functional specialization reflected by changes in gross cortical anatomy can be found in musicians who possess absolute pitch. In these musicians, the upper back portion of the left temporal lobe (*Wernicke region*) is larger in than that of musicians without absolute pitch (Schlaug et al., 1995b). Using MEG, the functional specialization of the auditory cortex has recently been demonstrated by Pantev et al. (1998). The number of auditory nerve cells involved in the processing of piano tones but not of pure sinusoidal tones was about 25% greater in pianists than in subjects who had never played an instrument. But it is not only cortical structures that are enlarged by early and prolonged instrumental training. Subcortical structures also seem to be highly affected. In professional musicians, the cerebellum, which contributes significantly to the precise timing and accuracy of motor commands, is also enlarged.

In summary, available evidence suggests that the central nervous system adapts to the challenging demands of professional musicianship during prolonged training. These adaptations are understood as brain plasticity. When training starts at an early age (before about 7 years), this adaptation affects brain anatomy in terms of the enlargement of certain brain structures involved in the respective skill. When training starts later, it modifies brain organization by rewiring neuronal webs and involving adjacent nerve cells to contribute to the required tasks. These changes result in enlarged cortical representations of, for example, specific fingers or sounds within existing brain structures.

Changes in Brain Organization While Practicing Music

Auditory Plasticity in Musicians

As mentioned earlier, the brain has the potential to reorganize its neural networks, in both the short and the long term, in response to experience and learning. Of the entire sensory system, the auditory system seems to be particularly adaptive. This is illustrated by the adaptation that results from routine ear training of musicians or the adaptation that follows experience with atypical acoustic stimuli.

Cerebral auditory plasticity has been reported in many research studies. The effects of plasticity are not restricted to a critical period in early life but also modulate functional auditory organization in adults. However, in general, the changes are more readily produced and are more stable in younger persons. This kind of dynamic neural plasticity can be shown in an experiment with a manipulated acoustic environment. In one study, adult subjects listened to music distorted by removal of a frequency band centered at one kilohertz for three hours. Immediately after the experiment, the number of auditory nerve cells found to respond to frequencies around one kilohertz was significantly diminished (Pantev et al., 1999). This demonstrates that even after a short exposure to unusual sounds the readiness to respond and the sensitivity of auditory nerve cells may be altered.

Just as the plastic changes mentioned earlier concern more basic auditory processes, musical learning is similarly accompanied by adaptive changes of neuronal networks. Furthermore, different teaching methods and learning attitudes during musical instruction are reflected in specific brain activation patterns. In order to clarify whether the *way music is learned* has any significant, contributory effect, we investigated the changes in brain activation patterns in a group of students who were learning to distinguish between correct and incorrect (balanced and unbalanced) phrases (i.e., the so-called musical periods that consist of corresponding parts, *antecedent* and *consequent*). Subjects were divided into three groups:

1. A *declarative (verbal) learner group* that received traditional instructions about the antecedent and consequent, as well as their tonal relation with respect to the closure of a complete or incomplete cadence, and whose instructions included verbal explanations, visual aids, notation, verbal rules, and some musical examples that were played to the subjects but never sung or performed
2. A *procedural learner group* that participated in musical experiences for establishing genuine musical representations by singing and playing, improvising with corresponding rhythmic and tonal elements, or performing examples from music literature
3. A *control group* of nonlearners who did not receive any instruction about or in music

Figure 5.3 shows the main results of the study. After learning, music processing in the verbally trained declarative group produced an increased activation of the left fronto-temporal brain regions, which may reflect inner speech and analytical, step-by-step processing. In contrast, the musically trained procedural group showed increased activation of the right frontal and bilateral parieto-occipital lobes, which may be ascribed to a more global way of processing and to visuo-spatial associations (Altenmüller & Gruhn, 1997). These results suggest that musical expertise influences auditory brain activation patterns and that changes in these activation patterns depend on the teaching strategies applied. In other words, the brain structures involved in music processing reflect the auditory learning biography—personal experiences accumulated over time. Listening to music, learning to play an instrument, formal instruction, and profes-

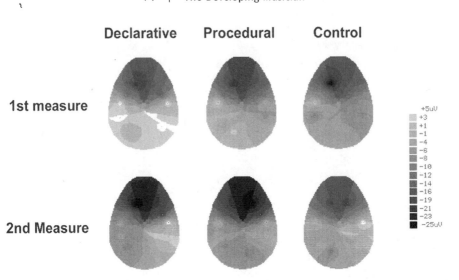

Declarative   Procedural   Control

1st measure

2nd Measure

Figure 5.3. Brain maps that demonstrate cortical activation patterns before (upper row) and after (lower row) learning in the declarative learning group, the procedural learning group, and the control group. Group statistics are displayed. Activation is dark; inactivation is white (see microvolt scale on the right). The brain diagrams are displayed as top views, frontal regions up, left hemisphere on the left, right hemisphere on the right. As illustrated, *declarative* (mainly verbally mediated) training leads to an increase in brain activity over the left frontal areas, whereas the *procedural* (mainly musically mediated) training produces an increase in activity over right frontal and bilateral parieto-occipital regions. In controls, overall activity decreased slightly.

sional training result in multiple and in many instances multisensory representations of music. These seem to be partly interchangeable and rapidly adaptive.

Sensory-Motor Plasticity and Sensory-Motor Learning

Our knowledge of the regions and mechanisms of the brain involved in sensory-motor learning is still incomplete. According to current concepts, all structures involved in motor control participate in the acquisition of new sensory-motor skills. Besides the motor areas in the cerebral cortex, the basal ganglia and the cerebellum also play an important role. It has been assumed since the nineteenth century that the cerebellum plays an important role in the acquisition of new motor skills. Such information was based on studies in which patients who were suffering from lesions of the cerebellum were found to be unable to increase the speed of a sequence of complex finger movements after practice. More recent evidence demonstrates that the cerebellum is involved in the selection, the sequence, and the timing of movements. Another functional system, which is equally important for the development and learning of fine finger movements, is the basal ganglia. Patients suffering from Parkinson's disease have deficits in learning new motor tasks, and—although they can improve the speed of complex movement patterns during practice sessions—they do not learn as quickly, and do not reach the level of performance of normal controls (Salmon & Butters, 1995). Caveat: the findings mentioned earlier are based on data obtained from patients who were suffering from brain lesions and do not take into account the acquisition of the extremely complex movement patterns necessary for professional musicianship.

It has been known for a long time that, with increasing complexity of finger movement sequences, the activity in the SMA and in the premotor area are enhanced (Roland et al., 1980). Using fMRI, Karni et al. (1995) investigated the learning of complex finger sequences similar to those necessary for piano playing. After 30 minutes of practice, the representation of the fingers in the primary motor cortex was increased. However, without further training, this effect diminished after one week with the hand representation returning to its previous size. In contrast, continuous practice resulted in a stable enlargement of the hand area in M1. This effect was specific for the daily trained sequence of complex finger movements and did not occur when the subjects improvised complex finger movements that were not subsequently repeated. Parallel to the enlargement of the hand area in the primary motor cortex, the size of the cerebellar hand representation diminished, suggesting that the cerebellum plays an important role only in the initial phase of motor learning.

Recent investigations have compared brain activation in professional pianists and nonmusicians. Hundt-Georgiadis and Cramon (1999), for example, studied brain activation during 35 minutes of short-term motor learning of a complex finger-tapping task that used the dominant right hand. They found that activation of the primary motor area during motor learning only increased among the pianists. Nonmusicians developed a temporary increase in activity during the first 7 to 14 minutes of training but, subsequently, a rapid attenuation of this activation. Furthermore, compared with nonmusicians, the motor learning of these pianists was accompanied by only small contributions from the supplementary motor areas and the cerebellar cortices. This finding is compatible with the idea that the anterior SMA is essential for setting up and executing complex motor programs prior to automatic performance. The pianists were able to rapidly and thoroughly learn the complex finger sequence, reaching a high degree of automaticity during the first minutes of motor learning.

Most interestingly, the motor cortex of the *untrained* hand was, at the same time, contributing to motor learning. This resulted in improved performance of the motor task in the untrained left hand in both pianists and nonmusicians. One of the most fascinating features of the human sensory-motor system relates to this phenomenon. Despite the clear somatotopic organization of the motor cortex, a movement can be learned with one extremity and performed with the other. Rijntjes and colleagues (1999) investigated subjects who wrote their signature with their right index finger and with their right big toe. The results of the fMRI study show that the movement parameters for these highly trained movements are stored in premotor and supplementary motor cortex adjacent to the right hand area in the primary motor cortex but are also accessible for the foot area. Thus somatotopy in secondary motor areas (SMA, PM) seems to be defined functionally—as abstract movement information independently of the executing limb (*Bewegungs-Ideen*)—and not on the basis of anatomical representations. Whereas these studies refer to explicit motor learning by trial and error and sensory feedback, implicit motor learning seems to be processed in a different way. When subjects were unaware of a motor learning task—because their attention was drawn to a different problem—activity of the basal ganglia correlated with motor learning.

None of the studies mentioned earlier take into account the special quality of musicianship and, in particular, the strong coupling of sensory-motor and auditory processing. Practicing an instrument means assembling, storing, and constantly improving complex sensory-motor programs through prolonged and repeated execution of motor patterns under control monitored of the auditory system.

Many professional pianists report that their fingers move more or less automatically when they are listening to piano music played by a colleague. In a cross-sectional experiment, we demonstrated that as a result of many years of practice, a strong linkage between auditory and sensory-motor cortical regions develops (Bangert, Parlitz, & Altenmüller, 1998). Furthermore, in a longitudinal study it was possible to follow up the formation of such neuronal multisensory connections along with piano training in beginner piano players. Nonmusicians who had never played an instrument before were trained on a computer piano twice a week over a period of 5 weeks. They listened to short piano melodies of a 3-second duration played in a five-tone range. They were then required, after a brief pause, to replay the melodies with the right hand as accurately as possible. After 10 minutes of training, listening to piano tunes produced additional activity in the central and left sensory-motor regions. In turn, playing on a keyboard produced additional activity in the auditory regions of both temporal lobes. These early signs of cortical plasticity during the first training session were not stable but stabilized within the subsequent 5 weeks of training. In the movement task, the most remarkable effect after 5 weeks was the development of additional activation of the right anterior temporal and frontal lobe. Since it has been demonstrated that this area is involved in the perception of pitch sequences, such activation might reflect the auditory imagery of sounds while moving the fingers on a soundless keyboard. In this context, it should be mentioned that the results of the experiment support the idea of the direct effectiveness of mental training on subtle sensory motor activation patterns represented in the central nervous system.

Many questions that concern the brain mechanisms of sensory-motor learning and processing during music performance remain to be clarified. It is still unclear, for example, how and where the rapid adjustment of the sensory-motor system to different spatial coordinates is processed when musicians switch between instruments of different sizes (e.g., from alto flute to piccolo). This phenomenon is referred to as response size or movement schema (Schmidt & Lee, 1999). Besides the aforementioned limb-independent storage of movement information in the secondary motor areas, the cerebellum may calculate a magnification or diminution factor. Another unsolved problem is the neuronal basis of the transition from guided slow movements, which are performed under steady sensory control, to fast, ballistic movements, which have to be performed without on-line sensory feedback. It is assumed that different brain regions produce these two types of movements and that the transition from one type to the other may be incomplete. This might explain why practicing guided movements while slowly and systematically increasing the tempo may finally hamper the execution of this movement at a very fast tempo. Although this has been recognized as a problem by many instrumental teachers, no research data are available on this topic. From an empirical standpoint, we would recommend, even at an early stage, rehearsing small segments of the movement pattern at a fast tempo. However, at the same time, the precise automation of difficult movements has to be practiced in a precisely guided slow tempo. For examples, see Cortot (1948).

Loss of Motor Control in Highly Trained Musicians

Approximately 1 in 200 professional musicians suffers from a loss of voluntary control of the extensively trained, refined, and complex sensory-motor skills— a condition generally referred to as *focal dystonia*, violinist's cramp, or pianist's cramp. In most cases, focal dystonia is so disabling that it prematurely ends the artist's professional career (Altenmüller, 1998; chapter 6 in this volume). Subtle loss of control in fast passages, finger curling (cf. Figure 5.4), lack of precision in forked fingerings in woodwind players, irregularity of trills, sticking fingers on the keys, involuntary flexion of the bowing thumb in strings, and impairment of control of the embouchure in woodwind and brass players in certain registers are the various symptoms that can mark the beginning of the disorder. At this stage, most musicians believe that the reduced precision of their movements is due to a technical problem. As a consequence, they intensify their efforts, but this often only exacerbates the problem.

Although the neurobiological origins of this disorder are not completely clarified, at present focal dystonia is understood as a cortical sensory-motor mislearning syndrome, caused by development and stabilization of disadvantageous nerve-cell connections in the sensory and motor brain regions, a condition generally referred to as *abormal plasticity* or *dysfunctional plasticity*. A study with trained monkeys (Byl, Merzenich, & Jenkins, 1996) demonstrated that chronic overuse and repetitive strain injury in highly stereotyped movements can actively degrade the cortical representation of the somatosensory information that guides the fine motor hand movements in primates. A similar degradation of sensory feedback information and concurrent fusion of the digital representations in the somatosensory cortex was confirmed in an MEG study conducted in musicians with focal dystonia, although these musicians had no history of chronic pain (Elbert et al., 1998). Therefore, additional factors such as a genetic predisposition and a certain susceptibility appear to play an important role in the development of focal dystonia

The most important and up to now unsolved question that concerns the therapy of musicians' dystonia is why this condition cannot be easily overcome by retraining and establishing new and appropriately functioning sensory-motor movement patterns.

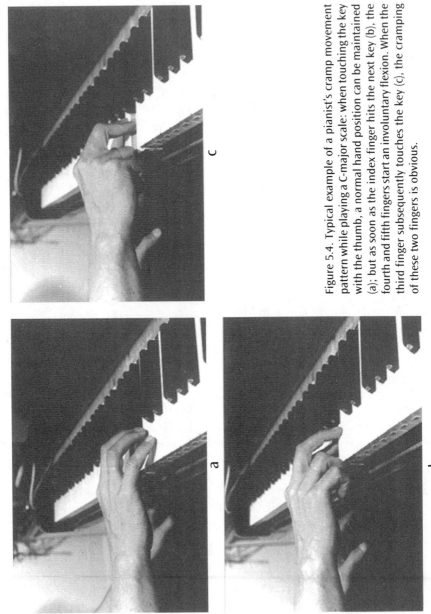

Figure 5.4. Typical example of a pianist's cramp movement pattern while playing a C-major scale: when touching the key with the thumb, a normal hand position can be maintained (a); but as soon as the index finger hits the next key (b), the fourth and fifth fingers start an involuntary flexion. When the third finger subsequently touches the key (c), the cramping of these two fingers is obvious.

Conclusions and Implications

At a time when brain research has become a key issue in science, the public is tempted to expect clear recommendations from brain studies that can be applied to teaching and learning. It is essential to be fully aware of the distinction between descriptions of how brains work and "think" (Calvin 1996; Pinker 1997) and prescriptions and recommendations on how to teach. As Gardner (1999, p. 60) has stated: "We could know what every neuron does and we would not be one step closer to knowing how to educate our children," since decisions in education are built upon value judgments. Science, however, deals with mindful theories, explanatory models, and empirical observations with no immediate link to educational values.

Nevertheless, research findings of changes in brain organization such as those described earlier may guide teachers' awareness toward optional directions of teaching and learning. In instrumental training, the main focus is generally placed upon the development of motor skills and how to automate patterns of movement. The main point here is that the brain is most flexible (or plastic) during the early years of childhood; later it becomes increasingly difficult to compensate for an underdeveloped disposition for motor skills and fine motor reflexes. Furthermore, as research has shown, the brain learns best when it is actively involved in exploring and experiencing the physical dimension of musical materials and actions. In "learning music musically" (Gruhn, 1997; Swanwick, 1999)—that is, in establishing genuine musical representations—singing and moving should be involved to enhance the aural-oral loop. As demonstrated by Bangert, Parlitz, and Altenmüller (1998), learning results in a network of coactivation where, at the very least, visual, sensory-motor, and aural representations are linked together. Learning strategies, therefore, depend on where the focus lies. If the main goal is concerned with the automation of motor skills, countless repetitions will support that process. The development of genuine musical representations that immediately represent musical properties as musical units but not in terms of visual or verbal features calls for a musical thinking that attributes intrinsic musical meaning to musical sound. This ability is called *audiation* by Gordon (1980). Mental musical representations define the physiological correlate of and prerequisite for music audiation. Audiation is the process by which one activates already-established familiar musical patterns that are stored as mental representations. Therefore, any learning efforts should be directed to establish mental images of sound prior to the training of mere motor or reading and writing skills.

Aural imagery is closely linked with musical practice, and the ability to do this depends on the level and amount of preceding practical experience. This is often misunderstood by parents who are impatient for immediate progress in expected practical skills. This may also happen when children do not read music literally (through associating letter names or syllables with notes) but rather look at the notation and play by ear along with what they imagine from the score in front of them. What may appear to be a failure of instruction actually manifests different approaches to music learning, which is best accomplished when students relate symbols (i.e., the notation) to sounds. In this manner, the perceived sound (i.e., the musical ear) guides the finger movements and instructs the students about what to play. Seen from this perspective, learning how to perform music musically not only is due to the effects of conditioning the best possible execution of motor skills but also integrates different types of representation (aural, visual, sensorimotor) into a more complex neuronal network. In the future, brain activation studies may help to develop educational strategies that foster a stronger connectivity among different brain areas by exploiting cross-modal representations.

Acknowledgments.   We are grateful to the coworkers of the Institute of Music Physiology and Performing Arts Medicine for stimulating ideas and many discussions on the topics of this contribution. The piano-learning experiment reported in the text has been conducted by Marc Bangert. The experiments on ear training and brain activation were carried out in collaboration with Dietrich Parlitz, to whom we owe Figure 5.3. Wendy Archer improved the English expression.

References

Altenmüller, E. (1998). Causes and cures of focal limb dystonia in musicians. *Journal of the International Society for the Study of Tensions in Performance (ISSTIP)*, *9*, 13–17.

Altenmüller, E., & Gruhn, W. (1997). *Music, the brain, and music learning.* Chicago: GIA.

Amunts, K., Schlaug, G., Jäncke, L., Steinmetz, H., Schleicher, A., Dabringhaus, A., & Zilles, K. (1997). Motor cortex and hand motor skills: Structural compliance in the human brain. *Human Brain Mapping, 5*, 206–215.

Bangert, M., Parlitz, D., & Altenmüller, E. (1998). Audio-motor integration in beginner and expert pianists: A combined DC-EEG and behavioral study. In N. Elsner and R. Wehner (Eds.), *Göttingen Neurobiology Report* (p. 753). Stuttgart: Thieme.

Byl, N. N., Merzenich, M. M., & Jenkins, W. M. (1996). A primate genesis model of focal dystonia and repetitive strain injury. *Neurology, 47*, 508–520.

Calvin, W. H. (1996). *How brains think.* New York: Basic Books.

Cortot, A. (1948). *F. Chopin, Etudes Op. 10.* Paris: Salabert.

Elbert, T., Pantev, C., Wienbruch, C., Rockstroh, B., & Taub, E. (1995). Increased cortical representation of the fingers of the left hand in string players. *Science, 270*, 305–307.

Elbert, T., Candia, V., Altenmüller, E., Rau, H., Sterr, A., Rockstroh, B., Pantev, C., & Taub, E. (1998). Alterations of digital representations in somatosensory cortex in focal hand dystonia. *NeuroReport, 9*, 3571–3575.

Gardner, H. (1999). *The disciplined mind.* New York: Simon & Schuster.

Gordon, E. E. (1980). *Learning sequences in music.* Chicago: GIA.

Gruhn, W. (1997). Music learning: Neurobiological foundations and educational implication. *Research Studies in Music Education, 9*, 36–47.

Hundt-Georgiadis, M., & Cramon, D. Y. (1999). Motor-learning related changes in piano players and non-musicians revealed by functional magnetic resonance signals. *Experimental Brain Research, 125*, 417–425.

Karni, A., Meyer, G., Jezzard, P., Adams, M. M., Turner. R., & Ungerleider, L. G. (1995). Functional MRI evidence for adult motor cortex plasticity during motor skill learning. *Nature, 377*, 155–158.

Marsden, C. D., Deecke, L., & Freund, H.-J. (1996). The functions of the supplementary motor area: Summary of a workshop. In H. Lüders (Ed.), *Advances in neurology: Vol. 70. Supplementary sensorimotor area* (pp. 477– 487). Philadelphia: Lippincott-Raven.

Pantev, C., Oostenveld, R., Engelien, A., Ross, B., Roberts, L. E., & Hoke, M. (1998). Increased auditory cortical representation in musicians. *Nature, 392,* 811–814.

Pantev, C., Wollbrink, A., Roberts, L. E. , Engelien, A., & Lutkenhoner, B. (1999). Short-term plasticity of the human auditory cortex. *Brain Research, 842,* 192–199.

Peretz, I. (1990). Processing of local and global musical information in unilateral brain-damaged patients. *Brain, 113,* 1185–1205.

Pinker, S. (1997). *How the mind works.* New York: Norton.

Rijntjes, M:, Dettmers, C., Buchel, C., Kiebel, S., Frackowiak, R. S., & Weiller, C. (1999). A blueprint for movement: Functional and anatomical representations in the human motor system *Journal of Neuroscience, 19,* 8043–8048.

Roland, P., Larsen, B., Lassen, N. A., & Skinhoi, E. (1980). Supplementary motor area and other cortical areas in organization of voluntary movements in man. *Journal of Neurophysiology, 43,* 118–136.

Rouiller, E. M. (1996). Multiple hand representations in the motor cortical areas. In A. M. Wing, P. Haggard, and J. R. Flanagan (Eds.), *Hand and brain* (pp. 99– 124). San Diego, CA: Academic Press.

Salmon, D. P., & Butters, N. (1995). Neurobiology of skill and habit learning. *Current Opinion in Neurobiology, 5,* 184–190.

Schlaug, G., Jäncke, L., Huang, Y., & Steinmetz, H. (1995a). Increased corpus callosum size in musicians. *Neuropsychologia, 33,* 1047–1055.

Schlaug, G., Jäncke, L., Huang, Y., & Steinmetz, H. (1995b). In vivo evidence of structural brain asymmetry in musicians. *Science, 267,* 699–701.

Schmidt, R. A., & Lee, T. D. (1999). *Motor control and learning: A behavioral emphasis* (3rd ed.). Champaign, IL: Human Kinetics.

Schuppert, M., Münte, T. F., Wieringa, B. M., & Altenmüller, E. (2000). Receptive amusia: Evidence for cross-hemispheric neural networks underlying music processing strategies. *Brain, 123,* 546–559.

Sergent, J. (1993). Mapping the musician brain. *Human Brain Mapping, 1,* 20–38.

Swanwick, K. (1999). *Teaching music musically.* London: Routledge.

6

Music Medicine

ALICE G. BRANDFONBRENER & JAMES M. KJELLAND

Most of the medical problems of musicians are the shared consequence of the specific instrument, performance technique, and repertoire interacting with the physical and psychological nature of the individual. The incidence of problems is greater for those instruments requiring more repetitive actions over a longer period of time and in all the risks that are increased by stress. Most frequent are musculoskeletal pain problems such as tendinitis, which typically resolve with simple measures like reduced activity, anti-inflammatory medication, and icing. Prevention is preferable to treatment for all these conditions but more research is needed to validate the techniques to be employed and to more precisely identify the causal factors. This requires close collaboration between medicine and music education.

Many, if not most, occupations are associated with some degree of personal medical risk, and music making is no exception. But it was not until the 1980s that attention became focused on music medicine. From the musicians' viewpoint, there was a certain degree of fear behind their reluctance to seek medical advice, fear of losing a career and fear of uninformed medical care. Most musicians know someone whose career was compromised or ended due to injury. Likewise, they may have themselves experienced or have heard of a colleague's negative medical experiences, which often resulted in a justifiable distrust of physicians. From the physicians' viewpoint, musicians with medical complaints often showed little or no observable pathology, and so the symptoms were often judged to be exaggerated and no diagnosis was made. Few physicians saw sufficient numbers of musicians to understand and properly assess their symptoms, especially in the context of their occupational demands, with the result that they frequently did not receive adequate or appropriate treatment.

In the 1980s this situation changed when musicians began to more openly discuss their medical problems. This was evident when two well-known and successful concert pianists, Leon Fleisher and Gary Graffman, disclosed to the public that they had medical problems that were severely affecting their ability to perform. This served to provide a kind of implicit permission for other musicians to acknowledge problems and to seek help without shame and with less apprehension. A case can also be made for an apparent increase in frequency of problems, but this is difficult to prove, since it is only recently that incidence data have become available. Concurrently, members of the medical community, many of whom were themselves musicians, came to recognize that the often-subtle complaints of musicians represented real pathology, albeit requiring special expertise to diagnose and treat appropriately. It was this coming together of many factors that led to the establishment and legitimizing of the new medical specialty of performing arts medicine.

Performing arts medicine has grown worldwide since the early 1980s. As of the beginning of the twenty-first century, there are clinical and research centers, national and international meetings and workshops, professional societies, and, in the United States, a peer-reviewed medical journal devoted entirely to the problems of performing artists (Harman, 1995). This is not to say that the evolution of performing arts medicine has been problem-free or that there is adequate financial support for its clinical or research endeavors. The growth of the field has been increasingly challenged by the money-saving efforts of medical insurers through limiting patient access to speciality consultations.

Because of its intrinsically multispecialty approach, there is no authorized training program or certification for becoming a performing arts medicine specialist and, therefore, there is no institutionalized quality control for its practice. Many medical students, therapists, and doctors in training spend elective time at one or another arts clinic or in a research lab to hone their skills. These experiences can obviously vary in quality and quantity. Among the goals for this new field are the development of criteria and standards for the practice and the teaching of performing arts medicine. In the meantime, those who are looking for information must keep in mind that performing arts medicine remains a discipline in the making; constructive criticism and questioning by practitioners, educators, and consumers are all necessary and appropriate.

While all musicians share certain occupational risks, there is a significant difference between the manifestations, diagnosis, and treatment of pathology in vocal versus instrumental musicians. For most of their medical problems the care of vocalists requires a different set of specialists than does that of instrumentalists. In fact, the level of science in the care of vocalists is more advanced than has been thus far achieved for other musicians. Singers have by necessity been more aware of their need for medical assistance, and problems of the vocal mechanism has long been a recognized area for subspecialization by laryngologists. There is a significant body of literature based on clinical experience and research, and a sophisticated technology has been developed for use in the diagnosis, assessment, and treatment of vocal problems and in vocal pedagogy (see chapter 16).

Incidence of Problems

With heightened interest in musicians' medical issues, a number of incidence studies of problems among different musical populations have been undertaken. Zaza (1998) reviewed 24 studies, of varying sizes and among different types of musical populations, from 1980 to 1996, but concluded that only 7 were methodologically reliable. Her review reports a prevalence that ranged from 39 to 87% of injuries in adult musicians and 17% in secondary school students. Two of the best studies were completed by Fishbein, Middlestadt, Ottani, Straus, and Ellis (1988) with players in professional U.S. orchestras and by Cayea and Manchester (1998), with conservatory students. Fishbein surveyed 2,212 musicians in 48 International Conference of Symphony and Opera Musicians (ICSOM) orchestras and reported that 76% had at least one serious medical problem that affected their playing. This study also included data on the relative incidence of problems in different orchestra sections, with the most problems occurring in strings, followed by woodwind, brass, and percussion. The data also reveal a higher incidence among female than male players and evidence that as the size of the string instrument grew, so did the likelihood of problems. While this was a factor especially in women, it also affected men. Although pianists are underrepresented among orchestral musicians and there has been no comparably large survey of pianists, the incidence of their problems appear to be around the same as in string players (Cayea & Manchester, 1998).

The Cayea and Manchester study of conservatory students was based on a review of the number of visits by music students to the health service for playing-related complaints during 14 academic years (1982–1996) and showed 8.3 injuries per 100 registered music performance students in an academic year. They also reported a higher incidence among women—8.9 as opposed to 5.9 in men, both per 100 students. The increased incidence in women may have several explanations, including that women more often seek medical help, have smaller hands, have hyperextensible joints, and have more responsibilities for nonoccupational activities than do men. From these data, as well as others, it is clear that youth is no protection against most of the medical problems experienced by musicians and, correspondingly, that being a musician carries risks at all ages.

Specific Medical Conditions and Their Treatment

Clinically, the medical problems that arise from playing instruments divide into three categories. Most common are *musculoskeletal pain syndromes* (which include *tendinitis*), followed by *nerve entrapments* and, last, *focal dystonias* (occupational cramps). The reported frequency varies with the nature of the practice. Larger clinics and those with a significant referral practice will see a proportionately greater number of patients with focal dystonias than those that see mostly students or those that have a small patient volume. The latter would see proportionately more pain syndromes, fewer nerve entrapments, and very rarely focal dystonias.

Muscoloskeletal Pain Syndromes

It is generally accepted among music medicine practitioners that the most frequent symptom that causes musicians to seek medical advice is pain, both acute and chronic. Hochberg et al. (1983) reported that 21 of 49 patients they reviewed complained of pain as their primary symptom, while Lederman (1994) reported that from 45 to 69% of 672 patients with musculoskeletal pain disorders, depending on the instrument played. In order of frequency the sites involved in musicians' pain syndromes are the arm, neck, and back, although it is also common to have problems concurrently in several sites, especially when the pain is chronic. Most of these disorders occur after overplaying of some sort, and are severe enough to affect playing but often are not symptomatic when not playing. Symptoms that persist more than a few days or progress should be evaluated by a physician to see if some specific treatment is indicated.

Appropriate treatment of muscle tendon pain problems is almost always medical rather than surgical, and while specifics will depend on the factors that led to the problem, much of this requires common sense as much as medical expertise. Often the use of antiinflammatory medications, such as ibuprofen, icing (ice packs), and some degree of rest are prescribed and will suffice. The need for rest, the hallmark of treatment, may be variable. After 30 years of experience, in most instances and for several reasons, the first author of this chapter has become a proponent of continuing some degree of customary musical activity rather than prohibiting all musical activity. This obviously does not apply to nonmusical trauma, in which there may have been actual tissue disruption, such as in fractures or severe sprains. There is no clinical or experimental data that is convincing of the merits of absolute rest, nor is there any rule of thumb for dictating the length of time for rest. My experience is that for both physical and psychological reasons it is more successful overall to allow a musician to play a little than not to play at all. Physically it helps retain facility so that when the symptom has resolved there is less need for excessive practice in order to return to the previous level of playing. Also, tissues retain elasticity, flexibility, and vascularity when used somewhat rather than when totally at rest. These syndromes do not usually lead to more serious problems, and the majority resolve in a matter of days or weeks at the most.

Nerve Entrapments

Nerve entrapments occur when a nerve is trapped in a particular location by some other tissue such as surrounding scar tissue or by inflamed and swollen tendons. These usually cause pain, sometimes quite severe, in the distribution of the affected nerve rather than only at the site of the entrapment (referred pain) and often are accompanied by a pins-and-needle sensation, sometimes by decreased sensation, and occasionally by weakness and atrophy (diminution in bulk) of affected muscles. However, some of these same symptoms may also occur in other conditions. Symptoms of nerve entrapments in musicians may be subtle or dramatic, especially when the problem is of long duration. Once a diagnosis is made, treatment depends on the degree of nerve impairment present. Often nonsurgical treatment will be successful, including rest, nonsteroidal antiinflammatories, occasionally cortisone, and splinting (see "Misdiagnosis and Mistreatment") for absolute rest. Whether or not surgery seems necessary, when and of what type is a question about which different well-qualified specialists may often be contradictory. This may necessitate obtaining multiple opinions. The most frequently entrapped nerve is the *median nerve* in the *carpal tunnel*, which lies beneath the fold where the palm of the hand meets the wrist. The carpal tunnel is a rigid structure, the floor and sides of which are wrist bones and the roof of which is formed by the transcarpal ligament, an unyielding piece of soft tissue. The contents of the canal include nine flexor tendons and the median nerve. When the tendons become inflamed and swollen they put varying degrees of pressure on the median nerve, causing the symptom complex known as *carpal tunnel syndrome*. Next in frequency of nerve entrapments is *cubital tunnel syndrome*, or entrapment of the *ulnar nerve*, at or in some cases slightly above the elbow. This is a less defined structure than the carpal tunnel, but essentially the nerve may become compressed by soft tissues in an area of relatively tight passage of the ulnar nerve. While these can often be diagnosed on clinical presentation alone, most practitioners rely on electrodiagnostic tests (*electromyograms* or *EMGs* and *nerve conduction velocity* or *NCVs*) for confirmation or refutation, as well as to follow the course of a particular entrapment. Carpal and cubital tunnel syndromes are typically treated with a degree of rest, often intermittent splinting, nonsteroidal antiinflammatory agents, occasionally cortisone injections, and physical or occupational therapy. If these methods fail or there is evidence of significant progression, operative intervention with release is indicated. Here there is usually a choice of the procedure as well as of the surgeon and, since this is always an elective procedure, musicians do well to fully inform themselves and to seek several opinions.

There is yet another diagnosis that may theoretically involve nerve entrapment, *thoracic outlet syndrome* (*TOS*), but in musicians especially this is an area of often-heated medical dispute, primarily because it does not fit the usual definition of nerve entrapment. *Thoracic outlet* refers to the area inside of the upper chest through which traverse the nerves and blood vessels that ultimately supply the arms. In some individuals this space may be compromised, due to the configuration of their shoulders, due occasionally to an extra rib, and most frequently due to a constantly changing factor, which is posture. When the space reduction is due to posture, unlike other nerve entrapments, the symptoms are intermittent based on position primarily of the shoulders. In some cases the symptoms of this postural TOS may be due to transient vascular rather than nerve compression. A diagnosis of TOS in musicians is typically made on the basis of often-vague pain that may be in the shoulder, back, or arm, with or without tingling; and, as it occurs in musicians, is rarely if ever accompanied by muscle weakness. Electrodiagnostic testing in these patients does not show nerve damage. Therefore, while physicians may at times suggest surgical release for documented carpal or cubital tunnel syndromes, only an occasional surgeon does not share the view of most physicians, which is to rarely, if ever, recommend surgery for the postural TOS that is typically seen in musicians. Conservative treatment consists of physical therapy with postural exercises, designed to help keep the shoulders back and down.

Focal Dystonias

The most serious medical problem that occurs in musicians is called focal dystonia, and its occurrence may well end or at least significantly impair professional performance careers. It is one of a group of conditions known as occupational cramps. *Focal* means "localized," and *dystonia* refers to abnormal muscle tone. The affected musician will note an inability to control a finger or fingers, primarily in one hand, which curl into the palm, often accompanied by a reciprocal extension of one or more of the other fingers. Among pianists, dystonias tend to affect fingers of the right hand, or the hand involved with the most activity. This occurs only while playing the instrument and does not affect other unrelated hand activities. In woodwind and brass players the condition may present as loss of control of muscles of the embouchure rather than in the fingers. The problem in the embouchure is often difficult to visualize, although sometimes one sees the curling up or pulling away of one side of the upper lip. The incidence among musicians is not known, but it is less common than the previous categories of medical problems discussed. In different consultative specialty practices dystonia patients have reportedly represented from 8 to 27% of the musician patients seen (Lederman, 1991; Brandfonbrener, 1995). The frequency is significantly greater among men than women, and it tends to occur during midlife but may occur earlier, although it is relatively uncommon before the midtwenties. The focal dystonias appear to represent an abnormality of the motor cortex in the brain rather than of the peripheral nerves (chapter 5). It does not extend to other areas of the body or affect the general health of the patient. In most instances all nonmusical activity is unaffected and one cannot detect any abnormality on routine examination. The cause is unknown, although there have been many theories, which range from a history of a previous, nonspecific injury to excess stress and tension in playing. While there are anecdotal reports of partial or complete resolution of symptoms, it is generally believed to be a permanent condition. To date, there is no specific therapy, although for some the injection of botulinum toxin (Botox) into the affected muscles has provided some temporary relief, but this needs to be repeated every few months to maintain even its partial effect (Cohen, Hallett, Geller, & Hochberg, 1989). Rest does not affect the symptoms of dystonia, nor does continuing to practice. Other treatments include the use of anti-Parkinson's medications as well as many alternative, nontraditional therapies, but none has yielded a cure or typically even enough relief to allow return to the previous performance level. A new treatment, called *constraint-induced movement therapy*, is reported to show promising results, but this was in a small series (five) of patients and needs further verification (Candia et al., 1999). Depending on the severity of their particular affliction, some musicians with dystonia can continue to play using selected repertoire, alternative fingerings, or modified instruments. All instrumental groups may be affected, but there is evidence that it occurs most, as do most other medical problems, in association with instruments that require the most repetitive muscle actions (Lederman, 1991).

Other Considerations in Assessment and Treatment

Psychosomatic Aspects

In virtually all matters of health there is a psychological component, in their cause as well as in their resolution. How we feel affects our health and our recovery for better and for worse. Depression is a major factor in injuries, both in cause and effect, as it is also an impediment to healing, especially in the context of chronic pain. Practitioners who see large numbers of musician patients note that a significant number of these patients have symptoms that are chronic and, as such, must be treated differently from symptoms that are more acute, that is, problems of more recent onset. These patients in particular need multidisciplinary physician input that includes those trained in physical medicine and rehabilitation and in psychiatry. The judicious use of tricyclic antidepressants is effective in musicians with chronic pain, as it is in chronic pain patients in general, along with exercise, psychotherapy, and often a period of musical retraining.

Misdiagnosis and Mistreatment

Some of the blame for the frequency of chronic problems appears due to inappropriate treatment or mistreatment of the acute problems. Musicians are sufficiently concerned and obsessed when they face a medical problem without physicians giving them further reasons to feel impaired by lengthy prohibitions against playing. In addition, musicians are likely to be noncompliant if the medical treatment seems unduly punishing, so that in the interests of compliance, working out a reasonable plan for reduced playing is usually both viable and pragmatic. Formulas for reduced playing can be devised, but individualization is more logical, depending on all the circumstances. Sometimes it may be advisable to splint the affected part, but there are a variety of ways to do this. Resting splints while useful for providing absolute rest have the disadvantage of causing stiffness and even atrophy if left on more than absolutely needed. Intermittent, or nocturnal splinting, is often sufficient and better. There are also dynamic splints that can be designed for the individual, allowing protection while playing. Splints worn only at night or intermittently, rather than constantly during the day, are less likely to cause weakness or stiffness. Some physicians favor the use of steroid injections (cortisone-type medications) in certain cases of tendinitis and other conditions. Other physicians, including the first author of this chapter, are reluctant to do this because of the possible long-range effects on tissue integrity, especially with multiple injections. Rarely, if ever, should steroid injections be used until more conservative methods have proven inadequate.

Contextual Diagnosis

Perhaps the single most important innovation utilized by practitioners of performing arts medicine is viewing medical problems in their performance context. Musicians often express their symptoms in musical terms, referring to problems playing octaves or double-stops, reduced endurance, change of range, or loss of tone quality or accuracy of pitch. Practitioners of performing arts medicine have learned that speaking and understanding musical language is often crucial. Most important, examining the patient playing the instrument is what defines a specialist in this field, in that most are expected to be familiar with the basics of positioning and technique requisite for playing each instrument. This sometimes may stretch beyond medical expertise into musical expertise, and many physicians and therapists welcome the input of music educators as participants or advisers in patient assessment. All of this takes more time than most traditional office visits, but it is this time and care upon which successful care of musicians is often predicated. Collaboration between medical and musical expertise is therefore essential to the healing process in music medicine. Due to the subtle and idiosyncratic nuances of the process of making music, the medical specialist cannot be expected to know and understand all of these aspects. This is analogous to sports medicine, where diagnosis and treatment are viewed from both medical and performance perspectives.

With musician patients it is essential to take a full medical history as well as a musical history. The former is because one cannot assume that an injury is due to a patient's occupation simply because he or she is a musician. Because musicians tend to be so aware of gradual decreases in function, nonoccupational pathology may present initially as a change in performance facility. Most problems seen among musicians do not stem from a single episode but are cumulative and caused by the interaction of several factors, such as the hours practiced, the intensity of practice, the instrument, the physical and mental properties of the musician, technique, and more. It is necessary to understand what musical maneuvers are compromised, the duration of symptoms, and about any musical changes (instrument, teacher, repertoire, schedule) that related in time to the occurrence of the symptom. Physicians are often at a loss to arrive at a precise diagnosis of musicians because of the lack of objective findings, such as swelling, loss of strength, sensation, or range of motion (ROM). Local tenderness may or may not be present. Examining the whole patient is essential, because playing musical instruments depends on the entire body; the problem in an arm may reside, for example, in weakness or tension in the more proximal musculature or joints or in the back. However, a diagnosis can usually be made on the basis of the history and physical diagnosis. Further testing is useful only to rule out other pathology. While magnetic resonance imaging (MRI) may show tissue swelling in tendinitis and other forms of musculoskeletal pain syndromes, it is rarely legitimate to resort to such extensive and expensive testing if clinical expertise alone will suffice. Likewise, electrodiagnostic tests, such as EMGs and NCVs, are useful only to rule out nerve entrapments or other pathology that can in many cases be done based on examination. Occasionally there may be a question of an underlying joint disorder, such as rheumatoid arthritis or osteoarthritis, or the effects of trauma, in which case X rays and/or blood tests may be indicated.

Risk Factors

Prevention of musicians' medical injuries and other problems largely involves understanding the risk factors. The risk factors can be partially divided into those that stem from the instrument and those that stem from the musician.

Instrument-Specific Risks. Factors that relate to the instrument include the posture with the instrument, the effort of supporting the static load of the instrument, the number of repetitions to depress keys or strings, and the force of the required airflow through the instrument. For a pianist, sitting too close or too far may be dictated by the demands of the technique or the body's proportions, but sitting too close or too far may affect the medical biomechanics as well as the technical. Clarinetists and oboists frequently have problems with their right thumbs, especially if they have small hands or if the thumb joints are hyperlax (double-jointed). The player then uses greater muscle tension to hold the instrument, which over time can result in overuse of the thumb muscles, as well as causing increased tension in the other fingers and the entire upper extremity. This hyperlaxity of finger joints can also adversely affect all instrumentalists (Brandfonbrener, 1990, 2000). Poor posture affects wind players by increasing the work of breathing. Many wind players have jaw pain, which is diagnosed as temperomandibular joint disease, or TMJ. While the problem may ultimately reside in the joint, prior to this the symptoms can usually be attributed to excess muscle tension in the masseter (chewing) and other embouchure muscles. Sometimes this is due to how the musicians position their jaws while playing and sometimes to problems with dental alignment, or both. In any problems of wind players that involve the temperomandibular joints of the jaw or the teeth, it is important to find expert dental advice, because poor advice can result in musically, if not dentally, disastrous procedures. Once again, when one is dealing with woodwind or brass players multiple opinions are appropriate before even seemingly routine extractions of third molars (wisdom teeth), or orthodenture to adjust malocclusions (Howard, 1989).

Risks That Stem from the Individual. The risks that the musician brings to playing may be of genetic origin, including body proportions, joint mobility, and finger length. Musicians who practice hours per day and are sedentary have a greater risk of upper extremity and back problems because the shoulder and back muscles, crucial to maintaining posture and arm support, are inadequately developed. As muscles fatigue, they become physically shorter, less flexible, and more subject to injury. Musicians who are emotionally tense tend to have tighter muscles, even before they start to play. There is evidence that how much time is spent in practice and its intensity are equally important as risk factors. Rapid increases in playing time, as at summer music festivals, for competitions, and for amateurs at workshops, have been documented as predisposing musicians to pain (Newmark & Lederman, 1987).

Repertoire that is technically more challenging, with long series of difficult chords and octaves for pianists, double-stops or thumb position for string players, and higher and longer sustained notes for wind players, is among risk factors that fall between those of the instrument and those intrinsic to the player. Finally, although this area is more complicated and difficult to subject to measurement of relative risk, based on clinical experience there is no question that the musician's overall ability and emotional status may be among the most critical risk factors for injuries to bear in mind.

Preventive Strategies

To date there are few studies that document the effectiveness of preventive measures. Spaulding (1988) reported work with conservatory students in Norway on posture and education that yielded promising results, even if on a modest scale. On a larger scale, Brandfonbrener and associates undertook a year-long prevention intervention with nine ICSOM (International Conference of Symphony and Opera Musicians) orchestras in 1989 (Brandfonbrener, 1997). Although the program was initially well attended, the participants gradually dropped out over the course of the year, so that while much interesting information was gathered, there were too few subjects left at the end to make any definitive comments about the effects on prevention. The difficulty in maintaining motivation in prevention of health problems is a universal fact of life.

Logically, the best time to attend to the prevention of musicians' injuries is during the early stages of education, so that efficient performance techniques and user-friendly postural habits, a positive attitude, and a healthy lifestyle can be instilled from the earliest lessons. Practice techniques such as pacing (e.g., taking frequent breaks), avoiding excessive repetitions, paying attention to posture, remaining aware of fatigue and tension, and maintaining an exercise routine, such as swimming, are helpful.

Physical Tension and Its Psychological Component

Excessive tension, muscular and emotional (often inseparable), is the most important risk factor for musicians' injuries. While both muscular and emotional tension can be prevented, they may have complicated roots that do not allow for simple solutions. On a routine basis, warming up, cooling down, and stretching help but should not be regarded as providing solutions for all playing-related problems. Yoga, the Feldenkreis method (see Nelson, 1989), and Alexander technique (see Mayers & Babits, 1987; Grey, 1991), as well as other schools of body awareness, are also helpful but frequently not enough. It is often essential, with musicians of any age, to attempt to understand the stresses that are contributing to emotional and muscular tension that have their origins in both musical and nonmusical sources. It will come as no surprise, then, that musicians themselves freely admit to perceiving great occupational stress (Middlestadt & Fishbein, 1988). This is not a call for amateur psychiatrists but rather a call for attention on the part of all involved in the music education process—including teachers, pedagogues, parents, and health-care professionals—to the role of psychological stress as a cause of musicians' medical problems. Although individuals are motivated to learn and achieve in many different ways, students should be taught about effective, energy-preserving methods of practice, warming up and cooling down, and stretching. Furthermore, where the pressure of competition might motivate one promising student, it could easily discourage another, with serious consequences. In ensemble classes there should also be periodic breaks and avoidance of long rehearsals. In addition, music directors should be implored to be sensitive to the long-term effects on morale and health of players when subjected to recurring demeaning, negative, and personal criticisms. Teachers and parents need to be aware of all these variables and how best to monitor them in the interests of the development of physically and psychologically healthy young musicians. How an instrument is played, how the individual has been taught, and the musician's state of health are all essential elements in good music education in both preventive and remedial conditions. Accordingly, music education meets music medicine.

Measuring Muscle Tension

As stated earlier, excess tension, regardless of its origins or reasons, is at the core of musicians' performance difficulties. Since muscle tension can be measured and followed through the technology of electromyography (EMG)—the measurement of electrochemical activity in muscles)—it would seem expedient to pursue research applications in this area further (Guettler, 1992; Heuser & McNitt-Gray, 1991, 1993, 1994; Kjelland, 2000; Levy, Lee, Brandfonbrener, Press, & Levy, 1992; Philipson, Sorbye, Larsson, & Kaladjev, 1990; Theim, Greene, Prassas, & Thaut, 1994). Furthermore, when use of EMGs is combined with various therapeutic interventions such as biofeedback, muscle tension can be significantly reduced (Druckman & Swets, 1988; Kjelland, 1986; Koehler, 1995; LeVine, 1988). The EMG biofeedback process involves the visual or auditory representation of muscle activity at a level that is beyond the subject's perceptibility. This representation can in turn be manipulated by the subject in a desired direction, thus altering muscle tension previously undetectable. Such technology and therapeutic intervention will always require the guidance and insight of an experienced teacher who is able to sort out fact from artifact in the process of nurturing genuine musical and technical development. Relaxation by itself without observable improvement in performance and/or physical comfort, and so on, is of no practical interest to music performance, just as it would not be to sports medicine. In fact, relaxation per se can be maladaptive if not carefully monitored in a performance context (Druckman & Swets, 1988; Kjelland, 1986). Studies such as that of Heuser and McNitt-Gray (1998) that involve, rather than exclude or bypass, the teacher in feedback process show much promise as a realistic adaptation of the traditional studio.

In this paradigm, the electromyograph contributes vitally important information for the teacher's use in diagnosing performance problems and prescribing alternative solutions.

Applications in Teaching and Performance

The future of performing arts medicine resides in the interaction between medical science and pedagogy if the health maintenance and care of musicians are to become more consistent and effective. With a solid foundation of scientific data, injuries from misuse of the body can be consistently minimized, and injuries from well-intended but sadly misinformed teaching and outmoded schools of technique will yield to validated healthful teaching principles. (Many performance injuries unfortunately can and do happen because students follow the teacher's directions to the letter instead of doing what might work best for them individually.) Obviously there is no teacher who would seek to injure a student, but with scientific knowledge the teaching profession can be more confident of the validity of certain pedagogical directives. Without such systematic examination of methodology, the music-teaching profession is destined to perpetuate its quasi-religious debates over which approach is better, further dividing the profession into various pedagogical schools of thought that impede meaningful long-term progress.

Such scientific validation does not and will not come quickly or easily. However, much is already known through the efforts of the relatively young field of music medicine research. The information in this chapter alone furnishes much for teachers to benefit from and be conscious of on behalf of their students. Just the fact that medical problems are independent of age should alert the teaching profession to the need for a greater awareness and sense of responsibility for detecting and referring students at the inception of significant symptoms. Validation of teaching practice must start with a thorough examination of those performers who are proven to be successful models (Druckman & Swets, 1988). From this, norms can be established for comparison to assess the physiological and psychological needs of those still developing and/or relearning musical skills and habits. This in turn will lead to the development of sound physiological, biomechanical, and psychological practices in music teaching.

References

Brandfonbrener, A. G. (1990). Joint laxity in instrumental musicians. *Medical Problems of Performing Artists, 5*, 117–119.

Brandfonbrener, A. G. (1995). Musicians with focal dystonia: A report of 58 cases seen during a ten-year period at a performing arts clinic. *Medical Problems of Performing Artists, 10*, 115–120.

Brandfonbrener, A. G. (1997). Orchestral injury prevention study. *Medical Problems of Performing Artists, 12*, 9–14.

Brandfonbrener, A. G. (2000). Joint laxity and arm pain in musicians. *Medical Problems of Performing Artists, 15*, 72–74.

Candia, V., Elbert, T., Altenmüller, E., Rau, H., Schafer, T., & Taub, E. (1999). Constraint-induced movement therapy for focal hand dystonia in musicians. *Lancet, 353* (9146), 42–43.

Cayea, D., & Manchester, R. (1998). Instrument-specific rates of upper extremity injuries in music students. *Medical Problems of Performing Artists, 13*, 19–25.

Cohen, L. G., Hallett, M., Geller, B. D., & Hochberg, F. (1989). Treatment of focal dystonias of the hand with botulinum toxin injections. *Journal of Neurology, Neurosurgery and Psychiatry, 52*, 355–363.

Druckman, D., & Swets, J. A. (Eds.) (1988). *Enhancing human performance: Issues, theories, and techniques.* Washington, DC: National Academy Press.

Fishbein, M., Middlestadt, S. E., Ottani, V., Straus, S., & Ellis, A. (1988). Medical problems among ICSOM musicians: Overview of a national survey. *Medical Problems of Performing Artists, 3*, 1–8.

Grey, J. (1991). *The Alexander technique.* New York: St. Martin's Press.

Guettler, K. (1992). Electromyography and muscle activities in double bass playing. *Music Perception, 9*(3), 2303–2309.

Harman, S. (1995). The evolution of performing arts medicine. In R. T. Sataloff, A. G. Brandfonbrener, and R. J. Lederman (Eds.), *Performing arts medicine* (2nd ed.) (pp. 1–18). San Diego, CA: Singular Press.

Heuser, F., & McNitt-Gray, J. L. (1991). EMG potentials prior to tone commencement in trumpet players. *Medical Problems of Performing Artists, 6*(2), 51–56.

Heuser, F., & McNitt-Gray, J. L. (1993). EMG patterns in embouchure muscles of trumpet players with asymmetrical mouthpiece placement. *Medical Problems of Performing Artists, 8*(3), 96–102.

Heuser, F., & McNitt-Gray, J. L. (1994). EMG changes in a trumpet player overcoming tone commencement difficulties: A case study. *Medical Problems of Performing Artists, 9*(1), 18–24.

Heuser, F., & McNitt-Gray, J. L. (1998). Enhancing and validating pedagogical practice: The use of electromyography during trumpet instruction. *Medical Problems of Performing Artists, 13*, 155–159.

Hochberg, F. H., Leffert, R. D., Heller, M. D., & Merriman, L. (1983). Hand difficulties among musicians. *Journal of the American Medical Association, 249*, 1869–1871.

Howard, J. A., & Lovrovich, A. T. (1989). Wind instruments: Their interplay with orofacial structures. *Medical Problems of Performing Artists, 4*, 59–72.

Kjelland, J. M. (1986). The effects of electromyographic biofeedback training on violoncello performance: Tone quality and muscle tension (Doctoral dissertation, University of Texas at Austin). *Dissertation Abstracts International, 47A*, 459A (University Microfilms No. DDJ86/09527)

Kjelland, J. M. (2000). Application of electromyography and electromyographic biofeedback in music performance research: A review of literature since 1985. *Medical Problems of Performing Artists, 15*, 115–118.

Koehler, W. K. (1995). The effect of electromyographic feedback on achievement in bowing technique (Doctoral dissertation). *Dissertation Abstracts International, 55A*, 2758A-9A (University Microfilms No. DA9502472)

Lederman, R. J. (1991). Focal dystonia in instrumentalists: Clinical features. *Medical Problems of Performing Artists, 6*, 132–136.

LeVine, W. R. (1988). Biofeedback in violin and viola pedagogy. In F. L. Roehmann and F. R. Wilson (Eds.), *The biology of music making: Proceedings of the 1984 Denver conference* (pp. 196–200). St. Louis: Magna Music Baton.

Levy, C. E., Lee, W. A., Brandfonbrener, A. G., Press, J., & Levy, A. E. (1992). Electromyographic analysis of muscular activity in the upper extremity generated by supporting a violin with and without a shoulder rest. *Medical Problems of Performing Artists, 7*(4), 103–109.

Mayers, H., & Babits, L. (1987, November). A balanced approach: The Alexander technique. *Music Educators' Journal,* 51–53.

Middlestadt, S. E., & Fishbein, M. (1988). Health and occupational correlates of perceived occupational stress in symphony orchestra musicians. *Journal of Occupational Medicine, 30,* 687–692.

Nelson, S. H. (1989). Playing with the entire self: The Feldenkreis method and musicians. *Seminars in Neurology, 9*(2), 97–104.

Newmark, J., & Lederman, R. J. (1987). Practice doesn't necessarily make perfect. *Medical Problems of Performing Artists, 2,* 142–144.

Philipson, L., Sorbye, M. D., Larsson, M. D., & Kaladjev, M. A. (1990). Muscular load levels in performing musicians as monitored by quantitative electromyography. *Medical Problems of Performing Artists, 5*(2), 79–82.

Spaulding, C. (1988). Before pathology: Prevention for performing artists. *Medical Problems of Performing Artists, 3,* 135–139.

Theim, B., Greene, D., Prassas, S., & Thaut, M. (1994). Left arm muscle activation and movement patterns in cellists employing a playing technique using rhythmic cueing. *Medical Problems of Performing Artists, 9,* 89–96.

Zaza, C. (1998). Playing-related musculo-skeletal disorders in musicians: A systematic review of incidence and prevalence. *Canadian Medical Association Journal, 158*(8), 1019–1025.

PART II

SUBSKILLS OF MUSIC PERFORMANCE

7

From Sound to Sign

GARY E. McPHERSON & ALF GABRIELSSON

One of the most contentious issues in music pedagogy concerns when and how to introduce notation to a beginning instrumentalist. Most current teaching introduces musical notation very early in the process, perhaps because many teachers believe that beginners who are taught by ear will never reach the same level of reading proficiency as children who are introduced to notation from their earliest lessons. In contrast, proponents of the *sound before sign* approach argue that children will have difficulty learning to read notation unless their musical knowledge is sufficiently developed for them to be able to relate the sound of what they can already play with the symbols used to represent them. Our review of literature results in the identification of six principles that can be used to develop the complex range of skills needed for a child to become musically literate.

A curious contradiction in music pedagogy is that teaching practice is often in conflict with theories of instrumental teaching about how to introduce notation to a child. Whereas most children learning an instrument in Western styles of education are introduced to musical notation from their very early lessons, prominent instrumental teachers throughout history have advocated that ear playing should be emphasized before the introduction of notation.

Historical Overview of Teaching Practice

Up until the mid-nineteenth century the teaching of instruments was regarded as a craft whereby knowledge was passed from one generation to the next by word of mouth, often through a form of musical apprenticeship. During this time, composers and teachers did not separate technical practice from more general musical skills; rather, the goal was to develop an all-round musician by inte-

99

grating technique with other aspects of general musicianship (Gellrich & Parncutt, 1998). Scales and arpeggios served as a means of learning the common vocabulary of musical language, and when passages were practiced in isolation from the music it was for the purpose of developing a range of musical skills, such as sight-reading, improvisation, and composition. For beginners, passages were often learned by ear rather than directly from reading musical notation. This process involved the rote learning of previously unknown pieces by imitating the teacher's model or the reconstruction of familiar music that had been internalized by repeated hearings or singing. (It should be noted that playing by ear is quite distinct from playing music from memory, which involves performing a piece that has been memorized as a result of repeated rehearsal of the notation. See further McPherson, 1995a, 1995b.) As skills developed, teachers would encourage their pupils to invent their own passages to develop the expressive and technical skills needed to master the musical language of the repertoire being learned (Gellrich & Sundin, 1993).

But changes occurred rapidly from around 1850 onward. The lithograph and high-speed printing machines were invented in 1818, and by 1830 it was possible to mass-produce relatively cheap scores in large quantities. Whereas few books of exercises had been published during the eighteenth century, from the second half of the nineteenth century they became common, and as a result the nature of learning to play changed quite dramatically. With access to new printed material the emphasis shifted from the development of skills in interpretation, improvisation, and composition to music as a reproductive art, with its resultant emphasis on technique and interpretation (Gellrich & Parncutt, 1998).

Once composers started to publish their exercises in method books, the oral tradition that had served musicians for centuries beforehand became irrevocably broken, and it was not long before pianists began to practice for long periods to develop specific technical skills that were often never applied when performing the literature. An unfortunate consequence was that exercises were often repeated endlessly during practice. Some students succeeded despite such mindless practice, while others, as we still see today, found it boring and uninspiring.

These comments highlight the changing emphasis in the use of technical exercises and how these were used by pianists to develop their craft. But this influence was soon felt on the full range of orchestral instruments. By the late 1800s, most beginning instrumental method books emphasized drill and technical material such as scales, rhythms, articulations, and finger exercises, with very little material of real melodic interest (Schleuter, 1997). One of the most consistent trends was to organize beginning method books according to the proportionality of note values whereby students were first taught a series of whole notes and whole note rests before graduating to half notes/rests, quarter notes/rests, and eventually eighth and sixteenth notes/rests (Schleuter, 1997). Modern method books place much more emphasis on learning repertoire, but the philosophy still tends to be based on the re-creation of music through a process of learning to read and develop technical skill from the very first lesson. The problem, according to Schleuter (1997), is that even today most instrumental method books associate fingerings with notation rather than fingerings with sound, perpetuate the mathematical relationships of proportional note values, emphasize note naming and theoretical concepts more than perceptual understandings, and separate technical skill from the process of learning to play actual music. In essence, they reinforce the notion of performance as a specialist craft in which technical development and knowledge of notation are valued above all else.

Advocates *of* Sound before Sign

Johann Heinrich Pestalozzi (1746–1827), who taught Swiss orphans after the French destruction of the canton of Unterwalden, was one of the first educators to profess that concepts should be taught through direct experience before the introduction of names or symbols (Abeles, Hoffer, & Klotman, 1994). Pestalozzi's ideas were introduced into North American schools by Joseph H. Naef, who had worked with Pestalozzi before emigrating around 1806. Naef founded an elementary school in 1809 that included music instruction as a basic subject and in 1830 outlined his "Principles of the Pestalozzian System of Music" at a meeting of the American Institute of Instruction. These included seven recommendations for teachers:

1. To teach sounds before signs and to make the child learn to sing before he learns the written notes or their names;
2. To lead him to observe by hearing and imitating sounds, their resemblances and differences, their agreeable and disagreeable effect, instead of explaining these things to him—in a word, to make active instead of passive in learning;
3. To teach but one thing at a time—rhythm, melody, and expression, which are to be taught and practiced separately, before the child is called to the difficult task of attending to all at once;
4. To make him practice each step of these divisions, until he is master of it, before passing to the next;
5. To give the principles and theory after the practice, and as induction from it;
6. To analyze and practice the elements of articulate sound in order to apply them to music; and
7. To have the names of the notes correspond to those used in instrumental music. (Abeles, Hoffer & Klotman, 1994, p. 11)

Other prominent music educators who were influenced by Pestalozzi's ideas include Lowell Mason, whose work as America's first public school music teacher helped to revolutionize music teaching. Mason was convinced that children should first experience music before learning to read notation. In England, similar calls have been a recurring theme (Pitts, 2000). One of the most articulate was Yorke Trotter (1914), who believed that a child "must first have the effect in his mind before he knows the symbols that should be used to express that effect" (p. 76).

From the second half of the twentieth century, Suzuki advocated that a child's musical education must begin as early as possible and be based on rote learning instead of note reading during the early stages of training. Grounding his method on how children learn their *mother tongue*, Suzuki developed a highly sequenced system of teaching whereby children learn to "speak" (i.e., play) before learning to read. In Suzuki's view, notation is only appropriate when it can be beneficial, such as when the music becomes so complex that children need a symbol system to help prepare their performance (Landers, 1980).

Kohut's (1985) *natural learning process* is in many ways similar to the *mother tongue* approach of Suzuki. According to Kohut, young infants learn how to walk by watching and observing their parents and then attempting to imitate them. Through a process of trial-and-error practice children eventually learn to coordinate the muscles and cognitive processes necessary to walk with minimum conscious effort. In Kohut's view, the same natural learning process that children use to develop skills in everyday tasks can be used for learning an instrument. The first step is for the children to develop a repertoire of *mental blueprints* through listening to various models, whether they be a peer or teacher or model they hear on a recording. These mental images are then retrieved when the children attempt to imitate the image formed mentally. It is this natural, innate inclination to learn by listening and reproducing by ear, rather than from notation, that Kohut believes is the key to effective musical learning (see also Schleuter, 1997).

Other prominent instrumental teachers argue that because young children have difficulty learning more than one thing at a time, it is pointless to both expose them to the complex variety of technical skills needed to manipulate an instrument while at the same time asking them to read and comprehend notation (e.g., Schleuter, 1997). Gordon (1997) even recommends delaying the introduction of notation for as long as it takes for a student to develop an extensive aural vocabulary of tonal and rhythmic patterns according to his *music-learning theory*. He believes that poor sight-reading ability does not result from poor instrumental technique but poor aural skills. This is because notation does not always look the way fingers move when reading notation and that a premature emphasis on notation actually prevents a student from learning to hear and comprehend music internally. In Gordon's approach, playing by ear and improvising are essential ingredients for effective learning during the early prenotation stages of a child's musical development.

Review of Psychological Literature

Ear Playing as Preparation for Music Literacy

James Mainwaring, a fellow of the British Psychological Society and prominent music educator, was among the first researchers to study the acquisition of ear-playing skills. During his career, Mainwaring attempted to clarify the cognitive processes associated with musical ability, and his studies in this area led him to question teaching practice, which he believed placed far too much emphasis on technical skill and the mechanized recall of music from the printed score (1931, 1947). He was convinced that learning an instrument should "proceed from sound to symbol, not from symbol to sound" (1951c, p. 12), based on his belief that the development of music literacy should involve processes similar to learning to speak and then read a language.

At the heart of Mainwaring's (1941, 1951a, 1951b, 1951c) concept of musicianship is the capacity of being able to "think in sound," which occurs when a musician is able to produce the mentally imagined sound, whether by playing by ear, improvising, or reading from musical notation. When reading musical notation, "thinking in sound" involves an ability to inwardly hear and comprehend notation separately from the act of performance. This concept is depicted in Figure 7.1, which highlights the important distinction between seeing notation and responding mechanically to produce the notated sound (i.e., working from symbol to action to sound) in contrast to seeing the musical notation and being able to hear the notation inwardly before reproducing it on an instrument (i.e., working from symbol to sound to action). The former method Mainwaring (1951b) believed to be typical of most instrumental teaching practice. However, it was the latter way of working that he advocated as the most efficient and effective means for developing a young player's overall musicianship .

For Mainwaring (1951a), the most musical way of teaching an instrument is to continually link sound with action. In the beginning stages of development, this means encouraging students to reproduce simple known tunes by ear, before they learn to read these songs from musical notation.

Mainwaring's ideas can be contrasted with teaching that introduces notation from the earliest lessons. Children as young as three can develop a basic understanding of the pitch elements of musical notation and relate this to the piano keyboard (Tommis & Fazey, 1999), so the issue is not whether young children can learn to read notation at an early age but whether they should learn it so early.

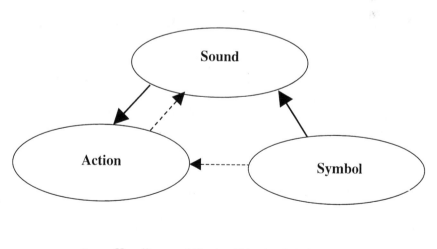

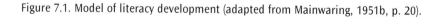 How literacy skills should be developed

Figure 7.1. Model of literacy development (adapted from Mainwaring, 1951b, p. 20).

One way of addressing this issue is to compare the acquisition of literacy skills in language with music, given that prominent methods such as the Suzuki approach are based on the premise that learning to speak and then read a language involves similar processes to learning to become literate in music. From a psychological perspective, Sloboda (1978) provides the most definitive starting point when he maintains that

> no-one would consider teaching a normal child to read while he was at a very early stage of learning spoken language. Yet it seems the norm to start children off on reading at the very first instrumental lesson without establishing the level of musical awareness already present. (p. 15)

According to Sloboda, musical sensitivity should be developed before the introduction of notation because "without some musical knowledge a beginner has no expectancies which can be used in reading" (p. 15).

By the time children enter first grade, they typically possess a solid command of the mechanics of their own language and are able to perceive and use an extensive vocabulary in excess of 5,000 words. They are therefore capable of beginning the process of learning to associate familiar words with the symbols used to represent them (Bruning, Schraw, & Ronning, 1999). By sounding out individual letters, spelling patterns, and words, children begin to recognize the spelling, sound, and meaning of particular words and over time are able to comprehend the meaning of complex sentences (Adams, 1990). If these processes are duplicated in music, then the process that leads to the introduction of musical notation would involve teaching children to perform familiar tunes by ear before they learn to sound out tunes they already know using notation. This is why Mainwaring (1951c) and others (e.g., Gordon, 1997; Kohut, 1985; Schleuter, 1997; Suzuki, 1983) advocated teaching known tunes by ear in familiar keys before the notation of these melodies are introduced to the child.

However, studies with children who are learning to read highlight the importance of metalinguistic capabilities—"knowledge about the uses of print, how print represents sounds, how words are formed, how sentences are put together, and how sentences become stories or reports" (Bruning, Schraw, & Ronning, 1999, p. 242). This form of awareness enables children to map the visual symbols of written language onto oral language and to thereby create meaning. Learning how to comprehend musical notation involves similar processes in that it requires knowledge about the use of notation, how notes represent sounds, how phrases are formed, how melodies are put together, and how melodies become compositions. Like reading text, learning to become musically literate involves more than linking visual cues with instrumental fingerings; otherwise instrumentalists become button pushers "to whom notation only indicates what fingers to put down rather than what sounds are desired" (Schleuter, 1997, p. 48).

This line of reasoning is underpinned by psychological literature (e.g., Dowling & Harwood, 1986) that shows that listeners do not perceive music on a note-to-note basis but as patterns according to well-known gestalt principles for perceptual organization. These principles have been observed in various types of musical performance. For example, when constructing a piece by ear, musicians work according to structural units, by rewinding their mental tape recorders to the beginning of a phrase every time they make a mistake (Bamberger, 1996, 1999; McPherson, 1993). Working in structurally meaningful units (e.g., phrases) is also how advanced instrumentalists rehearse music from notation (Gabrielsson, 1999; Gruson, 1988; chapter 10 in this volume).

Based on her extensive research with children, Bamberger (1996, 1999) concludes that young learners must first gain experience in playing musical patterns before they learn to decontexualize these patterns into individual notes, because the "units of perception" that novices intuitively attend to when processing music are "structurally meaningful entities such as motives, figures, and phrases," not individual notes (p. 42). Bamberger's advice can be compared with how beginners normally correct performance errors when reading notation. In the very early stages of learning a new piece, they will often stumble over individual notes and continue playing, sometimes so slowly or hesitantly that they no longer perceive the music they are attempting to play as a complete phrase or melody (McPherson, 1993; McPherson & Renwick, 2000). Beginning instrumentalists find it baffling and frustrating to learn music in this way, especially in situations where they are taught to "start out by listening for, looking at, and identifying the smallest, isolated objects" and to "classify and measure with no context or functional meaning" (Bamberger, 1996, p. 43). Asking beginners to focus on notation too early, according to Bamberger (1996), means asking them to "put aside their most intimate ways of knowing—figures, felt paths, context and function" (p. 44). Too early an emphasis on notation can therefore lead to a decreased aural sensitivity to the natural unified patterns that children spontaneously observe when listening to music.

Related evidence shows that notation should not be taught in isolation of perception because of the danger that children will be forced to make choices beyond their competence and will tend to do so in contradiction of their perception. This was demonstrated by Davidson, Scripp, and Welsh (1988), who asked a group of 12-, 15-, and 18-year-olds to sing and then notate songs such as "Happy Birthday." Students who were receiving private instrumental tuition plus music theory classes tended to work conceptually. They defied their perception of the song to produce a transcription, for example, that started and finished on middle C (rather than F) because they believed that if "Happy Birthday" started on C, then it must be in C major and should therefore end on C. As these students got older, they relied more on what they know theoretically about music rather than what they heard and knew perceptually, with the result that they made surprisingly inaccurate transcriptions of familiar melodies. In contrast, students exposed to an approach to instrumental learning that integrated aural development with literacy skills were more inclined to work perceptually and their notations were more accurate and generally improved across the age groups.

To extend these findings we can consider how easily beginners are able to attend to and integrate knowledge from a number of sources. Like reading text, learning to decode musical notation is a complex skill that in the beginning stages involves processes that are not instant and automatic but rather conscious and deliberate (Samuels, 1994). However, unlike reading, where a novice can focus on decoding the visual symbols, learning to perform music involves two competing and nonautomated tasks: learning to read musical notation at the same time as learning to manipulate an instrument. In this type of situation, there are constraints on the amount of information beginners can think about at any one time, how long they will be able to hold it in their mind before it is lost, and how quickly they can process new information (Shaffer, 1999; Sweller, van Merrienboer, & Paas, 1998). To complicate this even further, vision tends to dominate and inhibit the processing of signals from other modalities (Posner, Nissen, & Klein, 1976; Smyth, 1984). Consequently, if children's attention is focused on reading notation, they may have few cognitive resources left to devote to manipulating their instrument and listening to what they are playing.

A common criticism of "sound before sign" approaches is that children will have difficulty integrating the knowledge required to read music when notation is introduced and therefore never achieve the same level of reading fluency as children exposed to notation from their first lesson. However, this folklore view may be misguided, given the literature cited earlier and also studies that show that children who learn "by ear" do not become less successful music readers (Glenn, 1999; McPherson, 1993; Sperti, 1970). For example, Glenn (1999) studied the progress of a group of sixth-grade beginning string students over a period of a full school year. The beginners were randomly assigned to one of two groups. The first group was taught without notation (i.e., using modeling and verbal explanation) for the first three months, after which notation was introduced, even though some time continued to be devoted to playing repertoire "by ear." The second group was taught with notation after a brief 2-week introduction to their instrument. For this group, the emphasis was on matching note names with instrumental fingerings and working through a method book. At the end of the study, the students were videotaped to compare their performance achievement. Results indicate that students in the "ear-playing" class performed as well as or better than students in the notation-based class on all performance evaluations, including the sight-reading measure. Importantly, however, students who were taught by ear in the initial stages were more likely to continue learning their instrument and were reported by their teacher to be more motivated and to enjoy their playing more than the other group. Based on her results, which support literature on how difficult it can be for beginning instrumentalists to learn two competing and nonautomated tasks at the same time, Glenn concludes that students should achieve a degree of automaticity in their playing before they are introduced to musical notation.

An Integrated Model

To this point, our review has focused on studies that provide evidence of the importance of ear playing in the beginning stage of learning an instrument. Clearly, this literature has many gaps, but there is one project that helps clarify the beneficial effects of ear playing on subsequent development. Based on Mainwaring's (1941, 1951a, 1951c) assertion that ear playing is the most fundamental of all the performance skills and that playing by ear can exert a positive influence on other styles of performance, McPherson (1993, 1995a, 1995b, 1996, 1997; McPherson, Bailey, & Sinclair, 1997) undertook a 3-year longitudinal study with a sample of 101 instrumentalists to examine relationships among five different aspects of musical performance and 16 environmental variables that prior research had suggested may influence their development. At the start of his study, the students were in school grades 7 to 12 (ages 11 to 18) and had been learning their instrument for approximately 2 to 6 years.

In order to reduce the large amount of information to a manageable and interpretable form, factor analysis was used to collapse the environmental variables into four distinct categories. First, *early exposure* described variables related to the quality and quantity of the students' early exposure to music, such as when and how they started learning, how long they had been playing, and whether they had learned another instrument before commencing. Second, *enriching activities* grouped variables associated with the students' reports of how frequently they played by ear and improvised, as well as whether they were electing classroom music at school in which composing was an important component. Students who reported higher average levels of daily practice were more likely to report higher levels of these types of informal activities. Third, *length of study*, included variables associated with the period the students had been playing their instrument and taking private lessons. Fourth, *quality of study* included the subjects' report of their interest and participation in various forms of singing, the number of ensembles they were performing with, and a report of how often they mentally rehearsed music in their minds away from their instrument.

McPherson reviewed available literature in order to develop a theoretical model that he could test empirically using results from the high school students' performances and interviews (see Figure 7.2). Results from the path analysis indicate that the model fits nicely with the data he obtained. This supports evidence of a number of causal relationships among the five skills and four environmental factors. As indicated in Figure 7.2, the model implies both direct and indirect effects. Direct effects are the unmediated relation between two variables (e.g., the influence of playing by ear on improvising is shown by a direct arrow). Indirect effects are the relation between two variables that are mediated by one or more other variables (e.g., the influence of playing by ear on improvising is also mediated through its effect on sight-reading and playing from memory). (A complete explanation is available in McPherson, 1993, and McPherson et al., 1997).

Early exposure exerted a positive influence on the instrumentalists' ability to play by ear and no direct influence on their ability to sight-read. As expected, *enriching activities*, which included variables associated with how often the instrumentalists played by ear and improvised during their practice, had a stronger impact on the skill of playing by ear and subsequently on the musicians' ability to improvise, than it did on sight-reading. *Quality of study* had only a weak influence on the abilities of playing by ear and sight-reading, while *length of study* had a moderate influence on the instrumentalists' ability to sight-read, as well as a strong direct influence on their ability to perform rehearsed music.

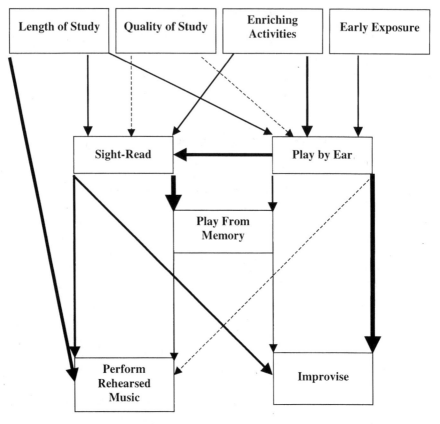

Figure 7.2. Path analysis of the McPherson theoretical model. In the simplified path diagram, path coefficients have been replaced by lines of differing thickness. Thicker lines represent stronger influences and thinner lines weaker relationships from one variable to the next as shown by the direction of the arrow.

Path analysis indicates that the skill of performing rehearsed music was most heavily influenced by the variables associated with *length of study*, plus the players' ability to sight-read. In contrast, the skill of improvising was most strongly influenced by the capacity of the musicians to play by ear (which had a strong direct path straight to improvising and a moderate indirectly effect via sight-reading and playing from memory).

Analysis of comments made by the less capable players show that they tended to use strategies that were independent of their instrument when preparing to play by ear (e.g., "While I listened to the tape I was trying to think in terms of what letter names the notes might be"). In contrast, more capable musicians were able to connect what they heard on the taped performances with the instrumental fingerings needed to execute these thoughts (e.g., "I just sing it in my head while I finger it through on my instrument"). Interestingly, McPherson's findings are in many ways similar to Davidson et al.'s (1988) explanation of how conceptual information can cloud perceptual awareness. In addition, the strong relationship McPherson reports between the students' ability to play by ear and sight-read is consistent with previous evidence (Luce, 1965; Priest, 1989) that ear playing may be more beneficial to the development of musicianship than sight-reading and also more receptive to training.

The results of McPherson's research support psychological and pedagogical assertions that the skill of playing by ear helps student musicians learn to coordinate ear, eye, and hand and to perform on their instrument what they see in notation and hear or imagine in their mind. Although continued refinement and testing of alternative models is needed to confirm the findings, this evidence suggests that teachers should recognize the importance of ear playing as an important facet of training that enhances overall musical growth and that provides for more enjoyable and meaningful learning.

Implications for Teaching

Developmental Level

There are a number of unresolved issues that arise from the discussion so far. Clearly, the dynamics of teaching play an important role in how quickly children will become literate, as do a variety of other intrapersonal and environmental catalysts that shape their development (see related chapters in this volume). However, since children start learning an instrument at widely different ages, some comments are appropriate about developmental issues. At the heart of arguments for the sound-before-sign sequence is the premise that sensory and/ or motor experiences should always precede the learning and use of symbols. Prominent theories of human development (e.g., Piaget, Bruner, Gardner) are in accord with this view, as are leading classroom music education methodologies (e.g., Dalcroze, Orff, Kodály). Hargreaves (1986), summarizing philosophies in music education that go back as far as Rousseau (1762), reinforces this view when he states:

> The intuitive experience and enjoyment of music should come first, such that the latter acquisition of formal musical skills occurs *inductively*, that is, as an integral growth of the child's experience. A good deal of traditional music education has worked deductively: the formal rules have been taught in the abstract, for example, through verbal description or written notation, rather than in the practical context of making the sounds themselves. (p. 215)

Bruning, Schraw, and Ronning (1999) explain that there are obvious developmental limits to how early children can be taught to read their language, but that most children start formal reading around the age of 6, after they have gained a great deal of prior experience in the use of their native tongue and reached the mental age necessary to maximize their success as readers. By this time their home experiences "will have prepared them with about 25 hours of storybook experience and perhaps 200 hours of general guidance about the form and nature of print" (Adams, 1994, pp. 89–90).

Obviously, a great deal of music learning takes place prior to formal lessons, and even very young children will come to their lessons having heard a vast amount of music in their everyday lives. However, the extent of a 6-year-old child's knowledge about how music can be represented in notation will typically be nowhere near the level of his or her understanding of how language can be represented in print. For this reason, in addition to the psychological literature cited earlier, there appears to be enough evidence to speculate that an emphasis on reading musical notation should not occur until a child is at least 6. Up until this age, teachers should emphasize rote teaching of pieces learned by ear in order to establish the important ear-to-hand coordination skills that provide a foundation for introducing notation later. In general, we believe that this rule should be extended to older age groups, although the length of time before introducing notation can be shortened, depending on how quickly they develop the necessary aural awareness and technical security on their instrument for them to be able to comprehend notation.

Prenotation Activities

In our view, two types of activities provide the foundation from which literacy skills can then be developed. First, during the early months (or weeks for older learners) of training, familiar pieces should be taught by rote and by repeated listening (many current methods books now include recorded examples of the literature being studied). In this stage the emphasis should be on encouraging beginners to sing and then play familiar repertoire on their instrument. Singing (either mentally or out aloud) is useful because it helps to establish a correct mental model that can guide children as they translate what has been memorized into the instrumental fingerings needed to perform it on an instrument. Singing should be a common and natural part of all early lessons. However, it should be noted that students need to progress from singing to linking singing with the fingerings needed to perform the piece on their instrument. Mentally and outwardly rehearsing (singing and fingering) a piece by ear develops a child's ability to experience sounds through gestures and touch, which Galvao and Kemp (1999) believe help integrate the body with the mind. If a teacher feels competent, then solfège can also be used to reinforce this transition from memorization (i.e., singing to a neutral syllable such as *la*) to comprehension (i.e., singing using sol-fa syllables and/or instrumental fingerings).

After these initial experiences, the notation of familiar pieces that children can already perform should be introduced gradually and in ways that challenge them to consider how and why notation is used in music. Asking students to invent their own notation for a piece they can already play provides a useful window from which to view their conceptual development. Such activities also "prompt the classification, organisation, and connections that enable the child to transform the concrete experience into one that can be represented in icons or symbols" (Gromko, 1994, p. 146). In general, a child's earliest experiences in learning notation should occur in isolation from the act of playing. Gradually, and stimulated by a variety of challenging activities, children should start to make connections between the sounds they can already play and the traditional notation used to represent them. Scanning and pointing to the melody of a piece being performed by the teacher, chanting or clapping rhythm patterns, and singing or fingering (either mentally or out aloud) phrases or melodies can each help develop the aural awareness needed for students to comprehend notation in meaningful ways.

In general, acquiring competence in reading and interpreting musical notation is best achieved via a three-way process of gaining fluency in playing music, then reading it, and then putting the two together.

Introducing Notation

After these steps have been reinforced through various activities, a child can begin to integrate playing with reading. It is probably best to start by introducing the notation of pieces a child can already perform, then move to pieces that he or she has not learned to play but already knows, before moving on to new, unfamiliar repertoire that demand more-sophisticated levels of processing.

Six general principles can guide teachers as they strive to develop the wide range of skills needed for their students to become musically literate. These principles are modeled on the work of Bruning et al. (1999, pp. 258–259), whose comments on teaching children to read are reinterpreted for beginning instrumental instruction:

1. *Approach the reading of notation as a meaningful activity.* Reading musical notation is a meaning-making act. Although children need to learn to decode notation and know, for example, that a quarter note is one beat in length, their developing skills need at all times to be linked to structurally meaningful entities such as phrases and melodies rather than individual notes. Children can lose track of the purpose of learning to read notation when the focus of their attention is on decoding signs and visual representations in terms of individual note values and theoretical relationships (e.g., understanding the proportions of note values or scale-pitch relationships). They need to be continually reminded of the basic reasons for acquiring music-reading skills—learning, communicating, and enjoyment.

2. *Take a broad perspective on literacy development.* Functional literacy, in terms of knowing where to put one's fingers as a result of seeing a visual cue on the score, represents only a limited understanding of how to comprehend musical notation. The goal should be to instill competence in the use of notation for all forms of thinking and expression. Focusing the child's attention on the flow of a melody, the expressive detail in a composition, or simply how to make a passage sound different helps to foster a more sophisticated awareness of the broader pur-

pose of musical notation and how it can be used to help an instrumentalist think, reason, and communicate musically. An important aspect of good teaching, therefore, is to focus on meaningful tasks that help develop both musical and cognitive competencies.

3. *Help young readers move toward automatic decoding.* As shown in the sight-reading chapter in this volume, skilled readers are able to quickly and accurately discern key features in the visual appearance of the score and then instigate the required motor action to perform them on their instrument. When these actions are automatic, it is easier to direct attention to higher level expressive elements that enhance one's performance. Explicit instruction in how to decode notation is important. Replaying passages to improve fluency is obviously important for improving performance ability, but it does not follow that drilling activities and endless repetition will lead to automaticity. Guided meaningful reading of a range of musical pieces in which the teacher directs a student's attention to the relevant technical and expressive characteristics embedded in the work itself helps to instill confidence in performance and knowledge that can be applied when performing other literature.

4. *Draw on children's domain and general knowledge.* All children have knowledge about music before they commence instruction. Reading notation is more likely to be meaningful when it connects with a child's prior experiences of music. For example, introducing the notation for a piece a child already knows and wishes to learn can provide a powerful incentive that helps the student learn to read more quickly, as well as decipher any new elements that are being introduced by the teacher. Encouraging young beginners to invent their own notations to represent pieces they can already perform provides them with the metamusical awareness that will enhance their progress toward understanding why traditional notation looks and works the way it does. Teachers should provide multiple ways for young learners to interact with and learn about notation so that it actually means something to them.

5. *Encourage children to develop their musical knowledge.* Effective teachers draw their students' attention to the many dimensions of musical notation and encourage them to reflect on their performance and to come up with different interpretations. Learning to read musical notation is a multifaceted process that hinges on knowledge activation, memory, and attention. Aural awareness enables students to map the visual symbols of the musical notation into the required actions that produce the sounds on their instrument. Memory facilitates comprehension of the larger scale structures of what is being performed, and attention enables the musician to focus on individual signs, phrases, and expressive detail in order to perform musically.

6. *Expect children to vary widely in their progress toward fluent reading.* No two children will ever be at exactly the same level of musical development. Some will struggle with learning to read notation, while others will pick up notational skills relatively easily. Unfortunately, children who do not pick up reading skills early in their development are often not given the types of remedial attention needed to correct their deficiencies. This does not mean, however, that they cannot

develop into competent musicians. As with any sophisticated skill, learning a musical instrument involves a complex mix of abilities, and every student will have strengths and weaknesses that impact on the rate at which, and, in turn, the likelihood that, they will continue learning.

Conclusion

The focus in this chapter has been on ear playing, which we believe teachers may be underestimating in terms of its benefits for developing literacy skills. Based on evidence cited in this chapter, we conclude that emphasizing notational skills too early can lead to a decreased sensitivity to the unified patterns that children spontaneously observe when listening to music. Notational skills should therefore never be taught in isolation from perception. In our view, stressing notation, with few opportunities to perform music by ear, or rote learning, with equally few opportunities to develop reading fluency, restricts overall musicianship and the types of skills needed for a musician to succeed long-term. Rather, we advocate a more integrated approach, where performing music by ear serves as preparation for literacy development in the beginning stages of musical involvement, and where performing with and without notation is encouraged during all subsequent levels of development.

Acknowledgments. We thank Daniel Kohut, Stanley Schleuter, and Jack Taylor, who each provided very helpful suggestions and insightful comments on an earlier version of this chapter.

References

Abeles, H. F., Hoffer, C. F., & Klotman, R. H. (1994). *Foundations of music education* (2nd ed.). New York: Schirmer.

Adams, M. J. (1994). *Beginning to read: Thinking and learning about print.* Cambridge, MA: MIT Press.

Bamberger, J. (1996). Turning music theory on its ear. *International Journal of Computers for Mathematical Learning, 1*(1), 33–55.

Bamberger, J. (1999). Learning from the children we teach. *Bulletin of the Council for Research in Music Education, 142,* 48–74.

Brunning, R. H., Schraw, G. J., & Ronning, R. R. (1999). *Cognitive psychology and instruction* (3rd ed.). Upper Saddle River, NJ: Prentice-Hall.

Davidson, L., Scripp, L., & Welsh, P. (1988). "Happy Birthday": Evidence of conflicts of perceptual knowledge and conceptual understanding. *Journal of Aesthetic Education, 22*(1), 65–74.

Dowling, W. J., & Harwood, D. L. (1986). *Music cognition.* Orlando, FL: Academic Press.

Gabrielsson, A. (1999). The performance of music. In D. Deutsch (Ed.) (2nd ed.), *The psychology of music* (pp. 501–602). San Diego, CA: Academic Press.

Galvao, A., & Kemp, A. (1999). Kinaesthesia and instrumental music instruction: Some implications. *Psychology of Music, 27*(2), 129–137.

Gellrich, M., & Parncutt, R. (1998). Piano technique and fingering in the eighteenth and nineteenth centuries: Bringing a forgotten method back to life. *British Journal of Music Education*, *15*(1), 5–24.

Gellrich, M., & Sundin, B. (1993). Instrumental practice in the 18th and 19th centuries. *Council for Research in Music Education*, *119*, 137–145.

Glenn, K. A. (1999). Rote vs. note: The relationship of working memory capacity to performance and continuation in beginning string classes. (Doctoral dissertation, the University of Northern Colorado). *Dissertation Abstracts International*, 60/04, 1010. (University Microfilms No. 9927738)

Gordon, E. E. (1997). *Learning sequences in music: Skill, content and patterns.* Chicago: GIA.

Gromko, J. E. (1994). Children's invented notations as measures of musical understanding. *Psychology of Music*, *22*(2), 136–147.

Gruson, L. M. (1988). Rehearsal skill and musical competence: Does practice make perfect? In J. A. Sloboda (Ed.), *Generative processes in music: The psychology of performance, improvisation, and composition* (pp. 91–112). Oxford: Clarendon Press.

Hargreaves, D. J. (1986). *The developmental psychology of music.* London: Cambridge University Press.

Kohut, D. L. (1985). *Musical performance: Learning theory and pedagogy.* Englewood Cliffs, NJ: Prentice-Hall.

Landers, R. (1980). *The talent education school of Shinichi Suzuki: An analysis.* Athens, OH: Ability Development.

Luce, J. R. (1965). Sight-reading and ear-playing abilities as related to instrumental music students. *Journal of Research in Music Education*, *13*(2), 101–109.

Mainwaring, J. (1931). Experiments on the analysis of cognitive processes involved in musical ability and in music education. *British Journal of Educational Psychology*, *1*(2), 180–203.

Mainwaring, J. (1941). The meaning of musicianship: A problem in the teaching of music. *British Journal of Educational Psychology*, *11*(3), 205–214.

Mainwaring, J. (1947). The assessment of musical ability. *British Journal of Educational Psychology*, *17*(1), 83–96.

Mainwaring, J. (1951a). Psychological factors in the teaching of music: Part 1: Conceptual musicianship. *British Journal of Educational Psychology*, *21*, 105–121.

Mainwaring, J. (1951b). Psychological factors in the teaching of music: Part II: Applied musicianship. *British Journal of Educational Psychology*, *21*(3), 199–213.

Mainwaring, J. (1951c). *Teaching music in schools.* London: Paxton.

McPherson, G. E. (1993). Factors and abilities influencing the development of visual, aural and creative performance skills in music and their educational implications. (Doctoral dissertation, University of Sydney, Australia). *Dissertation Abstracts International*, 54/04-A, 1277. (University Microfilms No. 9317278).

McPherson, G. E. (1995a). The assessment of musical performance: Development and validation of five new measures. *Psychology of Music*, *23*(2), 142–161.

McPherson, G. E. (1995b). Redefining the teaching of musical performance. *Quarterly Journal of Music Teaching and Learning*, *6*(2), 56–64.

McPherson, G. E. (1996). Five aspects of musical performance and their correlates. *Council for Research in Music Education*, *127*, 115–121.

McPherson, G. E. (1997). Cognitive strategies and skills acquisition in musical performance. *Council for Research in Music Education, 133*, 64–71.

McPherson, G. E., Bailey, M., & Sinclair, K. (1997). Path analysis of a model to describe the relationship among five types of musical performance. *Journal of Research in Music Education, 45*(1), 103–129.

McPherson, G. E., & Renwick, J. (2000). Self-regulation and musical practice. In C. Woods, G. B. Luck, R. Brochard, F. Seddon, and J. A. Sloboda (Eds.), *Proceedings of the Sixth International Conference on Music Perception and Cognition*. Keele, UK: Keele University, Department of Psychology. CD-ROM.

Pitts, S. (2000). *A century of change in music education: Historical perspectives on contemporary practice in British secondary school music*. Aldershot, UK: Ashgate.

Posner, M. I., Nissen, M. J., & Klein, R. M. (1976). Visual dominance: An information-processing account of its origins and significance. *Psychological Review, 83*(2), 157–171.

Priest, P. (1989). Playing "by ear": Its nature and application to instrumental learning. *British Journal of Music Education, 6*(2),173–191.

Rousseau, J. J. (1762). *Emile, or On education*. London: Dent.

Samuels, S. J. (1994). Toward a theory of automated information processing in reading, revisited. In R. B. Ruddell, M. R. Ruddell, and H. Singer (Eds.) *Theoretical models of processes of reading* (4th ed). (pp. 816–837). Newark, DE: International Reading Association.

Schleuter, S. (1997). *A sound approach to teaching instrumentalists* (2nd ed.). New York: Schirmer.

Shaffer, D. R. (1999). *Developmental psychology: Childhood and adolescence* (5th ed.). Pacific Grove, CA: Brooks/Cole.

Sloboda, J. A. (1978). The psychology of music reading. *Psychology of Music, 6*(2), 3–20.

Smyth, M. M. (1984). Perception and action. In M. M. Smyth and A. M. Wing (Eds.), *The psychology of human movement* (pp. 119–152). London: Academic Press.

Sperti, J. (1970). Adaptation of certain aspects of the Suzuki method to the teaching of the clarinet: An experimental investigation testing the comparative effectiveness of two different pedagogical methodologies. (Doctoral dissertation, New York University). *Dissertation Abstracts International, 32/03, 1557.* (UMI No. 7124833)

Suzuki, S. (1983). *Nurtured by love* (2nd ed.). New York: Smithtown.

Sweller, J., van Merrienboer, J., & Paas, F. (1998). Cognitive architecture and instructional design. *Educational Psychological Review, 10*(3), 251–296.

Tommis, Y., & Fazey, D. M. A. (1999). The acquisition of the pitch elements of music literacy skills by 3–4 year-old pre-school children: A comparison of two methods. *Psychology of Music, 27*(2), 230–244.

Yorke Trotter, T. H. (1914). *The making of musicians*. London: Herbert Jenkins.

8

Improvisation

BARRY J. KENNY & MARTIN GELLRICH

Depending upon its sociocultural function, the term improvisation incorporates a multiplicity of musical meanings, behaviors,
and practices. A feature common to all improvisation, however,
is that the creative decisions of its performers are made within the
real time restrictions of performance itself. Improvisation is therefore considered to be a performance art *par excellence*, requiring
not only a lifetime of preparation across a broad range of musical
and nonmusical formative experiences, but also a sophisticated
and eclectic skills base. The chapter reflects on psychological
models and their attempts to simulate improvising processes and
constraints, the means by which improvisers acquire performance
skills, improvisation as part of a larger, co-collaborative creative
endeavor, recent studies highlighting the benefits of improvisation in a learning situation, and improvisation as a means of revi-
talizing Western education. Practical implications and an integrated model for learning to improvise are discussed in the final
section.

When improvisers talk about their music, they often draw upon linguistic metaphors grounded in communication or rhetoric (Berliner, 1994; Monson, 1996).
The culturally agreed upon constraints that make this spontaneous rhetoric
possible distinguishes improvisation from most other forms of music making.
Of these constraints, the most important is time itself, which determines that
improvised creation must occur simultaneously with its performance (see Pressing, 1998). Such temporal constraints necessitate a series of efficient mechanisms
designed to facilitate improvising in real time. From a psychological perspective, these constraints fall into two broad categories—*internally* (i.e., psychologically) and *externally* (i.e., socioculturally) generated.

Aside from the more obvious cognitive (i.e., memory) and physiological (i.e.,
motor skills) constraints that affect improvisation, the most important *internal*

constraint is the *knowledge base* (see Figure 8.1). This warehouse of previously learned material is what the performer knows and brings to the performance, such as the "musical materials and excerpts, repertoire, sub skills, perceptual strategies, problem-solving routines, hierarchical memory structures and schemas, generalized motor programmes" (Pressing, 1998, p. 53) that have been acquired and developed through conscious deliberate practice. The knowledge base used by improvising musicians typically involves the internalization of source materials that are idiomatic to individual improvising cultures. Examples of such pedagogic source material include the Persian *Radif*—a "guide to improvisatory techniques, formal patterns, and overall structure of performances" (Nettl, 1998, p. 14)—and in jazz the transcribed solos of distinguished musicians.

Referents, however, are associated with or specific to a particular performance: the external, culturally supplied forms that assist with the transmission of improvised ideas. These points of departure include a range of musical and nonmusical (i.e., graphics) stimuli that, whether sounded or not, ultimately become deeply embedded in a musician's internalized creative resources (Nettl, 1974). The musical referents of jazz, for example, are its cyclical, often 32-bar song structures (i.e., jazz standards), its chords (and rules that govern treatment of their extensions), and its characteristic rhythmic patterns (Pressing, 1998). Two of the referent's most important functions are its ability to limit improvisational choices according to appropriate guidelines and its role in building perceptual paradigms for listener appreciation (Sloboda, 1985).

The latter of these two functions is particularly important, in that most improvisations are filtered through formal structures already familiar to listeners. In contrast to knowledge bases, which performers are not typically aware of during performance (because they are internalized and automated), referents influence improvisers more directly, providing the formal and musical material unique to each improvisation. However individual one artist's interpretation of the jazz standard "Body and Soul" may be, for example, it is still likely to share many similarities with another artist's version, thereby providing a perceptual degree of commonality for listeners. The same cannot be said for each artist's knowledge base, which may be as unique as each musician's experiences and personalities.

Skilled improvisers are adept at manipulating listeners' predetermined expectations of referents for expressive purposes through, for example, ironic interpretation or adherence to or denial of expectation. The gratification or frustration of these expectations in turn generates musical emotion, which in itself may play a key role in determining musical meaning (Meyer, 1973; Narmour, 2000). The perceptual frameworks that govern listener expectation in improvised music may range anywhere between concrete notated compositional forms and the amorphous musical shapes and sounds that are deeply embedded in any culture's collective unconscious (Monson, 1996). As Westendorf (1994) observes, the perceptual frameworks of jazz improvisation, for example, include not only groups of individual notes but also generalized contour shapes, where any number of melodic fragments can potentially trigger standardized patterns of expectation (see also Dowling & Harwood, 1986).

As suggested in Figure 8.1, the two key constraints of improvisation—knowledge bases and referents—work together to generate new musical structures. This diagram also illustrates the spillage between the two. Referents, for example, are likely to become part of knowledge bases through prolonged exposure and repetition. Similarly, listeners make synchronous connections between their perception of the initial referent (through prior exposure) and its modified variant—the improvisation itself.

Flow States, Risk Taking, and Kinesthesia

> Pepper forgot everything, just blew and blew, shaking all over—a state reminiscent of the horses of the gods—being possessed to the extent that they became their specific orisha, assuming all their particular dance movements and behaviours. This forgetting of oneself is a state that many improvisers strive to attain. (Floyd, 1995, p. 139)

The ecstatic state described in this quote by Floyd, where improvising artists surrender to the creative moment itself, is well documented in the psychological literature and by no means unique to musical creativity. Jazz pianist and practicing psychologist Denny Zeitlin admits this to be his state of mind when playing the piano (Csikszentmihalyi & Rich, 1997). As Csikszentmihalyi and Rich explain, these *peak experiences* or *flow states* assist improvisers, to move not only beyond the literal texts of referents but also beyond their own cognitive limits in non–flow states. Furthermore, this quasi-narcotic flow state may be one of the most important reasons that motivate improvising musicians to persevere with their craft, despite the often-adverse conditions it is produced under. Once possessed by the moment, musicians begin to forget personal problems, lose critical self-consciousness, lose track of time, and eventually feel that the activity in which they are engaged is worth doing for its own sake (Csikszentmihalyi

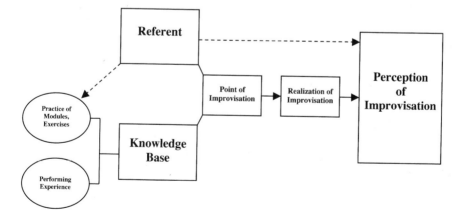

Figure 8.1. Referents, knowledge bases, and listener expectation.

& Rich, 1997). Aside from unlocking creative improvising in one of its most emancipated forms, flow states may therefore also play a key role in motivation and hence a predisposition or inclination toward further artistic development.

As a creative endeavor that occurs in real time, improvisation often involves the necessary disguising and making musical sense of mistakes. The old jazz adage that it's not a mistake if you play it twice is symptomatic of this approach. Mistakes suggest a more pervasive undercurrent that informs all improvisational creativity—risk taking. For many improvisers, risk taking provides a self-induced state of uncertainty where repetition and predictable responses become virtually impossible. In a landmark publication on this issue, Sudnow (1978) documented the frustrating process he underwent when acquiring and applying improvising skills. On his journey to become a professional musician, Sudnow reflects on the difficulty of acquiring knowledge bases from aural sources, the technical constraints of particular instruments (i.e., the black and white keys of a piano), the effect these constraints have on improvised response, and the relationship between spontaneously created material and improvised filler.

Sudnow's most important finding was that a conscious application of his internalized knowledge base resulted in what he terms "frantic" playing, where each distinct chord in the harmonic series of the song being improvised on triggered its own preconceived strategic plan, a plan inefficiently spilling over into and frustrating the plans of the next adjacent chord. Sudnow found that one way to unlearn this triggered response was to jettison his knowledge base, to let his hand go wherever it wished in a process where the intuitive shape of his hands and ears guided musical responses. Once he started taking more risks, Sudnow found more "right" notes falling under his fingers and his playing at last began to emulate the relaxed, idiomatic, and coherent sound typical of more-experienced players.

While Sudnow's introspective methodology is open to criticism, his findings nevertheless draw attention to significant psychological processes that complement and inform the automation of knowledge bases. Performance that incorporates flow states and risk taking may in fact hold the key to achieving optimal levels of musical communication, providing a clue as to why some musicians are able to access their knowledge bases more fluidly and creatively than other similarly skilled but less inspired improvisers. Berliner (1994) refers to the attainment of this heightened level of performance as being "within the groove [where] improvisers experience a great sense of relaxation, which increases their powers of expression and imagination. They handle their instruments with athletic finesse, able to respond to every impulse" (p. 389).

Surprisingly little research has been undertaken in the related area of *kinesthesia*, the sense of where parts of the body are with respect to one another. Our current understanding of complex muscular interactions and their relationship to instrumental performance is at best rudimentary; what little is known suggests a far subtler integration of mind and body than previously thought, where "what appears to be a simple act of throwing or catching an object actually involves the interaction of several feedback mechanisms" (Galvao & Kemp, 1999, p. 133). This suggests that some of the research on improvisation that makes connections between simple motoric movement and musical structures, thereby often informing technical pedagogy, may have to be rethought in terms of a more holistic conception of technique. Only then may we more fully understand why some musicians are able to move beyond technical automation to arrive at a more direct and meaningful form of communication.

Theoretical and Generative Models of Improvisation

What are improvisers thinking about at the precise moment of creation? In short, we still do not really know. As Johnson-Laird (1988) observes, in order to improvise efficiently and idiomatically, the subconscious knowledge base processes that generate improvisation need to be sufficiently automated and submerged "without any internal representation of an intermediate form" (p. 211). The fact that improvisers themselves cannot access their own subconscious processes at the moment of creation poses enormous practical problems for researchers. In addition, the creative impetus for improvisation often depends on volatile performance variables (e.g., interaction with audience, fellow musicians, acoustic considerations), all of which are extremely difficult to replicate under controlled experimental conditions or reliably account for with postevent analysis. To date, such practical considerations have precluded any serious examination of the thinking-aloud verbal protocols of improvising musicians.

In order to better understand and replicate the theoretical constructs that generate improvisation, researchers have attempted to model its salient features. Johnson-Laird's model (1991), itself based on a computer simulation of an improviser's knowledge base, sheds light on the mechanisms that assist with spontaneous creation. He argues that if the knowledge base is sufficiently internalized (in long-term memory) and automated (through practice and performance experience), the resources used to generate surface melody are ultimately freer to focus on developing coherence and structural unity. One of his model's strengths is that its ideology is grounded in cognitive load theory (i.e., the finite cognitive processing capacity of multiple tasks), which, given the multiple constraints that govern improvisation, seems to make good sense.

Significantly, Johnson-Laird's model shares a number of conceptual similarities with Chomsky's (1968) linguistic models. At the first or deepest level, improvisers commit basic structures (i.e., chord theory, prelearned formulas) to memory. At the second level, improvisers make aesthetic feedback decisions that concern the structure of the referent, such as which significant notes are to be targeted. At the third or surface level, improvised melody is generated (Johnson-Laird, 1991). In a computer program designed to test the theory, Johnson-Laird found that surface-level functions (i.e., improvised melody) required less computational processing power than the internalized functions that generated them.

Clarke's (1991) three-stage cognitive model of improvisation outlines a hierarchy of thought processes. These are employed proportionately according to the level of structure demanded by the improvising genre and/or the artistic inclinations of the improviser. These conceptual thought processes articulate various proportions of freedom and constraint and can be extended from a generalized understanding of jazz genres to include most global improvising genres. Clarke's three categories, which loosely resemble Kernfeld's (1981) much-cited theoretical genres of jazz, can be summarized as follows.

1. *Repertoire selection*: Formulaic improvising characteristic of bebop. In its crudest form, improvisers automatically associate prelearned formulas with either particular chords (i.e., C major seventh) or chord classes (i.e., major sevenths in general). When integrated with other types of improvisation, repertoire selection provides a potent means for binding disparate thematic material, a momentary resting point for improvising musicians (when inspiration momentarily fails) and a unique body of recurring motivic material that identifies particular musicians.

2. *Hierarchical*: Song form–generated improvising structures (i.e., referents) characteristic of both bebop and hard bop. These fixed forms supply not only the chord sequences that frame most improvised responses in Western improvised music but also the melodic structures associated with their original form (i.e., the original melody of "Body and Soul"). In its most emphatic form—*melodic paraphrase*—improvised responses are tantamount to variations or permutations of the original referent.

3. *Motivic*: Chain-associative improvising characteristic of modal and free jazz. In motivic improvising, motives develop linearly, with each new unit of improvisation drawing upon improvised material produced either immediately before the improvised event or within recent memory. The most overt form of motivic improvising is a series of melodic sequences in transposition.

It is interesting to read Clarke's hierarchical categories of improvisation in the light of Johnson-Laird's model. Taken together, they not only account for the basic generative mechanisms of improvisation but also further illuminate our current understanding of what constraints govern different improvising styles and forms. Figure 8.2 represents an attempt to combine these two theories together with the first author's own concerns with performance and group variables. These additions include the obvious starting point for the improvisation—the referent—in addition to other factors that affect initial input, such as performance variables (i.e., audience participation, venue, acoustics) and group creative input.

In this combined model, it is evident that *repertoire selection* processes the initial referent as a series of disjointed sections, with each section drawing a selected response from the basic structures. Both *hierarchic* and *motivic* improvising initially processes the referent (i.e., R) more holistically. This composite entity naturally requires more intermediary consideration than repertoire selection (which essentially bypasses the evaluation stage). It is also much more likely to frame improvisational responses to the degree that they will be perceived by listeners as similar to the original referent (i.e., R1). The main difference between hierarchic and motivic improvising occurs at the point of production. Once the referent has been processed hierarchically, new material (often another chorus

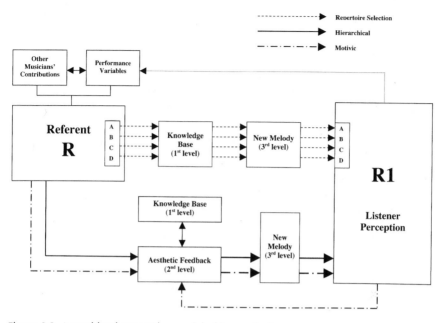

Figure 8.2. A combined generative model of improvisation.

of the same referent) is required to continue the process. In motivic improvising, any material generated as an end-point response—no matter how dissimilar to the original referent—can potentially feed back into the evaluative stage, thereby generating new improvisations. The diagram also suggests that all improvisation perceived by listeners in some way feeds back into the overall process through audience feedback, which in turn affects the future creative decisions of group participants.

A Model of Mental Processes During Improvisation

As the preceding models demonstrate, improvisation operates most effectively when realized through an efficient network of constraints, all of which assist improvisers in making effective, appropriate, and meaningful choices within the restrictions of real-time improvising. But how is the potential to improvise further constrained by our own finite physical and cognitive resources? As Pressing (1998) observes, improvisation operates as "an interruptible associative process based on the ongoing evaluation of previous musical events" (p. 56). What physical and cognitive constraints, then, is this feedback mechanism subject to?

The second author of this chapter has developed a speculative model of cognitive processes during improvisation where any combination of eight potentially different types of processes can be observed to occur. Improvisers typically shift from one process to another but cannot combine two or more simultaneously (see Heuer, 1996).

1. *Short-term anticipation*: At any point in the improvisation, musical events are anticipated within a time interval we estimate to be around 1 to 3 seconds. However, these anticipated notes cannot be sounded for a minimum of 0.3 second after the decision has been made (Gellrich, 2001b; see also psychological research on the refractory period: Welford, 1952; and from reading musical scores: Sloboda, 1985; Goolsby, 1994).
2. *Medium-term anticipation*: Musical events that occur within a 3- to 12-second time span (i.e., the next phrase or period) may be anticipated and projected into the future. (Again, these times are estimates and have not been substantiated by experimental evidence. The length of the time span will also depend on the length of the next musical phrase or period.)
3. *Long-term anticipation*: Projection of long-term plans for the remainder of the improvisation.
4. *Short-term recall*: Musical events that have occurred over the last few seconds can be recalled, in a process where concentration is focused on prior events (Gellrich, 2001a).
5. *Medium-term recall*: Musical events that have occurred within the last 4, 8, or 16 measures can be recalled so as to provide an accurate recollection of the previous musical phrase.
6. *Long-term recall*: Improvisers are able to recall the entire improvisation from its genesis up to the present moment.
7. *Flow status*: Improvisers are able to concentrate solely on what is being created at that particular moment.
8. *Feedback processes*: Musical ideas for future projected improvisation may be gathered from that which can be previously recalled. An example is an initially unintended ("wrong") note, recalled from previous performance, that the improviser decides to reiterate. Such recollections may further include a substantial amount of musical material held in medium- and long-term recall. This concept of feedback may be further extended to include the ongoing evaluation of musical events in the light of information held in medium- and long-term recall. An example of this kind of feedback occurs in jazz improvisation, where tones (of the scale) associated with the next adjacent chord in the series are sounded over the present chord. However temporarily dissonant such a practice may at first appear, it proves to be an effective means of preparing and linking adjacent chords.

In the course of performance, improvisers potentially draw on any number of these eight cognitive processes, provided that their decisions are made quickly and as a series (i.e., from one note to the next but not simultaneously). The second author's unpublished interviews with expert improvisers and personal analysis of his own improvisations suggest that the most commonly occurring activities are short- and medium-term anticipation and flow status. The other five cognitive processes generally occur when the improviser is able to master enough conscious control for their execution—for example, during

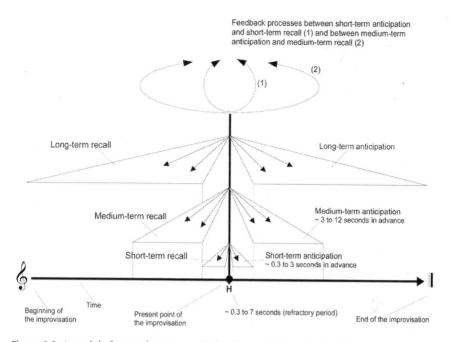

Figure 8.3. A model of mental processes during improvisation. Feedback processes between anticipation and short-term recall (1) and between medium-term musical concept and medium-term recall (2).

slower phrases or phrases with pauses and when prelearned patterns are articulated automatically.

Practical Implications

The Challenges of Teaching Improvisation

How does one teach a student to move beyond the text of knowledge to the fluid context in which it can be most fruitfully applied? Two pedagogical approaches—*deliberate practice* and *transcendence*—help answer this question. Much of the existing research on the pedagogy of improvisation so far has been concerned with deliberate practice. Transcendence can be understood as a heightened state of consciousness that moves beyond the confines of (thereby often jettisoning) the accumulated knowledge base itself. It is a state of consciousness that, like deliberate practice, can be encouraged and cultivated at the outset of an improviser's development; it need not be delayed until the final stages of an artist's development, as deliberate-practice research implies. While transcendence states, akin to the flow states discussed earlier, are more difficult to define and research, they nevertheless provide a cogent alternative to deliberate practice and play an important role in any well-rounded practice regime (see concluding section of this chapter).

Placing deliberate practice and transcendence states in opposition is not to say, however, that one does not require or ultimately lead to the other. As Berliner (1997) observes, improvisation involves a "lifetime of preparation in the rigors of musical thinking" so that musicians are able to "respond artfully, as well as spontaneously, when improvising" (p. 37). The skill acquisition and developmental processes detailed in Berliner (1994), however, move well beyond the *individual* learning of knowledge bases to include a wider, collaborative learning environment. In this environment, social interaction produces true innovation and musical meaning. The problem for educators is how to replicate these complex sociocultural phenomena in institutionalized educational settings.

Deliberate Practice

The traditional approach has been to instill as much improvising technique as possible (usually in a one-on-one setting) in the hope that it might equip *individuals* with sufficient material to cope with the unpredictable nature of *group* improvising. Much evidence supports deliberate practice as a necessary means of acquiring improvising skills, and hence expertise (Weisberg, 1999; Pressing, 1998; Lehmann & Ericsson, 1997). Through the correct levels of motivation and challenging situations, such individually tailored practice provides scaffolded targets for the accruement of improvisational skills. Ways in which a musician may practice deliberately include "working with a teacher in a directed situation, but also by aural absorption of examples of expert performance, study of theory and analysis, and interactive work in peer group ensembles during rehearsal and performance" (Pressing, 1998, p. 48).

One of the main aims of deliberate practice is to encourage improvisational expertise through the intensive development of internalized knowledge bases. The difference between expert and nonexpert improvisers is in how sophisticated, automated, and personalized these structures become (Kratus, 1989). Novice improvisers, for example, tend to access materials from the knowledge base in a diachronic and literal fashion by repeating prelearned motives parrot fashion or out of context, whereas experienced improvisers are able to make sophisticated hyperconnections between prelearned material. Borko and Livingston (1989) demonstrate this principle effectively in their observations of expert teachers of mathematics. Not only are the knowledge bases of these teachers more synthetic and dynamic than those of less experienced teachers, but they are also able to better anticipate questions and genuinely respond to the dynamics of the larger learning situation. For musicians, these hyperconnections can be effectively developed through well-established deliberate-practice routines—for example, practicing chord voicings in all inversions and spacings or motivic formulas practiced in all keys (Pressing, 1998).

Jazz is still the primary method of teaching improvisation in Western education and the chord-scale formulaic method the most widely practiced means of achieving this. It is therefore worthwhile to assess the success of this method as a case study for teaching improvisation in Western educational settings as a whole. To put it simply, the chord-scale method attempts to constrain an improviser's choice of individual melodic notes to an array of scales or modes suggested by the predefined chord sequence of the referent. For example, minor seventh chords—such as D minor seventh (D, F, A, C)—are said to best suggest Dorian modes, such as D Dorian (D, E, F, G, A, B, C), simply because Dorian modes represent supersets of this particular chord type (i.e., minor sevenths). The methodology's basic aim, like deliberate practice itself, is to provide improvisers with as much working material as possible. Significantly, its ideological precepts support the ideology that informs generative models of jazz improvisation based upon multiple constraints, where chords are seen to elicit any number of potential internalized responses. As Birkett (1995) explains, however, "While [the chord-scale method] certainly gives students notes to play, it does not seem to offer any reasons for playing anything in particular" (p. vi). Offering a knee-jerk approach to each successive chord in a series, the methodology's randomness significantly contradicts the "tension and resolution relationships" suggested by extended harmonic passages (Birkett, 1995, p. 25) and, as Sudnow's (1978) experience shows, ultimately only produces a frantic and disconnected style of playing.

This methodology's often-uncritical acceptance points to a more serious trend in the use of improvisation in educational settings—that of theoretical modeling inhibiting improvised response (Kenny, 1999). It is evident that a great deal of improvisation that emanates from many performing institutions today appears to be more concerned with preparing improvisers for every foreseeable eventuality than with developing individual improving voices. The effects that 30 years of this type of pedagogy has had on the language of jazz, for example, is articulated by Lou Donaldson:

> All players are sounding alike today. They're all working out of Oliver Nelson's book. They play mechanical sequences of changes that will fit anything. When they get to a chord change, they skate through it. They work out clusters of notes, whole-tone patterns and things, to get through it. . . . They don't have a feeling for tonal centres in music anymore, or they just improvise on the harmony in ways that have nothing to do with the song. (Berliner, 1994, p. 280)

Donaldson's quote illustrates the downside of repetition and imitation as an appropriate means of acquiring improvising skills. As Martinez, Malbran, and Shifres (1999) assert, once a mental image has been shaped "incorrectly" for the first time, subsequent repetitions fail to clarify its structure, instead only serving to reimprint the original unidiomatic errors. In other words, initial learning experiences may play a crucial role in determining how creatively such knowledge bases are ultimately applied. The implication for improvisational pedagogy is that it may be difficult to unlearn material once it has been compounded through countless repetitions and private practice. A solution to this seeming impasse is not simply to build connections between already-internalized material but also to encourage individual improvising voices from the outset (Birkett,

1995). As Berliner's classic anthropological study of the jazz scene demonstrates, extensive aural immersion, semistructured experimentation and active participation in improvising genres almost always take place prior to the systematic acquisition of theoretical principles (Berliner, 1994).

Children's Play and Group Improvising

Many of the mechanisms used by human beings in everyday problem-solving tasks are improvisatory in nature, a concept that has recently been articulated as "everyday creativity" (Sawyer, 1999). Children's play provides a fascinating window into improvised creation in one of its most unmediated forms. For example, Baker-Sennett and Matusov (1997) asked six Grade 2 and 3 girls to make up their own version of *Snow White* with minimal authoritarian intervention or guidance. Left to their own devices, these children first set the material itself aside to concentrate on the social dynamics that would ultimately facilitate the improvising process, such as the procedures they might use to resolve conflicts. Once a collaborative atmosphere had been established, the children proceeded to cooperatively improvise much of the play's structure in character. Baker-Sennett and Matusov found that a lack of authoritarian intervention produced as much cohesion and efficiency as a teacher-led control situation, if not more. Aside from the enormous educational benefits of involving children in the creation of new knowledge, these children were also aware of their privileged role as creative participants. Displaying similar artistic temperaments to adult creators, they paid special attention to the dramatic consequences of their choices and endlessly debated and workshopped the best possible solution to a problem.

A similar relaxation of authoritarian control in improvisation is discussed by Smith (1998), who investigated Miles Davis's creation of a ritualized performance space. Davis's success as a mentor and bandleader was based on similar principles to those exhibited by the children, especially his ability to exploit the semistructured possibilities of group creativity. Just as a lack of predictable control provided a point of focus for the children making up *Snow White*, musicians in Davis's groups were impelled, through Davis's refusal to provide certainty, to engage in a heightened form of group cohesion and creativity. In the absence of traditional hierarchical (top-down) leadership structures, on the one hand these musicians were freer to actively participate in creative contributions, while on the other they needed to listen and defer to one another's projections more closely than before. Not surprisingly, these interchanges gave rise to a subtle and efficient form of communication that paradoxically focused even greater attention on Davis himself than before, cementing his pivotal role as group mentor and instigator of new ideas.

Baker-Sennett and Matusov's and Smith's research draws attention to the social interactive variables of improvisation, without which the development of individual knowledge bases is relatively ineffectual. This research also demonstrates that improvisation can provide a potent means of harnessing intrinsic motivation in group (educational) settings. As Sternberg (2000) observed, educators may be selling many apparently unpromising students short by unduly emphasizing "memory and analytical abilities" above "creative and practical abilities" (p. 255). By concentrating more on their given abilities (as opposed to capabilities), students may start to perform better across a broad range of educational and personal areas "because they can use their abilities more effectively, and because the greater interest of the material better motivates them to learn" (Sternberg, 2000).

The overtraining of predictable learned responses is perhaps the greatest shortcoming when learning to improvise. Most improvised performance, however, takes place in dynamic, group-based settings where

> each has to listen and respond to the others, resulting in a collaborative, and intersubjectively generated performance . . . [where] no one acts as the director or leader, determining where the performance will go; instead, the performance emerges out of the actions of everyone working together. (Sawyer, 1999, p. 194)

One of the suggestions that emanated from these findings is that group performance activities must complement solitary practice. While far greater amounts of solitary practice may prove beneficial in fostering the technical and theoretical principles of notated music, improvisation requires a greater emphasis on performance (and group experience) itself. After all, improvisational creativity most often ultimately takes place in a performance environment, not in the practice room, and the ability to react to and generate music from dynamic and unpredictable variables is one of the distinguishing features of improvisation.

An Integrated Model for Learning to Improvise

One of the greatest challenges that face improvising musicians is their need to attend to several motoric and musical aspects simultaneously while improvising. Among other things, these aspects include harmony, patterns, melodies, form, musical expression, coordination of both hands (piano), and rhythm.

Although psychological research suggests the possible division of conscious control between two different aspects (Heuer, 1996; Pashler & Johnston, 1998), many improvisers that the second author has interviewed report that they normally can only consciously monitor one aspect at a time. This suggests that while one aspect is monopolizing conscious attention, the others must proceed unconsciously in the background. As improvisations unfold, musicians shift concentration from one aspect to another (Heuer, 1996), with conscious focus held on each aspect for only a fraction of a second. Such findings have profound consequences for the teaching and learning of improvisation. Because of these limitations on conscious control, the teaching of improvisation needs to be divided into different areas, all of which must be developed systematically and in parallel (Gellrich, 1995). Only after having mastered the ability to consciously control each aspect separately can improvisers control all aspects simultaneously and unconsciously with the added ability to switch between them.

Two basic stages in the acquisition of improvising skills can be distinguished, both of which can be understood in terms of a linguistic analogy. In the first stage of learning a language words and grammatical rules are acquired, and in the second students explore their various possibilities of combination and application. Improvisers similarly need to first master the hardware of improvisation: patterns, parts of melodies, chord progressions, modulations, voicings, counterpoint, and the coordination between chord progressions and melodic patterns. Only then can the software of improvisation be developed—systematic rules that assist with constructing melodies, phrases, and larger musical ideas, working with motifs, and establishing relationships among different parts of the improvisation. Both the hardware and the software of improvisation, which together play a key role in the formation of the knowledge base, must be practiced systematically and separately. The more musical equivalents of words and grammatical rules an improviser is able to acquire and master, the richer the ensuing language of the improvisations will be.

Once a musician has assimilated newly acquired material such as a motive or a chord progression into the knowledge base, it is necessary to apply it as soon as possible in a practical context. Each particular musical aspect of improvisation requires different working time and attention to detail. Players of melodic instruments, for example, need to intensively practice melodic patterns in different tonalities (Gellrich, 1992; Gellrich & Parncutt, 1998). This not only builds more complex connections between preexisting materials already in the knowledge base but also is an effective means of kinesthetic reinforcement (Gellrich, 1992; Gellrich & Parncutt, 1998). These patterns ultimately lie under the fingers to the extent that musicians are able to divert attention away from technique altogether. Similar precepts can be applied to guitar, organ, and piano players and their automation of chord voicings.

For improvisation to remain vital and truly spontaneous, it is important not only that the knowledge base is constantly updated and sophisticated but also that improvisers learn to transcend it. Only then are improvisers able to unconsciously avoid predictable responses and react spontaneously to less predictable variables such as other musicians' knowledge bases and audience variables. In order to avoid predictable responses, musicians need to devote practice time to exercises and activities that encourage creativity and risk taking and, most important, replicate the improvising environment, where mistakes and disaster recovery occur on a regular basis. For example, if a pianist accidentally lands on a dissonant or nonfunctional chord, this can become the starting point for a series of exercises that revolve around resolving such chords with the optimal voice leading. In this way mistakes ultimately become the catalysts for creativity, where new accidental figures and chord progressions potentially enter the ever-increasing richness and complexity of the knowledge base. One of the best forums for risk taking and self-challenge is group improvisation, where improvisers need to constantly reassess projected responses in relation to the creative contributions of other individuals and the collective group.

A further aspect worth exploring is associative improvisation. Inspiration for improvisation can be derived from a number of artistic resources other than music, such as dance, movement, poetry, films, comics, and pictures. There are clearly a multiplicity of factors beyond the purely musical that affect and shape the creative impulses of great improvisers. Seminal tenor saxophonist Joe Henderson illustrated this with his holistic experience of improvisation:

> I've probably been influenced by nonmusical things as much as musical things. I think I was probably influenced by writers, poets? . . . You know how to use quotation marks. You know how you quote people as a player. You use semicolons, hyphens, paragraphs, parentheses, stuff like this. I'm thinking this when I am playing. I'm having a conversation with somebody. (Floyd, 1995, p. 141)

Aside from its self-evident risk-taking benefits, such nonmusical, associative improvising may prove a useful tool in integrating improvisational hardware and software.

One of the greatest challenges that face improvisers in the current climate of global improvisation is to develop an individual improvising voice. With so many competing and culturally diverse styles to choose from, the question is where to begin. In the era before global communication, such problems of identity were never encountered by, for example, cultures where improvisational practices developed in comparative geographic isolation and across much greater historical time frames. So as to avoid the disorienting effect of competing influences, we suggest that in the initial stages students learn to improvise in one particular style, in a similar way that children naturally gravitate toward expressing themselves in certain musical forms. In this way, developing improvisers learn to initially speak in their mother tongue. Students should also study compositions in this style and learn to use elements of these as a means of increasing the range of ideas for their own improvisations. The skills honed under such a control situation can then be extended to improvising across a number of different styles. After having learned to improvise first in a particular style and then in a number of different styles, improvisers learn to develop both an individual and richly eclectic voice. Figure 8.4 demonstrates the connection between the different areas of teaching and learning improvisation discussed here.

Conclusion

The implications that the latest research in music psychology have for the pedagogy of improvisation are wide-ranging and interdisciplinary. This research suggests an integrated learning approach, combining the best aspects of deliberate practice theory with established cultural practices such as risk taking and group creativity. As for the discipline of music psychology itself, there are promising signs of interdisciplinary integration and cooperation, manifest in two recent monographs dedicated to improvisation, both of which reflect its dynamic, multifaceted, and interdisciplinary concerns (Nettle & Russell, 1998; Sawyer, 1997). A possible area for future improvement could be a greater level of cooperation and information sharing between music theory and music psychology, both of which are essentially responsible for generating theories on improvisation, theories that

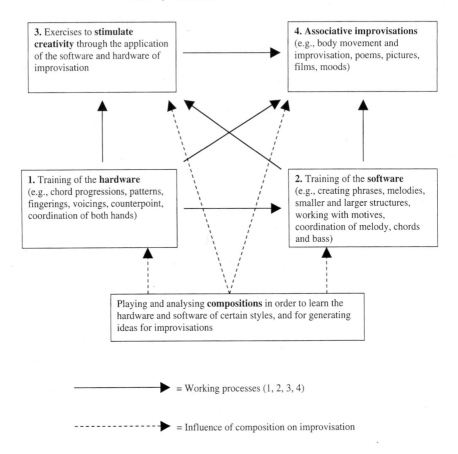

Figure 8.4. An integrative model of learning improvisation.

often translate into pedagogy. Another promising area is the psychological study of group dynamics. As improvisation is essentially about the collaborative creation of shared rhetoric, further research in this area can only improve the little we currently know about the cognitive aspects of group creativity.

References

Baker-Sennett, J., & Matusov, E. (1997). School performance: Improvisational processes in development and education. In R. K. Sawyer (Ed.), *Creativity in performance* (pp. 197–212). Greenwich, CT: Ablex.

Berliner, P. (1994). *Thinking in jazz : The infinite art of improvisation*. Chicago: University of Chicago Press.

Berliner, P. (1997). Give and take: The collective conversation of jazz performance. In R. K. Sawyer (Ed.), *Creativity in performance* (pp. 9–41). Greenwich, CT: Ablex.

Birkett, J. (1995). *Gaining access to the inner mechanisms of jazz improvisation.* Doctoral dissertation, Open University, Milton Keynes.

Borko, H., & Livingston, H. (1989). Cognition and improvisation: Differences in mathematics instruction by expert and novice teachers. *American Education Research Journal, 26,* 473–498.

Chomsky, N. (1968). *Language and mind.* New York: Harcourt, Brace & World.

Clarke, E. F. (1991). Generative processes in music. In J. A. Sloboda (Ed.), *Generative processes in music: The psychology of performance, improvisation, and composition* (pp. 1–26). Oxford: Clarendon Press.

Csikszentmihalyi, M., & Rich, G. (1997). Musical improvisation: A systems approach. In R. K. Sawyer (Ed.), *Creativity in performance* (pp. 43–66). Greenwich, CT: Ablex.

Dowling, W. J., & Harwood, D. W. (1986). *Music cognition.* New York: Academic Press.

Floyd, S. A., Jr. (1995). *The power of black music: Interpreting its history from Africa to the United States.* New York: Oxford University Press.

Galvao, A., & Kemp, A. (1999). Kinaesthesia and instrumental music instruction: Some implications. *Psychology of Music, 27*(2), 129–137.

Gellrich, M. (1992). *Üben mit Lis(z)t–Wiederentdeckte Geheimnisse aus der Werkstatt der Klaviervirtuosen.* Frauenfeld: Im Waldgut.

Gellrich, M. (1995). Umrisse zu einer Methode der Improvisation. *Ringgespräch über Gruppenimprovisation, 61,* 5–10.

Gellrich, M. (2001a). Psychologische Aspekte von Wahrnehmungsprozessen beim Instrumentalspiel. In M. Gellrich (Ed.), *Neue Wege in der Instrumentalpädagogik* (pp. 320–394). Regensburg: ConBrio.

Gellrich, M. (2001b). Über den Aufbau und die Koordination stabil-flexibler Spielbewegungen beim Instrumentalspiel. In M. Gellrich (Ed.), *Neue Wege in der Instrumentalpädagogik* (pp. 250–319). Regensburg: ConBrio.

Gellrich, M., & Parncutt, R. (1998). Piano technique and fingering in the eighteenth and nineteenth centuries: Bringing a forgotten method back to life. *British Journal of Music Education, 15*(1), 5–24.

Goolsby, T. (1994). Eye movement in music reading. Effects on reading ability, notational complexity, and encounters. *Music Perception, 12,* 77–96.

Heuer, H. (1996). Doppeltätigkeiten. In O. Neumann and A. F. Sanders (Eds.), *Aufmerksamkeit* (pp. 163–222). Göttingen: Hogrefe.

Johnson-Laird, P. N. (1988). Freedom and constraint in creativity. In R. J. Sternberg. (Ed.), *The nature of creativity* (pp. 202–219). Cambridge: Cambridge University Press.

Johnson-Laird, P. N. (1991). Jazz improvisation: A theory at the computational level. In P. Howell, R. West, and D. Cross (Eds.), *Representing musical structure* (pp. 291–325). New York: Academic Press.

Kenny, B. (1999). Jazz analysis as cultural imperative (and other urban myths): A critical overview of jazz analysis and its relationship to pedagogy. *Research Studies in Music Education, 13,* 56–80.

Kernfeld, B. (1981). *Adderley, Coltrane and Davis at the twilight of bebop: The search for melodic coherence, Vols. 1 and 2.* Doctoral dissertation, Cornell University.

Kratus, J. (1989). A time analysis of the compositional processes used by children aged 7–12. *Journal of Research in Music Education, 37*(1), 5–20.

Lehmann, A., & Ericsson, K. A. (1997). Research on expert performance and deliberate practice: Implications for the education of amateur musicians and music students. *Psychomusicology, 16*(1–2), 40–58.

Martinez, I., Malbran, S., & Shifres, F. (1999). The role of repetition in aural identification of harmonic sequences. *Bulletin for the Council of Research in Music Education, 141*, 93–97.

Meyer, L. B. (1973). *Explaining music*. Berkeley: University of California Press.

Monson, I. (1996). *Saying something*. Chicago: University of Chicago Press.

Narmour, E. (2000). Music expectation by cognitive rule-mapping. *Music Perception, 17*(3), 329–398.

Nettl, B. (1974). Thoughts on improvisation: A comparative approach. *Musical Quarterly, 60*, 1–19.

Nettl, B. (1998). An art neglected in scholarship. In B. Nettl and M. Russell (Eds.), *In the course of performance: Studies in the world of musical improvisation* (pp. 1–23). Chicago: University of Chicago Press.

Nettl, B., & Russell, M. (Eds.). (1998). *In the course of performance: Studies in the world of musical improvisation*. Chicago: University of Chicago Press.

Pashler, H., & Johnston, J. C. (1998). Attentional limitations in dual-task performance. In H. Pashler (Ed.), *Attention* (pp. 155–189). East Sussex: Psychology Press.

Pressing, J. (1998). Psychological constraints on improvisational expertise and communication. In B. Nettl and M. Russell (Eds.), *In the course of performance: Studies in the world of musical improvisation* (pp. 47–67). Chicago: University of Chicago Press.

Sawyer, R. K. (Ed.). (1997). *Creativity in performance*. Greenwich, CT: Ablex.

Sawyer, R. K. (1999). Improvised conversations: Music, collaboration, and development. *Psychology of Music, 27*(2), 192–216.

Sloboda, J. A. (1985). *The musical mind: The cognitive psychology of music*. Oxford: Clarendon Press.

Smith, C. (1998). A sense of the possible: Miles Davis and the semiotics of improvised performance. In B. Nettl and M. Russell (Eds.), *In the course of performance: Studies in the world of musical improvisation* (pp. 261–289). Chicago: University of Chicago Press.

Sternberg, R. J. (2000). In search of the zipperump-a-zoo. *Psychologist, 13*(5), 250–255.

Sudnow, D. (1978). *Ways of the hand: The organisation of improvised conduct*. Cambridge, MA: Harvard University Press.

Weisberg, R. (1999). Creativity and knowledge: A challenge to theories. In R. Sternberg (Ed.), *The handbook of creativity* (pp. 226–250). Cambridge: Cambridge University Press.

Welford, A. T. (1952). The "psychological refractory period" and the timing of high speed performance: A review and a theory. *British Journal of Psychology, 43*(1), 2–19.

Westendorf, L. (1994). *Analysing free jazz*. Doctoral dissertation, University of Washington.

9

Sight-Reading

ANDREAS C. LEHMANN & VICTORIA McARTHUR

From a psychological viewpoint, sight-reading involves perception (decoding note patterns), kinesthetics (executing motor programs), memory (recognizing patterns), and problem-solving skills (improvising and guessing). Sight-reading skills seem to be highly trainable and differences in sight-reading ability can be explained through differences in the amount of relevant experience and the size of the knowledge base (e.g., repertoire). The ability to perform with little or no rehearsal may be regarded as a reconstructive activity that involves higher-level mental processes. These are primarily initiated by visual input but also by conceptual knowledge and specific expectations. Common problems in sight-reading of pitches, rhythm, articulation, and expression are enumerated along with suggestions for their remediation through the use of technical equipment, practice of isolated parameters, and strategic preparations for playing.

When musicians speak of sight-reading, not all of them have the same activity in mind. Some might consider only the very first time one reads or plays through an unfamiliar piece to be true sight-reading, while others would allow the definition of sight-reading to encompass play-throughs after more extensive preparation. A conductor might even consider sight-reading to be the activity of silently reading through a score while imagining or performing appropriate conducting movements.

Rather than attempting a definitive circumscription of sight-reading, it is more helpful to picture a continuum of rehearsal, where playing a piece of music without any preparation would be located on one end of the scale while performing it after rehearsal to the point of overlearning would be located at the other end. One could limit the description of sight-reading somewhat by requiring that the music be physically played (gestured, softly voiced, or otherwise sounded) at an acceptable tempo and with appropriate expression, thereby excluding the mere deciphering of the notation, especially the tediously slow groping for notes with nothing more in mind than to internalize the piece. One could restrict sight-reading even further to those activities where the performer intends to approximate the final product as closely as possible.

The preceding description of sight-reading situates the skill of sight-reading within its naturally occurring music-making context. For example, during entrance auditions at music schools professional accompanists are confronted with scores that they may have already encountered on previous occasions. Also, professional musicians in studio orchestras, where music is being produced for soundtracks or other recordings, frequently play unrehearsed scores. At both professional and amateur levels, sight-reading commonly occurs when a choir or ensemble embarks on a new piece and the conductor wants to gain a rough impression of how it will sound before engaging in detailed rehearsal. Sometimes musicians might select new repertoire by sight-reading several works to ascertain which are the most suitable for their purposes.

While most musicians in the Western tradition sight-read to some extent, they often forget that it is the gap between each person's ordinary level of rehearsed performance and the same person's ability to perform at first sight that is the problem. The smaller this gap is, the better the sight reader.

History

Sight-reading is not exclusively a phenomenon encountered in traditional Western art music but has been part of any culture that possesses music notation and literate musicians. Only exclusively oral cultures have no need for sight-reading, and some musical traditions that are otherwise improvisatory, such as those of India and Indonesia, use notation only for didactic purposes.

It is important to remember that systems of musical notation are highly culture-specific and what they capture and which instructions they contain vary considerably. Since these systems only partially indicate what needs to be played, musicians must use their extensive knowledge and skills to accurately interpret the symbols. The reasons for the emergence of notations and their historical developments are well documented (see any music dictionary or encyclopedia).

In the nineteenth century, composer-performers such a Felix Mendelssohn Bartholdy and especially Clara Schumann began the tradition of publicly performing what we now call repertoire, namely, well-rehearsed (often to the point of memory) existing pieces by other composers. Prior to this, solo and ensemble performers were accustomed to playing new scores at first sight (*prima vista*) and extensive rehearsals like those of today were uncommon. This was due to several reasons: the musical idioms were familiar, most music was not performed more than a few times, composers were afraid of plagiarism by orchestral musicians, and so on. As a result, works written by someone other than the performer were generally sight-read.

Not only was sight-reading a prerequisite skill then, but outstanding sight-reading abilities, especially among child performers, have always had the aura of unexplainable feats. Extreme proficiency was considered a characteristic of prodigies and a marker of high levels of musical aptitude. For example, Lord

Barrington described W. A. Mozart's exceptional sight-reading abilities in a scientific report. Unusually good sight-reading skills are also attributed to Felix Mendelssohn-Bartholdy, Carl Czerny, Franz Liszt, and many others. For various reasons sight-reading has lost its place in public recitals, but it is to this day an indispensable part of any serious audition and subsequent training for musicians; piano accompanists and studio orchestra musicians are proficient at it, and it is even the focus of a few lesser known competitions.

Research Issues

The most interesting and simple question for the individual musician is: why are some people good sight readers and others not? Furthermore: how is sight-reading ability acquired and how can we improve sight-reading performance based on what we know about its development? Yet before we can answer these questions, we have to study the exact nature of sight-reading. Is it a simple matching of notes to fingers, or is the process more complex? Also, we need to identify what distinguishes good from less good readers.

Research on sight-reading has been a recurring topic since empirical research in music emerged, and it is also a common topic in publications aimed at music teachers. Some authors align themselves with research on reading, some with other psychological and educational aspects. As of late, the *development* of sight-reading skills has also attracted some attention (for reviews see Sloboda, 1984; Lehmann & Ericsson, 1996; Waters, Underwood, & Findlay, 1997; see also numerous music education dissertations). Our review of the literature will first cover the mental and physical task demands and the process of sight-reading and then outline the acquisition and development of sight-reading abilities.

Basics on Looking and Perceiving

We know from vision and reading research that people do not perceive the world around them the way a camera would, namely, as a coherent sharp picture of the whole field of vision (see Smith, 1994, for a good introduction). Instead, our field of vision has a small area (*fovea*) where the objects are in focus and then a blurrier circle of peripheral vision (*parafovea*), which by no means covers the entire field of vision. Research indicates that some information in the parafoveal area can be processed in addition to that of the focal area. Depending on the viewing distance from eye to object (e.g., the printed page), the area of focus varies in size but covers less than two degrees of the field of vision. In order to view an entire image, our eye performs larger and smaller discrete movements—called *ocular saccades*—at a rate of about four to six per second. With each saccade the focus moves from one point of *fixation* to the next; picture a flashlight being pointed to different locations in a dark room. Our brain then assembles the picture and creates the perfect illusion of a coherent environment. It creates meaningful connections between isolated elements by so-called *Gestalt principles* that apply equally well to vision and to sound (Bregman, 1990; or see any introductory psychology text).

Our perceptual systems (auditory and visual) develop early in life and operate on the basis of two kinds of processes. One is a *data-driven* or *bottom-up* process, which enables us to perceive the physical properties of an object such as shapes, sizes, and pitches, and one is a *conceptually driven* or *top-down* process, which interfaces with things we have learned and stored in long-term memory. In music sight-reading, the data-driven process would automatically take care of the decoding of pitch and duration information, with unusual complex stimuli requiring (and attracting!) more attention than familiar and simple ones, while the conceptually driven processes would allow the musician to develop hypotheses about the structure of the stimulus and anticipate continuations. Thus where we look (or don't look) is determined partly by the physical properties of the stimulus itself, which is what *bottom-up* means, and partly by what we expect or need to see in order to process the score, which is what *top-down* refers to.

Given the speed demands in sight-reading, it is doubtful that these two kinds of note-reading processes can be consciously controlled. In fact, even top–down processes such as expectations are likely to become automated in skilled performance. The two processes and their interaction are likely to develop with training. As a parallel, one learns that the tonic generally follows the dominant seventh chord in common practice, and one's perceptual system learns to look for indicators of such progressions. In this way, dominant seventh chords start to attract attention to themselves and facilitate subsequent note recognition and processing.

Subskills of Sight-Reading

Similar to other complex skills such as playing tennis, sight-reading is not a unitary skill but should rather be regarded as a collection of subskills that can be discussed and studied separately (e.g., Lehmann & Ericsson, 1993, 1996; Sergent et al., 1992; Waters, Townsend, & Underwood, 1998). Let us assume that sight-reading comprises certain perceptual, kinesthetic, memory, and problem-solving skills.

Perceptual Skills

In visual tasks, eye-movement recordings have been used to uncover individual differences in attentional processes that in turn can account for differences in level of performance (eye movements are recorded by means of special infrared cameras). In general, better readers will scan (or parse) the page more efficiently than less skilled readers. Although it is difficult to compare the various studies on eye movements during reading music because they have employed markedly different experimental methods and tasks, we will attempt a cautious summary of results.

Better sight readers require shorter and fewer fixations to compare or encode material for execution because they are able to grasp more information in one fixation (e.g., Waters et al., 1997). As a result, readers do not fixate on all notes but also fixate on blank areas between two notes. One study demonstrates that better sight readers' fixations were also directed across line and phrase boundaries, whereas less proficient readers tend to focus on individual notes (Goolsby, 1994). Also, better readers' eye movements go further ahead in the score, but also check on themselves by returning to the current point of performance. Less proficient readers search around for information and try to make sense out of what they see, while efficient readers seem to know what to look for (Goolsby, 1994).

Earlier studies demonstrated that readers of contrapuntal music tend to follow individual melodic lines more horizontally, while in homophonic music chords are scanned vertically, chord by chord (Weaver, 1943). Of course, the exact visual patterns while reading vary somewhat from one person to another. Other researchers have found that staves in piano music are read separately (Furneaux & Land, 1997). Surely the eye does not know the difference between the two types of music (contrapuntal and homophonic), but the reader has to invoke different strategies to read the music. Eye-movement data also show that, with increasing familiarity with the music fixations become shorter and eye movements longer, presumably because part of the information is already known.

These eye-movement studies can help us to better understand data from experiments about looking ahead (*perceptual span*). One of the first things investigated was how long subjects can continue playing after removal of the printed page, a measure that has been termed *eye-hand span*. This perceptual span for single-line melodies encompasses about six or seven notes for good readers but only three or four notes for less-skilled readers (Sloboda, 1984; Goolsby, 1994; for reviews), corresponding to roughly one second of music (Furneaux & Land, 1997). Once the notes are deciphered by the perceptual system, the associated storage devices in memory (*buffers*) organize their content in musically meaningful units (*chunks*). Note that those chunks are not necessarily encoded with one single eye fixation! Larger perceptual spans point to larger chunks in memory, which means that the players can devote more attention to the solution of other performance problems, for example, reassuring themselves of unclear passages or planning fingerings and jumps.

Sloboda (1984) found that the eye-hand span is not a fixed measure but grows and shrinks according to the musical structure. If a musical phrase exceeds the average span by a few notes, the span will grow to encompass the end of the phrase; if the end of a musical phrase lies closer than the average span, it will shrink. Thus the eye-hand span tends to coincide with phrase boundaries, which shows how higher level expectations ("end of phrase coming up") influence the way notes are grouped together when sight-reading ("get notes to end of phrase").

A recurring finding, not only with regard to perceptual performance in sight-reading, is that more expert subjects are more accurate and rapid than novices in many tasks related to the perception, the comparing of visual information, and so on—and that this difference is greater when the structure of the stimulus material is meaningful or familiar to the experts. "Meaningful" here means that the person can store a note sequence (e.g., C–E–G–E–C) by relating elements within this sequence in a sensible way (e.g., triad on C, up and down) instead of having to re-member each note separately. This phenomenon is strongly related to the chunking process referred to earlier. When the information is scrambled or random and no meaning is apparent, even experts become slower and less accurate. Novices usu-ally do not show this differentiated response to the stimulus properties, because they cannot extract the meaning. This means that prior knowledge about triads facilitates their recognition (visually, kinesthetically, and aurally).

A rarely investigated aspect of sight-reading is the influence of auditory per-ception (feedback) on performance. Theoretically, auditory feedback should not play a role in sight-reading, since no possibility for error correction exists. That would appear to explain why the removal of auditory feedback does not seem to cause sight-reading performance to deteriorate significantly (Banton, 1995). In an experiment, pianists sight-read music and at the same time repeated infor-mation that was presented over headphones. If sight-reading were reliant on creating an internal auditory representation of the music, this task should have caused interference—but it did not. Thus, in a self-paced performance, sight readers relied on their visual senses (i.e., the printed score) and did not need the auditory ones (i.e., the output they are producing). However, it has already been mentioned that the perceptual performance is only in part dependent on the physical properties of the printed stimulus but instead is heavily driven by expectations and prior knowledge of musical form and of the purely musical prop-erties of the (meaningful) stimulus. The truth probably lies in the middle: playing without feedback is essentially possible when the music is not very complicated, but feedback probably serves as a cue for creating expectations about the next notes, leading to a more musical performance.

Kinesthetic Skills

An often encountered belief about good sight-reading is that better sight readers have specific tactile or kinesthetic skills that allow them, at least on the piano, to orient themselves on the instrument without the help of visual monitoring. (Other instrumentalists cannot easily look at their instruments anyway, even when playing rehearsed music.)

Some authors have addressed eye and head movements made by poor sight readers, because these may interrupt visual contact with the score. What hap-pens if subjects do not look at their hands? Researchers in typing have shown that even skilled typists' performance deteriorates when visual feedback (oppor-tunity to monitor hand movements) is removed. It is therefore not surprising to find similar results in piano music sight-reading, namely, that the number of errors increases significantly when visual feedback is inhibited (Banton, 1995; Lehmann & Ericsson, 1996). However, pianists who are good at accurately per-forming large jumps on the keyboard tend to do so regardless of whether visual feedback is present or not (Lehmann & Ericsson, 1996). This suggests that kines-thetic ability is acquired in the course of piano training and is not a prerequisite for sight-reading and that avoiding unnecessary glances at the keyboard will improve performance.

Recall and Memory

It is almost paradoxical to talk about memory in sight-reading, since the very nature of sight-reading would seem to contradict the importance of recall. Yet when a piece is sight-read several times, memory becomes important. Remember that sight-reading is performance with little or no rehearsal; thus the repeated playing of a piece by an accompanist would *not* generally violate this basic assumption about the nature of sight-reading. In this case, good recall would facilitate improvement on subsequent play-throughs, and even for repeating or highly similar sections within a piece.

In fact, over repeated play-throughs with expert pianists performances on the first and subsequent play-throughs indicated that better sight readers learned the piece more quickly than less-skilled readers (Lehmann & Ericsson, 1996). This faster learning can be attributed to their superior ability to grasp the structure. Also, when subjects performed an unexpected fill-in-the-blanks task that required them to remember what they had just sight-read, recall scores were consistent with scores on the sight-reading task. The performance on the fill-in-the-blanks task was also correlated with results from a subsequent memory experiment with the same subjects. These findings agree with those from other studies that showed that experts display superior recall on domain-specific material, even when they are not explicitly asked to memorize (cf. Waters et al., 1998, for another sight-reading study).

Problem Solving

Musical problem solving is especially necessary in sight-reading, where not always all the notes can be clearly identfied and where external demands on the musician (for example, when playing with an accompanist or soloist) divert some attention away from the reading task. In such instances, the reader has to guess, simplify, or improvise. These processes have in common that the reader is actively reconstructing the musical material rather than simply taking it off the page and duplicating it on the instrument. Reconstruction of incomplete patterns is a fundamental perceptual-psychological, or Gestalt-psychological, process. For example, you can easily recognize an object when it is seen through a picket fence provided you are familiar with the everyday appearance of the hidden object. Your perception seems to put back the missing parts of the pattern that are obscured by the pickets.

One striking early finding in this respect is *proofreader's error*, a phenomenon we know from language reading that Sloboda (1976) investigated in music. A proofreader's error is the oversight of a mistake in a (highly) familiar word. By the way, did you notice the misspelling in the word *identfied* in the previous paragraph? Sloboda gave subjects a simple tonal piano part to sight-read in which several notes had been altered by a step; if played as written it would have sounded rather awkward. Yet subjects who performed the music at sight unintentionally corrected the altered notes to match their expectations, which meant back to the original pitches. Moreover, the number of falsely corrected notes increased with additional trials, although one would have hypothesized the opposite.

Another piece of evidence comes from an experiment where pianists were asked to sight-read a piece in which several notes had been erased (Lehmann & Ericsson, 1996). Again, similar to the fill-in-the-blanks task described earlier, the performances were scored for correctly inferred (improvised) notes. Not only did subjects who scored highly on the inference task also tend to be better sight readers, but also the number of correctly inferred notes increased statistically on a second attempt of filling in the blank. Despite their complete lack of information as to the required notes, better sight readers somehow assimilated the structure of a piece with its redundancies and were able to create appropriate passages on the fly.

Unlike computer keyboardists, whose fingers are consistently mapped to the keys, music keyboardists have to cope with the problem of the inconsistent mapping of fingers to keys. It appears that better sight readers use more appropriate fingerings at first sight and that on consecutive play-throughs the fingerings are optimized with regard to the upcoming musical context, which is (naturally) unknown at the first encounter (Lehmann & Ericsson, 1995; Sloboda et al., 1998).

Individual Differences in Musicians' Ability to Sight-Read

From anecdotal accounts in biographies and from casual observations, we know that there have existed and still exist large individual differences in sight-reading abilities. Some authors even talk of virtuoso pianists who cannot read music fluently, while outstanding sight readers are found even among mediocre pianists (e.g., Wolf, 1976). This observation probably applies to most instruments.

Relation to Other Musical Skills

Contrary to the aforementioned anecdotal evidence, the research literature suggests that better sight readers tend to be better performers (see Lehmann & Ericsson, 1993, for a discussion). In fact, moderate to high associations (correlations) are found among sight-reading performance, playing from memory, and performing rehearsed music in students of clarinet and trumpet (McPherson, 1995), sight-reading and rehearsed performance in clarinet students (Watkins, 1942), and sight-reading and amount of music committed to memory after one hour of deliberate memorization (Nuki, 1984). However, other authors failed to find such relations (Lehmann & Ericsson, 1993, 1996).

We could speculate that it is possible to find associations among specific subskills of sight-reading at one expertise level but not at another. Since the task demands of sight-reading differ from those of other musical activities, strong relationships among different activities are unlikely. However, especially among beginners there may be limiting factors in basic musical skills that constrain performance of all activities. For example, for a trumpet student who does not match notes and valve combinations fluently, even proficient reading or great improvisatory powers will not be beneficial—he just can't get it out! Yet at higher skill levels, where basic skills are no longer an issue, divergent musical backgrounds and long-term training differences (see later) may lead to an idiosyncratic skill profile, where sight-reading may be well developed in some people but not in others. For nonkeyboard instrumentalists, sight-reading opportunities may not be as plentiful as for pianists, leading to less of a gap between people who can and people who cannot.

Acquisition of Sight-Reading Skills

Educators and musicians in general are interested in whether or not sight-reading abilities can be acquired and, if so, how we can optimize this learning process. The first issue is an empirical one, and we will present some evidence that suggests that training and experience are important predictors for sight-reading achievement. The second question will be addressed in more detail in the last part of this chapter.

Banton (1995) found that frequency of self-reported sight-reading practice coincided with better sight-reading results in the expected direction, namely, that more is better. Another author (Kornicke, 1992) found that self-reported sight-reading experience was moderately associated with the results of a sight-reading test with college pianists. Unfortunately, neither of the authors took into account the level of general music experience or assessed the type of practice activity in which subjects might have engaged. Still, these findings support music teachers' advice to improve sight-reading by doing it frequently (see Lehmann & Ericsson, 1996, for references).

A more recent study was done in which college-level pianists sight-read an accompaniment to a prerecorded solo part and were interviewed about their musical backgrounds (Lehmann & Ericsson, 1996). When trying to explain individual differences in sight-reading performance, the authors found that sight-reading proficiency was primarily associated with the number of hours engaged in accompanying-related activities up to the point of the interview and with the current size of the pianists' accompanying repertoire. Conversely, age, accumulated piano practice (a proven indicator of level of performance among experts), and performance on isolated subskills (e.g., improvisation, recall, and kinesthetic ability) did not predict performance. This suggests that even performance on the named subskills can be viewed as a result of training and that sight-reading is not enabled by a fortuitous predisposition (talent) (chapter 1).

Thus experience is important, but other evidence suggests that this is not the whole story. We can observe that when someone sight-reads extensively but only at a particular, unchanging level of difficulty, then this person will not improve despite the accumulation of experience. This is the case among amateurs, be it in music or in sports. However, when this experience is combined with deliberate training efforts, be it through the choice of increasingly difficult reading material or through the strategic building up of a suitable accompanying repertoire, then the correlation between experience and level of sight-reading can be expected to increase (see Lehmann & Ericsson, 1996, for details).

Sight-Reading as a Reconstructive Process

The various research strands enable us to develop a cognitive model of sight-reading that is both consistent with research findings and of practical interest to music practitioners. The research suggests that we should view sight-reading as a twofold process. First, the performer encodes the printed music in terms of its structural and technical properties in the course of a complex reconstructive process, and second, he or she produces appropriate physical actions. The ability to execute these two processes does not emerge suddenly but rather as the result of extended training.

For the initial stages of the reconstructive process, the performer visually scans the music, relying partly on highly automated mental processes that allow the almost effortless encoding of typical features of the music. During this process musical features are recognized as patterns and matched to pertinent information already stored in long-term memory. One example would be the left-hand patterns in classical piano music called Alberti basses: here the pianist simply has to identify the notes involved and for how long the pattern is sustained. Gestalt principles such as continuation and proximity are likely to guide and facilitate this recognition process. The motor (physical) component necessary to perform the recognized pattern is well entrenched, and the pianist can focus on expression, accuracy, and the synchronization with other players.

Further processing only becomes necessary when the musician deliberately attempts to read information that is not easily matched with preexisting patterns or when visual complexity impairs the automatic deciphering of the music. In this case, the sight reader has to actively reconstruct the music based on partially extracted information and prior knowledge. The importance of prior knowledge and expectancies can be judged from proofreader's errors and the ability to guess correct continuations.

It may be that the musicians' main problem in sight-reading is to supply enough patterns and rules from memory for the described semiautomatic deciphering and pattern-matching process, so that most of the music is executed effortlessly. The remaining attentive and cognitive resources can then be deployed in strategic ways to cope with those notated events that remained unprocessed or only partially processed. Experts are better at this because they have optimized this intricate process and they have the necessary knowledge base of rules and patterns.

Of course, some cognitive resources must also be allocated to the coordination of timing and expression in much the same way that they would be in rehearsed music performance. To coordinate their timing, musicians have to integrate movement and note processing, and to create musical expression they rely on a set of standard devices that they intuitively apply (such as slowing at the end of phrases: chapter 13). Any remaining attentive capacity can then be used to improve other aspects of the performance, such as the monitoring of internal states (anxiety, expressive ideas) or the conscious listening to oneself and other musicians (building expectations, noting mistakes for future correction).

Pedagogical Applications

There are roughly a hundred sight-reading studies in the music education literature. Mapping these to psychological research is difficult, because educators have often implemented and validated their intuitions about teaching methods without detailing why their methods work (or fail to work). In the following suggestions, which are informed by the large amount of available literature, we draw most heavily on the idea that sight-reading has its unique skill demands and that learning to sight-read should emphasize those demands.

Practicing for Performance Versus Sight-reading

In a previous paragraph we addressed the relation between sight-reading skills and other musical activities. Wolf (1976) found only a weak association between sight-reading achievement and general performance achievement. In light of the fact that general instrumental performance and sight-reading require different subskills, it may be practical to show less experienced students some important differences between their sight-reading practice and their practice for performance. Consequently, teaching sight-reading should encourage the simulation of representative situations in which sight-reading occurs. Table 9.1 summarizes some important differences that we have identified as well as others when practicing a rehearsed piece and when practicing sight-reading.

Some of the aspects mentioned in Table 9.1 pertain to the task demands of sight-reading (points 1, 2, and 4) and some to general musical considerations (points 3 and 5). A good bit of improving one's sight-reading is forming habits that are in line with the performance conditions. For example, not stopping and not looking (unless something bad happened) are mostly a matter of breaking old habits. In practicing for performance, we look at our hands even when the notes are correct. One should not do that in sight-reading because it interrupts the visual contact with the score. The big picture is not something we get the first time, because we have to rely on previous experiences, thus repetition, in order to know what the big picture could be like. Generating such an overview may be done by listening to the piece (or similar pieces) in order to help build correct expectations that in turn will guide our perceptual system. This is especially true for twentieth-century music.

Table 9.1 Comparison of strategies used by pianists when practicing for rehearsed performance and for sight-reading.

	Practicing for Performance	Practicing Sight-reading
1	Correct your mistakes.	Maintain rhythm and meter.
2	Look at hands when playing.	Avoid looking at hands.
3	The details are important.	The big picture is important.
4	Correct fingering is crucial.	Get to notes however you can.
5	Avoid errors and omissions.	Errors and omissions are OK.

Allocating Attention

Figure 9.1 may exemplify the different levels of attention and processes during sight-reading that we have addressed earlier. We are focusing on technical difficulties rather than artistic (or aesthetic) difficulties that are more prominent for rehearsed performance. Panel (a) of the figure describes what may be a *low-demand* sight-reading task—that is, one in which the note patterns, as well as other features in the context such as the key and meter, frequently occur in many other pieces of music. It is likely that our brain will quasi-automatically decode and implement these sequences with low cognitive involvement. Panel (b) depicts a *moderate-demand* sight-reading task. In this example, the sight reader is constrained regarding his or her autonomous control of timing as well as choice of expressive features, given the additional task of playing in an ensemble. The performer may now be less able to aurally anticipate what is coming up, due to the need to consciously attend to the additional player's performance. Panel (c) represents a *high-demand* sight-reading task. The patterns as well as other features in the musical context are unusual for Western art music; thus they are unlikely to have been rehearsed to the point of automaticity by the performer (see Waters et al., 1998, for a discussion of the cognitive underpinnings of these

(a)

(b)

(c)

Figure 9.1. Illustrative examples of (a) low-demand, (b) moderate-demand, and (c) high-demand sight-reading for piano.

processes). It is not difficult to imagine that each task (corresponding to panels a to c) imposes different demands on perception and cognition.

Obviously, these examples are simplified and real-life music will combine aspects of all three examples. Reading music is somewhat like reading words: we have automated certain processes and actively engage in building mental models of the situation. Actively engaging in sight-reading in situations that mirror real life will ultimately create all the necessary memory traces and speed up relevant retrieval and reconstruction processes. The most important aspect, and we know this from research on expert performance, is keeping the practice tasks challenging. The following section will outline some sight-reading problems and solutions, which, applied to increasingly difficult reading material, will satisfy what we know about skill acquisition.

Specific Sight-Reading Problems and Solutions

Few instructors teach sight-reading explicitly, and those who do have methods based on their intuition (and their personal reading problems). Not surprisingly, the traditional goals of most sight-reading pedagogy (Burmeister, 1991; Colwell, 1992; McArthur, 1996; Spillman, 1990) generally match the research areas described earlier. Teachers address problems that relate to visual pattern recognition (often termed music theory) and/or motor action generation (the practice of technique) with novice sight readers. In addition, teachers traditionally have urged less skilled sight readers to simply sight-read as much as possible (e.g., accompanying, participating in ensembles, etc.) in order to acquaint themselves with both the music literature as well as appropriate sight-reading strategies and techniques.

Common pattern perception problems often involve misjudging sizes of melodic and harmonic intervals. Suggested strategies for remediation involve verbalizing interval names and scales prior to playing, isolating the interval identification problem via flash-card or computer-generated drill, playing pitches only without regard to rhythm, and identifying melodic patterns prior to playing.

There appears to be a strong association between rhythmic ability and sight-reading performance (Boyle, 1970; Elliott, 1982). The inability to accurately perform rhythm (also maintain tempo and meter) may be tackled via tapping or clapping of rhythm alone (or other forms of rhythmic body movement), writing counts in the music score, drawing vertical lines that indicate note alignment, reading practice that involves the metronome or a MIDI playback device such as a sequencer, or playing in accompanying or ensemble situations with living, breathing performers.

The inability of some sight readers to perform articulation and/or dynamics can have multiple causes. Sometimes especially younger players simply choose not to attend to these seemingly minor details. When this occurs, having players actually notate in the score the expressive features exhibited in either a live or recorded performance enhances sensitivity to these features in their own performance. If the cause for unexpressive performance is attention overload, often simply slowing the tempo or only performing pitch or rhythm notation will solve the problem.

Probably the most common problem seen in sight readers is that of *stuttering*, or backing up to correct omissions or errors. The solutions offered by pedagogues for this problem all have to do with forcing the performer to continue playing: for example, performing only the notes that occur on designated beats, thus forcing the eyes to arrive on time at future beats, and reading while another person covers up the notation immediately as it is played both make it impossible for eye movement to regress. Playing with live or electronic (metronome, MIDI recordings) ensemble members is an aid here also. Another way of improving the flow of performance is to pair up with another musician and sight-read increasingly difficult material.

Actually taking one's eyes off the music momentarily in order to glance down at the keyboard is a disputable point in sight-reading lore. Some advocate training the sense of touch by consciously practicing the music with the goal of playing it perfectly without the benefit of sight; others simply advocate keeping the chin and head level when glancing down. Regardless, losing one's place through loss of visual connection with the music is the cause of many errors in sight-reading and a relatively simple problem to remedy—just don't look.

While the foregoing examples represent remedies to local problems, they will in our opinion ultimately lead the reader to develop good intuitions about the musical grammar, frequent and infrequent patterns, and how it feels to play them. This learning process will have to be supplemented with a lot of music listening that provides stylistic and idiomatic templates against which the musical score can be compared. Contrary to what teachers hope to achieve through offering look-ahead exercises to their students (e.g., Burmeister, 1991), the larger perceptual span and all other characteristics of expert sight readers are a result of repeatedly solving low-level problems with great concentration and trying to contextualize them.

Conclusion

Our review shows that neither is the juggling of multiple tasks during sight-reading a completely unexplainable feat nor should outstanding sight-reading abilities be considered an indicator of some extraordinary musical talent. But, rather, we know that expert sight readers have had extensive experience with sight-reading tasks and have acquired a large knowledge base (repertoire of rules and patterns) to draw from. In the course of their development as sight readers, they have come to know large amounts of patterns (visual, kinesthetic, aural), have solved countless musical problems (reading, fingering, ensemble coordination), and have developed the ability to manage all situational demands of performing.

Educators should focus more attention on sight-reading pedagogy and continue to develop materials and training methods that enable students to narrow the gap between their level of rehearsed performance and ability to sight-read. Despite the fact that sight-reading is not in high demand in our public concert life and that it is only applicable to musical traditions that possess notated music, it does offer musicians a possibility to survive in an economic situation that demands the ability to learn music quickly, if not at sight. And it also enables musicians of all levels to perform together for their own enjoyment as well as that of others.

Acknowledgment. We thank Christoph Wünsch for the musical excerpts.

References

Banton, L. (1995). The role of visual and auditory feedback during the sight-reading of music. *Psychology of Music, 23*(1), 3–16.

Boyle, J. D. (1970). The effect of prescribed rhythmical movements on the ability to read music at sight. *Journal of Research in Music Education, 18,* 307–318.

Bregman, A. S. (1990). *Auditory scene analysis: The perceptual organization of sound.* Cambridge, MA: MIT Press.

Burmeister. E. (1991). *Keyboard sight reading.* Mountain View, CA: Mayfield.

Colwell, R. (Ed.). (1992). *Handbook of research on music teaching and learning.* New York: Schirmer.

Elliott, C. A. (1982). The relationship among instrumental sight reading ability and seven selected predictor variables. *Journal of Research in Music Education, 30*(1), 5–14.

Furneaux, S., & Land, M. F. (1997). The role of eye movements during music reading. In A. Gabrielsson (Ed.), *Proceedings of the 3rd Triennial ESCOM Conference* (pp. 210–214). Uppsala, Sweden: Uppsala University.

Goolsby, T. (1994). Profiles of processing: Eye movements during sightreading. *Music Perception, 12,* 97–123.

Kornicke, L. E. (1992). An exploratory study of individual difference variables in piano sight-reading achievement. (Doctoral dissertation, Indiana University). *Dissertation Abstracts International, 53,* 12A (University Microfilms No. 9301458)

Lehmann, A. C., & Ericsson, K. A. (1993). Sight-reading ability of expert pianists in the context of piano accompanying. *Psychomusicology, 12*(2), 182–195.

Lehmann, A. C., & Ericsson, K. A. (1995). Fingerings in piano performance as evidence for the mental representation of music: A preliminary study. In D. Wessel (Ed.), *Proceedings of the 1995 SMPC conference* (p. 2). Berkeley: University of California Press.

Lehmann, A. C., & Ericsson, K. A. (1996). Structure and acquisition of expert accompanying and sight-reading performance. *Psychomusicology, 15,* 1–29.

McArthur, V. H. (1996, March/April). New music for study: Piano methods and sight-reading, Part I. *Piano and Keyboard, 179,* 59–61.

McPherson, G. E. (1995). The assessment of musical performance: Development and validation of five new measures. *Psychology of Music, 23*(2), 142–161.

Nuki, M. (1984). Memorization of piano music. *Psychologia, 27,* 157–163.

Sergent, J., Zuck, E., Terriah, S., & MacDonald, B. (1992). Distributed neural network underlying musical sight-reading and keyboard performance. *Science, 257,* 106–109.

Sloboda, J. A. (1976). The effect of item position on the likelihood of identification by interference in prose reading and music reading. *Canadian Journal of Psychology, 30,* 228–236.

Sloboda, J. A. (1984). Experimental studies of music reading: A review. *Music Perception, 2,* 222–236.

Sloboda, J. A., Clarke, E. F., Parncutt, R., & Raekallio, M. (1998). Determinants of fingering choice in piano sight-reading. *Journal of Experimental Psychology: Human Perception and Performance, 24*(1), 185–203.

Smith, F. (1994). *Understanding reading: A psycholinguistic analysis of reading and learning to read* (5th ed.). Hillsdale, NJ: LEA.

Spillman, R. (1990). *Sight-reading at the keyboard.* New York: Schirmer.

Waters, A. J., Townsend, E., & Underwood, G. (1998). Expertise in musical sight-reading: A study of pianists. *British Journal of Psychology, 89,* 123–149.

Waters, A. J., Underwood, G., & Findlay, J. M. (1997). Studying expertise in music reading: Use of a pattern-matching paradigm. *Perception & Psychophysics, 59*(4), 477–488.

Watkins, J. G. (1942). *Objective measurement of instrumental performance.* New York: Teachers College Press.

Weaver, H. (1943). A study of visual processes in reading differently constructed musical selections. *Psychological Monographs, 55,* 1–30.

Wolf, T. (1976). A cognitive model of musical sight-reading. *Journal of Psycholinguistic Research, 5,* 143–171.

10

Practice

NANCY H. BARRY & SUSAN HALLAM

Musicians practice to gain technical proficiency, learn new repertoire, develop musical interpretation, memorize music, and prepare for performances. Based on available empirical research, we describe appropriate practicing and learning strategies that can be incorporated into regular music teaching to encourage students to become autonomous learners. Research demonstrates that practice is more effective when musicians engage in metacognition (reflecting upon their own thought processes); employ mental practice in combination with physical practice; approach practice in an organized, goal-oriented manner; study and analyze scores; plan relatively short and regular practice sessions; are intrinsically motivated; and listen to appropriate musical examples including professional recordings and/or teacher demonstrations. Students may also benefit from understanding the relationship between time spent practicing and achievement, and the nature and the importance of motivation. The old adage *practice makes perfect* may not necessarily be true, because repetition of ineffective practice strategies can yield disappointing results.

> *If I don't practice for one day, I know it; if I don't practice for two days, the critics know it; if I don't practice for three days, the audience knows it.*
>
> Ignacy Jan Paderewski,
> *An Encyclopedia of Quotations About Music*

Practice is defined as "repeated performance or systematic exercise for the purpose of learning or acquiring proficiency" (Cayne, 1990, p. 787). In many contexts, such as sports and psychology, *training* and *practice* are often used synonymously. However, since *practice* is the term traditionally used by musicians to describe systematic rehearsal, that term will be used in this chapter.

The notion that practice is required for skill development is of course very old. Scientific interest in the nature of practice and its relationship to the transition from novice to expert performance has only emerged within the past 100 years or so, with a growing body of studies across diverse disciplines (Hallam, 1997b, 1997c; Jørgensen & Lehmann, 1997). Research has shed light upon the ways that expert musicians practice, but, at present, no longitudinal data on how different styles of practice lead to better performance are available, although there is some evidence that professional musicians can attain equally high standards of performance by adopting a variety of approaches to practice (Hallam, 1995b). While practice is certainly a relevant topic for all musical genres, this chapter is limited to Western/European musical traditions, because until now most psychological research has concentrated on Western music.

Managing Practice Time

To acquire musical skill it is essential to practice. The question that has concerned researchers is, therefore, not whether practice is necessary but to what extent it is necessary. Some researchers have argued that attainment simply increases with practice and, consequently, that accumulated practice time can directly predict achievement (Ericsson, Krampe, & Tesch-Römer, 1993; Sloboda et al., 1996).

Total Duration of Practice

Achieving high levels of musical expertise requires considerable practice. Typically, 16 years of practice are required to achieve levels that will lead to international standing in playing an instrument (Sosniak, 1985). The individual usually begins to play at a very early age, with about 25 hours of practice being undertaken weekly by adolescence, increasing to as much as 50 hours. However, there is considerable individual variation (Ericsson et al., 1993; Sloboda et al., 1996). Some research (Hallam, 1998a; Williamon & Valentine, 2000) has suggested that while cumulative practice may be a good predictor of the overall level of expertise attained, it may not predict the quality of performance at any point in time. There is also evidence that the practice undertaken and required for different instruments varies (Jørgensen, 1997b).

Organization of Practice Time

Psychological literature on distribution of practice time for motor skills suggests (Oxendine, 1984):

- Practice distributed over time is generally more efficient for learning and performance than massed practice (i.e., a great deal of practice in a limited time frame, such as cramming just before a lesson).
- Proficiency developed over a long period of time is retained better than proficiency developed within a short time period.

- Relatively short practice sessions are generally more effective than longer practice sessions. Of course, this varies with the age and skill level of the musician.
- Short practices are best for short, simple tasks, but longer and more complex tasks require longer practice sessions.
- A high level of motivation enables one to benefit from longer and more concentrated practice than would be possible with less motivation.
- Individuals who are more competent in a particular activity can effectively practice that activity for longer periods than individuals who are less competent. Also, older children can practice longer than younger children. However, even very advanced musicians are subject to mental and physical fatigue and are advised to distribute practice over time.
- The optimal practice duration is longer for some group activities (such as ensembles) than for individual activities because in group activities the individual may not be playing the entire time.

Some researchers (Mumford et al. 1994) have concluded that practice must be distributed across time to allow for deep, higher level thinking in which the individual actively constructs ideas about how to approach a particular task. Distributed practice may be essential when educators work with novices who lack well-developed knowledge structures and when students must begin to generate and apply new concepts. However, this study also revealed that massed practice may prove useful under two conditions: if the goal of training is a particular behavior rather than understanding and for experts who already possess the requisite knowledge structures.

Cognitive Strategies

Mental Practice

Mental practice involves cognitive rehearsal of a skill without physical activity. Oxendine (1984) described three different forms of mental practice: (1) review that immediately precedes, follows, or coincides with the performance, (2) formal or informal rehearsal between periods of physical practice, and (3) decision making relating to the strategy-making phases of the activity that occur during (or between) periods of physical practice or performance. A review of the mental practice literature (Weinberg, 1982) revealed the following principles of mental practice for motor skill acquisition. Mental practice is more effective:

- If the learner has some prior experience with the task or with a similar task
- During the early stages of learning when the student is just beginning to formulate ideas about the task and during later stages when more complex strategies have developed
- If the learner can express the task verbally
- If the learner has been taught proper techniques of mental practice such as focused concentration and visualization
- When used in combination with physical practice
- If mental practice sessions are brief

- When individuals also imagine responses in the muscles that would actually perform the movement

In music, mental practice techniques are most effective when combined with physical practice (Coffman, 1990; Ross, 1985; Rubin-Rabson, 1941c). However, more research is needed to ascertain the role of mental practice in relation to interpretation and expression.

Analysis

Analytical study of the music prior to physical practice, in which aspects such as key, meter, and familiar patterns are noted, may increase performance accuracy (Barry, 1992), and reduce the number of physical trials required to achieve technical proficiency (Rubin-Rabson, 1941b). Studies of sight-reading support the notion that mental analysis and rehearsal, such as scanning the music to identify possible obstacles and making oneself consciously aware of the key and time signatures, help musicians to play more accurately (e.g., McPherson, 1994). Teachers should encourage their students to apply a variety of analysis strategies before playing, particularly in the early stages of learning a new piece.

Metacognition

Metacognition refers to the learner's knowledge about learning itself (i.e., thinking about thinking). This is central to practice. Metacognitive skills are concerned with the planning, monitoring, and evaluation of learning, including knowledge of personal strengths and weaknesses, available strategies (task-oriented and person-oriented), and domain knowledge to assess the nature of the task and evaluate progress toward the goal (Hallam, 2001b).

The level at which a musician is able to engage in metacognition seems to be a function of musical expertise. Expert musicians have well-developed metacognitive skills that encompass technical matters, interpretation, performance, learning, concentration, planning, monitoring, and evaluation (Nielson, 1999). Novice musicians demonstrate less metacognitive awareness, with the amount and structure of their practice tending to be determined by external commitments such as examinations (Hallam, 1997a).

Novice musicians are often unaware of errors. When they can identify errors, they initially correct them by repetition of the single wrong note. Later small sections (a half-bar or a bar) are repeated. Finally, error correction changes to a focus on difficult sections that are then worked on as units. In the early stages of learning, novices have problems identifying difficult sections and tend to practice by simply playing through the music. This has been confirmed in a range of settings (Gruson, 1988; Hallam, 1997a; Renwick & McPherson, 2000).

Beginners demonstrate little or no self-regulation in their practice (McPherson & Renwick, 2000). Initially, they tend to focus on playing notes that are at the correct pitch, but as their expertise develops attention is then directed to rhythm, other technical aspects of playing, and later dynamics, interpretation, and the expressive elements of playing (Hallam, 2001a).

Students become aware of specific strategies for practice before adopting those strategies spontaneously. This is known as a *production deficiency* (Flavell, Beach, & Chinsky, 1966). Changes in strategy use seem to be more closely linked to developing expertise than age (Hallam, 1997a, 1997c), in particular the development of appropriate aural schemata. Prior to this, learning about the nature of particular strategies and how to adopt them is not productive because students have no conception of when they are making errors. Once a certain level of expertise has been attained, however, students develop approaches to practice that mirror those of professionals. There is a greater concern with interpretation, and individual differences emerge in approaches and orientations to practice (Hallam, 1997a).

Individual Differences

Several researchers have studied differences in learning styles and approaches to practice. Hallam (1997a) found differences in orientation to practice, approach to detailed practice, and interpretation in professional musicians, all of which were equally effective. McLaughlin (1985) concluded that there was no single method that professional musicians adapted when transferring embouchure control, air support, tonguing, and vibrato production from one woodwind instrument to another, and Cantwell and Millard (1994) identified deep and surface approaches to learning in 14-year-old musicians. A later study (Sullivan & Cantwell, 1999) analyzed the relationships among high levels of planning, strategy use, and deep and surface approaches to learning. In two tasks, one with traditional notation, the other with a nontraditional graphic score, a deep approach was consistently linked with high-level cognitive strategies and a high level of planning. The deep approach was consistently more effective.

Different types of structure or practice organization may be best for optimal skill development in particular students (Kane, 1984). A study of practice strategies, individual differences in cognitive style, and gender (Barry, 1992) found that students who followed a detailed practice procedure (structured practice) made more improvement in the accuracy and musicality of their musical performances than did those students who practiced without benefit of a specific structure. This was particularly evident in field-dependent males (students having difficulty identifying an image embedded within a complex visual field).

Practice Activities

What Is the Purpose of Practice?

In music, practice is necessary to enable musicians to acquire, develop, and maintain aspects of technique, learn new music, memorize music for performance, develop interpretation, and prepare for performance. A key purpose of practice is to enable complex physical, cognitive, and musical skills to be performed fluently with relatively little conscious control, freeing cognitive processing capacity for higher order processing (e.g., communicating interpretation).

Three stages are generally recognized in the development of a motor skill (Fitts & Posner, 1967). In the cognitive-verbal-motor stage, learning is largely under cognitive, conscious control, requires effort, is deliberate, and may require verbal mediation. During the associate stage, the learner begins to put together a sequence of responses to produce a desired outcome. This becomes more fluent over time. In the autonomous stage, the skill becomes automated and appears to be carried out without conscious effort.

Recently the term *deliberate practice* has been used to specify the type of practice associated with the development of expert skills in a variety of areas such as computers, sports, and music (Ericsson, 1997; Ericsson et al., 1993; Pranger, 1999). According to this conceptualization, deliberate practice requires the identification of a specific goal at an appropriate difficulty level for the individual, meaningful feedback, and opportunities for repetition and correction of errors (Ericsson, 1997). Deliberate practice is highly focused and requires great effort and concentration.

Learning a New Piece of Music

Another purpose of practicing for all musicians is to learn new repertoire. Several studies have addressed the issue of how musicians learn new music. These studies (Chaffin & Imreh, 1997; Hallam 1995a, 1995b, 1997a; Miklaszewski, 1989, 1995; Wicinski, 1950) taken together suggest:

- Most musicians tend to acquire an overview of the music they are to learn in the early stages of practice of a new work, in a way that depends on their ability to develop an internal aural representation of the music from examination of the score alone.
- The structure of the music determines how it is divided into sections for practice.
- The more complex the music, the smaller the sections.
- As practice progresses, the units become larger.
- A hierarchical structure appears to develop, in which the performer's notions about the ideal performance are gradually integrated into a coherent whole. This plan is guided by musical rather than technical considerations.
- There is considerable individual diversity in the ways that musicians practice.
- The way that practice progresses also depends on the nature of the task. Musicians approach the task of learning contemporary music differently from that of learning older music. They generally find it more difficult and place greater emphasis upon cognitive strategies (specific strategies about how to approach the task) (Miklaszewski, 1995; Hallam, 1995b).

Developing Interpretation

Such research as there is suggests that musicians adopt two main approaches to developing interpretation: intuitive and analytic. If an intuitive approach is adopted, interpretation evolves during the course of learning to play the piece and is based on intuition. When an analytic approach is adopted interpretation is based on extensive listening to music, comparison of alternative interpretations, and analysis of the structure of the music. Here interpretation can be developed with little actual physical practice taking place. Some musicians adopt both approaches to developing interpretation, although they tend to exhibit a preference for one (Hallam, 1995a).

Memorizing Music

A further purpose of practice can be to memorize music for performance. The evidence suggests that while much memorization takes place as practice proceeds, musicians may have to adopt additional strategies toward the end of the learning process to consolidate their learning, particularly if the music is long and complex (Chaffin & Imreh, 1997; Miklaszewski, 1995).

The strategies adopted depend on the nature of the task and the context within which the music is to be performed (Hallam, 1997b). Musicians report being more likely to rely on automated aural memory without resort to cognitive analysis if the piece is short, simple, and to be performed in a relatively unthreatening environment, such as an informal concert. The evidence also suggests that changes in memorization practice strategies occur as expertise develops (chapter 11 in this volume; Hallam, 1997b; McPherson, 1996).

Preparing for Performance

While most practice is in preparation for performance, some musicians adopt specific practice strategies to prepare, such as playing through as if in performance conditions, recording or videotaping themselves. We know relatively little about the effectiveness of such strategies, although there is considerable evidence that being well prepared is important (Bartel & Thompson, 1994).

Teaching Students to Practice Effectively

The Teacher

Music teachers acknowledge the importance of practice and report that they discuss specific practice techniques with their students. A survey of 94 applied music teachers (Barry & McArthur, 1994) found that most teachers encouraged students to use different approaches to practice, to begin a piece slowly and gradually increase the tempo, and to analyze a new piece before playing it. Teachers also tended to encourage students to mark their music, set specific practice goals for each practice session, have two or more short daily practice sessions instead of one longer session, and practice with the metronome. Responses that regarded other aspects of practice were varied, suggesting the lack of a shared systematic pedagogy.

A study (Barry, 2000) of the relationship between student–teacher interactions in the college music lesson and subsequent individual student practice behaviors revealed that student practice habits were influenced to a limited degree by their teacher's advice, but the most powerful influence was the teacher's instruction style. What the teachers actually did during the lessons (e.g., the teacher demonstrating a particular technique or having the student try a particular approach) had a more profound influence upon their students' practice than what they said.

Providing Examples

Hearing high-quality examples may prove beneficial in guiding practice for student musicians who have not internalized an appropriate ideal for musical performance. Music educators have stressed the importance of teacher demonstration to provide students with aural examples. This can be very useful for beginning students, but at a later stage the provision of a single example may force students into stereotypical performances and deter them from developing their own interpretations (Hallam, 1998a).

Teacher demonstration can certainly provide a useful resource for students, but many music teachers may lack the skills necessary to demonstrate on every instrument that they are called upon to teach (Kohut, 1973). Teachers may not have sufficient time to demonstrate every instrument during every class and cannot be available to demonstrate during students' home practice sessions (Linklater, 1997). There is considerable interest, therefore, in the effects of providing students with taped performance models (examples) to use in conjunction with individual practice. One experiment (Zurcher, 1975) provided beginning instrumentalists with cassette tapes that contained instructions, reminders, and model play-along performances of the music. Model-supported practice was significantly more effective than traditional practice on gross pitch discrimination, pitch matching, rhythmic discrimination, and time spent in practice. Additional studies (Dickey, 1992; Kendall, 1990) also support the use of aural models as an aid to musical development. In contrast, Anderson's (1981) study of tape-recorded aural examples for home practice failed to reveal any significant differences between sight-reading and performance skills of young clarinet students who used taped examples and those with no taped examples.

A more recent study (Linklater, 1997) investigated the effects of home practice that used three different types of examples (model videotape, model audiotape, audiotape with nonmodeling/accompaniment only) on the performance achievement of beginning clarinet students. The students in the videotape group scored significantly higher on visual and physical performance criteria immediately after practicing with examples and also scored higher on performance criteria based on tone quality and intonation in subsequent delayed longitudinal assessments than did students in the nonmodeling group.

Motivating Students to Practice

There are complex relationships among motivation, achievement and practice (Hallam, 1997c; 1998b). McPherson, Bailey, and Sinclair (1997) found that students who reported higher levels of daily practice were more likely to improvise, play music by ear, compose, and elect to take music classes at school. Likewise, O'Neill (1997) observed that higher achieving beginning instrumental music students practiced more during a 2-week diary period than lower achieving students. She also found a relationship between children's motivational processes and effective music practice. Achievement is related not only to the length of time spent practicing but also to the quality of that practice.

Given that increasing the amount of time engaged in practice can contribute to an increase in musical achievement, musicians and researchers have investigated a number of different motivational approaches. On the one hand, a study (Rubin-Rabson, 1941a) that compared the effects of verbal encouragement or cash payment with a control group (with no special incentive to practice) found no significant differences among the three conditions in the amount of students' practice time. On the other hand, Wolfe (1987) found that behavioral contracts in which students enter into a formal agreement with parents and the teacher could be an effective way to motivate students to practice.

Student motivation to practice may be increased by allowing students to make certain choices. One project (Brandstrom, 1995) allowed piano students to set their own goals regarding improvement, repertoire, and time. These university students also engaged in self-evaluation of the same three elements through written comments and reflections. Project evaluation indicated that most of the students held favorable attitudes about the project, believing that they had become better pianists and had developed greater independence and planning ability. Greco (1997) found that using student-selected repertoire arranged in appropriate keys and tessitura resulted in an increase in practice time and a decrease in attrition rate for second- and third-year instrumental music students in Grades 5 and 6 (see also chapter 3 in this volume).

Supervised Practice

There is evidence to suggest that for the young or novice musician supervised practice can be more effective than practice carried out without supervision. Research indicates a strong relationship between youngsters' musical development and the direct involvement of parents and nurturing, supportive teachers (O'Neill, 1997; Sosniak, 1985). Studies (Brokaw, 1983; Davidson, Howe, Moore, & Sloboda, 1996; chapter 2 in this volume) have also revealed a significant relationship between the achievement of young instrumentalists and the amount of parental supervision of home practice. Supervision by other adults may also be helpful. A study of adolescent instrumentalists (Barry, 1992) compared the musical performance improvement (melodic accuracy, rhythmic, accuracy, and musicality) of students who followed a structured practice program under adult supervision with that of students who practiced with no supervision. The supervised group achieved greater gains for melodic accuracy, rhythmic accuracy, and musicality. While supervised practice can be quite helpful for some individuals, it can be detrimental as students become more mature and seek greater independence.

Structured Practice

Practice is most effective when it is governed by an appropriate framework or structure. However, student musicians may not have sufficient knowledge to determine an optimal framework for practice. One study (Barry, 1990) compared student instrumentalists' performance improvement under three different practice conditions. Students who used a structured approach to practice (teacher-designed and self-designed) were able to correct more performance errors than students who did not employ any structured practice. Students who used the teacher-designed approach had the highest scores of all.

Conclusion

Efficient and effective practice is central to the development of musical expertise. Musicians engage in practice for a number of reasons, such as gaining technical proficiency, learning new repertoire, developing musical interpretation, memorizing music, and preparing for performance. Fluency is achieved through effective practice, with complex tasks eventually becoming automated.

Practice is most effective when it is deliberate and mindful. Acquiring metacognitive skills is central to effective and efficient practice. The literature suggests that these skills cannot be developed independently of musical skills and knowledge and that in the early stages of learning the two are irrevocably intertwined.

Teachers have a crucial role to play not only in assisting students in acquiring musical expertise but also in developing knowledge of appropriate practicing and learning strategies and supporting students in becoming autonomous independent learners. The ways that this can be achieved will depend to some extent on the age of the student (Hallam, 1998a). The younger they are, the more directed supervision they need. As their expertise increases, it is important to encourage autonomy in learning and the acquisition of a range of strategies that will assist in developing effective practice and preparation for performance. The evidence to date, however, suggests that most musicians do not feel that their training has assisted them in developing metacognitive skills (Hallam, 1992; Jørgensen, 1997a).

The following suggestions for musicians who wish to practice more effectively (and teachers who wish to guide their students toward greater achievement) are based upon evidence from a wide range of literature sources:

- Engage in metacognition—become mindful about practicing and related physical and mental processes. Be consciously aware of your own thought processes.
- Approach practice systematically. Do not go about practice haphazardly. Practice is more effective when it is structured and goal-oriented.
- Engage in mental practice (cognitive rehearsal) in combination with physical practice.

- Invest time in score study and analysis, particularly when beginning a new piece.
- Plan regular practice sessions with several relatively short sessions distributed across time.
- Acknowledge the relationship between time spent practicing and achievement and set out to invest the time necessary.
- Be aware of the importance of motivation. When teachers and parents allow students to make some choices about goals and repertoire, student motivation is likely to increase.
- Listen to high-quality models of musical performance. This is particularly important for beginning musicians. Parents and teachers should invest in a library of fine recordings and, if capable, play and/or sing often for their charges.
- Support and nurture young musicians. Parents and teachers should demonstrate keen interest and involvement in music study and practice.

Musicians may take for granted the old adage that "practice makes perfect." However, literature in both psychology and music indicates that not only the amount of time invested in practice but also the manner in which one approaches practice will have a bearing on an individual's level of musical development. While this may be stating the obvious, the important element here is that musicians stand to improve their skills by paying careful attention to increasing their own ability to learn how to learn.

References

Anderson, J. N. (1981). Effects of tape recorded aural models on sight-reading and performance skills. *Journal of Research in Music Education, 29*(1), 23–30.

Barry, N. H. (1990). The effects of different practice techniques upon technical accuracy and musicality in student instrumental music performance. *Research Perspectives in Music Education, 1*, 4–8.

Barry, N. H. (1992). The effects of practice strategies, individual differences in cognitive style, and gender upon technical accuracy and musicality of student instrumental performance. *Psychology of Music, 20*(2), 112–123.

Barry, N. H. (2000, February). *Behind closed doors: What really goes on in the practice room.* Paper presented at the meeting of the Southern Chapter of the College Music Society, Lafayette, LA.

Barry, N. H., & McArthur, V. (1994). Teaching practice strategies in the music studio: A survey of applied music teachers. *Psychology of Music, 22*(1), 44–55.

Bartel, L. R., & Thompson, E. G. (1994). Coping with performance stress: A study of professional orchestral musicians in Canada. *Quarterly Journal of Music Teaching and Learning, 5*(4), 70–78.

Brandstrom, S. (1995). Self-formulated goals and self-evaluation in music education. *Bulletin of the Council for Research in Music Education, 127*, 16–21.

Brokaw, J. P. (1983). The extent to which parental supervision and other selected factors are related to achievement of musical and technical-physical characteristics by beginning instrumental music students. (Doctoral dissertation, University of Michigan). *Dissertation Abstracts International*, 43/10-A, 3252. (University Microfilms No. 0534271)

Cantwell, R. H., & Millard, Y. (1994). The relationship between approach to learning and learning strategies in learning music. *British Journal of Educational Psychology, 64*(1), 45–63.

Cayne, B. S. (Ed.). (1990). *The new Lexicon dictionary of the English language.* New York: Lexicon.

Chaffin, R., & Imreh, G. (1997). "Pulling teeth and torture": Musical memory and problem solving. *Thinking and Reasoning, 3*(4), 315–336.

Coffman, D. D. (1990). Effects of mental practice, physical practice, and knowledge of results on piano performance. *Journal of Research in Music Education, 38*(3), 187–196.

Davidson, J. W., Howe, M. J. A., Moore, D. G., & Sloboda, J. A. (1996). The role of parental influences in the development of musical performance. *British Journal of Developmental Psychology, 14*, 399–412.

Dickey, M. R. (1992). A review of research on modeling in music teaching and learning. *Bulletin of the Council for Research in Music Education, 113*, 27–40.

Ericsson, K. A. (1997). Deliberate practice and the acquisition of expert performance: An overview. In H. Jørgensen and A. C. Lehmann (Eds.), *Does practice make perfect? Current theory and research on instrumental music practice* (pp. 9–51). Oslo: Norges Musikkhøgskole.

Ericsson, K. A., Krampe, R. T., & Tesch-Römer, C. (1993). The role of deliberate practice in the acquisition of expert performance. *Psychological Review, 100*(3), 363–406.

Fitts, P. M., & Posner, M. I. (1967). *Human performance.* Belmont, CA: Brooks/Cole.

Flavell, J. H., Beach, D. R., & Chinsky, J. M. (1966). Spontaneous verbal rehearsal in a memory task as a function of age. *Child Development, 37*, 283–299.

Greco, V. (1997). *Investigation of the effects of student-selected repertoire on the practice habits of instrumental music students.* M. A. Action Research Project, Saint Xavier University. (ERIC Document Reproduction Service No. ED418049).

Gruson, L. M. (1988). Rehearsal skill and musical competence: Does practice make perfect? In J. A. Sloboda (Ed.), *Generative processes in music: The psychology of performance, improvisation, and composition* (pp. 91–112). Oxford: Clarendon Press.

Hallam, S. (1992). *Approaches to learning and performance of expert and novice musicians.* Unpublished doctoral dissertation, Institute of Education, University of London.

Hallam, S. (1995a). Professional musicians' approaches to the learning and interpretation of music. *Psychology of Music, 23*(2), 111–128.

Hallam, S. (1995b). Professional musicians' orientations to practice: Implications for teaching. *British Journal of Music Education, 12*(1), 3–19.

Hallam, S. (1997a). Approaches to instrumental music practice of experts and novices: Implications for education. In H. Jørgensen and A. C. Lehmann (Eds.), *Does practice make perfect? Current theory and research on instrumental music practice* (pp. 89–108). Oslo: Norges Musikkhøgskole.

Hallam, S. (1997b). The development of memorisation strategies in musicians: Implications for education. *British Journal of Music Education, 14*(1), 87–97.

Hallam, S. (1997c). What do we know about practicing? Toward a model synthesizing the research literature. In H. Jørgensen and A. C. Lehmann (Eds.),

Does practice make perfect? Current theory and research on instrumental music practice (pp. 179–231). Oslo: Norges Musikkhøgskole.

Hallam, S. (1998a) *Instrumental teaching: A practical guide to better teaching and learning.* Oxford: Heinemann.

Hallam, S. (1998b). The predictors of achievement and dropout in instrumental music tuition. *Psychology of Music, 26*(2), 116–132.

Hallam, S. (2001a) The development of expertise in young musicians: Strategy use, knowledge acquisition and individual diversity. *Music Education Research, 3*(1), 7–23.

Hallam, S. (2001b). The development of metacognition in musicians: Implications for education. *British Journal of Music Education, 18*(1), 27–39.

Jørgensen, H. (1997a). Teaching/learning strategies in instrumental practice: A report on research in progress. In J. A. Taylor (Ed.), *Transatlantic roads of music education: World views* (pp. 47–51). Tallahassee, FL: CMR.

Jørgensen, H. (1997b). Time for practicing? Higher level students' use of time for instrumental practicing. In H. Jørgensen and A. C. Lehmann (Eds.), *Does practice make perfect? Current theory and research on instrumental music practice* (pp. 123–140). Oslo: Norges Musikkhøgskole.

Jørgensen, H., & Lehmann, A. C. (Eds.). (1997). *Does practice make perfect? Current theory and research on instrumental music practice.* Oslo: Norges Musikkhøgskole.

Kane, M. (1984). Cognitive styles of thinking and learning: Part two. *Academic Therapy, 20*(1), 83–92.

Kendall, M. J. (1990). A review of selected research literature in elementary instrumental music education with implication for teaching. *Journal of Band Research, 25*, 64–82.

Kohut, D. L. (1973). *Instrumental music pedagogy: Teaching techniques for band and orchestra directors.* Englewood Cliffs, NJ: Prentice-Hall.

Linklater, F. (1997). Effects of audio- and videotape models on performance achievement of beginning clarinetists. *Journal of Research in Music Education, 45*(3), 402–414.

McLaughlin, D. B. (1985). An investigation of performance problems confronted by multiple woodwind specialists. (Doctoral thesis, Columbia University Teachers College, New York). *Dissertation Abstracts International, 46*/09-A, 2610. (University Microfilms No. 8525495)

McPherson, G. E. (1994). Factors and abilities influencing sightreading skill in music. *Journal of Research in Music Education, 42*(3), 217–231.

McPherson, G. E. (1996). Five aspects of musical performance and their correlates. *Bulletin of the Council for Research in Music Education, 127*, 115–121.

McPherson, G. E., Bailey, M., & Sinclair, K. E. (1997). Path analysis of a theoretical model to describe the relationship among five types of musical performance. *Journal of Research in Music Education, 45*(1), 103–129.

McPherson, G. E., & Renwick, J. M. (2000). Self-regulation and musical practice: A longitudinal study. In C. Woods, G. B. Luck, R. Brochard, F. Seddon, and J. A. Sloboda (Eds.), *Proceedings of the Sixth International Conference on Music Perception and Cognition.* Keele, UK: Keele University, Department of Psychology. CD-ROM.

Miklaszewski, K. (1989). A case study of a pianist preparing a musical performance. *Psychology of Music, 17*(2), 95–109.

Miklaszewski, K. (1995). Individual differences in preparing a musical composition for public performance. In M. Manturzewska, K. Miklaszewski, and A. Biatkowski (Eds.), *Psychology of music today* (pp. 138–147). Warsaw: Fryderyk Chopin Academy of Music.

Mumford, M. D., Costanza, D. P., Baughman, W. A., Threlfall, K. V., & Fleishman, E. A. (1994). Influence of abilities on performance during practice: Effects of massed and distributed practice. *Journal of Educational Psychology, 86*(1), 134–144.

Nielsen, S. (1999). Learning strategies in instrumental music practice. *British Journal of Music Education, 16*(3), 275–291.

O'Neill, S. A. (1997). The role of practice in children's early musical performance achievement. In H. Jørgensen and A. C. Lehmann (Eds.), *Does practice make perfect? Current theory and research on instrumental music practice* (pp. 53–70). Oslo: Norges Musikkhøgskole.

Oxendine, J. B. (1984). *Psychology of motor learning* (2nd ed.). New York: Appleton-Century-Crofts.

Pranger, H. M. (1999). How adults develop computer skills: An extension of deliberate practice theory. (Doctoral dissertation, University of Connecticut.). *Dissertation Abstracts International, 59/09-A*, 3321. (University Microfilms No. 9906558)

Renwick, J. M., & McPherson, G. E. (2000). "I've got to do my scale first!": A case study of a novice's clarinet practice. In C. Woods, G. B. Luck, R. Brochard, F. Seddon, and J. A. Sloboda (Eds.), *Proceedings of the Sixth International Conference on Music Perception and Cognition*. Keele: Keele University, Department of Psychology. CD-ROM.

Ross, S. L. (1985). The effectiveness of mental practice in improving the performance of college trombonists. *Journal of Research in Music Education, 33*(4), 221–230.

Rubin-Rabson, G. (1941a). Studies in the psychology of memorizing piano music: IV. The effect of incentive. *Journal of Educational Psychology, 32*, 45–54.

Rubin-Rabson, G. (1941b). Studies in the psychology of memorizing piano music: V. A comparison of pre-study periods of varied length. *Journal of Educational Psychology, 32*, 101–112.

Rubin-Rabson, G. (1941c). Studies in the psychology of memorizing piano music: VI. A comparison of two forms of mental rehearsal and keyboard overlearning. *Journal of Educational Psychology, 32*, 688–696.

Sloboda, J. A., Davidson, J. W., Howe, M. J. A., & Moore, D. G. (1996). The role of practice in the development of performing musicians. *British Journal of Psychology, 87*(2), 287–309.

Sosniak, L. A. (1985). Learning to be a concert pianist. In B. S. Bloom (Ed.), *Developing talent in young people* (pp. 19–67). New York: Ballantine.

Sullivan, Y., & Cantwell, R. (1999). The planning behaviours of musicians engaging traditional and non-traditional scores. *Psychology of Music, 27*(2), 245–266.

Weinberg, R. S. (1982). The relationship between mental preparation strategies and motor performance: A review and critique. *Quest, 33*(2), 195–213.

Wicinski, A. A. (1950). Psichologiceskii analiz processa raboty pianista-ispolnitiela and muzykalnym proizviedieniem (Psychological analysis of piano performer's process of work on musical composition). *Izviestia Akademii Piedagogiceskich Nauk Vyp, 25*, 171–215.

Williamon, A., & Valentine, E. (2000). Quantity and quality of musical practice as predictors of performance quality. *British Journal of Psychology, 91*(3), 353–376.

Wolfe, D. E. (1987). The use of behavioral contracts in music instruction. In C. K. Madsen and C. A. Prickett (Eds.), *Applications of research in music behavior* (pp. 43–50). Tuscaloosa: University of Alabama Press.

Zurcher, W. (1975). The effect of model-supportive practice on beginning brass instrumentalists. In C. K. Madsen, R. D. Greer, and C. H. Madsen (Eds.), *Research in music behavior: Modifying music behavior in the classroom* (pp. 131–138). New York: Teachers College Press.

11

Memory

RITA AIELLO & AARON WILLIAMON

There is extensive biographical and anecdotal information on the memory of exceptional musicians, but only recently has there been systematic psychological research, and this has mostly focused on pianists. Historical reasons for performing from memory can be traced to Clara Wieck Schumann and Franz Liszt. General theories of expert memory can help us understand how expert musicians memorize music. Auditory, kinesthetic, and visual information contribute to musical memory. Recent psychological research suggests the importance of explicitly analyzing the score. Memory strategies depend on the skill of the performer and the style and difficulty of the music to be memorized. The ability to memorize seems to be enhanced by studying music theory and analysis. Learning to improvise in the style of the music could also be helpful.

During the last century, several pianists and piano pedagogues have written on how to memorize music. Matthay (1913, 1926), Hughes (1915), and Gieseking and Leimer (1932/1972) described three principal ways in which performers can learn music when preparing for a memorized performance: *aurally*, *visually*, and *kinesthetically*. Aural memory (i.e., auditory memory) enables individuals to imagine the sounds of a piece, including anticipation of upcoming events in the score and concurrent evaluations of a performance's progress. Visual memory consists of images of the written page and other aspects of the playing environment. Pianists and other keyboard players, for instance, may remember positions of the hand and fingers, the look of the chords as they are struck, and the patterns made upon the keyboard as they are played. Kinesthetic memory (i.e., finger, muscular, or tactile memory) enables performers to execute complex motor sequences automatically. For pianists, it is facilitated by extended training of the fingers, wrists, and arms and can exist in two forms: (1) position and movement from note to note and (2) sense of key resistance (Hughes, 1915). All these pianists and teachers stressed that no really intelligent memorizing is possible without a knowledge of musical structure, including harmony, counterpoint, and form. They insisted that aural, visual, and kinesthetic memory could not function properly without this knowledge (Gieseking & Leimer, 1932/1972; Hughes,1915; Matthay, 1913, 1926).

In addition to the study of structure, Gieseking and Leimer emphasized the importance of mental rehearsal when memorizing a piece. They recommended that students learn to memorize pieces by visualizing them through silent reading and prepare for their technical execution through visualization before beginning to play them at the keyboard. The authors illustrated their method with detailed examples from the music of J. S. Bach and Beethoven.

Clearly, performances from memory involve complex interactions among the aforementioned methods of memorizing music. This chapter explores systematic and psychological research that has evaluated such combinations and approaches. Overall, the existing literature on how to memorize music for performance is scarce, and what has been written has focused mainly on pianists. Nevertheless, other instrumentalists can relate to this information in terms of their own memory performance strategies. For singers the interaction of music and text is central in memorizing their repertoire (Ginsborg, 2000). Although space limitation does not allow us to evaluate this interaction adequately, singers could find this chapter useful as a general background.

Why Perform from Memory?

Until the nineteenth century, when musicians played in public they either improvised the music or read from the score. While it would have been preposterous during the time of Bach, Haydn, and Mozart for musicians to perform their music in public from memory, the Romantic period was marked by a trend toward the individuality of the solo performer, and it is in this era that acclaimed pianists such as Clara Wieck Schumann (1819–1896) and Franz Liszt (1811–1886) began to play in concerts without the score (Schonberg, 1963). Since the early twentieth century the majority of solo pianists and violinists have not used the score when giving performances of the standard repertoire. It is widely acceptable, however, for a contemporary work to be performed using the score.

Performing from memory can be a difficult and anxiety-provoking task. So why do performers insist on doing it? A number of performers and pedagogues have argued that there are fulfilling musical justifications for this tradition. Some of these arguments have been purely practical in their nature. For example, memorizing music dispenses with cumbersome page turns and enables musicians to monitor visually aspects of their performance such as posture and hand positions. Other arguments have focused on specific musical and communicative advantages to memorizing music, claiming for instance that memorization allows performers to develop more freely their own expressive ideas and to communicate those ideas more effectively to audiences (see Bernstein, 1981; Hallam, 1995; Hughes, 1915; Matthay, 1913, 1926).

In an investigation of some of the practical benefits of performing from memory, Williamon (1999b) asked a group of listeners to evaluate videotaped performances of a cellist playing the Preludes from Bach's *Cello Suites* nos. I, II, and III. The performances were divided into five conditions that differed in terms of memorization and visual information available to audience members. In some memorized performances, for example, an empty music stand was used, suggesting to the audience that the performer was reading from the score. The study revealed that audiences preferred memorized performances to nonmemorized performances. Moreover, audience members with musical training rated memorized performances higher than nonmusicians in terms of communicative ability, thus suggesting that listeners who were musicians may have been better equipped to pick up subtle communication cues embedded in performances from memory. In addition, the findings are consistent with the notion that enhanced visual communication (e.g., a view of the performer that is not obstructed by a music stand) augments audiences' experiences at large (Davidson, 1993, 1994).

General Psychological Research on Memory

Classic Studies

Current knowledge and theories of memory rely heavily on the findings and terminology of classic studies by Ebbinghaus and by Bartlett. With himself as the sole subject, Ebbinghaus (1885/1964) learned lists of nonsense syllables (e.g., MIB, DAK, BOK) over a period of several years. From a set of some two thousand of these stimuli, he constructed lists of a dozen or so syllables and would read them aloud in time with the beat of a metronome. After reading a given list, he would attempt to recall the items at various time intervals, measuring the number of times he had to repeat a list until recall was faultless. Not surprisingly, Ebbinghaus found that the longer the list, the more he needed to repeat the trials to reach perfect recall. Moreover, he found that the longer the interval of time between the original learning and its subsequent recall, the greater the amount of forgetting that occurred. This relationship between memory retention and time after learning is known as Ebbinghaus's forgetting curve. It shows a sharp decline in retention for up to 10 hours after the original learning and then a much more gradual decline across following weeks. The immediate practical implication of this for any student is that material should be rehearsed soon after it is newly learned to avoid such rapid forgetting.

Bartlett (1932) became interested in the kinds of information that people remember rather than the number of trials needed to memorize that information. Instead of asking individuals to learn lists of nonsense syllables, Bartlett used meaningful stimuli such as words, objects, and stories and measured the extent to which people's memories of these changed over time. His method of repeated reproduction, for instance, required participants to read an unusual story from folktale or myth and later recall the story after various periods of time. Bartlett found that recall was often characterized by omissions, simplifications, and transformations, thus demonstrating that memory is often vague and incomplete. For the most part, participants' errors changed the story into more familiar and conventional forms. Bartlett was able to show, therefore, how individuals are able to fill gaps in memory by making logical inferences.

In more recent research, memory has broadly been classified into short-term memory (STM) and long-term memory (LTM). STM is, simply put, the type of memory used when retaining information for only a short period of time (e.g., for 10 seconds). The short-term store can be loosely equated with the concepts of attention and consciousness, and has a working memory component that can be used to manipulate information (see Baddeley, 1986). Working memory is essential for such cognitive tasks as speaking or reading (Baddeley, 1979; Fletcher, 1986) and, in the case of music, for sight-reading.

Across a wide variety of conditions, STM is limited to about seven plus or minus two chunks (Miller, 1956), with a chunk being a unit of information that functions as a single meaningful stimulus. For example, Simon (1974) reported that he was unable to recall the following list correctly after just one presentation because it represented nine chunks of information, an amount that typically exceeds STM capacity: Lincoln, Milky, Criminal, Differential, Address, Way, Lawyer, Calculus, Gettysburg. However, when Simon rearranged the words into four chunks of information—Lincoln's Gettysburg Address, Milky Way, Criminal Lawyer, Differential Calculus—the words were more easily recalled because the four chunks fit comfortably within STM.

LTM is a more-or-less permanent repository of information. It allows us to retain and recall information over long periods of time. Moreover, it is this store that lies at the heart of the exceptional feats of memory often displayed by skilled musicians and expert performers in other fields as discussed later.

Expert Memory

Several theories have been put forth to explain how experts are able to develop and maintain their sometimes-extraordinary memory abilities. Chase and Simon's (1973) chunking theory proposes that superior memory abilities are underpinned by a vast knowledge base specific to the activity. Information in this knowledge base is continually collected and stored into chunks that often become associated with specific physical actions and commands.

The skilled memory theory of Chase and Ericsson (1982) was subsequently proposed to address certain shortcomings of chunking theory. Skilled memory theory asserts that remarkable displays of memory result from the creation and efficient use of mechanisms called *retrieval structures*. These mechanisms can only be acquired under restricted circumstances. First, individuals must be able to store information in LTM rapidly. This requires a large body of relevant knowledge and patterns for the specific type of information involved. Second, the activity must be familiar, so that individuals can anticipate future demands for the retrieval of relevant information. Third, individuals must associate the information to be recalled with appropriate retrieval cues. This association permits the activation of a particular retrieval cue at a later time, and thus partially reinstates the conditions of learning so that the desired information can be retrieved from LTM. Only after individuals organize the set of retrieval cues can a retrieval structure be formed, thereby enabling them to "retrieve stored information efficiently without lengthy search" (Ericsson & Staszewski, 1989, p. 239).

Extensive research that supports skilled memory theory has been carried out to study the memory capacities of chess players at various levels of expertise. A close investigation of what master chess players do reveals that they abstract meaningful units from the very same material that less experienced players view as separate, single events. In fact, if chess pieces are placed randomly (i.e., in positions that could not have been reached using permissible moves in a game of chess), both experienced and inexperienced chess players score poorly in remembering the positions on the board (Chase & Simon, 1973). Let us illustrate this point within the context of reading and remembering words (Lindsay & Norman, 1977). In reading and remembering the words *Well Tempered Clavier*, inexperienced readers might attempt to learn or process 19 separate letters or three words, while musically experienced readers would immediately recognize that what they read is the title of one work by J. S. Bach. However, when reading and remembering *Llew Derepmet Reivalc* (these are the same three words as *Well Tempered Clavier* but written in reverse) both experienced and inexperienced readers would be at a similar disadvantage.

As a musical example, while inexperienced pianists might strive to remember all the individual notes that occur in the right and left hands in a certain measure, experienced pianists might easily recognize that those notes constituted a cadential formula in a particular tonality. Their knowledge of harmony, together with their advanced keyboard skills, would enable them to play these notes with ease. Basic examples of such chunks in music include scales and arpeggios. Musicians spend hours practicing these so that they can easily recognize and execute them when sight-reading or committing a piece to memory. This process of chunking allows for rapid categorization of domain-specific patterns and accounts for the speed with which experts recognize the key elements in a problem situation. Skilled memory theory has commonly been accepted as accounting for exceptional memory (Anderson, 1990; Baddeley, 1990; Carpenter & Just, 1989; Ericsson & Kintsch, 1995; Newell, 1990; Schneider & Detweiler, 1987). Although subsequent psychologists (e.g., Ericsson & Kintsch, 1995) have extended skilled memory theory to address some of its limitations, the description of the mechanisms that underlie exceptional feats of memory displayed by skilled performers has remained unaltered. For example, a musician who is performing a composition from memory will rely heavily on a hierarchically organized set of preformed retrieval cues (based perhaps on the music's formal structure) to ensure that information is retrieved reliably and efficiently. This retrieval structure may form and develop throughout the course of extensive practice of the piece.

A multitude of issues, however, must be addressed before the skilled memory theory, or any theory of general expertise for that matter, can adequately explain the cognitive processes that govern musical memory. Recent research on music performance has begun to address these issues.

Music-Psychological Research on Memory

Mnemonics, Mental Representation, and Structure

Musicians use mnemonics extensively. Glancing through any music theory book one sees how frequently musicians use mnemonics to remember the formal structure of a piece. For example, a binary form is outlined as AB, a ternary form ABA, and a theme and variations is A, A', A'', A''', and so on. The formal structure of J. S. Bach's *Goldberg Variations* can be remembered according to the plan used by the composer: two variations in free style are followed by a canonic variation, and the final variation is a *quodlibet*.

Music psychologists have used the terms *internal* and *mental representation* to describe the cognitive mechanisms used by musicians. Clarke (1988) asserted that performers retrieve and execute compositions using internal representations. He proposed that to play from memory performers must understand a piece at many different levels, from a complete overall hierarchical memory of the entire piece down to the smallest detail. However, given that it would be impossible for anyone to access the memory of an entire piece at any one time during performance, it is likely that a performer will activate his or her memory of a piece one section at a time, shifting between sections as the performance progresses. As a general rule, "the depth to which the generative structure is activated is directly related to the structural significance of phrase boundaries lying close to, or at, the player's current musical location" (p. 5). In the middle of a deeply embedded musical phrase, for instance, a performer may primarily be concerned with the detailed structure of connections within the phrase itself. Therefore, only a region of low-level generative connections would be active, rather than high-level structural information. Conversely, at a phrase boundary a performer may need to know how the previous and subsequent phrases relate to one another and to the overall structure of the piece. At such a moment, "a small area of low-level structural connections may be active, sufficient to specify the immediate succession of events to be played, together with a section of the higher levels of generative structure specifying larger-scale relationships" (p. 4). Therefore when learning a piece, performers must strive to develop their memory of the overall structure of the composition, and of the way phrases and sections follow and relate to one another.

Lehmann and Ericsson (1995) have provided evidence that internal representations are not only formed and used during performance but can be manipulated. They measured general memorization ability by counting the number of trials required to perform two note-perfect renditions of excerpts from Schubert's Sonata for Violin and Piano, Op. 137. The researchers found significant correlations between memorization ability and ability with other musical tasks (i.e., playing faster and slower than the notated tempo, playing right and left hands individually, and transposing into other keys). They suggested that these abilities are mediated by an underlying mental representation that permits encoded information to be reproduced and manipulated accurately.

Chaffin and Imreh (1994, 1996a, 1996b, 1997) systematically observed the practice of Imreh, a concert pianist, to determine whether she formed an internal representation when memorizing J. S. Bach's Italian Concerto (Presto) and whether that representation was hierarchically ordered. They examined the pianist's videotaped practice on the piece and her concurrent and retrospective commentary on her practice. In doing so, they confirmed Ericsson and Kintsch's (1995) prediction that skilled performers use hierarchically ordered retrieval schemes to recall encoded information. Chaffin and Imreh found—through their direct observations of practice and the pianist's commentary—that she organized her practice and subsequent retrieval of the Presto according to its formal structure (i.e., Italian rondo form); in her practice she started and stopped more frequently at structural boundaries than in the middle of sections, and she compared the various repetitions of the A and B themes. The pianist's knowledge of the movement's formal structure allowed her to remember when repetitions occurred and the subtle changes between each successive occurrence.

Chaffin and Imreh's research is the first to demonstrate that principles of expert memory (see Chase & Ericsson, 1982; Ericsson & Oliver, 1989) apply to concert soloists. Several issues remain to be resolved with respect to how these cognitive mechanisms relate to musical skill. In particular, how does the formation and use of such structures change as musicians acquire greater levels of overall competence? How do retrieval structures change across the practice process as musicians progressively learn a given composition for performance?

A recent paper by Williamon and Valentine (in press) addressed these questions by examining the practice of 22 pianists—spread across four levels of skill—as they prepared an assigned composition for a memorized performance. In general, the results indicate that the pianists segmented their assigned composition into meaningful sections and reported using those sections in both practice and performance. Empirical examinations of the pianists' practice confirmed their reports in that they, like the concert soloist in Chaffin and Imreh's study, used the music's structure to guide their practice in preparing for the required memorized performance. Despite individual differences in the pianists' identification of structure, the findings held true for all participants. Furthermore, they were greatest for those at higher levels of skill, they increased over the practice process, and their use correlated positively with assessments of performance quality (as judged by expert evaluators). Therefore, the identification and continued use of meaningful structure in practice—regardless of what that structure may be—seems to be an ability that develops with musical competence.

In investigating how experienced pianists and intermediate piano students reported memorizing the same pieces from the piano repertoire, Aiello (2001) found that experienced pianists were more able than the piano students to describe how they memorized piano compositions in terms of the musical structure and reported more often than the piano students that they had memorized the music using some aspects of visual, auditory, or kinesthetic memory. The piano students had difficulties explaining how they had memorized the pieces at all and reported that they relied mostly on rote memory. Experienced pianists tend to conceptualize a composition into independent but linked sections that create a coherent (i.e., meaningful) musical structure, and they organize their practice to start and stop at the beginnings of sections rather than at any point within the piece. Novice pianists, instead, are more likely to approach a composition as an amorphous whole or as a series of independent notes (Gruson, 1988).

Three interview studies have demonstrated the extent to which professional musicians employ the analysis of the score when memorizing. Hallam (1997) interviewed 22 freelance professional orchestral musicians and 55 novice string players. She found that the strategies adopted by the professional musicians to memorize a composition were related in part to the difficulty of the piece. When memorizing a short, simple piece, some of them felt confident in relying on automated processes, but to memorize longer, more complex works such as a concerto, all of them tended to adopted a more analytic approach. However, the inexperienced musicians reported memorizing by using only repetition and automated process. None of them reported analyzing the music to memorize it. Similarly, Aiello (1999) examined the methods used by professional pianists to memorize piano pieces. They all emphasized that analyzing the score carefully and having a clear idea of the musical structure were the most important and reliable aids to memorization. When concert pianists were asked to give suggestions on how to memorize Bach's Prelude in C Major from Book I of the *Well Tempered Clavier*, they all recommended analyzing the chord progression upon which this piece is based (Aiello, 2000a, 2000b).

In sum, the data of Chaffin and Imreh (1994, 1996a, 1996b, 1997), Chaffin, Imreh, and Crawford (2002), Williamon and Valentine (in press), Williamon (1999a), Hallam (1995,1997), and Aiello (1999, 2000a, 2000b), alongside the theoretical proposals of Chase and Ericsson (1982) suggest that for experienced performers studying the structure of a given composition in detail will provide the most secure foundation for memorizing a work.

Music educators and music theorists have long stressed to performers the importance of studying the structure of musical compositions. Cook (1989), for example, has argued that

> the ability to set aside details and see large-scale connections appropriate to the particular musical context, which is what analysis encourages, is an essential part of the musician's way of perceiving musical sound. For the performer, it is obvious that analysis has a role to play in the memorization of extended scores, and to some extent in the judgment of large-scale dynamic and rhythmic relationships (p. 232).

The Role of Musical Style

When playing from memory, performers draw on not only their knowledge of the composition they are performing but their general knowledge of the musical style in which the piece is written. The style of a composition seems to influence how performers approach memorizing the music. When memorizing a contemporary work, some concert pianists report relying even more on their analytic memory to recall the unique patterns of the composition. Others, instead, depend more on kinesthetic memory because they find that they have to repeat the piece more to have it in their fingers. The pianist Seymour Bernstein articulated a number of difficulties that can be found when memorizing contemporary and serial music and concluded that unless composers incorporate into their writing logical motivic developments, performers are forced to invent their own melodic associations or, indeed, to rely exclusively on their automatic pilot (Bernstein, 1981, p. 258).

Atonal pieces tend to be based on patterns and sonorities that are unique to the piece itself more so than tonal compositions. Not surprisingly, the research with concert pianists shows that they find atonal compositions more difficult to memorize than tonal music (Aiello, 1999; Miklaszewski, 1995). These findings are in agréement with the remarks made by the acclaimed pianists Claude Frank and Rudolf Firkusny during interviews many years ago. Claude Frank noted, "I do not memorize music easily that I do not hear thoroughly. For example, some contemporary music. I can force myself to memorize, but it's hard work, and I tend to forget easily" (Marcus, 1979, p. 59). And Rudolf Firkusny commented, "When you are memorizing complex modern works, the harmonies are more complicated and anything but what you expected. Then you need much more concentration" (Noyle, 1987, p. 84). As psychological research has shown, the more a sequence of items is presented in an unpredictable order, the more difficult it will be for a subject to remember it (Chase & Simon, 1973; Simon, 1974).

Different Kinds of Memory

The information that we process when hearing music, reading a score, and playing an instrument creates memories. But are auditory memory, visual memory, and kinesthetic memory equally valuable in helping us to perform without the score? Which of these memories should we concentrate on to be sure to achieve our goal? The systematic psychological data on this question are scarce. Although most professional pianists report creating dependable memory strategies by relying mainly on the analysis of the musical structure, some also describe using aspects of auditory, visual, or kinesthetic memory to memorize. Others reveal using combinations of these types of memories (Marcus, 1979; Noyle, 1987). Research in cognitive psychology would support the notion that the more ways in which musical information is encoded, the more associations and connections will be formed to that information and, therefore, the more likely an individual is to remember it.

In their methods for memorizing piano music Matthay (1913, 1926) and Gieseking and Leimer (1932/1972) emphasized the importance of auditory and visual memory above kinesthetic memory. Gieseking and Leimer explained: "The fingers are the servitors of the brain, they perform the action the brain commands. If, therefore, by means of a well-trained ear, it is clear to the brain how to execute correctly, the fingers will do their work correctly" (p. 20). In fact, kinesthetic memory seems to be the one that is most questioned by concert pianists. André Watts noted, "I'm very mistrustful of tactile memory. I think it's the first that goes" (Noyle, 1987, p. 147). Watts's comments are in agreement with Leon Fleisher's opinion: "I think probably the least reliable, in terms of public performance, is finger memory, because it's the finger that deserts one first" (Noyle, 1987, p. 97). Kinesthetic memory may be the most helpful to enable children to perform without the score, and is also what adult music students and inexperienced musicians report relying on to memorize (Aiello, 2000a, 2001; Hallam, 1997). Concert pianists, however, report depending on it only when playing fast virtuoso passages, because at a very fast tempo the automated response is occurring faster than the performer can think about it (Aiello, 1999).

Implications for Performers and Teachers

By and large, detailed discussions on how to memorize music tend not to be an integral part of the music lesson. Most piano teachers do not spend much time discussing how to memorize the repertoire they assign to their students. Many piano students simply memorize by rote even after they have achieved quite a good level of technical proficiency. Often students do not question at all how they memorize. And piano teachers, seeing that the students have memorized the assigned piece, do not question how the goal was obtained (Aiello, 1999, 2000a, in preparation).

If the students' instrumental technique is more advanced than their theoretical understanding of what they are memorizing, how can they memorize by applying reflection and analysis? Rote learning can bring immediate results. For example, children trained in the Suzuki method can perform pieces from memory after just a few months of music training. And this is certainly a very rewarding and valuable musical experience for the child.

But there comes a time when the benefits of rote learning may fall short of the desired outcome because rote learning does not require a rich, profound understanding of the material (Aiello, 1999, in preparation; Hallam, 1997; chapter 7 in this volume). For memory to become reliable and long-lasting, a deeper understanding is essential. Therefore, we strongly recommend an active dialogue between the teacher and the student on the memory strategies being used by the student and how they may be improved. Students should be encouraged to question how they memorize so that they can better understand how memory works. Taking into account the students' learning styles, teachers can help them achieve this goal.

While many professional musicians use the analysis of the music structure as their primary basis for memorizing a piece, it is not unusual for some students to start memorizing a composition without having analyzed the overall plan of the piece. Students will benefit from studying a composition's structure as the basis for developing their memory strategies (Aiello, 1999, in preparation; Chaffin & Imreh, 1997; Gieseking & Leimer, 1932/1972; Hallam, 1995, 1997; Marcus, 1979; Matthay, 1913, 1926). They should come to value the importance of describing and analyzing all the theoretical aspects of the pieces to be memorized. When asked to discuss the music they practice and perform from memory, some students reveal that they have not fully integrated into their piano playing what they learned in music classes other than their piano lessons. It seems as if some students tend to compartmentalize what they learn in theory classes, analysis classes, and their piano lessons into separate domains, not seeing that there is a common denominator to musical knowledge. Those students who do not fully integrate the various components of their musical knowledge fail to make the inherent connection between music performance and music theory, the same connection, in fact, that has been shown to be an integral part of how concert soloists memorize successfully (Aiello, 1999, 2000b). On the one hand, this is a sad commentary on education at large. On the other hand, it is encouraging to know that, as teachers, we can improve our students' abilities to memorize by helping them integrate what they have learned from various sources. The instrumental teacher can help students understand that *there really is* a relationship between performance and theory. Some students may benefit from hearing their instrumental teachers give very explicit explanations about the musical structure of the piece they play and analyzing the piece along with the teacher during the instrumental lesson.

In addition, teachers might encourage their students to develop their auditory memory, explaining that above all, music *is* sound. Gieseking and Leimer placed training the musical ear as a foundation of their method and wrote, "Listening to one self is the most important factor of the whole of music study" (p. 10). Matthay, too, emphasized the fundamental value of developing the ear when learning to memorize. He warned: "There is nothing more fatal for our musical sense, than to allow ourselves—by the hour—to *hear* musical sounds without *listening* to them" (1913, p. 5). He explained how effective listening implies *pre*-listening all the time as to what the sounds should be. Whether the music to be performed is heard inwardly from memory, or is read from the score, or is heard externally, students must be aware that all playing always involves the ear (Priest, 1989; chapter 7 in this volume).

Furthermore, learning how to improvise can be helpful for memorizing music because improvisation requires having internalized the characteristics of a particular musical style to the point of being able to create a novel piece spontaneously. While in the past keyboard performers were expected to know how to improvise well, today relatively few classically trained piano students are expected to develop advanced improvisatory skills (Gellrich & Parncutt, 1998; chapter 7 in this volume). In interviews conducted with seven concert pianists, six of them considered their improvisatory skills to be helpful in the process of memorization; interestingly, even the pianist who reported that she did not know how to improvise thought that improvisation could be helpful for others (Aiello, 1999). The relationship between improvisatory skills and memorization skills could be researched further and could be addressed more frequently within the context of the piano lesson. In sum, students may be taught that memory is based on knowledge, on information that has been internalized meaningfully, and on the connections that are made between different aspects of what one knows and senses.

But where can a piano teacher start when students are not aware of the various types of memories that they could develop and are not able to integrate effectively the various components of their musical knowledge? A way to encourage a student become more cognizant of memory strategies could be for the teacher to ask: "What specific suggestions would you give to a technically proficient fellow student to help him or her memorize this piece?" In her teaching,

Aiello has found that asking this question helps students become more aware of what strategies they use when memorizing a piece. This question can make them channel their own memorization strategies into specific instructions that must be explicit enough for a fellow piano student to understand and to follow. Based on the teaching experience of the first author of this chapter, the following suggestions have been found to be helpful in teaching students how to memorize.

Suggestions Based on the Analysis of the Piece

- Describe and analyze the piece in terms of its macrostructure (the overall form) and microstructure (movements, sections, major themes, sequences, characteristic intervals, modulations, key areas, rhythmic patterns, dynamics, phrasing, etc.) (see Matthay 1913, 1926; Gieseking & Leimer, 1932/1972).
- Learn the landmarks of the piece. Describe where they occur in the piece and why. What leads to them? What occurs after them?
- Describe in detail how the various sections of each movement (or of the piece) are linked together.
- Highlight and describe the melodic and rhythmic patterns in the piece. Explain what they contribute to the music.
- Use markers of different colors to highlight the various themes or voices and their recurrences in the piece. Describe what you did and why.
- Discuss in detail the harmonic structure of the piece (modulations, key regions).
- Mark the closures and the points of tension and resolution in the piece. Describe them.
- Describe the gestures and the dynamics of the piece and how they are related to the overall structure of the composition.
- Based on the analysis and the characteristics of the piece, describe what strategies would be best for memorizing this particular piece. Explain why.
- Memorize in sections. Use the formal structure of the piece to create logical sections.

Suggestions Based on the Performance of the Piece

- Practice each hand separately, and describe what each hand is supposed to play.
- Rehearse the piece mentally. Practice away from the piano visualizing the score, visualizing the keyboard, and most of all *hearing* the music in your mind (Gieseking & Leimer, 1932/1972).
- Sing the various themes or voices. Sing one voice while playing another; sing the melody while playing the accompaniment.
- Play at a slow tempo, *reflecting* upon the structure and the various patterns in the piece.
- Move to the rhythm, the tempo, and the gestures of the music.
- Learn to improvise in the style of the music to be memorized. Through the development of improvisatory skills students can acquire additional means of encoding information based on the characteristics of a particular musical style. The knowledge and the instrumental dexterity required

to improvise according to a given style can help students in developing their memory strategies and in overcoming a memory lapse during a performance. Overall, knowing how to improvise in the style of a memorized piece can contribute to a musician's knowledge and therefore can add to a performer's sense of confidence.

These suggestions may be of more use to some performers than to others. Furthermore, some teachers may realize that only some of these strategies may be suited for a particular student, given his or her learning style. Regardless, we want to stress that by learning to reflect on how they memorize and by acquiring multiple systems to remember a piece students may gain a deeper understanding of how their memories work. Teachers can be the catalysts in this important educational process.

References

Aiello, R. (1999). Strategies for memorizing piano music: Pedagogical implications. Work in progress presented at the Eastern Division of the Music Educators National Conference, New York, NY.

Aiello, R. (2000a). The analysis of the score as a basis for memory. Poster presented at the Music Cognition / Music Pedagogy Group, Society for Music Theory, Toronto, Canada.

Aiello, R. (2000b). Memorizing two piano pieces: The recommendations of concert pianists. In C. Woods, G. Luck, R. Brochard, F. Seddon, and J. A. Sloboda (Eds.), *Proceedings of the Sixth International Conference on Music Perception and Cognition.* Keele, UK: Department of Psychology, Keele University.

Aiello, R. (2001). Playing the piano by heart: From behavior to cognition. In R. J. Zatorre and I. Peretz (Eds.), *The Biological Foundations of Music.* Annals of the New York Academy of Sciences, *930,* 389–393.

Aiello, R. (in preparation). Reflections on learning music.

Anderson, J. (1990). *Cognitive psychology and its implications.* San Francisco, CA: Freeman.

Baddeley, A. D. (1979). Working memory and reading. In P. A. Kolers, M. E. Wrolstad, and H. Bouma (Eds.), *Processing of visible language,* Vol. 1. New York: Plenum.

Baddeley, A. D. (1986). *Working memory.* Oxford: Clarendon Press.

Baddeley, A. D. (1990). *Human memory: Theory and practice.* Boston: Allyn & Bacon.

Bartlett, F. C. (1932). *Remembering: A study in experimental and social psychology.* Cambridge: Cambridge University Press.

Bernstein, S. (1981). *With your own two hands: Self-discovery through music.* New York: Schirmer.

Carpenter, P. A., & Just, M. A. (1989). The role of working memory in language comprehension. In D. Klahr and K. Kotovsky (Eds.), *Complex information processing* (pp. 31–68). Hillsdale, NJ: Erlbaum.

Chaffin, R., & Imreh, G. (1994). *Memorizing for performance: A case study of expert memory.* Paper presented at the Third Practical Aspects of Memory Conference, College Park, MD.

Chaffin, R., & Imreh, G. (1996a). Effects of difficulty on practice: A case study of a concert pianist. Poster presented at the Fourth International Conference on Music Perception and Cognition, McGill University, Montreal, Canada.

Chaffin, R., & Imreh, G. (1996b). Effects of musical complexity on expert practice: A case study of a concert pianist. Poster presented at the Thirty-seventh Meeting of the Psychonomic Society, Chicago.

Chaffin, R., & Imreh, G. (1997). "Pulling teeth and torture": Musical memory and problem solving. *Thinking and Reasoning, 3*(4), 315–336.

Chaffin, R., Imreh, G., & Crawford, M. (2002). *Practicing perfection: Memory and piano performance.* Mahwah, NJ: Erlbaum.

Chase, W. G., & Ericsson, K. A. (1982). Skill and working memory. In G. H. Bower (Ed.), *Psychology of learning and motivation,* Vol. 16. New York: Academic Press.

Chase, W. G., & Simon, H. A. (1973). The mind's eye in chess. In W. G. Chase (Ed.), *Visual information processing* (pp. 215–281). New York: Academic Press.

Clarke, E. F. (1988). Generative principles in music performance. In J. A. Sloboda (Ed.), *Generative processes in music* (pp. 1–26). Oxford: Clarendon Press.

Cook, N. (1987). *A guide to musical analysis.* New York: W. W. Norton.

Davidson, J. W. (1993). Visual perception and performance manner in the movements of solo musicians. *Psychology of Music, 21,* 103–113.

Davidson, J. W. (1994). Which areas of a pianist's body convey information about expressive intention to an audience? *Journal of Human Movement Studies, 26,* 279–301.

Ebbinghaus, H. (1885/1964). *Memory.* New York: Dover.

Ericsson, K. A., & Kintsch, W. (1995). Long-term working memory. *Psychological Review, 102,* 211–245.

Ericsson, K. A., & Oliver, W. (1989). A methodology for assessing the detailed structure of memory skills. In A. M. Colley and J. R. Beech (Eds.), *Acquisition and performance of cognitive skills* (pp. 193–215). Chichester, UK: Wiley.

Ericsson, K. A., & Staszewski, J. J. (1989). Skilled memory and expertise: Mechanisms of exceptional performance. In D. Klahr and K. Kotovsky (Eds.), *Complex information processing* (pp. 235–267). Hillsdale, NJ: Erlbaum.

Fletcher, C. R. (1986). Strategies for the allocation of short-term memory during comprehension. *Journal of Memory and Language, 25,* 43–58.

Gellrich, M., & Parncutt, R. (1998). Piano technique and fingering in the eighteenth and nineteenth centuries: Bringing a forgotten method back to life. *British Journal of Music Education, 15*(1), 5–23.

Gieseking, W., & Leimer, K. (1932/1972). *Piano technique.* New York: Dover.

Ginsborg, J. (2000, August). *Off by heart: Expert singers' memorization strategies and recall for the words and music of songs.* Paper presented at the Sixth International Conference on Music Perception and Cognition, Keele University, UK.

Gruson, L. M. (1988). Rehearsal skill and musical competence: Does practice make perfect? In J. A. Sloboda (Ed.), *Generative processes in music* (pp. 90–112). Oxford: Clarendon Press.

Hallam, S. (1995). Professional musicians' approaches to the learning and interpretation of music. *Psychology of Music, 23*(2), 111–128.

Hallam, S. (1997). The development of memorisation strategies in musicians: Implications for education. *British Journal of Music Education, 14*(1), 87–97.

Hughes, E. (1915). Musical memory in piano playing and piano study. *Musical Quarterly, 1,* 592–603.

Lehmann, A. C., & Ericsson, K. A. (1995). Expert pianists' mental representation of memorized music. Poster presented at the Thirty-sixth Annual Meeting of the Psychonomic Society, Los Angeles, CA.

Lindsay P., & Norman, D. (1977). *Human information processing: An introduction to psychology.* New York: Academic Press.

Marcus, A. (1979). *Great pianists speak.* Neptune, NJ: Paganiniana.

Matthay, T. (1913). *Musical interpretation: Its laws and principles, and their application in teaching and performing.* Boston, MA: Boston Music.

Matthay, T. (1926). *On memorizing and playing from memory and on the laws of practice generally.* Oxford: Oxford University Press.

Miklaszewski, K. (1995). Individual differences in preparing a musical composition for public performance. In M. Manturzewska, K. Miklaszewski, and A. Bialkowski (Eds.), *Psychology of music today* (pp. 138–147). Warsaw: Fryderyk Chopin Academy of Music.

Miller, G. A. (1956). The magic number seven, plus or minus two: Some limits on our capacity for processing information. *Psychological Review, 63,* 81–93.

Newell, A. (1990). *Unified theories of cognition.* Cambridge, MA: Harvard University Press.

Noyle, L. (1987). *Pianists on playing: Interviews with twelve concert pianists.* Metuchen, NJ: Scarecrow.

Priest, P. (1989). Playing by ear: Its nature and application to instrumental learning. *British Journal of Music Education, 6*(2), 173–191.

Schneider, W., & Detweiler, M. (1987). A connectionist / control architecture for working memory. In G. H. Bower (Ed.), *Psychology of learning and motivation,* Vol. 21 (pp. 54–119). New York: Academic Press.

Schonberg, H. (1963). *Great pianists from Mozart to the present.* New York: Simon & Schuster.

Simon, H. A. (1974). How big is a chunk? *Science, 183,* 482–488.

Williamon, A. (1999a). *Preparing for performance: An examination of musical practice as a function of expertise.* Unpublished doctoral dissertation, University of London.

Williamon, A. (1999b). The value of performing from memory. *Psychology of Music, 27,* 84–95.

Williamon, A., & Valentine, E. (in press). The role of retrieval structures in memorizing music. *Cognitive Psychology.*

12

Intonation

STEVEN J. MORRISON & JANINA FYK

Rather than an isolated ability, intonation is an amalgam of several sub-skills including pitch discrimination, pitch matching, and instrument tuning. Success at these skills depends on many factors including musical experience and the nature of the task presented. However, ability in any one of these areas is not clearly related to ability in the others. The skill that musicians demonstrate at isolated intonation-related tasks does not necessarily reflect their performance within a typical, complex musical setting. Within a real musical context, mature performers deviate considerably from common standards of pitch measurement, suggesting that absolute pitch accuracy should not be the ultimate goal in this area of musical development. The ability to identify and produce the most appropriate pitch within a given musical context may emerge parallel to general musical development as students' awareness of the performers around them increases and they develop their own concepts of ideal performances.

Intonation is an imprecise term. When teachers or performers consider intonation, they may be addressing one or more of several skills that fall under this general heading.

At the most basic aural level, they may be referring to *pitch discrimination*, which can be defined as the ability to distinguish between two successive pitches or two dissimilar examples of a single pitch. For example, students may be presented with a C and a C♯ and asked to identify the higher pitch. Or they may be given an A at 440 Hz and an A that is 15 cents flat (436.2 Hz) and asked to decide if there is a difference.

Or, combining aural and performance skills, focus may be on *pitch matching*, where one attempts to reproduce exactly a given pitch. This may involve isolating one pitch at a time or, occasionally, a sequence of individual pitches. Though the target is usually at unison, students may be requested to produce an octave or an intervening interval such as a fourth or fifth. Tuning may be regarded as a sort of ritualized pitch matching that usually takes place near the beginning of instrumental rehearsals. Procedures for tuning differ from ensemble to ensemble. Some may be very teacher-directed, others more student-centered. Some may be assessed by machine, others by the teacher's ear, and still others by the students' ears. The target may be an A (for orchestras), a B♭ or F (for bands), or, for the tuning of string instruments, an interval series.

Finally, we arrive at *intonation*. For the purposes of this chapter, this will refer to the manipulation of pitches and intervals within a real musical context. It is often measured relative to the *just, Pythagorean*, or *equally tempered* systems. Pythagorean tuning is theoretically derived from combinations of perfect octaves (with frequency ratios of exactly 1:2) and perfect fifths (with frequency ratio 2:3); just intonation from combinations of octaves, fifths, and major thirds (with frequency ratio 4:5); and equal temperament by dividing the octave into 12 equal semitones; for a thorough examination of tuning systems, see Barbour (1951). Intonation is necessarily culture-bound, assessed relative to the norms and according to the criteria of a given musical tradition. Because much of the research literature has focused on Western classical music, the scope of this chapter is necessarily limited to that one tradition. This chapter will survey what research has revealed about each of the component skills identified earlier (pitch discrimination, pitch matching, and intonation), with discussions of how they are demonstrated by developing and advanced musicians, and how findings may impact music teaching.

An Overview of Research

Pitch Discrimination

Good intonation is characteristic of a musically *sensitive* performance; it supports the beauty and expressive qualities of the sound. But it is not a prerequisite for a musically *comprehensible* performance, one in which the basic musical elements are discernible to a listener. For a performance to be comprehensible to a listener, it must convey reasonably accurate and specific information that includes relationships among simultaneous pitches (as in chords) and successive pitches (as in melodies). For this information to be understood, listeners must be capable of pitch *discrimination*. (For a detailed examination of perceptual research related to intervals, scales, and tuning, see Burns, 1999).

The most minute level of discrimination ability is described through the measurement of *just noticeable differences of frequency*, or *JND*. Magnitude of the JND threshold can vary depending on a listener's musical experience and training and the testing procedures used. Given favorable experimental conditions, listeners have been found to identify differences smaller than 2 cents (0.02 semitone) (Fyk, 1982; Rakowski, 1978; Vos, 1982). Placing pitches in a musical context—a chord or a melody, for example—affects discrimination accuracy, though exact results have varied. Accuracy may be impaired by the increased information to which the listener must attend (Watson, Kelly & Wroton, 1976). Alternatively, the presence of more musical information may allow the listener to make a more thorough evaluation (Wapnick, Bourassa, & Sampson, 1982).

In order to understand the musical information being conveyed in a performance, listeners must not only identify pitches as same or different but must also sort pitches according to melodic or harmonic function. Such sorting requires the listener to disregard strict pitch accuracy and focus instead on the intervallic relationship between pitches according to learned conventions. Within a given scalar convention several pitches quite close in frequency might be identified as the same pitch insomuch as we would call them by the same note name. Similarly, within a familiar harmonic or melodic context several intervals quite close in size might be assessed as the same interval. Researchers have labeled this phenomenon *categorical* or *zonal* perception (Fyk, 1995; Garbuzov, 1948; Siegel & Siegel, 1977).

This phenomenon has been likened to perception of vowels and consonants in speech (Burns & Ward, 1978; Rakowski, 1990). When conversing with other people, we can comprehend their meaning even if their pronunciation of *th* or *ay*, for example, differs from our own. Similarly in music, we will usually recognize the identity of an interval or tone even if it is considerably out of tune. For example, we give intervals of 280 and 320 cents the same identity (minor third). The pitches 280 and 320 cents above C are both identified as E♭/D♯. This is true even though we perceive that the two intervals or pitches are not identical. In this way we are able to recognize "Ode to Joy" whether it is performed by a beginning band or the Berlin Philharmonic.

Pitch discrimination ability can be affected by variables that include intensity (Sergeant, 1973), timbre (e.g., simple vs. complex synthesized tones in Platt & Racine, 1985), direction of error (Geringer & Witt, 1985; Kelly, 2000), tempo, and tone duration (Fyk, 1985). Tone quality in particular has been found to play a significant role in listeners' perceptions of absolute pitch and interval size. Listeners tend to misinterpret tone quality errors as pitch inaccuracy and pitch errors as poor tone quality (Geringer & Worthy, 1999; Madsen & Geringer, 1976, 1981; Wapnick & Freeman, 1980). Clearly performance skills such as embouchure, breath support, and even posture—skills not directly associated with pitch manipulation (i.e., finger placement, slide position)—contribute significantly to what listeners recognize as an in-tune performance. We may also speculate that the very term *in-tune performance* is less precise than it would seem. To many listeners, in-tuneness might be a more global assessment of musical quality than just pitch precision.

Pitch Matching

Perception of small differences among pitches is a separate skill from manipulation of pitches to minimize those differences. While discrimination requires a listener to assess pitch relationships from a more or less detached vantage point, *pitch matching* requires an individual to take an active role in the shaping of sounds. The individual still acts as a listener, of course, but the focus becomes assessment of the results of one's own actions rather than the examination of an external sonic artifact.

Skill at both pitch discrimination and pitch matching has been found to be better among musicians than in nonmusicians (Brown, 1991; Fastl & Hesse, 1984; Spiegel & Watson, 1984) and among more experienced musicians rather than those with less experience (Madsen, Edmonson, & Madsen, 1969; Platt & Racine, 1985; Tieplov, 1947). This might be expected since matching pitch using an instrument or the voice is a task performing musicians would be required to perform regularly. Nonperformers, however, may infrequently or never have to face this challenge.

Despite these findings, no significant relationship has been found between pitch discrimination skills and success at pitch matching. Preschool and fourth-grade students who were grouped according to success on a pitch discrimination pretest subsequently completed a vocal pitch-matching task (Geringer, 1983). Except for a moderate positive correlation found among the highest ability fourth-graders, no significant relationship was found between results of the two tasks. Similarly, only the most accurate of 28 10-year-old singers demonstrated a relationship between pitch-matching accuracy and understanding of pitch concepts (Fyk, 1985).

Geringer and Witt (1985) asked secondary-level, postsecondary, and professional string performers to tune to a given pitch and then provide a verbal assessment of the accuracy of the tuning stimulus compared to an equally tempered standard. Though the more experienced players demonstrated more frequent agreement between their tuning and verbal judgment, neither group showed strong agreement between the two tasks. In another study, undergraduate and graduate woodwind players performed an eight-note melodic fragment along with a stimulus tape, listened to recordings of the resulting duets, and attempted to identify out-of-tune tone pairs (Ely, 1992). Again there was no significant correlation between the accuracy of their performances and their success at identifying pitch errors.

Even relationships between seemingly similar tasks have proven elusive. In a series of studies that tested middle school, junior high, and senior high wind players, subjects attempted to match a single target pitch using both their instrument and a variable-pitch electronic keyboard (Yarbrough, Karrick, & Morrison, 1995; Yarbrough, Morrison, & Karrick, 1997). Though performance on both tasks was more accurate for each successive level of experience, no correlation was found between subjects' instrument and keyboard scores. A similar procedure was used with choir students when junior high school boys attempted to match a target pitch with both their voice a variable-pitch electronic keyboard (Demorest, 2000). Again, no significant relationship was found between accuracy of vocal responses and accuracy of keyboard responses. Much research of this type has necessarily focused on broad groups of school-aged musicians. Perhaps, as some results suggest (Fyk, 1985; Geringer, 1983), clearer relationships among the various skills related to pitch will be found by concentrating future research efforts on the most advanced performers. Though a purely speculative question, might it be that the *interactions* of skills such as pitch discrimination and pitch matching may be part of what *defines* advanced performers?

Adding the Musical Context

It is unlikely that musicians at any level approach the singing of a song or the playing of a melody as an extended series of pitch-matching tasks. When a performer is faced with placing pitches within a musical setting an array of considerations is introduced that may impact pitch accuracy. (For an extended program of research in this area, see Geringer and Madsen, 1987). For less-experienced performers, the number of competing demands may be so great that attention is not available to monitor fine pitch adjustments. For more experienced performers, especially the most advanced artists, not only can they monitor fine pitch adjustments, but they can also make those adjustments to serve what they believe to be the best and most expressive musical ends (Fyk, 1995).

Experienced musicians demonstrate a tendency toward sharp performance when compared to an equally tempered standard in both solo and accompanied settings (Geringer, 1978; Geringer & Witt, 1985; Kantorski, 1986; Yarbrough & Ballard, 1990). This tendency appears to emerge among students over the first four years of performance study (Yarbrough, Karrick, & Morrison, 1995). It is most frequently observed in the performance of intervals of a third or larger, while intervals smaller than a third are often compressed (summarized in Burns, 1999). Other evidence suggests that even listeners prefer performances in which pitches are sharper and intervals are wider than an equally tempered standard (Sundberg, 1982). The octave in particular has been the focus of considerable attention. Both performers and listeners tend to favor octaves that are larger than the pure 1:2 ratio (e.g., Burns & Campbell, 1994), a phenomenon referred to as octave stretching.

It seems clear that the pitch choices advanced performers make do not conform to a specific tuning system. Nevertheless, these choices are considered acceptable and even preferable (Karrick, 1998). Most recent evidence suggests that intonation in Western music is typically closer to equal temperament (Karrick, 1998; Rakowski, 1990) though some results find the Pythagorean system to be an equally good fit (Loosen, 1993). Given these and other similar results, it is probably inappropriate to say that performers play *in* a given system. Rather, it is more accurate to identify the system closest to a given performance.

Among less-advanced performers, pitch accuracy appears to be compromised by the demands of a musical setting. Primary and secondary school band students performed an eight-measure melody in unison along with a prerecorded equally tempered model (Morrison, 2000). Four target pitches, identical in pitch class, were extracted from each response—one pitch approached from above, one from below, one repeated, and one of extended duration. There were no differences in accuracy among the four pitches. There was also a high positive correlation among the four pitches. Many of the students were also asked to tune their instrument to a single target pitch before playing the melody, similar to the tuning procedure they carry out in their daily band class. Students at all levels performed the single pitch significantly more accurately. Though the exact context of each pitch did not appear to have an impact on student performances, the overall addition of a musical context significantly affected student's accuracy.

Other findings suggest that melodic direction does have a significant effect on pitch accuracy. Advanced string instrumentalists have been observed to perform descending whole-tone tetrachords significantly sharper than ascending tetrachords when compared to an equally tempered standard (Kantorski, 1986; Sogin, 1989). Conversely, Yarbrough and Ballard (1990) found that advanced string players performed significantly sharper when ascending than descending. Overall pitch deviation was assessed by Madsen (1966), who found that primary, secondary, and postsecondary vocalists, pianists, and violinists, sang descending scales more closely to an equally tempered standard than ascending patterns. Along with melodic direction, melodic range may significantly impact pitch accuracy. Advanced performers have demonstrated greater pitch variation across registers than between each other (Fyk, 1995).

Improving Pitch-Matching and Intonation Skills

Several common characteristics have been identified among performers who demonstrate good pitch accuracy. First, as discussed earlier, accuracy appears to improve with experience. Beginning instrumental students have demonstrated difficulty accurately matching a single pitch with their instrument (Yarbrough et al., 1995). As shown in Figure 12.1, from that point improvement in accuracy appears to continue for at least seven years (Yarbrough et al., 1997). It was also noted that students who took private instrumental lessons in addition to participating in an ensemble performed more accurately.

Several issues remain unclear. First, it is not known whether private instruction improves pitch skills or students who study privately spend more time performing and, therefore, develop accuracy more quickly. Alternatively, students who are more successful at pitch-related tasks may find performance rewarding enough to seek individual instruction. Second, in light of the overall trend toward improved accuracy with experience, it remains unclear whether experience itself contributes toward improved pitch skills or students who are not successful at such tasks tend to quit their school music programs earlier in their performance careers. This conclusion may be supported by studies that did not find that experience alone resulted in more accurate performance (Brittin, 1993; Duke, 1985).

The placement and characteristics of target pitches also affect accuracy. Corso (1954) observed no difference in accuracy when advanced instrumental performers attempted to tune to simultaneous or preceding target pitches. Cassidy (1989) found that students tuned simultaneous octaves at least as well as unisons. While instrumentalists appear to be little affected by the timbre of the target pitch (Ely, 1992), timbre has a greater effect on the pitch-matching accuracy of young vocalists. Primary school children have been found to be more successful performing a minor third (G–E) following a child or female model rather than a male model (Yarbrough, Green, Benson, & Bowers, 1991). However, a male falsetto model has been found to be effective (Yarbrough et al. 1995). Among young students, at least, it appears advantageous to present students with unison pitch targets.

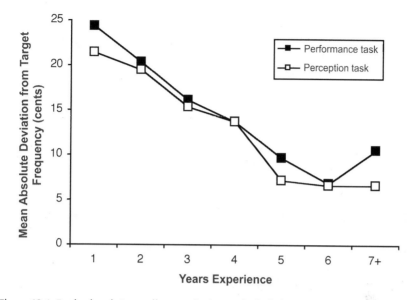

Figure 12.1. Beginning, intermediate, and advanced wind players' mean absolute cent deviation scores when matching a target pitch with their instrument (dark squares) and an electronic keyboard (white squares). Students with greater experience show more accuracy on both tasks. (Adapted from Yarbrough, Morrison, & Karrick, 1997. Copyright 1997 the University of Illinois, used by permission.)

The presence of vibrato in a target stimulus has also been found to affect the accuracy of pitch responses. Brown (1991) asked musicians and nonmusicians to match pitches presented with wide and narrow vibrato. Responses of the two groups were significantly different, with musicians' responses generally above the mean pitch and nonmusicians' responses at or below mean pitch. This contradicts other research in which the mean frequency was identified as the best match within a vibrato tone (Brown & Vaughn, 1996; Shonle & Horan, 1980). At the early stages of music instruction, the presence of vibrato may be a source of confusion. Yarbrough, Bowers, and Benson (1992) found that both certain and uncertain singers in kindergarten through Grade 3 responded more accurately to a nonvibrato adult female vocal model than to a child vocal model or an adult female model using vibrato. Uncertain singers particularly benefited from the nonvibrato model.

In an effort to improve pitch accuracy, ensembles generally tune at the outset of a rehearsal or performance. At the beginning of this chapter we identified tuning as unique from other pitch-related tasks, though its prominence within the rehearsal context suggests belief in a strong link between an ensemble's accuracy at tuning and their pitch accuracy in performance. To examine students' ability to transfer pitch information from the tuning process to a performance situation, Morrison (2000) recorded high school wind instrumentalists individually performing a familiar eight-measure melody along with a prerecorded model. Before performing, the students either (1) tuned their instrument to a target pitch, (2) were verbally instructed to perform as in tune as possible, or (3) received no information or tuning opportunity. No differences were found in the accuracy of their performances. Similar results were reported by Geringer (1978), who found that cautioning undergraduate and graduate music students about tuning did not significantly improve the accuracy of their performance. Surprisingly, even rehearsal did not improve the pitch accuracy of primary, secondary school, and undergraduate students' performances of ascending and descending scales (Madsen, 1966).

Specific feedback, rather than instructions alone, has been found to improve pitch-matching accuracy. Among 32 musically experienced and inexperienced adults, visual and aural feedback given across four treatment sessions was found to improve subjects' ability to adjust an electronic tone to match a target pitch (Platt & Racine, 1985). First-year college students also demonstrated improved pitch-matching skills after taking part in aural skills coursework that emphasized instructional feedback (Fyk, 1987).

Development of Intonational Skill

As stated earlier in this chapter, the musical characteristic we refer to as intonation represents pitch manipulation within a real musical context. Perhaps the improvement in this skill observed over time and experience reflects developing musicians' ability to interact within larger and larger musical environments. The following model proposes a view of how development of pitch manipulation skills parallels the growth of a young musician's musical context. Within this model the extent of young performers' musical awareness corresponds with the areas of musical skill to which they can attend. These, in turn, help the teacher to identify appropriate learning objectives.

Young musicians at the most basic level of performance operate within a very limited context, focusing solely on themselves and their actions. This is not surprising given the array of cognitive challenges they are suddenly facing. As depicted in Figure 12.2, attention is often consumed with their *internal self*—the feeling of manipulating an instrument or the process of producing a sound. These experiences are novel and, at first, feel awkward and unnatural. Members of beginning ensembles often wander off into their own worlds of tempo, melody, and rhythm, oblivious to the ensemble's disjointed results. Even the sounds that emerge from their own instruments (including the voice) are often overlooked in favor of attending to the physical demands of basic sound production.

At the next level, students become more aware of their *external self*—the different kinds of sounds they are able to produce, the results of their physical processes. They are able to select from and perform a variety of pitches that have become part of their repertoire and are able to discriminate between what is generally right and what is definitely wrong. Trumpet players can make judgments about which partial should be played; violinists can make decisions about correct finger placement. These judgments may be at a gross level—should that be an F or an F♯?—but they show a significant shift of attention toward self-generated musical information.

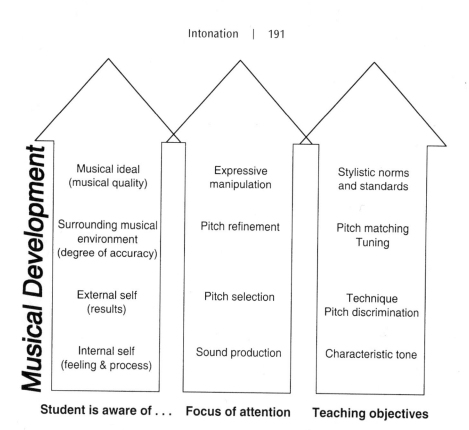

Figure 12.2. Model that describes the growth of pitch manipulation skills within the overall context of musical development.

The expansion of the musical context continues as young musicians match the sounds they are making to the sounds happening around them. They are comfortable enough with their own technique that they can attend to the *surrounding musical environment*. Accuracy is assumed as degree of accuracy becomes the focus. Not only can performers at this level select the proper pitch, but they can refine that pitch so that it matches a reference point established by other members of the group or some other external sound source (e.g., an electronic tuner).

At the most advanced stage, students can not only compare the relationship between their sounds and that of others around them, but they can also compare that comparison to an abstract standard, a *musical ideal*. They can manipulate their own actions so that the result is not only correct but also expressive. At this point, the musical context has extended beyond their immediate environment to include an awareness of historical and cultural—in short, professional—standards. Taken together with key findings that emerge from research surveyed earlier in this chapter, this model offers potential guidance for music teaching and performance.

Implications for Teaching

Tone Quality Affects Perception of Pitch Accuracy

If intonation is a process that demands at least three levels of awareness—the performers' own actions, the actions of those around them, and an abstract model of ideal performance—then it would seem well beyond the grasp of novice performers. However, that is if we limit our view of intonation to the active process of pitch manipulation. Let us instead view intonation as a result of other active processes—particularly production of a characteristic tone—that, when executed successfully, result in a more in-tune performance. Certainly intonation-as-action is one of the ultimate goals of music performance instruction, but intonation-as-result can be a realistic outcome along the way.

The development of good, characteristic tone quality is a skill within reach of even the most inexperienced beginner. As a result of the development of good tone quality, performers and performing ensembles are likely to produce performances that sound more in tune. Tone quality is a direct consequence of skills that reside at the foundation of performance instruction: correct posture, breath technique, vowel formation, embouchure, bow grip, and instrument carriage. Most important, students can successfully practice and demonstrate these skills by focusing solely on their own actions, a key characteristic of early musical development.

Pitch Discrimination and Manipulation Skills Are Not Clearly Related

It seems reasonable to suggest that it is the interaction among pitch discrimination, pitch matching, and melodic and harmonic pitch placement (the task to which we have specifically applied the term *intonation*) that results in an in-tune musical performance. Indeed, the model presented earlier depicts these subskills as sequential building blocks toward performance proficiency. However, it may not be accurate to say that all students must demonstrate high achievement in each of these areas in order to produce a successful final result.

Students' skills at pitch discrimination or isolated pitch matching are often used as predictors of their contribution to a performance ensemble or future success in music. As only limited correlation has been found among these skills, it may be inappropriate to speculate on achievement in one area by assessing achievement in another. For example, the flute player who can usually match any given target pitch may struggle to play a unison melodic line with the rest of the woodwind section. The vocalist who can perform a vast repertoire of songs with impeccable intonation may be less successful at distinguishing between slightly flat or slightly sharp tones if sung by someone else. The only relationships that have emerged are among students at the highest level of musical achievement. The first-chair trumpet player in the school's top band and the soprano section leader in the school's top choir would be the most likely individuals to demonstrate strong skills in all areas. But even in these cases, results suggest that such assumptions cannot be made with complete confidence.

Pitch Accuracy Is Affected by the Presence of a Musical Context

One key to effectively addressing pitch issues is to correctly match the teaching strategy with the desired outcome. Take, for example, a trombone section experiencing difficulty with a unison countermelody. One strategy might be to ask the section to tune each individual pitch in isolation, removing the variables of tempo, rhythm, dynamics, articulation, and pitch function. Another strategy might be to ask them to identify the location, source, and direction of the pitch discrepancies.

Unfortunately, these strategies may only succeed in developing the students' skills at pitch matching or discrimination. Morrison (2000), after observing that instrumentalists were more accurate performing an isolated B♭—a traditional band tuning pitch—than performing a G as part of a simple melody, suggested that students become very accurate at the specific skills that they are directed to practice. In this case, students probably had considerable experience matching isolated pitches in general and the tuning B♭ in particular. Would results have been different if students tuned to other pitches during rehearsal or if the tuning B♭ was directly transferred into a short melody?

A better strategy would be to simplify only a minimum of performance parameters, thereby retaining as much of the surrounding musical environment as possible. Slowing the tempo, eliminating dynamic contrasts, or thinning the texture by reducing the number of other parts playing might be enough simplification to allow the players to focus their attention on pitch accuracy. Identifying certain individual notes as anchors or landmarks may also serve the same function. However, consider a final, sustained unison at the conclusion of a choral work. In this case, pitch matching is exactly the skill in question. In this example, taking the pitch out of context and isolating it in time and function might, indeed, be an appropriate strategy for improving accuracy.

Pitch Accuracy Is Aided by Clear Models

To successfully and accurately place a pitch within a musical context, it is first necessary to identify what that pitch should be. For the least-experienced performers the target pitch can be obscured by obstacles that, in any other situation, would be appropriate. Expecting inexperienced singers to echo back a melodic passage presented with vibrato one octave higher than they are asked to respond presents a sequence of challenges—finding a pitch within the vibrato, then displacing the pitch into their own range, then matching it—that may not easily be mastered. Students have the best chance to respond successfully if the model presented is as close as possible to the response they are expected or able to make.

Specific Feedback Improves Pitch Skills

The successful implementation of any effective teaching or practice strategy necessarily includes feedback. Feedback may be in the form of a comment or gesture from the teacher, it may be the swaying needle or blinking light of an electronic tuner, or it may be performers' own assessment of themselves. In the short term, feedback can help students make adjustments that result in accurate pitch placement. On a more permanent level, continued constructive feedback over time allows students to learn the norms and standards against which their performance is judged, what accurate tuning *is*, how good intonation *sounds*. Experience may have a profound effect on students' pitch sensitivity not only because they have spent so much time mastering their instrument but also because they have gained an understanding of the musical goals toward which they are working.

The Most Accurate Pitch Is Not Always the Most Preferred Pitch

Though it would seem that pitch *accuracy* is the overall goal addressed in this chapter, it might be better to say that pitch *control* is the ultimate goal toward which musicians should strive. Performance practices of the most highly trained musicians and listening preferences of the most discriminating audiences demonstrate that pitch discrepancies are an accepted and even desirable component of the best musical performances. In short, truth is subjective when it comes to pitch.

A teacher's or performer's overreliance on an external standard such as an electronic tuner or its corresponding theoretical tuning system may limit the type of pitch flexibility characteristic of expert performances. The conductor who subjects every pitch in a melodic passage to electronic analysis may be choosing the wrong analysis tool, since the assessment of good intonation appears to be more a product of listener evaluation than mathematical precision. That is not to say that attention to pitch accuracy should be minimized. It may be more desirable that musicians have the *ability* to match a target pitch exactly (with a 0 cent deviation from a presented model) than that they *perform* it that way every time. In a real musical context, intonation appears to be more negotiation than conformity.

Intonation cannot be addressed by rehearsal strategies alone. Along with ensemble skills, performance experience helps students gain knowledge of their own instrument, be it a trombone, a viola, or a voice. Each instrument, other than those with fixed pitches, has its own tendencies and eccentricities. As students progress, success at pitch accuracy will be influenced by knowledge of such details. Nevertheless, execution of an in-tune performance—regardless of which definition of the term we are using—ultimately depends on the ability of performers to assess what is happening around them and to respond accordingly.

References

Barbour, J. M. (1951). *Tuning and temperament: A historical survey*. East Lansing: Michigan State College Press.

Brittin, R. V. (1993). Effects of upper- and lower-register accompaniment on intonation. *Journal of Band Research, 29*(1), 43–50.

Brown, J. C., & Vaughn, K. V. (1996). Pitch center of stringed instrument vibrato tones. *Journal of the Acoustical Society of America, 100*(3), 1728–1735.

Brown, S. F. (1991). Determination of location of pitches within a musical vibrato. *Bulletin of the Council for Research in Music Education, 108*, 15–30.

Burns, E. M. (1999). Intervals, scales, and tuning. In D. Deutsch (Ed.), *The psychology of music* (2nd ed., pp. 215–264). San Diego, CA: Academic Press.

Burns, E. M., & Campbell, S. L. (1994). Frequency and frequency ratio resolution by possessors of relative and absolute pitch: Examples of categorical perception? *Journal of the Acoustical Society of America, 96*(5), 2704–2719.

Burns, E. M., & Ward, W. D. (1978). Categorical perception—phenomenon or epiphenomenon: Evidence from experiments in the perception of melodic musical intervals. *Journal of the Acoustical Society of America, 63*(2), 456–468.

Cassidy, J. W. (1989). The effect of instrument type, stimulus timbre, and stimulus octave placement on tuning accuracy. *Missouri Journal of Research in Music Education, 26*, 7–23.

Corso, J. F. (1954). Unison tuning of musical instruments. *Journal of the Acoustical Society of America, 26*(5), 746–750.

Demorest, S. M. (2000, March). *Pitch-matching performance of junior high boys: A comparison of perception and production.* Paper presented at the MENC National Biennial In-Service Conference, Washington, DC.

Duke, R. A. (1985). Wind instrumentalists' intonational performance of selected musical intervals. *Journal of Research in Music Education, 33*(2), 101–112.

Ely, M. C. (1992). Effects of timbre on college woodwind players' intonation performance and perception. *Journal of Research in Music Education, 40*(2), 158–167.

Fastl, H., & Hesse, A. (1984). Frequency discrimination for pure tones at short durations. *Acustica, 56*, 41–47.

Fyk, J. (1982). Perception of mistuned intervals in melodic context. *Psychology of Music*, Special Edition, 36–41.

Fyk, J. (1985). Vocal pitch-matching ability in children as a function of sound duration. *Bulletin of the Council for Research in Music Education, 85*, 76–89.

Fyk, J. (1987). Duration of tones required for satisfactory precision of pitch matching. *Bulletin of the Council for Research in Music Education, 91*, 38–44.

Fyk, J. (1995). *Melodic intonation, psychoacoustics, and the violin.* Zielona Góra, Poland: Organon.

Garbuzov, N. A. (1948). Zonal nature of the pitch perception. In *Problems of physiological acoustics*, Vol. 1 (pp. 138–152). Moscow: USSR Academy of Sciences.

Geringer, J. M. (1978). Intonational performance and perception of ascending scales. *Journal of Research in Music Education, 26*(1), 32–40.

Geringer, J. M. (1983). The relationship of pitch-matching and pitch-discrimination abilities of preschool and fourth-grade students. *Journal of Research in Music Education, 31*(2), 93–100.

Geringer, J. M., & Madsen, C. K. (1987). Programmatic research in music: Perception and performance of intonation. In C. K. Madsen and C. A. Prickett (Eds.), *Applications of research in music behavior* (pp. 244–253). Tuscaloosa: University of Alabama Press.

Geringer, J. M., & Witt, A. C. (1985). An investigation of tuning performance and perception of string instrumentalists. *Bulletin of the Council for Research in Music Education, 85*, 90–101.

Geringer, J. M., & Worthy, M. D. (1999). Effects of tone-quality changes on intonation and tone-quality ratings of high school and college instrumentalists. *Journal of Research in Music Education, 47*(2), 135–149.

Kantorski, V. J. (1986). String instrument intonation in upper and lower registers: The effects of accompaniment. *Journal of Research in Music Education, 34*(3), 200–210.

Karrick, B. (1998). An examination of the intonation tendencies of wind instrumentalists based on their performances of selected harmonic intervals. *Journal of Research in Music Education, 46*(1), 112–127.

Kelly, N. E. (2000, August). *Detecting intonation errors in familiar melodies.* Paper presented at the Sixth International Conference on Music Perception and Cognition, Keele University, UK.

Loosen, F. (1993). Intonation of solo violin performance with reference to equally tempered, Pythagorean, and just intonation. *Journal of the Acoustical Society of America, 93*(1), 525–539.

Madsen, C. K. (1966). The effect of scale directon on pitch acuity in solo vocal performance. *Journal of Research in Music Education, 14*(4), 266–275.

Madsen, C. K., Edmonson, F. A., & Madsen, C. H. (1969). Modulated frequency discrimination in relationship to age and musical training. *Journal of the Acoustical Society of America, 46* (6, pt. 2), 1468–1472.

Madsen, C. K., & Geringer, J. M. (1976). Preferences for trumpet tone quality versus intonation. *Bulletin of the Council for Research in Music Education, 46*, 13–22.

Madsen, C. K., & Geringer, J. M. (1981). Discrimination between tone quality and intonation in unaccompanied flute/oboe duets. *Journal of Research in Music Education, 29*(4), 305–313.

Morrison, S. J. (2000). Effect of melodic context, tuning behaviors, and experience on the intonation accuracy of wind players. *Journal of Research in Music Education, 48*(1), 39–51.

Platt, J. R., & Racine, R. J. (1985). Effect of frequency, timbre, experience, and feedback on musical tuning skills. *Perception and Psychophysics, 38*(6), 543–553.

Rakowski, A. (1978). *Categorical perception of the pitch in music.* Warsaw: State Higher School of Music.

Rakowski, A. (1990). Intonation variants of musical intervals in isolation and in musical contexts. *Psychology of Music, 18*(1), 60–72.

Sergeant, D. (1973). Measurement of pitch discrimination. *Journal of Research in Music Education, 21*(1), 3–19.

Shonle, J. I., & Horan, K. E. (1980). The pitch of vibrato tones. *Journal of the Acoustical Society of America, 67*(1), 246–252.

Siegel, J. A., & Siegel, W. (1977). Categorical perception of tonal intervals: Musicians can't tell sharp from flat. *Perception and Psychophysics, 21*(5), 399–407.

Sogin, D. W. (1989). An analysis of string instrumentalists' performed intonational adjustments within ascending and descending pitch set. *Journal of Research in Music Education, 37*(2), 104–111.

Spiegel, M. F., & Watson, C. S. (1984). Performance on frequency-discrimination tasks by musicians and nonmusicians. *Journal of the Acoustical Society of America, 76*, 1690–1695.

Sundberg, J. (1982). In tune or not? A study of fundamental frequency in music practice. In C. Dahlhaus and M. Krause (Eds.), *Tiefenstruktur der Musik* (pp. 69–97). Berlin: Technical University of Berlin.

Tieplov, B. M. (1947). *Psychology of musical aptitude.* Moscow: Academy of Pedagogical Sciences of the RSFSR.

Vos, J. (1982). The perception of pure and mistuned musical fifths and major thirds: Thresholds for discrimination, beats, and identification. *Perception and Psychophysics, 32*(4), 297–313.

Wapnick, J., & Freeman, P. (1980). Effects of dark-bright timbral variation on the perception of flatness and sharpness. *Journal of Research in Music Education, 28*(3), 176–184.

Wapnick, J., Bourassa, G., & Sampson, J. (1982). The perception of tonal intervals in isolation and in melodic context. *Psychomusicology, 2*(1), 21–37.

Watson, C. S., Kelly, W. J, & Wroton, M. W. (1976). Factors in the discrimination of tonal patterns. II. Selective attention and learning under various levels of stimulus uncertainty. *Journal of the Acoustical Society of America, 60,* 1176–1186.

Yarbrough, C., & Ballard, D. (1990). The effect of accidentals, scale degrees, direction, and performer opinions on intonation. *Update: Applications of Research in Music Education, 8(2),* 19–22.

Yarbrough, C., Bowers, J., & Benson, W. (1992). The effect of vibrato on the pitch-matching accuracy of certain and uncertain singers. *Journal of Research in Music Education, 40*(1), 30–38.

Yarbrough, C., Karrick, B., & Morrison, S. J. (1995). Effect of knowledge of directional mistunings on the tuning accuracy of beginning and intermediate wind players. *Journal of Research in Music Education, 43*(3), 232–241.

Yarbrough, C., Morrison, S. J., & Karrick, B. (1997). The effect of experience, private instruction, and knowledge of mistunings on the tuning performance and perception of high school wind players. *Bulletin of the Council for Research in Music Education, 134,* 31–42.

Yarbrough, C., Morrison, S. J., Karrick, B., & Dunn, D. E. (1995). The effect of male falsetto on the pitch-matching accuracy of uncertain boy singers, grades K–8. *Update: Applications of Research in Music Education, 14*(1), 4–10.

Yarbrough, C. M., Green, G. A., Benson, W., & Bowers, J. (1991). Inaccurate singers: An exploratory study of variables affecting pitch-matching. *Bulletin of the Council for Research in Music Education, 107,* 23–34.

13

Structural Communication

ANDERS FRIBERG & GIOVANNI UMBERTO BATTEL

The communication of structure in musical expression has been studied scientifically by analyzing variations in timing and dynamics in expert performances. The underlying principles have been extracted and models of the relationship between expression and musical structure formulated. For example, a musical phrase tends to speed up and get louder at the start and to slow down and get quieter at the end; mathematical models of these variations can enhance the quality of synthesized performances. We overview the dependence of timing and dynamics on tempo, phrasing, harmonic and melodic tension, repetitive patterns and grooves, articulation, accents, and ensemble timing. Principles of structural communication (expression) can be taught analytically by explaining the underlying principles and techniques with computer-generated demonstrations, or in traditional classroom or lesson settings by live demonstration.

Variations in timing and dynamics play an essential role in music performance. This is easily shown by having a computer perform a classical piece exactly as written in the score. The result is dull and will probably not affect us in any positive manner, although there may be plenty of potentially beautiful passages in the score. A musician can, by changing the performance of a piece, totally change its emotional character, for example, from sad to happy (chapter 14). How is this possible, and what are the basic techniques used to accomplish such a change? The key is how the musical structure is communicated. Therefore, a good understanding of structure—whether theoretic or intuitive—is a prerequisite for a convincing musical performance.

This chapter surveys the basic principles and techniques that musicians use to convey and project music structure (see also overviews in Gabrielsson, 1999; Palmer, 1997). We will only consider auditory communication and leave out visual cues in concert performances (see chapter 15). Another issue only briefly covered is perception—the extent to which subtle variations in performance are perceived by the listener. Our focus will be on topics that have been the subject of systematic research and that can be useful for music students and teachers. Largely for practical reasons, this research has tended to focus more on traditional classical music than other styles, timing more than other parameters such as dynamics and articulation, and piano performance more than that of other instruments. Nonetheless, most of the results obtained, and hence most of the principles presented here, seem to have a universal character and may be applied to a wide variety of genres and instruments.

Concepts and Terms

How can music performance be studied scientifically? We base our analysis primarily on information available in the sound alone. All cues for musical communication are contained in sound, which in turn can be described and quantified in terms of physical variables such as the duration and sound level of each tone.

Tone duration is the time interval between the physical start of the tone (*onset*) and the end of the same tone (*offset*), that is, the sounding duration of a tone. More important for timing in music is the *interonset interval* (*IOI*), defined as the time interval between the onset of the tone and the onset of the immediately following tone. In other words, IOI is the sum of a tone's physical duration and the pause duration between the offset of the tone and the onset of the next (see Figure 13.1). IOI is easy to measure in MIDI recordings and can also be estimated from audio recordings using computer software.

To find out if a tone is lengthened or shortened in performance, measured IOI values are compared with the note values given in the score. A *nominal*

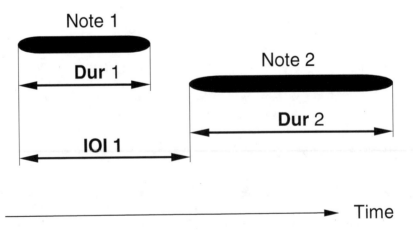

Figure 13.1. Definition of interonset interval (IOI) and duration (Dur) for two successive tones.

performance (or deadpan performance) is defined as a direct translation of the score into physical variables, where all notes of the same note value have the same *nominal IOI*, derived from the *global tempo* (tempo marking or mean tempo). In a nominal performance, for example, an eighth note is always exactly half as long as a quarter note. A nominal performance often serves as a reference point for research on musical timing. Timing variations relative to a nominal performance can be analyzed either tone by tone or as changes in *local tempo*, conceived as a continuously varying function of time (*tempo curve*).

Conventional Western notation developed historically within the physical and cognitive constraints of performance and sight-reading. It deliberately fails to describe music in too much detail, since that would make it too difficult to read. This means that it is not possible to define nominal values for articulation and dynamics in conventional scores. Another consequence is the development of *performance conventions*—standard (but generally style-specific) interpretations of notational symbols that are not evident in the score itself. For example, strings of eighth notes in a jazz score are typically performed unevenly in long-short patterns (*swing*).

What are the basic building blocks of musical structure? Most tonal music has a hierarchical phrase structure, sometimes simply called *grouping*. The slowest level is the entire piece, which is then divided and subdivided into sections, phrases, subphrases, and melodic groups. Superimposed upon this is usually a *metrical hierarchy*: the beat or *tactus* (corresponding to when you tap your feet) is grouped, usually in groups of two or three, into measures and groups of measures. The beat can also be divided into subbeats. Phrasing and meter are theoretically independent, although phrase and metric boundaries often coincide, reinforcing the overall perceived grouping (Lerdahl & Jackendoff, 1983) (see Figure 13.2).

Figure 13.2. Phrase structure and metrical structure in an excerpt from Haydn's Symphony no. 104. The dots represent the hierarchical metrical structure. The top level in the figure is the beat level, the second the measure level, and the third and fourth are hypermetric levels. The hierarchical phrase structure is shown with brackets. The top level in the figure is the fastest, with only a few tones in each phrase or group. The slowest level corresponds to the whole phrase. (From Lerdahl & Jackendoff, 1983. Copyright 1983 MIT Press, used by permission.)

Commonalities Among Performers and Between Repetitions

What are the similarities and differences in separate performances of the same piece? When discussing interpretation, the emphasis is often placed on performance differences. However, even musicians who are considered to interpret music quite differently may produce remarkably similar patterns of timing and dynamics (Repp, 1992).

Musical structure is reflected in physical variables in a number of ways. Figure 13.3 illustrates the variation of IOI and dynamics in two performances of the same piece. We see that both pianists express the phrase structure by lengthening and softening the tones (*ritardando* and *diminuendo*) at the end of each melodic gesture, in measures 4 and 8. The slowing and softening are more pronounced at the end of the whole phrase and are quite substantial and thus clearly perceptible. The differences in interpretation between the pianists are largely seen in variations within phrases and on a note-to-note level.

It is often argued that a repeated passage should be performed differently in both cases. This is, however, not generally confirmed in measurements. On the contrary, there are often striking similarities between the first and second presentation of a thematic group. This is also true for the repetition of a whole piece on different occasions. In Figure 13.3, the differences between the two performances are very small and, at least for timing, are below the perceptual limits in most cases.

Basic Principles and Techniques

Tempo

Global tempo can vary substantially in different renditions of the same piece by different performers. In commercial recordings of both Schumann's "Träumerei" and Chopin's Etude in E Major, Op. 10, No. 3, the fastest tempo was about twice as fast as the slowest (Repp, 1992, 1998b). Clearly tempo is influenced not only by tempo indications but also by the performer's interpretation, in particular by the intended motional and emotional character (chapter 14).

Collier and Collier (1994) investigated tempo in jazz by analyzing a large number of commercial jazz recordings. They found that *double time* (doubling of tempo, sometimes introduced into an improvisation to produce a contrasting passage or to increase the intensity) corresponded to a tempo ratio of 2.68:1—well above a mathematical doubling of tempo.

When the global tempo of a performance is changed, patterns of local timing variations may also change. For example, there may be a tendency toward more expressive timing variation (relative to tempo) at slower tempi (Repp, 1995). Also, the perceptual or motor limits of tone duration may alter the expressive pattern.

Phrasing

In music from the Romantic period, large variations in local tempo are an essential part of the performance tradition. Phrases often start slow, speed up in the

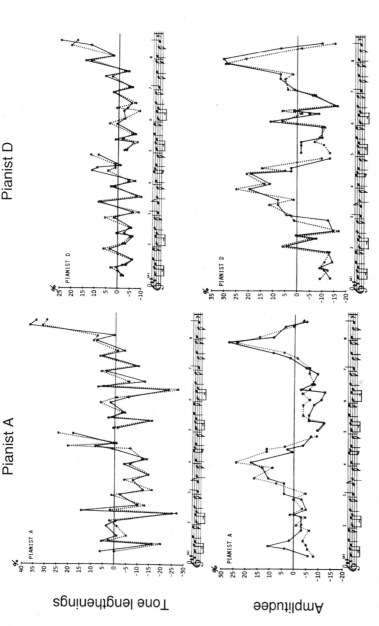

Figure 13.3. The first eight measures of Mozart's Piano Sonata K. 331, as performed by two pianists. The upper graphs illustrate the timing, with the vertical axis showing the deviation in IOI of each tone relative to nominal duration. The lower graphs illustrate the dynamic variation, with the vertical axis showing the peak amplitude of each tone relative to the mean of all tones in each performance. The first performance is represented by full lines and the repetition by dashed lines. (Adapted from Gabrielsson, 1987. Copyright 1987 Royal Swedish Academy of Music, used by permission.)

middle, and slow down again toward the last tone (e.g., Henderson, 1936; Repp, 1992). Dynamic variations tend to follow a similar pattern: soft in the beginning, loud in the middle, and softer toward the end of the phrase (see Figure 13.3) (Gabrielsson, 1987).

These typical shapes of timing and dynamics are observed in a majority of performances of Romantic music and are important for conveying the basic phrase structure to the listener. The *ritardando* at the end can communicate the phrase level, with typically a more pronounced *ritardando* at the end of a musical unit of longer duration or at a slower hierarchical level. This is clearly the case in Figure 13.3, where pianists A and D both lengthen the tones more at the end of the example than in the middle. The dynamic variation follows a similar pattern. In this way, not only the phrase boundaries but also their hierarchical level—and hence the hierarchical phrase structure of the whole piece—can be communicated, just by changing tempo and dynamics. Similar principles are found in speech, where lengthening is used to communicate phrase and sentence boundaries.

The exact amount and shape of the variation over the phrases is an important issue for the performer to decide. In Figure 13.3, both pianists slow down at the phrase boundaries but follow different tempo curves. For example, pianist A lengthens the final tones in each subphrase more than pianist D. Different shapings of local tempo or dynamics can entirely change the character of a performance, signaling different expressive intentions (Battel & Fimbianti, 1998).

Several models of these typical tempo variations have been developed. The first computational model was presented by Todd (1985, 1989; see also Windsor & Clarke, 1997; Penel & Drake, 1998) and accounted for the variation of measure duration over phrases. Todd (1992, 1995) later developed a revised model based on a different mathematical function, which he argued was more closely related to a metaphor of physical motion. Friberg (1995) modified Todd's first model so that it may be applied at the note level, introducing several extra parameters to account for individual variations. In Figure 13.4, this *phrase arch* model is fitted to three different piano performances of Schumann's "Träumerei" measured by Repp (1992). As can be seen in the figure, the model catches most of the individual variation regarding phrasing but misses local variations on the note level.

Phrasing in Baroque music typically involves smaller variations in local tempo than in Romantic music. Baroque music tends to have a more motoric, metrical character (as does most contemporary jazz and pop), suggesting the metaphor of a mass moving at a constant speed, creating a kind of musical momentum. This natural coupling of motion and music has been investigated in an intuitive way in a number of publications (overview in Shove & Repp, 1995). Looking for direct couplings between the physical world and music, Friberg and Sundberg (1999) discovered a close connection between how a runner stops and how Baroque music stops at a final *ritardando*. They found that the average velocity of the runner and the average local tempo closely followed the same curve: their model could account for the deceleration both of individual runners and of individual music performances. Moreover, participants in listening experiments

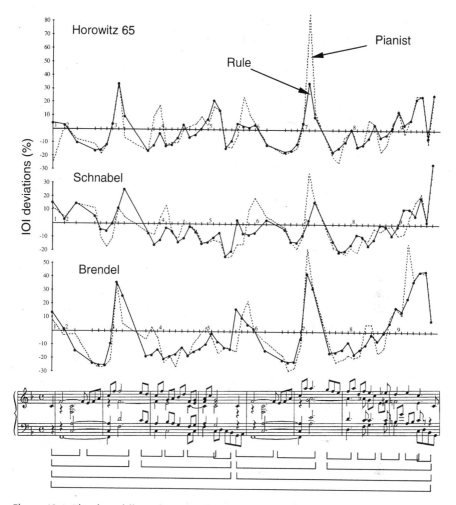

Figure 13.4. The dotted lines show the deviations in IOI from nominal values for performances of Schumann's "Träumerei" by three different pianists. The solid lines show predicted IOI deviations according to the phrase arch model. The predictions have been fitted to the three performances by adjusting the parameters of the model. The brackets below indicate the grouping analysis used in the model.

preferred final *ritardandi* that corresponded to the stopping runners, suggesting, in this case, a close coupling to physical motion.

The fastest level in the phrase hierarchy consists of small melodic units of a few notes each. Grouping (i.e., segmentation) at this level tends to be quite ambiguous, often with several possible interpretations. So communication of this structure can be subject to more individual interpretation than, say, communication of longer phrases. One example is found in Mozart's A-major sonata (Figure 13.3), where many performers chose the first five notes as a group while others chose the first four notes, giving the second group an upbeat. This ambiguity may be due to contradictory perceptual cues from different aspects of the musical structure, such as the melodic contour or the meter, and can be resolved in performance by inserting a micropause between the last tone of one phrase and the first of the next, which both interrupts the sound and delays the onset of the following tone (Friberg, Sundberg, & Frydén, 1987; Friberg, Bresin, Frydén, & Sundberg, 1998; Clarke, 1988).

A deceptively simple performance principle is *the higher, the louder* (Sundberg, Friberg, & Frydén, 1991). The origin of this principle appears to be physical: wind instruments (including the voice) tend to produce louder tones at higher pitches, even though effort or input pressure is held constant. Often the most important tone in a phrase is also the highest in pitch. In this case, the high-loud principle produces natural-sounding phrasing (cf. Windsor & Clarke, 1997; Palmer, 1996a; Krumhansl, 1996).

Harmonic and Melodic Tension

The notion of musical tension is common to both music theory and music psychology. Many authors claim that the contrast between tension and release is a major source of musical interest. Tension is coupled to expectancy; an unexpected tone or chord creates tension (Krumhansl, 1990). A number of sources that contribute to harmonic and melodic tension have been identified. A partial list is given in Table 13.1 (cf. Bigand, Parncutt, & Lerdahl, 1996).

Several models have been developed to address tension. For case 2(i), Sundberg, Friberg, and Frydén (1991) defined the *harmonic charge* of a chord as a weighted

Table 13.1. A list of tonal relationships that contribute to melodic and harmonic tension.

Case	Relationship	Increased Tension For:
1	between keys	(i) a modulation to a key that is distant on the circle of fifths (ii) a modulation to a scale with few tones in common with the original scale
2	between chords;	(i) chords more distant from the key on the circle of fifths chord relative to key (comparing roots) (ii) chromatic chords, or chords that include tones foreign to the prevailing scale (iii) successive chords that have few tones in common
3	tone relative to chord	(i) tones that are more distant on the circle of fifths from the root of the chord (ii) tones foreign to the diatonic scale associated with the chord
4	simultaneous tones in a chord	chords that contain more dissonant intervals
5	melodic contour	unexpected melodic turns

sum (root most important) of the distance between the tones of the chord and the prevailing tonic on the circle of fifths. They then allowed local tempo to slow down and sound level to increase in areas of high harmonic charge (Friberg, 1991), creating a kind of harmonic phrasing (see Figure 13.5).

For case 3(i), Sundberg et al. (1991) defined *melodic charge* as an increasing function of the distance on the circle of fifths. The performance model increases the sound level, IOI, and—if applicable—the extent of vibrato in proportion to the calculated melodic charge (Friberg, 1991).

A complex model that takes into account most of the aspects in Table 13.1 was formulated by Lerdahl (1996). This model explained the majority of variation in subjects' ratings of perceived tension in a Mozart sonata (Krumhansl, 1996).

The most common way to communicate tension seems to be to emphasize notes or areas of relatively high tension, as in the models of harmonic and melodic charge described earlier. However, it is difficult to trace the origins of variations of timing and dynamics measured in real performances, since the various tension concepts often are coupled to each other and to the phrasing structure. For example, chords more distant from the key are more often found in the middle of phrases, while chords close to the key are more often found in the beginning or in the end of the phrase. Also, phrasing tends to dominate performance expression, which makes it hard to isolate the more subtle details such as the expression of melodic or harmonic tension.

Analyzing a performance of a Mozart sonata, Palmer (1996a) found a weak correspondence between predictions of Lerdahl's model and observed timing (IOI): positions of high tension were emphasized by lengthening. An additional finding was that relatively dissonant chords were often performed by delaying the melody by as much as 100 ms. The purpose of this performance strategy could

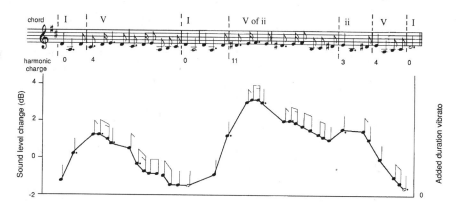

Figure 13.5. The harmonic charge model applied to a theme from Schubert's "unfinished" symphony. Sound level and vibrato rate increases and tempo decreases with increasing harmonic distance from the tonic. Note the peak in harmonic charge at the most distant chord (V of II) on the circle of fifths.

either be to reduce the perceptual dissonance of the chord (as Palmer suggested) or to emphasize the melody tone by delaying it (see "Accents" later).

Repetitive Metrical Patterns and Grooves

Music that is rhythmically regular often exhibits consistent patterns of timing and dynamics within metrical units such as the measure. For example, if the first beat in each measure is accentuated, a dynamic pattern is formed that is repeated in each measure. This kind of patterning is often associated with dance, suggesting that these patterns serve to characterize the motional character of the piece.

Patterns in Triple Meter. In performances of both a Beethoven minuet (Repp, 1990) and a Chopin nocturne (Henderson, 1936), the pianists played the second beat late and the third beat early, forming a long–short–long pattern.

In patterns of a half note followed by a quarter note in $\frac{3}{4}$ time, or a quarter note followed by an eighth note in $\frac{6}{8}$, the ratio of the IOIs of the long and short tones is usually in the range from 1.7:1 to 1.9:1—consistently smaller than the nominal 2:1. This has been found in performances of Swedish folk music as well as Mozart and Chopin (Gabrielsson, 1987; Gabrielsson, Bengtsson, & Gabrielsson, 1983; Henderson, 1936), (see Figure 13.3; note the characteristic zigzag patterns in the timing graphs). Sundberg et al. (1991) called this effect *double duration* and incorporated it into a performance model.

A different pattern is found in Viennese waltzes: they are usually performed with an early second beat, thus forming a short–long–intermediate timing pattern for the three beats in the measure. This pattern was first systematically investigated by Bengtsson and Gabrielsson (1983), who also observed a hypermetric timing pattern spanning two measures that reflects how these waltzes are danced, as well as the underlying harmonic structure.

Two-note Patterns. In jazz, Baroque, and folk music, it is common to apply a long–short pattern to consecutive eighth notes (or the shortest prevalent note value). In Baroque music, this performance convention is referred to as *notes inégales* (Hefling, 1993). Drummers playing typical comping patterns in jazz perform different ratios between consecutive eighth notes depending on global tempo. At slow to medium tempi, the ratio tends to be about 3:1 (dotted eighth + sixteenth), dropping to 1:1 (even eighth notes) at fast tempi (Friberg and Sundström, in press). At the same time, the soloist uses smaller ratios than 2:1. Surprisingly, the ratio of 2:1, implied by the often-mentioned triplet feel of swing, was not observed in these experiments.

Duration Contrast. Contrary to the double duration principle described earlier, the contrast between long and short tones is often *increased* by a lengthening of comparatively long notes and a corresponding shortening of comparatively short notes (Taguti, Mori, & Suga, 1994). However, duration contrast applies to *all* notes, while double duration applies only to the 2:1 pattern. In the case of a repeated rhythmical figure, duration contrast will appear as a repetitive timing pattern. Duration contrast can also be applied backward: depending on the performer's intention, the contrast may instead be decreased (chapter 14). A model was formulated by Sundberg et al. (1991).

Articulation

Articulation—at least in the sense of *staccato* versus *legato*—may be defined mathematically as the ratio of tone duration to IOI. Articulation strongly affects motional and emotional character (De Poli, Rodà, & Vidolin, 1998; Battel & Fimbianti, 1998; chapter 14 in this volume).

The duration of *staccato* tones has been found to correspond on average to about 40% of the IOI (or note value) in typical performances of a Mozart andante movement for piano (from Sonata K. 545; Bresin & Battel, 2000). When pianists were asked to play the same piece *brillante* or *leggero*, the duration decreased to 25% (*staccatissimo* range), while in *pesante* performances the duration approached 75% of IOI (*mezzo staccato* range). The typical value of 40% is in nice agreement with C. P. E. Bach's (1753/1957) observation that *staccato* notes should be played with less than 50% of their nominal duration.

In *legato* playing on the piano, successive tones often overlap—both keys are down for a short period of time. The amount of overlap (in milliseconds) increases with IOI and pitch interval size (Repp, 1997; Bresin and Battel, 2000). Bresin and Battel also found that the overlap time was used for expressive purposes: the pianists used more overlap when instructed to play *appassionato* than *piatto* (flat). Overlap is also dependent on direction of melodic motion; descending melodic patterns are usually played with more overlap than ascending patterns (Repp, 1997; Bresin, 2000).

Bresin (2000) also found an interesting link between articulation and physical locomotion. The overlap time of the feet in walking was found to vary qualitatively in the same way as in *legato* articulation. Flying time in running (the time during which neither foot is in contact with the ground) was similarly found to be related to detached time in *staccato* articulation. Based on these measurements, Bresin (2000) was able to formulate models for *staccato*, *legato*, and tone repetition.

Accents

The meaning of the term *accent* varies considerably in music-theoretic literature. Two main categories can be identified: immanent accents and performed accents (cf. Parncutt, in press; Lerdahl & Jackendoff, 1983). An *immanent accent* is evident from the structure of the score itself, meaning that even if the score is performed nominally, these positions will be perceived as accented. For example, immanent accents may occur on notes in metrically strong positions, on comparatively long notes, on the second tone of an upward leap, on the top tone of a melodic turn, or at increased harmonic tension (melodic immanent accents: Thomassen, 1982; Huron & Royal, 1996).

A *performed accent* is added by the performer relative to the nominal performance. This definition is closer to the common use of the term. Performed accents seem primarily to be used to reinforce immanent accents. This was confirmed in simple melodies (Drake & Palmer, 1993). However, in more complex (real) music, only weak couplings between performed and immanent accents have been found: only when positions interacting with the grouping structure were disregarded was it possible to get statistical significance in piano performances of Schumann's "Träumerei" (Penel & Drake, 1998). This finding may indicate that the concept of melodic accent is only a cue that leads to the forming of melodic groups. In fact, cues for immanent accents and cues for making automatic melodic grouping are similar (e.g., Friberg et al., 1998; Cambouropoulos, 1998).

Perhaps the most obvious way to perform an accent is to increase loudness. In the case of instruments where the loudness envelope can be varied (such as winds, strings, and voice), there are several possibilities, including a loudness increase at the beginning of the tone and a shorter attack time. Timing can also be used in several ways to emphasize a tone: (1) by lengthening the tone; (2) by delaying the onset, that is, lengthening the preceding tone (IOI) and possibly inserting a micropause before the accented note; and (3) by playing the accented note more *legato* (Henderson, 1936; Clarke, 1988; Drake & Palmer, 1993). In addition, a change in articulation such as one *legato* note surrounded by *staccato* notes may signal an accent (cf. Lerdahl & Jackendoff, 1983).

Ensemble Timing

In polyphonic classical music, it is often important to highlight the melody. An obvious way is to play it louder. However, timing is also an effective method. If two tones are presented at almost the same time, the first will be perceptually emphasized (Rasch, 1978). This technical device, commonly referred to as *melody lead*, has been observed in string and wind trios, as well as in piano performances. The melody is typically played about 20 ms ahead of the other voices, within the range of about 7 to 50 ms (Rasch, 1979; Palmer, 1996b; Vernon, 1936).

The opposite often happens in jazz: soloists deliberately play behind the beat. At each quarter-note beat, the soloist was delayed relative to the ride cymbal by up to about 100 ms at slow tempi (Ellis, 1991; Friberg & Sundström, in press). At the same time, the soloist and drummer were synchronized at the upbeats, that is, on the eighth notes between the beats. The purpose here is probably not to highlight the soloist, which in this style is clearly audible, due to either large spectral differences or the use of microphones. Rather, this timing combination creates both the impression of the laid-back soloist often strived for in jazz and at the same time an impression of good synchronization (see Figure 13.6).

Classification and Purpose of Performance Variations

Non-notated variations in timing and dynamics (deviations from the nominal performance) can be divided into two main types (cf. Juslin, Friberg, & Bresin,

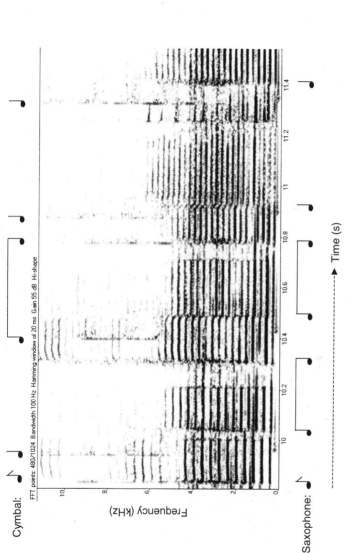

Figure 13.6. A spectrogram of a short passage of "My Funny Valentine" performed by Miles Davis Quintet, 1964, that illustrates the timing relation between the ride cymbal and the soloist in jazz. The cymbal onsets appear as vertical lines in the high-frequency part of the graph. The saxophone onsets appear as breaks, or vertical shifts, in the horizontal lines in the lower part of the graph. In this example, cymbal is being played with a swing ratio of about 4:1 and the saxophone with a swing ratio of approximately 3:2. The downbeat saxophone tones are delayed relative to the cymbal by about 100 ms, but on the upbeats the cymbal and the saxophone are synchronized.

in press). *Expressive variations* are deliberately meaningful or communicative (but not necessarily conscious). *Nonexpressive variations* are of two kinds: *variations due to technical limitations* of the instrument and the performer and *random variations* (including imperfections in the perceptual timing and motor system). Neither of these last two have a deliberate communicative function; they may tell us something about the performer's abilities, but this is of course unintentional. Nevertheless, they can be important for the naturalness of a performance.

Expressive variations can be classified according to their apparent communicative purpose. They may either communicate the *structure* of the music or express its *character*. We use the term *character* to refer to either the *emotional* (happy, sad, etc.) or *motional* (urgent, calm, swingy, etc.) implications of the music. Emotional character is dealt with in more detail in chapter 14.

Sundberg (2000) identified two main underlying principles for communicating musical structure. The first involves the *differentiation* of pitch and duration. Categorical perception is improved by increasing the difference between categories, such as stretching the frequencies of scale tones or playing short notes even shorter (e.g., duration contrast, high loud). The second principle involves the *grouping* of notes in phrases, metrical units, or harmonic areas. For example, phrases are often performed with a *diminuendo* at the end. This increases efficiency of the musical communication by introducing redundancy; the phrase boundaries are often recognized even without this cue.

Structure and character are not necessarily independent. Character can be characterized in terms of *how* the structure is communicated. In fact, most of the cues described in chapter 14 for communicating different emotions can be realized by the techniques for structural communication described in this chapter (Bresin & Friberg, 2000; Battel & Fimbianti, 1998).

Applications in Music Pedagogy

As outlined in this chapter, music psychology research has over the past years accumulated a substantial body of knowledge about music performance that could be incorporated into music teaching. Knowledge of the basic principles of structural communication is possibly more important in earlier stages of instrumental learning; once these principles are mastered, both in theory and in performance, it may be easier to develop an individual voice and allow the more interesting development of an artist's individual personality to come to the fore (see Figure 13.7) (Andreas C. Lehmann, personal communication).

Teaching Theory of Structural Communication

Each of the basic principles and techniques described earlier can be explained and discussed in terms of generality and individual differences. Consider phrasing as an example. A teacher might explain how performers introduce small *ritardandi* or *diminuendi* at the end of phrases and increase their extent at the end of sections. This archetypal phrasing is not so easy to hear from just listen-

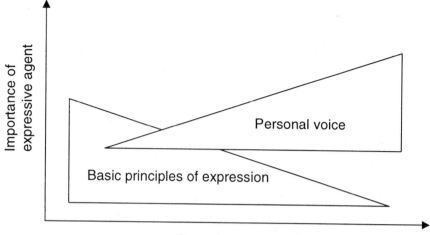

Figure 13.7. Relative importance, at different stages during performance studies, of the basic principles of communicating musical structure and character and the musician's personal voice or individual approach to musical interpretation (adapted from Andreas C. Lehmann, personal communication).

ing to recordings and can come as a surprise, even to musicians. It is also useful to show measurements of performances by well-known musicians such as in Figure 13.3 and 13.4 so that students understand that the same principles are also used in top-level performances. Other aspects of structural communication, such as articulation and timing patterns, can be taught in a similar way.

The use of sound examples generated by computer-based performance models (e.g., www.speech.kth.se/music/performance/) allows each aspect (e.g., phrasing) to be studied and listened to in isolation. Graphs that show the variation of dynamics and timing also help the student to hear and understand what is happening. A computer program such as *Director Musices* (Friberg et al., 2000) allows a teacher to directly apply phrasing rules to any music example, with the flexibility of changing the extent and parameters—all in real time and all in the classroom. Students can then judge for themselves how much variation of timing and dynamics is appropriate for the interpretation of a given phrase. Regardless of their musical training or ability to read notation, students can listen to differences between different renditions of a given passage and learn to focus their auditory attention on one aspect. Thus the suggested pedagogical approach may be useful not only for teaching performance but also for teaching relevant auditory skills.

Performance Studies

Once the theoretical concepts have been explained, the various performance principles could be practiced separately. If musical tension is selected, a student or teacher might first make an analysis of tension–relaxation patterns in a piece and think about different ways in which tension could be appropriately communicated or expressed in a particular performance on a given instrument. Then the student could practice emphasizing the tension–relaxation patterns in different ways (e.g., timing, dynamics). For example, one could, as an exercise, emphasize harmonic tension but otherwise play without expression. This can extend the student's expressive vocabulary and facilitate the creation of different emotions or patterns of implied movement (cf. chapter 14).

The importance of feedback for efficient learning is well known. Using computer analysis tools, the variations of timing and dynamics in students' performances can be measured and shown graphically. This could help students to evaluate, for example, how well their variations of dynamics and timing communicate intended patterns of tension and relaxation. Commercial recordings can also be analyzed in this way, but the methods of analysis and the required software tools depend on which instrument and structural aspect is being studied.

A majority of the principles of structural communication can be studied with just a microphone connected to a computer using commercial or free software. Ensemble timing, such as observing the amount of lead or lag for each performer, can be illustrated in a spectrogram program (e.g., Soundswell, www.hitech.se; Wavesurfer, www.speech.kth.se/wavesurfer). An example was given in Figure 13.6. Illustrations of dynamics and articulation can be obtained by computing a smoothed RMS value of the audio signal, a feature found in several audio wave editors.

Studying interonset timing and local tempo variations is currently a little bit more complicated. Here it is necessary to compute for each note the deviations of IOI relative to the nominal value. The IOIs and durations can be obtained from a MIDI-equipped instrument (e.g., a Disklavier piano from Yamaha, Zeta string instruments, an electric guitar MIDI controller, or an acoustic instrument with an audio-to-MIDI converter) connected to a computer. A program such as POCO (Desain, Honing, & Heijink, 1997; Honing, 1990; stephanus2.socsci.kun.nl/mmm/) can match the values to the score so that deviations are obtained.

Pianists may find an instrument such as the Yamaha Disklavier useful for the study of structural communication. This is essentially an acoustic piano in which the timing and dynamics of each key pressure can be registered on a computer. The computer can also control the instrument so that a recorded performance can be listened to directly on the instrument. The Disklavier has been used regularly by the second author of this chapter in teaching advanced courses in piano performance (Battel et. al., 1998). One such course consisted of two parts: (1) music performance analysis, and (2) analytical methods for performance. The participants played the first 10 bars of Mozart's Sonata K. 333 in B♭ Major on the Disklavier. Variations in dynamics and timing produced by the players were displayed on a computer screen. The data were compared to those of the second author's performance recorded earlier on a Disklavier and to those produced by a performance rule system implemented in MELODIA (Bresin, 1993). Finally, the musical meaning of performance variables in the historical period, style, and performance tradition of the composer was analyzed and discussed.

In summary, recent research on music performance has opened up a range of new possibilities for teaching expression in the sense of structural communication. The development of new software tools for this purpose would further facilitate the use of the computer as a complement in the classroom.

References

Bach, C. P. E. (1753/1957), edited by L. Hoffman-Erbrecht. *Versuch über die wahre Art, das Clavier zu spielen.* Leipzig: Breitkopf & Härtel.

Battel, G. U., Canazza S., Fimbianti, R., & Rodà, A. (1998). III. Modalités de l'expérience. In Gruppo Analisi e Teoria Musicale: Quand une analyse schenkerienne est-elle utile aux interprètes? *Revue Belge de Musicologie 52*, 331–334.

Battel, G. U., & Fimbianti, R. (1998). How to communicate expressive intentions in piano performance. In A. Argentini and C. Mirolo (Eds.), *Proceedings of the XII Colloquium on Musical Informatics* (pp. 67–70). Gorizia: Associazione di Informatica Musicale Italiana.

Bengtsson, I., & Gabrielsson, A. (1983). Analysis and synthesis of musical rhythm. In J. Sundberg (Ed.), *Studies of music performance* (pp. 27–60). Stockholm: Royal Swedish Academy of Music.

Bigand, E., Parncutt, R., & Lerdahl, F. (1996). Perception of musical tension in short chord sequences: The influence of harmonic function, sensory dissonance, horizontal motion, and musical training. *Perception & Psychophysics, 58*(1), 125–141.

Bresin, R. (1993). MELODIA: A program for performance rules testing, teaching, and piano score performance. In G. Havs and I. Pighi (Eds.), *Proceedings of the X Colloquium on Musical Informatics* (pp. 325–327). Milano: Associazione di Informatica Musicale Italiana.

Bresin, R. (2000). *Virtual virtuosity: Studies in automatic music performance.* Unpublished doctoral dissertation, Royal Institute of Technology, Stockholm.

Bresin, R, & Battel, G. U. (2000). Articulation strategies in expressive piano performance. Analysis of legato, staccato, and repeated notes in performances of the Andante movement of Mozart's Sonata in G major (K 545). *Journal of New Music Research, 29*, 211–244.

Bresin, R., & Friberg, A. (2000). Emotional coloring of computer controlled music performance. *Computer Music Journal, 24*(4), 44–62.

Cambouropoulos, E. (1998). *Towards a general computational theory of musical structure.* Doctoral Thesis, Faculty of Music and Department of Artificial Intelligence, University of Edinburgh.

Clarke, E. F. (1988). Generative principles in music performance. In J. A. Sloboda, (Ed.), *Generative processes in music* (pp. 1–26). Oxford: Clarendon Press.

Collier, G. L., & Collier, J. L. (1994). An exploration of the use of tempo in jazz. *Music Perception, 11*(3), 219–242.

De Poli, G., Rodà, A., & Vidolin, A. (1998). Note-by-note analysis of the influence of expressive intentions and musical structure in violin performance. *Journal of New Music Research, 27*(3), 293–321.

Desain, P., Honing, H., & Heijink, H. (1997). Robust score-performance matching: Taking advantage of structural information. In *Proceedings of the 1997 International Computer Music Conference* (pp. 337–340). San Francisco, CA: CMA.

Drake, C., & Palmer, C. (1993). Accent structures in music performance. *Music Perception, 10*, 343–378.

Ellis, M. C. (1991). An analysis of "swing" subdivision and asynchronization in three jazz saxophonists. *Perceptual and Motor Skills, 75*, 707–713.

Friberg, A. (1991). Generative rules for music performance: A formal description of a rule system. *Computer Music Journal, 15*(2), 56–71.

Friberg, A. (1995, May). Matching the rule parameters of Phrase arch to performances of "Träumerei": A preliminary study. In A. Friberg and J. Sundberg (Eds.), *Proceedings of the KTH Symposium on Grammars for Music Performance* (pp. 37–44). Stockholm: Royal Institute of Technology.

Friberg, A., Bresin, R., Frydén, L., & Sundberg, J. (1998). Musical punctuation on the microlevel: Automatic identification and performance of small melodic units. *Journal of New Music Research, 27*(3), 271–292.

Friberg, A., Colombo, V., Frydén, L., & Sundberg, J. (2000). Generating musical performances with Director Musices. *Computer Music Journal, 24*(3), 23–29.

Friberg, A., & Sundberg, J. (1999). Does music performance allude to locomotion? A model of final *ritardandi* derived from measurements of stopping runners. *Journal of the Acoustical Society of America, 105*(3), 1469–1484.

Friberg, A., Sundberg, J., & Frydén, L. (1987). How to terminate a phrase: An analysis-by-synthesis experiment on the perceptual aspect of music performance. In A. Gabrielsson (Ed.), *Action and perception in rhythm and music* (pp. 49–55). Stockholm: Royal Swedish Academy of Music.

Friberg, A., & Sundström, A. (in press). Swing ratios and ensemble timing in jazz performance: Evidence for a common rhythmic pattern. *Music Perception.*

Gabrielsson, A. (1987). Once again: The theme from Mozart's piano sonata in A major (K. 331). A comparison of five performances. In A. Gabrielsson (Ed.), *Action and perception in rhythm and music* (pp. 81–103). Stockholm: Royal Swedish Academy of Music.

Gabrielsson, A. (1999). The performance of music. In D. Deutsch (Ed.), *The psychology of music* (2nd ed.) (pp. 501–602). New York: Academic Press.

Gabrielsson, A., Bengtsson, I., & Gabrielsson, B. (1983). Performance of musical rhythm in $\frac{3}{4}$ and $\frac{6}{8}$ meter. *Scandinavian Journal of Psychology, 24*, 193–213.

Hefling, S., E. (1993). *Rhythmic alteration in seventeenth- and eighteenth-century music:* Notes inégales *and overdotting.* New York: Schirmer.

Henderson, M. T. (1936). Rhythmic organization in artistic piano performance. In C. E. Seashore (Ed.), *Objective analysis of musical performance, University of Iowa Studies in the Psychology of Music*, Vol. 4 (pp. 281–305). Iowa City: University of Iowa Press.

Honing, H. (1990). POCO: An environment for analysing, modifying, and generating expression in music. In *Proceedings of the 1990 International Computer Music Conference* (pp. 364–368). San Francisco, CA: CMA.

Huron, D., & Royal, M. (1996). What is melodic accent? Converging evidence from musical practice. *Music Perception, 13*, 489–516.

Juslin, P., Friberg, A., & Bresin, R. (in press). Toward a computational model of performance expression: The GERM model. *Musicae Scientiae.*

Krumhansl, C. L. (1990). *Cognitive foundations of musical pitch.* New York: Oxford University Press.

Krumhansl, C. L. (1996). A perceptual analysis of Mozart's piano sonata K282: Segmentation, tension, and musical ideas. *Music Perception, 13*, 401–432.

Lerdahl, F. (1996). Calculating tonal tension. *Music Perception, 13*, 319–364.

Lerdahl, F., & Jackendoff, R. (1983). *A generative theory of tonal music.* Cambridge, MA: MIT Press.

Palmer, C. (1996a). Anatomy of a performance: Sources of musical expression. *Music Perception, 13*(3), 433–453.

Palmer, C. (1996b). On the assignment of structure in music performance. *Music Perception, 14*(1), 23–56.

Palmer, C. (1997). Music performance. *Annual Review of Psychology, 48*, 115–138.

Parncutt, R. (in press). Accents and expression in piano performance. *Systemische Musikwissenschaft. Festschrift Jobst P. Fricke zum 65. Geburtsdag.* Frankfurt: Peter Lang.

Penel, A., & Drake, C. (1998). Sources of timing variations in music performance: A psychological segmentation model. *Psychological Research, 61*, 12–32.

Rasch, R. A. (1978). The perception of simultaneous notes such as in polyphonic music. *Acustica, 40*, 21–33.

Rasch, R. A. (1979). Synchronization in performed ensemble music. *Acustica, 43*, 121–131.

Repp, B. H. (1990). Patterns of expressive timing in performances of a Beethoven minuet by nineteen famous pianists. *Journal of the Acoustical Society of America, 88*(2), 622–641.

Repp, B. H. (1992). Diversity and commonality in music performance: An analysis of timing microstructure in Schumann's "Träumerei." *Journal of the Acoustical Society of America, 92*(5), 2546–2568.

Repp, B. H. (1995). Quantitative effects of global tempo on expressive timing in music performance: Some perceptual evidence. *Music Perception, 13*(1), 39–57.

Repp, B. H. (1997). Acoustics, perception, and production of legato articulation on a computer-controlled grand piano. *Journal of the Acoustical Society of America, 102*(3), 1878–1890.

Repp, B. H. (1998a). The detectability of local deviations from a typical expressive timing pattern. *Music Perception, 15*(3), 265–289.

Repp, B. H. (1998b). A microcosm of musical expression: I. Quantitative analysis of pianists' timing in the initial measures of Chopin's Etude in E major. *Journal of the Acoustical Society of America, 104*, 1085–1100.

Shove, P., & Repp, B. H. (1995). Musical motion and performance: Theoretical and empirical perspectives. In J. Rink (Ed.), *The practice of performance: Studies in musical interpretation* (pp. 55–83). Cambridge: Cambridge University Press.

Sundberg, J. (2000). Grouping and differentiation. Two main principles in the performance of music. In T. Nakada (Ed.), *Integrated human brain science: Theory, method application (music)* (pp. 299–314). Amsterdam: Elsevier.

Sundberg, J., Friberg, A., & Frydén, L. (1991). Common secrets of musicians and listeners—an analysis-by-synthesis study of musical performance. In P. Howell, R. West, and I. Cross (Eds.), *Representing musical structure* (pp. 161–197). London: Academic Press.

Taguti, T., Mori, S., & Suga, S. (1994). Stepwise change in the physical speed of music rendered in tempo. In I. Deliège (Ed.), *Proceedings of the 3rd International Conference on Music Perception and Cognition, Liège* (pp. 341–342). Liège, Belgium: ESCOM.

Thomassen, M. T. (1982). Melodic accent: Experiments and a tentative model. *Journal of the Acoustical Society of America, 71*, 1596–1605.

Todd, N. P. McA. (1985). A model of expressive timing in tonal music. *Music Perception, 3*, 33–58.

Todd, N. P. McA. (1989). A computational model of rubato. *Contemporary Music Review, 3*, 69–88.

Todd, N. P. McA. (1992). The dynamics of dynamics: A model of musical expression. *Journal of the Acoustical Society of America, 91*(6), 3540–3550.

Todd, N. P. McA. (1995). The kinematics of musical expression. *Journal of the Acoustical Society of America, 97*(3), 1940–1949.

Vernon, L. N. (1936). Synchronization of chords in artistic piano music. In C. E. Seashore (Ed.), *Objective analysis of musical performance, University of Iowa Studies in the Psychology of Music*, Vol. 4 (pp 306–345). Iowa City: University of Iowa Press.

Windsor, W. L., and Clarke, E. F. (1997). Expressive timing and dynamics in real and artificial musical performances: Using an algorithm as an analytical tool. *Music Perception, 15*(2), 127–152.

14

Emotional Communication

PATRIK N. JUSLIN & ROLAND S. PERSSON

To communicate specific emotions to listeners, performers simultaneously manipulate a range of musical parameters. The research findings on emotional expression in music may be organized according to a theoretical framework that describes the communicative process in terms of E. Brunswik's (1956) *lens model*. We discuss traditional strategies for teaching expression including the use of metaphors, aural modeling, and felt emotion and conclude that these strategies rarely provide informative feedback to the performer. A new, empirically based approach to teaching expression called *cognitive feedback* is outlined and its efficacy evaluated. The goal is to provide performers with the tools they need to develop their own personal expression.

With regard to musical performances, experience has shown that the imagination of the hearer is in general so much at the disposal of the [performer] that by help of variation, intervals, and modulation he may stamp what impression on the mind he pleases.

Francesco Geminiani, cited in Meyer,
Emotion and Meaning in Music

Of all the subskills that make up music performance, the ones associated with emotional communication are often viewed as the most elusive. They go right to the core of why people engage in musical behavior, either as performers or as listeners. The performance of a piece of music is crucial in shaping its emotional expression. Thus the emotional impact of particularly expressive performers—for example, C. P. E. Bach, Niccolò Paganini, and Jimi Hendrix—has always been a source of great fascination. What is the origin of their expressiveness? How is it achieved?

It should be noted at the outset that there are different uses of the word *expression* in the literature. In studies of music performance, *expression* has been used to refer to the systematic variations in timing, dynamics, timbre, and pitch that form the *microstructure* of a performance and differentiate it from another performance of the same music (Palmer, 1997; chapter 13 in this volume). The word *expression* has also been used to refer to the *emotional* qualities of music as perceived by listeners (Davies, 1994). These two senses of the word are of course related in that performers use systematic variations in performance parameters to convey emotions to listeners.

Much has been written about expression in music—far more than we can hope to cover in this chapter. A review of the literature, from antiquity to modern times, reveals a variety of ideas about what music is able to express: emotion, beauty, motion, expressive form, energy, tension, events, religious faith, personal identity, and social conditions. In this chapter, we have chosen for pragmatic reasons to focus on expression of emotion and also limit our review to psychological research. One final limitation reflects the focus of this volume: while not wishing to deny the crucial role of the composer, we shall focus on how the *performer* contributes to emotional expression in music. (For a discussion of the composer, see Juslin & Sloboda, 2001, section 3.)

Questions about music and emotion have occupied humans ever since antiquity. The ancient Greeks argued that specific musical features are associated with specific emotions. This notion received its most precise formulation in the *doctrine of the affections* during the seventeenth and eighteenth centuries (cf. Mattheson, 1739/1954). Since then, conceptions of musical emotions have changed, throughout history, along with changing conceptions of emotions in general (e.g., eighteenth-century affect as a rationalized emotional state in contrast to nineteenth-century emotion as personal and spontaneous expression, see Cook & Dibben, 2001). Influential modern theories of music and emotion include Langer (1942), Meyer (1956), Cooke (1959), and Clynes (1977). Empirical research on emotional expression in music has been conducted for a century, including the pioneering studies by Hevner (1936). This work explored the expressive properties of various musical features, such as pitch or mode (for a review, see Gabrielsson & Juslin, in press). From this research we have learned much about how different aspects of a musical composition may influence emotional expression but less about how different aspects of a *performance* may influence expression.

Few studies have investigated how performers conceptualize and assign meaning to a piece of music while preparing it for performance. However, both empirical research (e.g., Persson, 1993; Woody, 2000) and biographical accounts (e.g., Blum 1977; Menuhin, 1996; Schumacher, 1995) confirm that performers often conceive of performance in terms of emotions and moods. Many performers consider expressivity to be one of the most important aspects of performance (Boyd & George-Warren, 1992; Persson, 1993).

Despite the strong emphasis on expressiveness among musicians, a number of studies suggest that expressive aspects of performance are neglected in music education. Specifically, teachers tend to spend much more time and effort on technical aspects than on expressive or aesthetic aspects (Persson, 1993; Tait, 1992). As a result, students may come to focus on expressive aspects fairly late in their artistic development (Woody, 2000). Critics often complain that young musicians acquire a high technical skill without being able to induce an emotional experience in the listener (e.g., Dubal, 1985). Consequently, music educators have been encouraged to devote more attention to emotion and expression in music (Reimer, 1989). Such a change of emphasis should lead to an increased concern with the actual strategies used to teach expressive skills of music performance. Teaching strategies form the *how* of music teaching; they involve vocabulary usage, various forms of modeling, and management procedures (Tait, 1992).

The objective of this chapter is to illustrate how psychological research on emotional communication in music performance might contribute to the development of more efficient teaching strategies aimed at the expressive aspects of performance. First, we summarize relevant research. Then, we describe a framework for organizing the findings. Finally, we consider how theory and research on expression might inform day-to-day teaching practice.

Research on Emotional Expression in Performance

Performers and listeners often discuss and compare musical performances in terms of their expressive aspects, and there are many treatises on performance practices that can be used to enhance emotional expressivity (e.g., Hudson, 1994). Therefore, it may come as a surprise that it is only recently that researchers have began to study this phenomenon. This may reflect the dominant influence of cognitive science in psychology in general and music psychology in particular, which has led to a focus on cognitive aspects of performance, such as structural representation (for a review, see Gabrielsson, 1999). However, renewed interest in emotion has led to increased interest in musical emotion also (Juslin & Sloboda, 2001), even in performance research.

Emotions are difficult to define and measure. Yet most researchers would probably agree that emotions consist of many components: cognitive appraisal, subjective feeling, physiology, expression, and action tendency (Oatley & Jenkins, 1996). For example, we may appraise an event as harmful that evokes feelings of fear and physiological reactions in our body; we may express this fear verbally or nonverbally and may also act in certain ways (e.g., running away) rather than others. There are two major approaches to conceptualizing emotions. According to the *categorical* approach, people experience emotions as categories that are distinct from one another (Ekman, 1992). The categorical approach thus focuses on the characteristics that distinguish emotions from one another. In contrast, the *dimensional* approach focuses on identifying emotions based on their placement on a small number of dimensions like *valence* (positive/negative) and *activation* (high/low) (Russell, 1980).

What is emotional communication? We reserve this term for situations where the performer intends to communicate an emotion to the listener. Accurate communication takes place to the extent that the performer's expressive intention is understood by the listener. This approach implies that expression and recognition of emotions should be studied in an integrated fashion. Accordingly, most studies in the domain have used the following procedure: The performer is asked to play a piece of music to express various emotions (e.g., sadness) chosen by the investigator. The performances are first recorded and later analyzed according to their acoustic characteristics. The performances are also judged by listeners to see whether they perceive the expression in accordance with the performer's intention. Thus, the focus in this research is on *perception* (rather than induction) of emotion.

Accuracy

The first question to face any researcher concerned with emotional communication in music is whether such communication is possible at all. In a pioneering study, Kotlyar and Morozov (1976) asked 10 opera singers to sing phrases from various pieces of music in such a way that they would communicate joy, anger, sorrow, and fear to listeners. Results show that the 10 musically trained listeners who judged the emotional expression of each performance were consistently successful at recognizing the intended expressions. Since then, several studies have confirmed that professional musicians are able to communicate emotions to listeners (Behrens & Green, 1993; Gabrielsson & Juslin, 1996; Juslin, 1997b, 2000; Juslin & Madison, 1999; Sundberg, Iwarsson, & Hagegård, 1995), but that there are considerable individual differences in expressive skill.

Few studies have reported the results in a manner that makes more precise estimates of communication accuracy possible. Juslin (1997c) used a forced-choice format to enable comparison with the results reported in studies of vocal expression of emotion. He found that the communication accuracy was 75% correct—about four times more accurate than would be expected by chance alone. This suggests—at least under ideal circumstances—that the accuracy of communication of emotion in music performance may approach the accuracy of facial and vocal expression (Johnstone & Scherer, 2000). Furthermore, the communicative process seems to be reliable regardless of the particular response format used to collect listeners' judgments (Juslin, 1997a).

Code Usage

A number of studies have attempted to describe the *code* (i.e., the acoustic means) that performers use to communicate emotions to listeners (Gabrielsson & Juslin, 1996; Juslin, 1997b; 2000; Juslin & Madison, 1999; Rapoport, 1996). One of the main findings is that the performer's expressive intention affects almost every aspect of the performance; that is, emotional expression in performance involves a sizable array of *cues* (i.e., pieces of information) that are used by performers and listeners. A summary of the code usage established in investigations so far is shown in Table 14.1. Included are the five emotions—happiness, sadness, anger, fear, tenderness—that have been studied most extensively. These emotions represent a natural point of departure because all are regarded as typical emotions by laypeople (Shields, 1984) and as *basic emotions* (i.e., innate and universal emotions) by scientists (Plutchik, 1994). The same emotions also appear occasionally as expression marks in musical scores (e.g., *festoso, dolente, furioso, timoroso, teneramente*).

The expressive cues shown in Table 14.1 include tempo, sound level, timing, intonation, articulation, timbre, vibrato, tone attacks, tone decays, and pauses. Both the mean level of a cue and its variability throughout the performance may be important for the expression. For example, sadness is associated with slow tempo, low sound level, *legato* articulation, small articulation vari-

Table 14.1. Cue utilization in communication of emotions (based on material presented in Juslin, 2001).

Emotion	Cue Utilization	Activity, Valence
Happiness	fast tempo, small tempo variability, *staccato* articulation, large articulation variability, high sound level, bright timbre, fast tone attacks, small timing variations, increased durational contrasts between long and short notes, rising microintonation, small vibrato extent	high, positive
Sadness	very slow tempo, *legato* articulation, small articulation variability, low sound level, dull timbre, large timing variations, reduced durational contrasts between long and short notes, slow tone attacks, flat or falling microintonation, slow vibrato, final *ritardando*, phrase *decelerando*	low, negative
Anger	high sound level, sharp timbre, spectral noise, fast tempo, *staccato* articulation, abrupt tone attacks, increased durational contrasts between long and short notes, no *ritardando*, sudden accents, accents on tonally unstable notes, *crescendo*, phrase *accelerando*, large vibrato extent	high, negative
Tenderness	slow tempo, slow tone attacks, low sound level, small sound-level variability, *legato* articulation, soft timbre, moderate timing variations, intense vibrato, reduced durational contrasts between long and short notes, final *ritardando*, accents on stable notes	low, positive
Fear	*staccato* articulation, very low sound level, large sound-level variability, fast tempo, large tempo variability, very large timing variations, bright spectrum, fast, shallow, irregular vibrato, pauses between phrases, sudden syncopations	moderate, negative

Note: This is a simplified description of the relationships established in studies of performers' and listeners' cue utilization in expression of emotion via music performance. For information about the precise definition and measurement of each cue, see Juslin (1999). The rightmost column shows each emotion's position on two emotion dimensions: *activity* (high vs. low) and *valence* (positive vs. negative) (e.g., Plutchik, 1994, chapter 3).

ability, slow tone attacks, and soft timbre (for a detailed review, see Juslin, 1999). Also, different tones in the melodic structure may be emphasized depending on which emotion the performer intends to express (Lindström, 1999). It is possible to simulate emotional expression in synthesized performances based on the findings in the table in such a way that listeners can accurately decode the intended emotion (Juslin, 1997c; Bresin & Friberg, 2000).

While Table 14.1 is limited to a few emotion categories, one can easily imagine how these categories may be combined or mixed in different ways and also how emotional expression may be altered during a performance (Juslin, 2001). Some of the cues shown in the table may be common knowledge to most performers, whereas other cues (e.g., those that have to do with the microstructure of the performance) are less obvious. The number of cues available, of course, depends on the instrument used. Furthermore, cue utilization is not completely consistent across performers, instruments, or pieces of music (Juslin, 2000).

Most studies in the field so far have focused on cues that are applied in much the same way and to much the same extent throughout a piece. However, it would seem intuitively that much of music's expressiveness lies in the way cue use changes during the course of the performance. Indeed, there seem to exist certain *expressive contours* (i.e., patterns of changes in tempo and dynamics) that are characteristic of specific emotions. Listening tests that employed systematic manipulations of synthesized (Juslin, 1997c) or real performances (Juslin & Madison, 1999) have shown that expressive contours can be used by a listener to decode emotional expression.

Performer Insight

An important question is whether music performers have any insight regarding their own cue utilization. It seems generally agreed that performers are usually not aware of the details of how their musical intentions are realized in performance (Sloboda, 1996). In the case of emotional communication, performers are not normally conscious of how they use the cues listed in Table 14.1 (Juslin & Laukka, 2000).

However, there are large individual differences among performers in this regard. Some performers seem to imagine themselves being in the emotional state that their performance is intended to express and just let things happen (Juslin & Laukka, 2000; Persson, 2001). For example, the Russian violist Yuri Bashmet commented, "Identify with the emotions and the notes—fearful as they are—will look after themselves" (Seckerson, 1991, p. 26). Other performers take a more analytical approach, explicitly pondering how to vary different cues. But to the extent that cues are used *implicitly*, this presents a problem for the teaching of expression, which relies predominately on verbal instruction (Tait, 1992; Woody, 2000).

A Theoretical Framework

One reason for the neglect of emotion in both performance research and music education may be the lack of relevant theories. In the following, we describe the only elaborated theoretical framework aimed specifically at emotional communication via performance, namely, the *functionalist perspective* (Juslin, 1997b; 2001).

Origin of the Code

Music performers are able to communicate emotions to listeners. What is it that makes this communication possible? Or, more specifically, what is the origin of the acoustical code used by performers? Arguably, the code reflects contributions from both nature and nurture.

Regarding nature, there is evidence for *innate brain programs* for vocal expression of emotion. Studies of the neurological substrates that underlie spontaneous vocalizations of emotion in monkeys and humans with brain lesions provide evidence of brain circuits that function to initiate innate affect vocalizations (Jürgens, 1992). We hypothesize that music performers communicate emotions to listeners by using the same acoustic code as is used in vocal expression. This hypothesis is supported by similarities in cue utilization between music performance and vocal expression (Juslin, 1999). For example, vocal expression of sadness involves slow speech rate, low voice intensity, and little high-frequency energy in the spectrum of the voice. Similar acoustic cues are used to express sadness in music performance (Table 14.1). Cross-cultural studies of vocal expression (Johnstone & Scherer, 2000) and music performance (Juslin, 2001) show that there are cross-cultural similarities. Thus there seems to exist an innate code for acoustical communication of emotion, which could explain why emotional expression is often regarded by music teachers as instinctive. If musicians are to apply this innate code to their performance, they need to understand the parallels between human voices and musical instruments and to learn sufficient technique to express emotions in accordance with the vocal code.

The second factor that governs emotional expression in performance is social learning or specific memories. This is a lifelong process that begins with the early interaction between mother and infant. When mothers talk to their infants, for example, if they want to calm their infant, they reduce the speed and intensity of their speech and talk with slowly falling pitch contours. If mothers want to express disapproval toward some unfavorable activity they employ brief, sharp, and *staccato*-like contours (Papoušek, 1996). Although the code used by mothers seems to be innate, the particular expressive style of the mother modulates the expressive style of the infant. This modulation of the expressive skills continues throughout life as one accumulates experience. Performers learn links between cues and extramusical aspects (e.g., motion, body language) through analogies (Persson, 1993; Sloboda, 1996; see also chapter 15 in this volume), which implies that extramusical life experiences are crucial in learning expressivity in performance (Woody, 2000).

Description of the Code

One way of capturing the crucial characteristics of the communicative process is to conceptualize it in terms of a variant of Brunswik's (1956) lens model. The lens model was originally intended as a model of visual perception that described the relationship between an organism and distal cues. However, it was later used mainly in studies of human judgment where the goal was to relate the judge's judgment strategy to a description of the judgment task (Cooksey, 1996).

The modified lens model (Figure 14.1) illustrates how performers *encode* (i.e., express) emotions by means of a set of cues (e.g., variations of tempo, sound level, and timbre) that are *probabilistic* (i.e., uncertain) and partly *redundant*. The emotions are *decoded* (i.e., recognized) by listeners who use these same cues to infer the expression. The cues are probabilistic in that they are not perfectly reliable indicators of the intended expression. Performers and listeners have to *combine* the cues for reliable communication to occur. However, this is not simply a matter of pattern matching, because the cues contribute in an additive fashion to listeners' judgments: Each cue is neither necessary nor sufficient, but the larger the number of cues used, the more reliable the communication. The redundancy among cues partly reflects how sounds are produced on instruments (e.g., a harder string attack produces a tone that is both louder and sharper in timbre).

In Figure 14.1, *accuracy* refers to the correlation between the performer's intention and the listener's judgment. *Matching* refers to the degree of similarity between the performer's and the listener's cue utilization, respectively. For

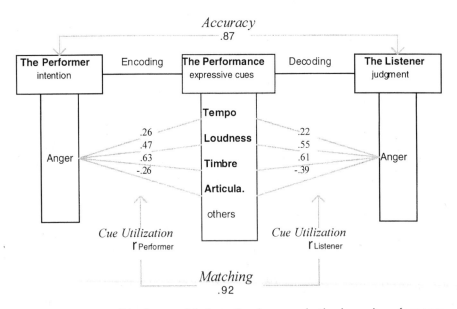

Figure 14.1. A Brunswikian lens model of emotional communication in music performance (adapted from Juslin, 1997b). The cue weights should be interpreted as follows: Positive (as opposed to negative) signs indicate, respectively for each cue, fast (vs. slow) mean tempo, high (vs. low) sound level, sharp (vs. soft) timbre, and *legato* (vs. *staccato*) articulation (for details regarding methodology, see Juslin, 2000).

successful communication to occur, the performer's cue utilization must be as similar as possible to the listener's cue utilization. For illustrative purposes, unpublished data have been inserted into Figure 14.1. As can be seen, there is a high correlation between intention and judgment, which means that the performer was successful in communicating anger to the listener. This is explained by the high level of matching between the performer's and the listener's cue utilization.

Brunswik's lens model has a number of important implications. First, we cannot expect perfect accuracy of communication. If cues are only probabilistic, that means that accuracy can only be probabilistic, too. Second, to understand why the communication is successful or not in a particular situation we have to describe both expression and recognition in terms of the same concepts. Third, because the cues are partly redundant, many different cue utilization strategies may lead to the same level of accuracy (Juslin, 2000). There is a virtue associated with this redundancy. Because there is no pressure toward uniformity in cue utilization, performers can communicate successfully with listeners without compromising their unique playing styles.

Applications in Music Education

Can Emotional Expression Be Learned?

Expertise in music performance is commonly seen as the synthesis of technical and expressive skills (chapter 7). However, technical aspects of playing are often regarded as learnable skills, whereas expressive aspects are regarded as being more instinctive. Many teachers view expression as something that cannot be taught—a view that is sometimes shared by their students: "There is no technique to perform expressively. You have to use your soul" (cited in Woody, 2000, p. 21).

This view probably stems from certain myths about artistic expression. One such myth is that expression is entirely subjective and passive in its genesis and has nothing to do with understanding (Howard, 1989). In this view, consistent with the romantic notion of art and artists as a kind of mystery, expression is seen as a hands-off affair that is best left alone. Hence, expression is wrongly believed to reflect a divine endowment—or talent—beyond learning and development (cf. Sloboda, 1996).

Although we often think of artistic expression in terms of individual talent, the criteria for what is regarded as high art ultimately reflect social construction. Nowhere is this more apparent than in an educational setting (Kingsbury, 1988). Part of the problem the music teacher faces resides in the tension between the subjective world of individual performers and the social and objective requirements of the educational setting. Hence, an important goal of any teaching strategy aimed at developing expressive skills should be to *relate* the subjective world of the performer (e.g., imagery, metaphor, emotion) to objective features of performance (e.g., articulation).

Emotional expressiveness in music is sometimes hard to describe in words, making it somewhat elusive to both research and teaching practice. Furthermore, it is probably true that expressive skills to some extent reflect the emotional sensitivity of the performer. But this does not imply that it is impossible to learn expressive skills through training. Studies that have addressed this issue have demonstrated that expressive skills *can* be improved by training (Marchand, 1975; Juslin & Laukka, 2000; Woody, 1999).

The idea that the learning of musical expression is best left untouched by conscious thought reflects a misunderstanding that pervades commonsense teaching (i.e., teaching that relies not on empirically derived models and knowledge but rather on tradition and folklore) and is typical of master performers who may never have received training on how to teach musicians (Persson, 1996). It is not realized that goal-directed strategies that initially are willfully applied normally undergo *automation* as a result of practice (Hallam, 1997). That is, although a performer may initially have to use cues in a conscious manner, soon the associations among cues and emotions become internalized by the performer and no longer require conscious control.

Traditional Strategies for Teaching Expression

Aural Modeling. Perhaps the most frequently used tool in conveying to students how something should be played is aural modeling. The teacher's performance provides a model of what is desired from the student, and the student is usually required to learn by imitating the teacher. Such strategies are usually achieved on the instrument or using the voice (e.g., singing a certain phrase). Although modeling is useful, it has some limitations. One is that the student is required to pick up the relevant aspects of the model. It may be difficult for a student to know what to listen for and how to represent it in terms of specific skills (Lehmann, 1997). Davidson and Scripp (1992) note that masterful performances are so compact and seamless that it is difficult to observe the subskills that support a fluent production.

Experiential Strategies. There are, however, a number of experiential teaching strategies also, which instead aim at conveying the subjective aspects of performing to a student. One such strategy is the use of *metaphors* to focus the emotional qualities of the performance by creating an emotional state within the performer (Davidson & Scripp, 1992). A teacher may, for example, say: "Well, I don't think the lover and his lass had much fun, do you? If a young girl and her boy go into the cornfields, they have other things in mind than playing cards surely!" (comment to a student singing Finzi's "It was a Lover and His Lass," in Persson, 1993, p. 328). Or a teacher may say: "Strange ... myths ... ghosts ... dragons ... eerie ... the unknown ... spine-chilling ... a drama ... Weber was an opera composer!" (comment to a student playing an instrumental piece by C. M. Weber, in Persson, 1993, p. 328). Although metaphors can be effective (Kohut, 1985), there are some problems with them. One problem is that metaphors depend on the performer's personal experience with words and images. Since different performers have different experiences, metaphors are often ambiguous.

Another teaching strategy endorsed by some teachers is to focus on the performer's *felt emotions*, trusting that these emotions will naturally translate into appropriate sound properties (Woody, 2000). Felt emotion, however, is no guarantee that the emotion will be successfully conveyed to listeners; nor is it necessary to feel the emotion in order to communicate successfully. As observed by Sloboda (1996), students rarely monitor the expressive outcomes of their own performances. Instead, they monitor their own intentions and "take the intention for the deed" (p. 121).

The Problem of Feedback.   Based on an extensive review of a century of research on skill acquisition, Ericsson, Krampe, and Tesch-Römer (1993) proposed three elements that are required in a learning task for it to qualify as *deliberate practice*: (1) clear task definition (2) informative feedback, and (3) opportunities for repetition and correction of errors. Our view is that traditional strategies for teaching expression are problematic mainly in that they do not provide informative feedback to the performer.

Technically, feedback can be defined as "the process by which an environment returns to individuals a portion of the information in their response output necessary to compare their present strategy with a representation of an ideal strategy" (Balzer, Doherty, & O'Connor, 1989, p. 412). It follows from this definition that many kinds of responses that teachers give their students (e.g., "put some expression into it!") do not actually constitute feedback. Thus we agree with Tait's (1992) astute conclusion that "teaching strategies need to become more specific in terms of tasks and feedback" (p. 532). Teachers need a pedagogical model that can guide the development of expressivity and emphasize its significance for successful communication with an audience.

Alternative Approaches to Teaching Emotional Communication

Teaching Theory of Emotional Communication.   One fairly straightforward way of taking advantage of performance research would be to teach the code description shown in Table 14.1. This description could be used as a springboard for exploring different interpretations and reflecting on what makes for a stunning or lackluster performance of a specific piece of music. The value of reflection and adoption of multiple stances toward a piece of art is often emphasized. True enough, simple application of the expressive principles in Table 14.1 may not result in living expression, but these principles can serve as the core from which subtler interpretations are developed with knowledge about the particular instrument, piece, style, and composer.

We believe that the ultimate goal should be to provide performers with the tools they need to develop their own personal expression. The performer may wish the interpretation of a given piece to be clear or ambiguous, stable or variable, specific or general, depending on the composition. Knowledge about the relationships between expressive cues and their emotional effects will help performers to reliably achieve desired listener responses. As in the visual arts, a performer may need to know the underlying principles and conventions in order to know how to vary them in an aesthetically pleasing manner.

Theory of emotional communication could usefully be taught to music students, based on the framework discussed earlier. A deeper understanding of the communicative process may be beneficial for the learning process. Rabinowitz (1988) argues that "knowledge about the how, where, and why of strategy use [is] important if students are to take control of their cognitive processing" (p. 234). Such knowledge about expressive skills makes it more likely that students retain the new knowledge and are able to apply it to new situations.

Cognitive Feedback.   Recall that emotional communication in music performance involves a number of acoustic cues that are used by both performers and listeners. Both expression and recognition of emotions are made by *integrating* these cues. Such integration requires knowledge about the relationships among performers, cues, and listeners. The notion of *cognitive feedback* (hereafter, *CFB*) is to allow the performer to compare a model of his or her cue utilization to an *optimal* model of cue utilization. This is, of course, a fundamental feature of feedback as such. However, how this is achieved is crucial. CFB was originally developed in studies of cognitive judgment (Cooksey, 1996). To illustrate how CFB works in a musical context, we summarize a study that evaluated the efficacy of the CFB strategy (for details, see Juslin & Laukka, 2000).

In the first phase of the study, eight amateur guitarists were asked to play a piece of music in such a way that they would communicate four different emotions to listeners. Their performances were recorded and analyzed in terms of acoustic characteristics. Listeners also rated each performance on scales that corresponded to the intended emotions. Then statistical analysis was used to model the relationships between (1) performers' intentions and cues and (2) cues and listeners' judgments. Finally, the performer and listener models were quantitatively related to each other (by means of the lens model equation; Cooksey, 1996). This made it possible to directly *compare* how performers and listeners used the cues in the performances (cf. Figure 14.1).

In the second phase of the study, half of the performers returned to the laboratory to receive CFB. This consisted of a description of the performer's cue utilization, the listeners' cue utilization, and the degree of matching between performer and listeners. Instances of mismatching between performer and listeners were explained to individual performers. For example, a performer would be told that "you used *staccato* articulation in your sadness expressions, but the listeners associated *legato* articulation with sadness. You should therefore try to play your sadness expressions with more *legato* articulation." In other words, the performers were given specific directions on how to alter their cue utilization to make it more similar to the listeners' cue utilization. The other half of the performers acted as control group and did not receive any feedback.

In the final phase, all performers returned to the laboratory to repeat the first task once more. That is, they were once again asked to perform a piece of music to communicate emotions to listeners. The goal was to see whether the performers who had received CFB had improved their communication accuracy more than the control group. Two kinds of criteria were used to evaluate the efficacy of CFB: (1) behavioral criteria (did CFB improve the performers' accuracy?) and (2) reaction criteria (how did the performers react to CFB?).

Figure 14.2 shows the results. As can be seen, *before* feedback there was no significant difference in accuracy between the groups. However, *after* feedback there was a significant difference in accuracy. CFB yielded about a 50% increase in accuracy after a single session. Furthermore, the performers reacted positively to the CFB and believed that it had really improved their skills. In contrast, the control group did *not* improve its accuracy, suggesting that simple task repetition leads to little improvement in this context. Improvement requires informative feedback.

There is often disagreement about whether teachers' instructions should address sound properties of the performance or experiential concepts. CFB resolves this problem because it *relates* the acoustical vocabulary to the experiential vocabulary. When using CFB, one is consensually establishing the extent to which a performance is successful in communicating a certain emotion, rather than relying on the judgment of a single person. The teacher's advice is provided automatically, as it were, from the statistical analysis of the communicative process. The analysis renders transparent much of the previously opaque process of communication—in particular, the combined and unique effects of the acoustic cues. Those effects are extremely difficult for a listener or performer to infer.

Applications of Cognitive Feedback

Among the benefits of CFB are that (1) its efficacy has been empirically demonstrated, (2) it is not subject to the changing ideals of individual teachers, and (3) it is consistent with empirically confirmed features of deliberate practice. Among the drawbacks of CFB—in the form described—are that CFB is complicated and time-consuming to carry out and requires special equipment for acoustic analyses. With both benefits and drawbacks in mind, there are various ways, present and future, of implementing CFB in teaching practice.

CFB as Computer-Assisted Teaching.   Applications of computer feedback for music performance have been around for some time, concerning, for instance, piano technique and intonation in singing (Hallam, 1997). However, none of the applications concern the expressive aspects of performance. Through the use of algorithms for automatic analysis of acoustic cues in performances and statistical models that simulate emotion judgments of various listener populations, CFB could be applied in teaching more swiftly. User-friendly software for this purpose is currently being developed in a research project at the Uppsala University led by the first author of this chapter. Computer-assisted teaching could serve as a complement to traditional teaching, allowing performers to experiment freely with interpretive ideas.

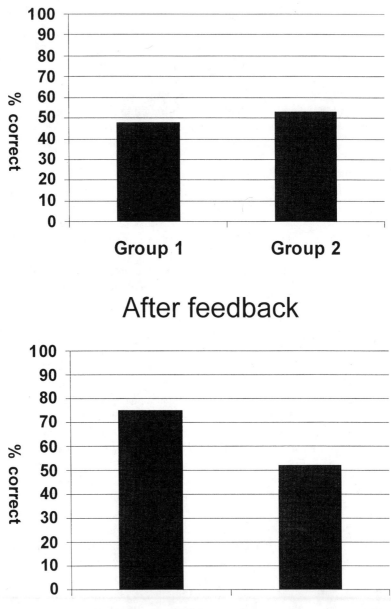

Before feedback

% correct

Group 1   Group 2

After feedback

% correct

Group 1 (CFB)   Group 2 (control)

Figure 14.2. Between-subjects comparisons of communication accuracy (% correct) for Group 1 (cognitive feedback, CFB) and Group 2 (control) before and after feedback (from Juslin & Laukka, 2000).

CFB in a Noncomputerized Setting. Prior to the production of appropriate software, the CFB strategy can still serve as a pedagogical tool, although without the exact and objective feedback provided by computer-assisted procedures. No statistics or computer programs are required when simply asking a group of students to perform a certain piece of music with the intention of communicating a number of emotions to a group of listening students, and then asking the listeners how they perceived the different performances. A discussion could follow that highlights the possible reasons that some performers seemed more successful in conveying their intentions than others using the cue utilization list (Table 14.1). The purpose of this exercise could be to make students *aware* of the many possibilities of expressiveness.

Toward an Integration of Technique and Expression

The world of Western art music, in particular, has tended to preserve what Renshaw (1986) terms a "museum culture," which has prompted many educators to focus on the technical aspects of performance. But it is likely that uncovering the nature and function of expression by research will help to restore the balance between technique and expression. However, we must not forget that expression is also a matter of learnable technique. Some of the differences among individuals in expressive ability reflect technical differences, but it is technique that allows artistic flexibility and is not likely to alienate the performer from the subjective experience of the music studied and performed.

In this chapter, we have not only presented possible teaching strategies in relation to developing expressive skills, but we have also endeavored to show that science and arts are neither opposites nor contradictory. However, in regard to finding specific applications of cognitive feedback, further research is needed. We therefore propose that qualitative studies of the subjective world of performers and quantitative studies of the communicative process should be pursued in combination. To achieve this, psychologists, educators, and musicians will need to work in close collaboration. This book may itself contribute to this very goal.

Acknowledgment. The writing of this chapter was supported by the Bank of Sweden Tercentenary Foundation.

References

Balzer, W. K., Doherty, M. E., & O'Connor, R. (1989). Effects of cognitive feedback on performance. *Psychological Bulletin, 106,* 410–433.

Behrens , G. A., & Green, S. B. (1993). The ability to identify emotional content of solo improvisations performed vocally and on three different instruments. *Psychology of Music, 21,* 20–33.

Blum, D. (1977). *Casals and the art of interpretation.* Berkeley: University of California Press.

Boyd, J., & George-Warren, H. (1992). *Musicians in tune: Seventy-five contemporary musicians discuss the creative process.* New York: Fireside.

Bresin, R., & Friberg, A. (2000). Emotional coloring of computer-controlled music performance. *Computer Music Journal, 24*(4), 44–62.

Brunswik, E. (1956). *Perception and the representative design of psychological experiments.* Berkeley: University of California Press.

Clynes, M. (1977). *Sentics: The touch of emotions.* New York: Anchor/Doubleday.

Cook, N., & Dibben, N. (2001). Musicological approaches to emotion. In P. N. Juslin & J. A. Sloboda (Eds.), *Music and emotion: Theory and research* (pp. 45–70). New York: Oxford University Press.

Cooke, D. (1959). *The language of music.* London: Oxford University Press.

Cooksey, R. W. (1996). *Judgment analysis.* New York: Academic Press.

Davidson, L., & Scripp, L. (1992). Surveying the coordinates of cognitive skills in music. In R. Colwell (Ed.), *Handbook of research on music teaching and learning* (pp. 392–413). New York: Schirmer.

Davies, S. (1994). *Musical meaning and expression.* Ithaca: Cornell University Press.

Dubal, D. (1985). *The world of the concert pianist: Conversations with 35 internationally celebrated pianists.* London: Victor Gollancz.

Ekman, P. (1992). An argument for basic emotions. *Cognition and Emotion, 6,* 169–200.

Ericsson, K. A., Krampe, R. T., & Tesch-Römer, C. (1993). The role of deliberate practice in the acquisition of expert performance. *Psychological Review, 100*(3), 363–406.

Gabrielsson, A. (1999). The performance of music. In D. Deutsch (Ed.), *The psychology of music* (2nd ed.) (pp. 501–602). San Diego, CA: Academic Press.

Gabrielsson, A., & Juslin, P. N. (1996). Emotional expression in music performance: Between the performer's intention and the listener's experience. *Psychology of Music, 24,* 68–91.

Gabrielsson, A., & Juslin, P. N. (in press). Emotional expression in music. In R. J. Davidson, H. H. Goldsmith, and K. R. Scherer (Eds.), *Handbook of affective sciences.* New York: Oxford University Press.

Hallam, S. (1997). What do we know about practising? Towards a model synthesising the research literature. In H. Jørgensen and A. C. Lehmann (Eds.), *Does practice make perfect? Current theory and research on instrumental practice* (pp. 179–231). Oslo: Norges Musikhøgskole.

Hevner, K. (1936). Experimental studies of the elements of expression in music. *American Journal of Psychology, 48,* 246–268.

Howard, V. A. (1989). Expression as hands-on construction. In H. Gardner and D. Perkins (Eds.), *Art, mind, and education* (pp. 133–141). Chicago: University of Illinois Press.

Hudson, R. (1994). *Stolen time: The history of tempo rubato.* Oxford: Clarendon Press.

Johnstone, T., & Scherer, K. R. (2000). Vocal communication of emotion. In M. Lewis and J. M. Haviland-Jones (Eds.), *Handbook of emotions* (2nd ed.) (pp. 220–235). New York: Guilford.

Jürgens, U. (1992). On the neurobiology of vocal communication. In H. Papoušek, U. Jürgens, and M. Papoušek (Eds.), *Nonverbal vocal communication* (pp. 31–42). Cambridge: Cambridge University Press.

Juslin, P. N. (1997a). Can results from studies of perceived expression in musical performances be generalized across response formats? *Psychomusicology, 16,* 77–101.

Juslin, P. N. (1997b). Emotional communication in music performance: A functionalist perspective and some data. *Music Perception, 14*, 383–418.

Juslin, P. N. (1997c). Perceived emotional expression in synthesized performances of a short melody: Capturing the listener's judgment policy. *Musicae Scientiae, 1*, 225–256.

Juslin, P. N. (1999). *Communication of emotion in vocal expression and music performance: Different channels, same code?* Manuscript submitted for publication.

Juslin, P. N. (2000). Cue utilization in communication of emotion in music performance: Relating performance to perception. *Journal of Experimental Psychology: Human Perception and Performance, 26*, 1797–1813.

Juslin, P. N. (2001). Communicating emotion in music performance: A review and a theoretical framework. In P. N. Juslin and J. A. Sloboda (Eds.), *Music and emotion: Theory and research* (pp. 309–337). New York: Oxford University Press.

Juslin, P. N., & Laukka, P. (2000). Improving emotional communication in music performance through cognitive feedback. *Musicae Scientiae, 4*, 151–183.

Juslin, P. N., & Madison, G. (1999). The role of timing patterns in recognition of emotional expression from musical performance. *Music Perception, 17*, 197–221.

Juslin, P. N., & Sloboda, J. A. (Eds.). (2001). *Music and emotion: Theory and research*. New York: Oxford University Press.

Kingsbury, H. (1988). *Music, talent, and performance: A conservatory system.* Philadelphia: Temple University Press.

Kohut, D. L. (1985). *Musical performance: Learning theory and pedagogy.* Englewood Cliffs, NJ: Prentice-Hall.

Kotlyar, G. M., & Morozov, V. P. (1976). Acoustic correlates of the emotional content of vocalized speech. *Soviet Physics: Acoustics, 22*, 370–376.

Langer, S. K. (1942). *Philosophy in a new key.* Cambridge, MA: Harvard University Press.

Lehmann, A. C. (1997). Acquired mental representations in music performance: Anecdotal and preliminary empirical evidence. In H. Jørgensen and A. C. Lehmann (Eds.), *Does practice make perfect? Current theory and research on instrumental practice* (pp. 141–163). Oslo: Norges Musikhøgskole.

Lindström, E. (1999, August). *Expression in music: Interplay between performance and melodic structure.* Paper presented at the Meeting of the Society for Music Perception and Cognition, Evanston.

Marchand, D. J. (1975). A study of two approaches to developing expressive performance. *Journal of Research in Music Education, 23*, 14–22.

Mattheson, J. (1739/1954). *Der vollkommene Capellmeister.* Bärenreiter: Basel.

Menuhin, Y. (1996). *Unfinished journey.* London: Methuen.

Meyer, L. B. (1956). *Emotion and meaning in music.* Chicago: University of Chicago Press.

Oatley, K., & Jenkins, J. M. (1996). *Understanding emotions.* Oxford, UK: Blackwell.

Palmer, C. (1997). Music performance. *Annual Review of Psychology, 48*, 115–138.

Papoušek, M. (1996). Intuitive parenting: A hidden source of musical stimulation in infancy. In I. Deliège and J. A. Sloboda (Eds.), *Musical beginnings: Origins and development of musical competence* (pp. 88–112). Oxford: Oxford University Press.

Persson, R. S. (1993). *The subjectivity of musical performance: A music-psycho-logical real world enquiry into the determinants and education of musical reality.* Doctoral dissertation, Huddersfield University, UK.

Persson, R. S. (1996). Brilliant performers as teachers: A case study of common-sense teaching in a conservatoire setting. *International Journal of Music Education, 28,* 1–15.

Persson, R. S. (2001). The subjective world of the performer. In P. N. Juslin and J. A. Sloboda (Eds.), *Music and emotion: Theory and research* (pp. 275–289). New York: Oxford University Press.

Plutchik, R. (1994). *The psychology and biology of emotion.* New York: Harper-Collins.

Rabinowitz, M. (1988). On teaching cognitive strategies: The influence of accessibility of conceptual knowledge. *Contemporary Educational Psychology, 13,* 229–234.

Rapoport, E. (1996). Emotional expression code in opera and lied singing. *Journal of New Music Research, 25,* 109–149.

Reimer, B. (1989). *A philosophy of music education.* Englewood Cliffs, NJ: Prentice-Hall.

Renshaw, P. (1986). Towards the changing face of the conservatoire curriculum. *British Journal of Music Education, 3,* 79–90.

Russell, J. A. (1980). A circumplex model of affect. *Journal of Personality and Social Psychology, 39,* 1161–1178.

Schumacher, M. (1995). *Crossroads: The life and music of Eric Clapton.* New York: Hyperion.

Seckerson, E. (1991, June). Yuri Bashmet as interviewed by Seckerson. *Gramophone,* 26–27.

Shields, S. A. (1984). Distinguishing between emotion and non-emotion: Judgments about experience. *Motivation and Emotion, 8,* 355–369.

Sloboda, J. A. (1996). The acquisition of musical performance expertise: Deconstructing the "talent" account of individual differences in musical expressivity. In K. A. Ericsson (Ed.), *The road to excellence* (pp. 107–126). Mahwah, NJ: Erlbaum.

Sundberg, J., Iwarsson, J., & Hagegård, H. (1995). A singer's expression of emotions in sung performance. In O. Fujimura and M. Hirano (Eds.), *Vocal fold physiology: Voice quality control* (pp. 217–229). San Diego, CA: Singular Press.

Tait, M. (1992). Teaching strategies and styles. In R. Colwell (Ed.), *Handbook of research on music teaching and learning* (pp. 525–534). New York: Schirmer.

Woody, R. H. (1999). The relationship between explicit planning and expressive performance of dynamic variations in an aural modeling task. *Journal of Research in Music Education, 47,* 331–342.

Woody, R. H. (2000). Learning expressivity in music performance: An exploratory study. *Research Studies in Music Education, 14,* 14–23.

15

Body Movement

JANE W. DAVIDSON & JORGE SALGADO CORREIA

Body movement plays a role in the construction, execution, and perception of musical performances. We explore the interface between technical matters of physical control and the expressive components of physical gestures and discuss the bodily origins of musical meaning, expressive performance, and musical skill acquisition. For example, bodily gesture and rhythm in proto-musical mother-child exchanges influence the development of thought and knowledge, and expressive slowing in music (ritardando) corresponds to the deceleration of runners coming to a halt. Specific movement gestures in music performance function as illustrative and emblematic cues and clearly indicate the focus of the performer's attention, whether on the narrative content of a song or on showing off to the audience. Thus, through body movement thoughts and concerns are communicated to the audience. Performers, educators, and students can use this knowledge to enhance their performing, teaching, and learning capacities.

All musicians use their bodies to interact with their musical instruments when performing music. The intention of this chapter is to show that the body is not only essential to the physical manipulation of the instrument for the accurate execution of music, but it is also vital in the generation of expressive ideas about the music. In addition, the body seems to be critical in the production and perception of information about the performer's concerns to coordinate with coperformers and audience and to engage in extramusical concerns on stage, for instance, preening display movements.

To begin the exploration of musical performance and the body, it is important to recall that parents rhythmically pat, bounce, and caress their babies and melodically vocalize softly to them in *motherese* (infant-directed speech). In essence, the movements and sounds are based on exchanges that utilize varying elements associated with expressive musical performance. The motherese develops into play and conversational turn taking (Papoušek, 1996). There is imitation, matching, elaboration, with all kinds of emotions being played out through pitch, rhythm, and movement variation for the giver and the receiver of the information. Trevarthen (1999–2000) has argued that these *proto-musical* experiences are critical in establishing physiological and emotional attunement so that the interactive patterns become salient and, therefore, meaningful.

Given Trevarthen's ideas, it may be that proto-musical behavior is vital for the general development of meaningful thoughts and actions. It would follow that a concrete and practical way of understanding music can be explored through bodily movement. To generate music, the formulation and execution of expressive ideas and qualities in movement is certainly necessary. By implication, this would suggest that the understanding of musical performance could be clarified or enhanced when the movements that produce the musical sounds are given due attention by both the performer and the audience.

In light of the preceding, it seems no accident that physical metaphors are commonly used in reference to music: "a punchy performance," a "flowing *legato*," for example. Johnson (1999), Clarke (2001), and Damasio (1999), from the disciplines of philosophy, music psychology, and neuroscience respectively, all concur that these metaphors are helpful in assisting us to relay how we experience music. For performers, teachers, and students, it seems that the movement metaphor may be a powerful tool in the development of a musical performance. We shall return to this and other points about strategies for developing meaningful performances later in the chapter when considering how musical expression may be taught through body movement. But after a brief presentation of a justification for the central importance of the body in the production and perception of musical performances it seems critical to examine both elements in detail.

Production of Body Movement in Performance

A motor program is conceived of as a hierarchical structure that translates information input into performed action. When we learn to play a musical instrument and then work on a specific piece of music, these programs are constructed and strengthened with rehearsal. It is now well documented that it takes in excess of 10,000 hours of technical and repertoire practice (see Ericsson, Krampe, & Tesch-Römer, 1993) to refine an instrumental technique to reach expertise (the professional standard to play in a symphony orchestra); and during this practice the development of motor programs interfaces with that of other cognitive skills such as memorization in order for the whole learning and playing process to become automated.

Examining different skilled performances made by typists and pianists, Shaffer (1982, 1984) explored how motor programs are organized. He discovered that in typing, sequences of key presses have definite timing profiles across performances of the same word sequences. He concluded that the movement control program elicits effects on the performance that are inevitable but expressive only of the individual's production of words. In piano performance, Shaffer (1984) concluded that some of the timing deviations from the metric pulse of the musical rhythm are, similarly, the inevitable expression of features of the motor program. However, he went on to illustrate that other timing profile variations are flexible in tone production. Though these features are themselves integrated into the motor program, they are seen as timing modifications intended to enhance the musical effect. These intentional variations can be increased or diminished but never totally removed. Thus two elements of motor programming coexist in musical performance: timing profiles directly related to simple execution and timing deviations for musically enhancing effects.

In line with Shaffer's evidence, it is essential to recognize that dynamics, intonation, and timbre, as well as timing, are manipulated according to an individual's performance interpretation, and indeed, it has been demonstrated that differently intentioned performances contain different quantities of dynamic variation that are consciously used and recognized by performers as expressive devices (Nakamura, 1987). As stated earlier, it seems that the expressive effects applied to musical structures may be, in some part at least, related to bodily sources. For instance, a mathematical model produced by Todd (1985) indicated that phrase-related tempo changes—the acceleration and deceleration of tones in a musical phrase—are directly proportional to their position in the musical phrase. For example, slowing at a phrase boundary occurs in a systematic and seemingly rule-governed manner. Later Todd (1992, 1995) modified the proposal, basing the new model of deceleration toward a musical phrase end on velocity in physical motion. Recently it has been discovered that the expressive device of slowing toward a musical phrase end may be linked to the human movement properties found when adults slow down and stop after running (Friberg & Sundberg, 1999).

So, considering the body in the production of music, it is critical that motor programs are well established. However, the body is much more than a mechanistic source of input and output. There is a vast array of movements and gestures that serve many purposes. For example, one study tracked how individual points of the body move in space each 0.20 s during a piano performance, investigating the playing of the same piece of music with three different expressive intentions labeled deadpan, normal, and exaggerated (Davidson, 1994; in press). The study revealed a relationship between the movement size and the intensity of the musical sound expression—the more exaggerated the expressive intention of the music, the larger the movement. This suggested a direct correlation between the expressive movement and the production of musical intensity, since these performances were regarded as sounding as well as looking more expressive. In addition, it was revealed that the performer made a constant rocking movement when playing, though this movement was barely visible in the deadpan condition.

There are several possible accounts for the different types of movement used by pianists. First, they could be regarded as being responsive to the sounds produced—that is, reflecting the sounds. In the case of the rocking, there may even be movements analogous to those of self-stimulation observed in speech (Ekman

& Friesen, 1969)—movements used by the performer to make him- or herself feel at ease in the social context of the performance and/or enjoy the musical sounds being made. Support for this idea comes in the finding that although the rocking movement is allied to the timing and some structural features of the music (Clarke & Davidson, 1998), it seems to be not strictly bound to the musical structure, so it may be connected to the performer's individual concerns as well as a reaction to the music.

However, in line with research that suggests that the body provides a source for the generation of musical expression (see Friberg & Sundberg, 1999), it seems that the pianist's movements may be indicators of the mental and physical intentions necessary to generate the expressive performance. Although research on the origin of physical expression is scant, by drawing a parallel between the research on general locomotion (all kinds of traveling patterns from walking to running) and movement in musical performance Davidson (in press) was able to develop a theory of physical expression in playing. Although musical expression (that is, a specifically performed and intended communication) is not equivalent to locomotion, the locomotion research examined how the characteristics of gender and identity were displayed and used for communicative ends and thus expressed in the movement patterns. It is on these grounds that a parallel was made between the research findings and movements of musical expression.

Cutting, Proffitt, and Kozlowski (1978) and Kozlowski and Cutting (1977) were interested in how observers used the visual information available in the locomotion patterns. The researchers used bands of reflective tape attached to all the major body joints and filmed in highly contrasting light conditions to produce observation data that showed movement patterns only, avoiding surface information like dress, hairstyle, and so forth. From these movement displays onlookers were initially asked to identify the walker's sex. Then, in a series of studies where the onlookers knew all the walkers, they were asked to identify the walkers by name. Onlookers were very good at determining sex and naming individuals from these minimal visual displays.

The researchers showed that any part of the walking movement cycle and any body joint shown as a two-second excerpt provides similar information expressive of either gender or identity. The results were explained by demonstrating that there is a point within the walker's body referred to as the *center of moment* that acts as a reference around which movements in all parts of the body are organized, and this center is different for men and women (Cutting et al., 1978). Davidson proposed that such a principle may be in operation in musical performance, the description providing a framework from which we can begin to understand the importance of the rocking movement in the pianist's performances. The idea is that there is a physical center for the expression of musical information, the rocking being a critical part of the generation of the musical expression.

From the analysis of the pianist's movements, Davidson noted that the rocking emanated from the hip region. Given the sitting position of a pianist, the hips represent the fulcrum for the pianist's center of gravity and therefore provide the pivotal point for all upper torso movements. This center of gravity seemed to be the central location for the generation of this overall physical expression: thus the hips may be the center of moment. Although only a single pianist was used in a detailed case study (Davidson, in press), previous studies had indicated that a range of individual performers make similar types of movements and modifications to them across different expressive interpretations, suggesting that generalizable findings can be assumed from the case-study material (Davidson, 1993, had studied the perception of violinists' movements).

Although some musicians appear to remain absolutely still when performing, data from many studies (Davidson 1991, 1993, 1994, 1997, in press) have shown that despite individual differences, when interviewed, many of the players said that the musical ideas they had were connected with the concept of a repetitive whole-body motion. It was an imagined sense of motion. Thus it could be that the movement may be internalized as well as externalized, and so it may be present to some degree. This idea links with that of Alexander Truslit, the German pedagogue:

> Musical motion is internal and encompasses the whole human being. It is not only an emotion [*Gemüts-Bewegung*] but also a true motion sensation. It must be distinguished from acoustic vibrations, from sympathetic resonance, from technical movements in playing an instrument, from the sequence of tones (which is only the outward manifestation of the inner process), and from conducting movements (though they merge partially with it). Musical motion can be likened to an invisible, imaginary dance. (Truslit, 1938, translated and presented by Repp, 1993, p. 51)

For Truslit, the movement metaphor for understanding and experiencing movement is of key importance. With the center-of-moment principle, the claim is that real or imagined motion is necessary to generate musical expression. This is a contentious idea, but nonetheless it brings together several allied propositions to produce a coherent theoretical proposal.

Related to the center-of-moment principle and in addition to the rocking motion, individually identifiable expressive locations have been discovered (see Davidson, in press). When these specific movements were closely examined in relation to the musical score, it was found, first, that they only occurred when a particular body part—the hand, for instance—was free to move, that is, when it was not tied to the technicalities of executing the music. Examples of these locations would be structural features like rests and sustained pedal notes. Second, the movements were all of a rotational nature—circling wrist movements and shoulder rotations, for instance. Third, these movements seemed to form a vocabulary of gestures in that they appeared across performances of different styles of music. They were not, however, allied in a one-to-one manner with musical features or pieces. There was a tendency for the performer to use the gestures in a variety of contexts and manners—sometimes small and slow, other times large and fast.

Further studies had refined the description of the center of moment by suggesting that different parts of the body convey similar expressive information at different hierarchical levels (Cutting & Proffitt, 1981). This finding could account for results obtained earlier that indicated that more localized movement is of a similar expressive type to that of the overall rocking motion.

Gellrich (1991) has explored how specifically learned gestures can furnish a musical performance with an expressive intention. From his perspective, it is apparent that many of the gestures are culturally learned, as are their associated meanings. It is certain, in all forms of music, that some elements of physical gesture are learned from shared cultural codes. They may be picked up from teachers, peers, or even observation of someone on TV. Technically, the gestures may be *superfluous* to the production of the music—a surface level of movement or a kind of rhetoric that the performer adds to the performance. It could be that the deep-level source of expression is the rocking movement and that the local expressive gesture is a means of adding to that.

While Davidson's is case-study work, it does seem that the findings may be generalizable, since the growing research literature on nonverbal gesture in conversation and social interaction indicates that gestures often have particular purposes and these are commonly understood and used within a specific social and cultural context (see Ellis & Beattie, 1986; Argyle, 1988). For instance, *emblems* (such as a raising of the eyebrows or a shoulder shrug) are typically used to reinforce what is being said. The movement vocabulary of gestures used in music could have some similar functions. For instance, within the context of jazz performance saxophonists often raise the bell of the instrument and close their eyes as a symbol of intense expression, usually getting louder. Some saxophonists make the physical gesture even when they cannot actually play any louder.

So it seems that the bodily production of music involves general motion and specific localized culturally learned gestures for technical, musical, and socially communicative purposes. Beyond production, it would appear that from a perceptual perspective, body movements can assist the degree of coordination between coperformers and aid audience comprehension of the musical performance.

Perception of Body Movement in Performance

It is now well documented that audiences can detect finely grained information about musical expression (timing, pitch, and dynamics modifications to structural features of the music) and intention (the emotional mood of the performer and the piece) from a musician's body movements when he or she is playing (Davidson, 1993, 1994, 1995). So embodied musical meaning seems to be both perceptually available and comprehensible to audiences. In fact, when audiences are not skilled as listeners they rely entirely on the visual information they receive, not being able to differentiate between musical intentions and aural information (Davidson, 1994).

In an attempt to assess whether all or parts of the movements of a musical performance are meaningful, Davidson (in press, b) explored whether the movement information of a pianist was available to observers in a continuous stream or it was limited to particular moments within a performance. It was discovered, on the one hand, that audiences reported the repetitive body rocking as being a continuously present and key source of expressive information, but on the other hand clips of only two seconds of visual material revealed that some moments were more obvious indicators of expressive intention than others, especially those moments that contained particular expressive gestures.

So it would appear that those movements used to produce a performance are informative of the musical meaning, as well as being generative of the musical intention itself. Consider the following anecdote about Glenn Gould (cited by Delalande, 1990) that explores the link between audience perception and the performer's use of his body. Gould's career fell into two distinct phases: an early period during which he gave concert tours as well as making sound recordings and a late period when he only worked in the recording studio. Looking at video footage from both periods, Delalande discovered that in the live performances Gould's movements had a degree of unpredictability but showed great fluency. In the sound-recording sessions, the movements were far more repetitive and fixed. It is possible that the earlier movements were for direct communicative intentions: literally demonstrating ideas to the audience. In the later performances, perhaps Gould was less socially motivated and was simply focusing on the best way to achieve a sound performance. Of course, this is only one possible interpretation of Gould's movements, but it nevertheless raises issues about the role of social interaction in shaping the production of the performance. Davidson and Good (1997; in press) discovered that when playing in small ensembles performers use their movement patterns to coordinate timing, dynamics and other expressive effects with their coperformers. So perception of coperformers has an influence on shaping the movement patterns, too.

The nature of the social mediation that goes on among performer, coperformer, and audience in the construction of the performance and the critical role of the body in shaping this have received very little attention in the psychology research literature. One relevant study is on the singer Annie Lennox (Davidson, 2001). Analysis showed that in addition to the specific movements related directly to the communication of the song—such as coordination signals and expressive gestures about the narrative content of the songs—some other types of movements were used purely for audience display or showing-off purposes. These involved a deliberate attempt to involve audience participation and had nothing to do with the song's narrative. For instance, there were moments when Annie Lennox danced playfully with her coperformers and came to the front of the stage, asking the audience members near the stage to clap along in time with the singing. Frith's (1996) analysis of pop singers' behavior showed that the pop singer constantly negotiates a communication of the song's narrative, a pop-star role with associated culturally defined behaviors, and his or her own individuality in the public forum.

Annie Lennox plays the role of a star in her use of showing-off or display gestures. She is a narrator-interpreter in her use of illustrative and emblematic gestures with the coperformers and audience. She is a coworker in her use of regulatory movements to coordinate musical entrances and exits. Internal self-concern also seems to be presented in Annie's adaptive gestures such as the self-stimulation involved in touching her face or caressing her body with her arms as she sings. The particular illustrative, emblematic, regulatory, and display gestures are specific to Annie and her personal experiences and thus also indicate critical information about an unique individual. However, the adaptive gestures seem to display inner personal states or characteristics, whereas the display, regulatory, and illustrative (emblematic) gestures are more audience (externally) oriented.

Summary

Presenting the findings of the body movement work in summary, it seems that musical skills involve issues of fluency and technique, yet in the live performance critical concerns appear to be how the performer presents him- or herself as:

- A communicator interacting with coperformers to regulate the performance so that it remains unified
- An individual interpreter of the narrative or expressive/emotional elements of the work being played
- A self with individual experiences and behaviors
- A public figure with a clear aim to interact with and entertain the audience

All of these factors together highlight the tremendous range of skills involved in performance and undoubtedly provide important insights into understanding *what* information is being communicated in a performance.

The literature surveyed shows how critical gestural movements are in the production of and perception of a performance and particularly underscores the role of social interaction in the construction of a performance through the discovery that different types of gestures are used for specific coperformer and audience engagement. It could well be that the presence of others promotes the use of these communicative gestures.

Another issue to emerge from this research is the juxtaposition of movements connected with self and self-adaptation and those connected with pure social display. It seems that different aspects of self and self-projection are revealed in the movements.

Thus far, the work presented has demonstrated that musical performance movements are of the following types: purely biomechanical (they can only occur when the body is free and ready to use them), individual (each person has his or her own style), and culturally determined (some of the movements are learned through imitation of others' behaviors in specific contexts and so have common presentations within the cultural context). Many of these performance movements have clear functions and meanings: to communicate the expressive intention (for instance, a sudden surge forward to facilitate the execution of a loud musical passage or a high curving hand gesture to link sections of the music during a pause); to communicate directly with the audience or coperformers about issues of coordination or participation (for example, nodding the head to beckon the audience to join in a chorus of a song or exchanging glances for the coperformer to take over a solo in a jazz piece); to signal extramusical concerns (for example, gesturing to the audience to remain quiet); to present information about the performer's personality, with his or her individualized characteristics providing important cues (muted contained gestures or large extravagant gestures, for example); and to show off to the audience.

In addition to the findings presented earlier, some performance movements with no specific value to the audience as interpretative cues are nevertheless the by-products of psychophysical, social, and cultural practices that surround performance—for example, standing rooted on both feet to be able to sing better. Although the audience may not read such cues in their assessment of the performance, taken together it is likely that such movements do add to the overall style and content of the performance.

A final point is that the body movements need to be presented at an optimal level. For example, it seems that too many movements might create an overly exaggerated performance and too few movements might make the performance appear stilted. Recall, for example, that although grand flourishing gestures were fashionable in nineteenth-century musical performance, Liszt was referred to by Glinka as an "exaggerator of nuance" (cited in Morgenstern, 1956, p. 129).

Bearing all of the findings discussed earlier in mind, the final section of this chapter considers their educational implications.

Working with the Body in Music Performance Teaching

Contemporary method books and study guides include diagrams of the correct positions and postures for holding musical instruments in order to play (see, e.g., Miller, 1996), but few of these texts provide information about how to use the body effectively to achieve a musically expressive performance or a charismatic and highly personalized interaction with the audience. However, there has been a historical interest in such matters. For instance, Pierre Baillot in his *L'art du violon* of 1834 (cited in Stowell, 1985) suggests that different types of movement are necessary to produce different musical tempi. For instance, the *adagio* tempo requires "more ample movements" than the *allegro*, where the notes are "tossed off," whereas in *presto* there is "great physical abandon."

Where an interest in the use of bodily gesture for musical interpretation has been expressed, it has typically been found when the author has an interest in the domain of dance and body alignment, with the most commonly cited source of inspiration for the practical being the teachings of Emile Jacques-Dalcroze (1865–1950), who points to body movement as crucial to the process of unifying the musical elements and focusing on musical expression. The Dalcrozian approach addressed the whole issue of musical meaning and musical communication:

What is the source of music? Where does music begin?
Human emotions are translated into musical motion.
Where do we sense emotions?
In various parts of the body.

How do we feel emotions?
By various sensations produced by different levels of muscular contraction and relaxation.
How does the body express these internal feelings to the external world?
In postures, gestures, and movements of various kinds. Some of these are automatic, some are spontaneous, others are the results of thought and will.
By what instrument does a human being translate inner emotions into music?
By human motion. (Jacques-Dalcroze writing in 1931, cited in Choksy, Abramson, Gillespie, & Woods, 1986, p. 31).

Some individual teachers may not agree with the Dalcrozian approach to teaching and learning music, but it does centralize the role of the body, connecting sounds to particular physical gestures. Recently Pierce (1994) has made a significant impact in the United States by adapting Dalcrozian principles for work with advanced musicians. Her approach involves teaching rhythm by experiencing the beat of pulse of music through pendular, swinging movements away from the instrument. The point of an exercise like this is to embody the full motion required to produce the attack point on the beat. That is, the student can feel the approaching downbeat and the surrounding moments in the body swing. So quite an abstract musical idea can be played out through the body. In another example, in order to achieve a *legato* line and to assist in the detection of a melody line that may be submerged in a harmony passage, students are asked to trace with the hand an analog to the shape of the melody, attending to weight and flow of the line to assist or draw attention to direction of melody and the surrounding harmonies and other textures.

Although we cannot comment on the efficacy of Pierce's work or, indeed, that of Dalcroze and others, we believe that these teachers draw on principles based on the human body and human nature that can assist development of a deeper base from which music technique and expression can be explored and understood.

In line with the range of ideas presented earlier, it becomes evident that there is not just one way to explore the body in music in order to improve technique, musical expression, and the presentation of self in performance, but rooted in the research discussed earlier in the chapter we now present some of our own methods for working with students to train their bodies. More detail about these practical ideas can be found in Correia (1999a, 1999b) and Davidson, Pitts, and Correia (2000), where experimental evidence that verifies the efficacy of the methods is presented.

Training Fluency of Movement. Without doubt, musicians need to be able to be aware of the muscular tensions or bad postural habits that may interfere with their playing. Thus, as a general principle, attempting to find the point of best equilibrium for head, neck, spine, pelvis, and legs is recommended as a good practical grounding for students to develop self-awareness in the overall posture of their bodies when preparing to play. These principles emerge out of the teachings of Alexander (1869–1943) and his principles on body alignment—the Alexander Technique.

Exploring Expressive Potential: The Narrative of the Musical Work.   Based on drama-style exercises (see Boal, 1992), students are asked to express different characters, affects, or states of mind suggested by the narrative of the piece they are learning. They do this first through physical gesture and then in their musical sounds.

Working on the Intention of Each Musical Phrase.   Once engaged and acquainted with the style and the overall atmosphere of the piece, the students are then asked to find *action metaphors* for each phrase or effect, trying to build up a nonverbal narrative in which every passage of the piece becomes meaningful and thus communicable through movement or physical gesture. Here the concepts of weight and flow are adapted from the movement analyst and choreographer Laban (1960), who attracted the student's attention to all the dynamic qualities of each movement as a means of understanding how forces act upon it and to give as broad an expressive palette as possible.

Directing an Interpretation: Conducting the Musical Expression of the Teacher.   Another means of using the body to gain insights into the musical expression is for the student to conduct the expression in the playing of the teacher, using the body as the means through which to get the teacher to make expressive sound changes to his or her playing. Trials and discussion are used to explore all the expressive nuances by gestures and/or movement.

Finding the Inner and Outer Personality in Movement.   Stategies to develop a sense of a public versus a private communication of one's self on stage has been central to the work of the actor (see Boal, 1992). It seems likely that some of the best performers are able to connect with the communicative principles necessary to achieve a good public presentation, while other individuals need to be aided. In music performance, teachers often ask their students to make their bodily gestures larger and more obvious to the audience so that the presentational component of the performance—its publicness—is clear. Difficulties in terms of both music production and perception seem to arise when the performer's behavior is either not sufficiently public for the concert environment or, on occasion, too large-scale and overt. Here issues of historical style and audience opinion can be explored.

Teacher's Body Movement Strategies to Develop Musical Expression in the Student.   A wide range of verbal *metaphors*—especially for situations where the expression has to do with inner motions or reactions (like contraction or tenderness) can be used by teachers to stimulate the student's imagination and bodily meaning. These metaphors usually captured physical qualities. For instance, Correia (1999b) reported one teacher as having said, "Play it as if you were throwing pebbles into a pond, and feel the ripples pulsing out of the center of your body to the bow."

Concluding Comments

The evidence presented in this chapter has shown the significance of body movement in the development, performance, and training of musicians. Interfacing empirical findings, theory, and some practical applications, we hope to have inspired readers to reappraise their use of movement in the training of musicians and in their own performances. The work we have covered is in no way meant to be prescriptive, rather a starting point from which further developments can and we believe should be made.

References

Argyle, M. (1988). *Bodily communication* (2nd ed.). London: Methuen.

Boal, A. (1992). *Games for actors and non-actors* (2nd ed.). London: Routledge.

Choksy, L., Abramson, R., Gillespie, A., & Woods, D. (1986). *Teaching music in the twentieth century.* Englewood Cliffs, NJ: Prentice-Hall.

Clarke, E. F. (2001). Meaning and specification of motion in music. *Musicae Scientiae*, 5(2), 213–234.

Clarke, E. F., & Davidson, J. W. (1998). The body in performance. In W. Thomas (Ed.), *Composition–performance–reception* (pp. 74–92). Aldershot: Ashgate.

Correia, J. S. (1999a). Embodied meaning: All languages are ethnic . . . *Psychology of Music*, 27, 96–101.

Correia, J. S. (1999b, September). *Making meaning: Teaching performers musical interpretation when working from a score.* Lucerne, Switzerland: European Society for the Cognitive Sciences of Music Conference on Research Relevant to Music Colleges.

Cutting, J. E., & Proffitt, D. R. (1981). Gait perception as an example of how we may perceive events. In R. D. Walker and H. L. Pick (Eds.), *Intersensory perception and sensory intelligence* (pp. 61–87). New York: Plenum.

Cutting, J. E, Proffitt, D. R., & Kozlowski, L. T. (1978). A biomechanical invariant for gait perception. *Journal of Experimental Psychology: Human Perception and Performance*, 4, 357–372.

Damasio, A. (1999). *The feeling of what happens.* Orlando, FL: Harcourt Brace.

Davidson, J. W. (1991). The perception of expressive movement in music performance. Unpublished doctoral dissertation, City University, London.

Davidson, J. W. (1993). Visual perception and performance manner in the movements of solo musicians. *Psychology of Music*, 21, 103–113.

Davidson, J. W. (1994). What type of information is conveyed in the body movements of solo musician performers? *Journal of Human Movement Studies*, 6, 279–301.

Davidson, J. W. (1995). What does the visual information contained in music performances offer the observer? Some preliminary thoughts. In R. Steinberg (Ed.), *Music and the mind machine: Psychophysiology and psychopathology of the sense of music* (pp. 105–114). Heidelberg: Springer.

Davidson, J. W. (1997). The social in musical performance. In D. J. Hargreaves and A. C. North (Eds.), *The social psychology of music* (pp. 209–228). Oxford: Oxford University Press.

Davidson, J. W. (2001). The role of the body in the production and perception of solo vocal performance: A case study of Annie Lennox. *Musicae Scientiae*, 5(2), 235–256.

Davidson, J. W. (in press). Understanding the expressive movements of a solo pianist. *Jahrbuch Musikpsychologie.*

Davidson, J. W., & Good, J. M. M. (1997, June). Social psychology of performance.

In A. Gabrielsson (Ed.), *Proceedings of the Third Triennial ESCOM Conference* (pp. 329–332). Uppsala, Sweden: University of Uppsala.

Davidson, J. W., & Good, J. M. M. (in press). Towards social psychology of string quartets. *Psychology of Music.*

Davidson, J. W., Pitts, S. E., & Correia, J. S. (2000). Reconciling technical and expressive elements in young children's musical instrument learning. *Journal of Aesthetic Education.*

Delalande, F. (1990, June). *Human movement and the interpretation of music.* Paper presented at the Second International Colloquium on the Psychology of Music, Ravello, Italy.

Ekman, P., & Friesen, W. V. (1969). The repertory of nonverbal behaviour: Categories, origins, usage, and coding. *Semiotica, 1,* 49–98.

Ellis, A., & Beattie, G., (1986). *The psychology of language and communication.* London: Weidenfield & Nicolson.

Ericsson, K. A., Krampe, R. T., & Tesch-Römer, C. (1993). The role of deliberate practice in the acquisition of expert performance. *Psychological Review, 100*(3), 363–406.

Friberg, A., & Sundberg, J. (1999). Does music performance allude to locomotion? A model of final *ritardandi* derived from measurements of stopping runners. *Journal of the Acoustical Society of America, 105*(3), 1469–1484.

Frith, S. (1996). *Performance rites.* Oxford: Oxford University Press.

Gellrich, M. (1991). Concentration and tension. *British Journal of Music Education, 8,* 167–179.

Johnson, M. (1999). Something in the way she moves: Musical motion and musical space. http://www.hf.uio.no/CMI-99/.

Kozlowski, L. T., & Cutting, J. E. (1977). Recognising the sex of a walker from a dynamic point-light display. *Perception and Psychophysics, 21,* 575–580.

Laban, R. (1960). *The art of movement and dance* (2nd ed.). London: Macdonald & Evans.

Miller, J. (1996). *The good brass guide.* London: Guildhall School of Music and Drama.

Morgenstern, S. (1956). *Composers on music.* London: Faber & Faber.

Nakamura, T. (1987). The communication of dynamics between musicians and listeners through musical performance. *Perception and Psychophysics, 41,* 525–533.

Papoušek, M. (1996). Intuitive parenting: A hidden source of musical stimulation in infancy. In I. Deliège and J. A. Sloboda (Eds.), *Musical beginnings: Origins and development of musical competence* (pp. 88–112). Oxford: Oxford University Press.

Pierce, A. (1994). Developing Schenkerian hearing and performing. *Integral, 8,* 51–123.

Repp, B. H. (1993). Music as motion: A synopsis of Alexander Truslit (1938) *Gestaltung und Bewegung in der Musik. Psychology of Music, 21,* 48–72.

Shaffer, L. H. (1982). Rhythm and skill. *Psychological Review, 89,* 109–122.

Shaffer, L. H. (1984). Timing in solo and duet piano performances. *Quarterly Journal of Experimental Psychology, 36,* 577–595.

Stowell, R. (1985). *Violin technique and peformance practice in late eighteenth and early nineteenth centuries.* Cambridge: Cambridge University Press.

Todd, N. P. McA. (1985). A model of expressive timing in tonal music. *Music Perception, 3,* 33–58.

Todd, N. P. McA. (1992). The dynamics of dynamics: A model of musical expression. *Journal of the Acoustical Society of America*, *91*(6), 3540–3550.

Todd, N. P. McA. (1995). The kinematics of musical expression. *Journal of the Acoustical Society of America*, *97*(3), 1940–1949.

Trevarthen, C. (1999–2000). Musicality and the intrinsic motive pulse: Evidence from human psychobiology and infant communication. *Musicae Scientiae*, Special Issue: Rhythm, Musical Narrative, and Origins of Human Communication, 155–215.

PART III

INSTRUMENTS AND ENSEMBLES

16

Solo Voice

GRAHAM F. WELCH & JOHAN SUNDBERG

One of the principal challenges for the singer is to acquire an understanding of how to develop and maintain a particular set of culturally specific musical behaviors using an instrument that is not visible and in which the functional components change physically across the lifespan. The singer's instrument has three components. The respiratory system is responsible for variations in loudness; changes in the pattern and frequency of vocal fold vibration are perceived as variations in pitch and voice quality; and changes in the configuration of the vocal tract are linked to resonance and carrying power. Although often interrelated (particularly in the untrained vocalist), these three functional characteristics are susceptible through education to focused development and conscious control.

The ability to use the voice to express music through singing is a characteristic of all known musical cultures. Each culture tends to value particular vocal timbres in the performance of its art music, such as the vocal sounds commonly associated with classical opera in the West, with the throat music of Tuva, or with blues. These vocal timbres are a selection from a much wider potential variety, indicating the inherent plasticity of the human voice. So one of the central issues in any consideration of solo voice performance is the development and maintenance of a particular set of culturally specific behaviors that use an instrument that is not visible and in which the functional components change physically across the life span. This chapter will examine the basic design of the vocal instrument (its anatomy, physiology, and psychological correlates), its function in singing, and the pedagogical implications for both teachers and performers.

Structure and Function

The vocal instrument (Figure 16.1) consists of three essential components: the *respiratory system*, the *vocal folds* and the *vocal tract* (the cavity formed by the spaces above the larynx, namely, the pharynx and the mouth, which are sometimes complemented by the nasal cavity) (cf. Sundberg, 1996). Together, their combined action determines the characteristics of perceived vocal sound in speech and singing.

The respiratory system is the energy source for human voice production. This system compresses the lungs to provide an upward-flowing air stream that sets the *vocal folds* (situated within the larynx) into vibration. The vibrating vocal folds chop the air stream into a pulsating airflow (Figure 16.1; *transglottal airflow*) called the *voice source*. This consists of a complex of simultaneously sounding pure tones, or *partials* of different frequencies. Since the relationship between the partials in voiced sounds corresponds exactly to the harmonic series, the partials are also called harmonics and the lowest is called the fundamental. These partials decrease in strength with their ascending frequencies (see glottal source spectrum in the figure). However, the voice source is filtered by the spaces of the vocal tract above the vocal folds. Depending on its configuration, the vocal tract enhances or suppresses particular partials and so forms (shapes) the output sound (see the radiated spectrum in the figure). Consequently, these vocal tract resonances are called *formants* (see figure). The properties of the voice source, plus the frequencies of the formants, enable us to perceive and label particular output sounds as vowels. Formants also characterize consonants, both voiced (e.g., *d*) and unvoiced (e.g., *t*). The combined action of the vocal folds and the vocal tract also creates the distinctive personal timbre that we perceive in a voice.

The Vocal Tract

At the lower end of the vocal tract is the *larynx*. The two vocal folds are located inside the larynx and are made up of muscles shaped as folds. Their horizontal and vertical dimensions change in relation mainly to pitch. Covered by a mucous membrane, the folds are approximately 3 mm long in newborn infants and grow at an average rate of 0.4 mm per year for females and 0.7 mm per year for males. With a disproportionate growth during puberty in males, adult female vocal folds are about 9 to 13 mm, compared to 15 to 20 mm in adult males (Titze, 1994). Vocal fold length and vibrating mass are crucial to the pitch range of the voice: the longer and thicker the vocal folds, the lower the pitch range. Consequently, because their vocal folds are smaller, young children have a higher vocal pitch range than adults. Although boys tend to have slightly longer vocal folds than girls, this difference appears not to be reflected in customary pitch ranges, as these are very similar. However, once puberty begins (at around the age of eight in some girls) and the relative physical dimensions increase, voice pitch lowers and diverges between male and female voices. This results in adult male voices' being approximately one fifth to one octave lower than those for adult females, depending on the singer's voice classification. (For example, the average spoken pitch of a typical soprano is near B_3 (247 Hz), a semitone below middle C or C_4, but the average spoken pitch of a typical tenor is about a fifth lower at E_3 (165 Hz), a sixth below middle C: Titze, 1994, p. 188.) Vocal fold length does not significantly depend on body height but is more related to the circumference of the neck (a function of body build). At the limits of vocal pitch range, there is an overlap between men and women in their sung vocal pitch ranges, and this is greater between altos and tenors than sopranos and basses (Titze, 1994, p. 187; see "Voice Source" later).

The vocal folds run horizontally from front to back within the *thyroid cartilage*. They are attached together at the front to the inside of the thyroid cartilage (Adam's apple) and at the back to two mobile cartilages (the *arytenoids*). When one is breathing silently, the arytenoid cartilages are moved apart (abduction) by the *opener* set of muscles (*posterior cricoarytenoid* muscles), allowing the air stream to flow freely. The gap between the two folds is known as the glottis. When one is speaking or singing, voiced sounds are produced when the *closer* muscles (the lateral *cricoarytenoid* and *interarytenoid* muscles) bring the arytenoid cartilages together and hence draw the posterior ends of vocal folds together (adduction), so that their edges vibrate in the air stream. The folds are abducted for unvoiced sounds (such as certain consonants) and adducted for voiced sounds (such as vowels). The muscles responsible for opening and closing the glottis are mainly located at the back of the vocal folds near the spine. As well as assisting in basic vocal fold vibration, this set of opener and closer muscles is also involved when changing the loudness of the voice.

The air pressure in the lungs is the main tool for varying vocal loudness: the higher the pressure, the louder the voice. The underlying mechanism is that a greater air pressure throws the vocal folds apart with a greater force, with the result that they then also close more quickly. If the closer muscles are fully activated and the opener muscles are relaxed, the vocal folds are kept tightly closed together. This requires much more effort from the air stream to push them apart. Eventually, even when the folds are firmly adducted, at high lung pressures it is usually possible to get some air between the vocal folds. The effort, however, bursts the folds apart and then snaps them back together, creating a bigger disturbance of the air, which is perceived as a louder voice and *pressed* phonation (also termed *hyperadduction* or overly tight vocal fold adduction: Harris et al., 1998).

The laryngeal *lengthener* and *shortener* muscles are essentially responsible for pitch change. The shortener muscles (the *thyroarytenoids*) are located within the vocal folds themselves. They have a horizontal orientation (front to back). When these contract, the result is a fatter, bulkier, shorter vibrating tissue that produces a lower pitch. In contrast, the lengthener muscles (the *cricothyroids*) have more of a vertical orientation and are attached near the front of the larynx, stretched between the thyroid and cricoid cartilages. The effect of the contraction of the lengthener muscles on the cartilages is to tilt and slide the thyroid cartilage forward and so stretch (lengthen) the vocal folds. In so doing, the fundamental frequency is raised.

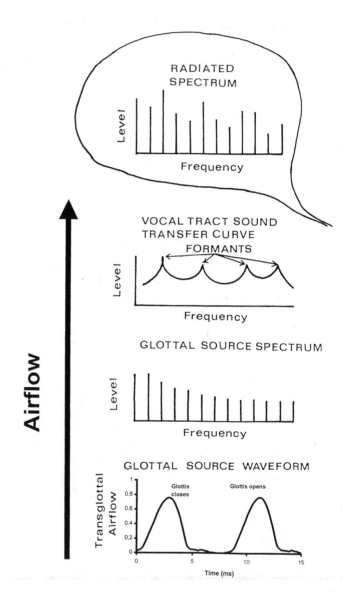

Airflow

RADIATED SPECTRUM

Level

Frequency

VOCAL TRACT SOUND TRANSFER CURVE FORMANTS

Level

Frequency

GLOTTAL SOURCE SPECTRUM

Level

Frequency

GLOTTAL SOURCE WAVEFORM

Transglottal Airflow

Glottis closes

Glottis opens

Time (ms)

Figure 16.1. (a) The respiratory system (lungs), (b) the vocal folds, and (c) the vocal tract. (Adapted from Sundberg, 1987. Copyright 1987 University of Illinois Press, used by permission.)

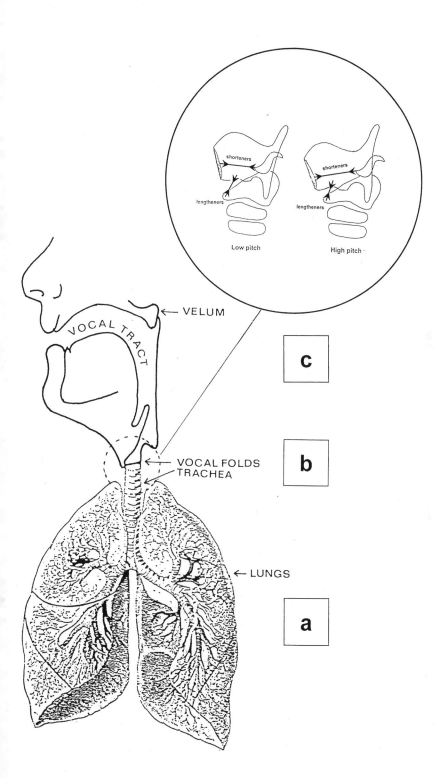

shorteners

shorteners

lengtheners

lengtheners

Low pitch

High pitch ·

VELUM

VOCAL TRACT

c

VOCAL FOLDS
TRACHEA

b

LUNGS

a

Effective coordinated action of each of these shortener and lengthener muscles is required for skilled voicing. When a voice becomes louder, the activation of the closer muscles is increased, while the activation of the lengthener muscles is reduced. The reason is that the increased airflow creates the louder snapping together of the vibrating vocal folds and so the lengthener and shortener muscles have to work harder in combination to resist the pressure from the lungs, either to maintain or to change pitch as well as intensity (see "Voice Source" later and also Thurman & Welch, 2000, pp. 394–408).

A few millimeters above the vocal folds there is another pair of folds, also covered by mucous membrane. These are called the *false vocal folds* or the *ventricular folds*. Between the vocal folds and the ventricular folds there is a small cavity known as the *laryngeal ventricle* (sometimes termed *epilarynx*). This links into the much larger pharyngeal space above. The ceiling of the pharynx is the *soft palate* (*velum*), which also serves as the gateway to the nasal cavities. Narrow channels in the ceiling of the nasal cavity lead up to other cavities, the maxillary and frontal sinuses, which are located in the bone structure of the skull. The pharynx leads into the oral cavity. Both these cavities have their shapes altered by the movement of the tongue and the jaw. Thus the pulsating air stream flows through a tube that consists of a group of linked chambers to produce particular vocal timbres.

With regard to differences between the sexes, an adult female vocal tract is about 15% to 20% shorter than its adult male counterpart. In particular, the female laryngeal ventricle (the space between the vocal folds to the false folds) and pharynx are shorter (Story, Titze, & Hoffman, 1997) than those of the male, while the mouth length difference between the sexes is less marked (Nordström, 1977).

Breathing

The lungs are elastic, spongy structures suspended in a vacuum in a sac within the rib cage. Because of the vacuum, their volume is enlarged. They contain a great number of small cavities linked by a system of air pipes, which join in the trachea, a tube that leads up to the vocal folds. Inhalation and exhalation correspond to decompression and compression of the lungs, which is performed by the respiratory system through forces generated by muscles, elasticity, and gravitation. Through muscle contraction, we can expand and contract the rib cage. As most of the lung surface is covered by the rib cage, small rib cage movements result in substantial compression or decompression. A large inspiratory muscle sheet, the diaphragm, constitutes the boundary between the rib cage and the abdomen. It originates along the lower edge of the rib cage and is vaulted into it. When contracting, it lowers the bottom of the rib cage by pushing the abdominal content downward and forward, which in turn expands the abdominal wall. Conversely, by contracting the abdominal wall muscles the abdominal content can be pushed back into the rib cage, thus compressing the lungs.

After a completely relaxed sigh, lung volume typically reaches the *functional residual capacity* (*FRC*), generally near 40% of maximum lung volume in an upright position. In singing and speech alike, we usually phonate at lung volumes above FRC, whereas phonating below FRC can feel uncomfortable. When trained singers learn new songs, they learn how to inhale and sing in order to avoid lung volumes below FRC. Small lung volumes are generally used in speech, whereas in classical singing phrases are often initiated at very high lung volumes. Moreover, classical singers tend to repeat their breathing patterns very consistently when they sing the same phrase. They seem to use the rib cage mainly for changing lung volume, though some singers appear also to make use of the abdominal wall (Thomasson & Sundberg, 1999).

The overpressure of air in the trachea generates an air stream through the *glottis* (the space between the vocal folds). The pressure just below the glottis, the *subglottal pressure*, provides the driving force of the voice and is the main tool for controlling vocal loudness: the higher the pressure, the louder the voice (as mentioned earlier). This pressure variation in singing needs to be quite accurate, as pressure affects pitch; failure to match a target pressure may result in pitch errors (singing out of tune). A classical singing exercise that involves *staccato* performance (short tones interleaved with short silent intervals) of ascending and descending triad patterns seems particularly appropriate to train the singer's subglottal pressure control in coordination with the control of the laryngeal muscles that regulate the fundamental frequency. During the silent intervals the vocal folds part, leaving the airways open, so lung pressure must then be reduced to zero to avoid a waste of air. In addition, high tones need higher pressures than low tones, so each tone usually needs a different pressure. Singers also use subglottal pressure variations to demarcate the tones in rapid sequences, as in legato *coloratura* singing. Then each tone receives its own pressure pulse, so that one pressure pulse is produced for each tone in synchrony with the fundamental frequency pattern. In quick tempi, these pressure pulses may be as short as 150 milliseconds (ms).

Voice Source

In voiced sounds, the voice source is a pulsating airflow (see waveform element in Figure 16.1). The voice source can be varied in several different ways with respect to fundamental frequency (perceived as pitch), amplitude of the spectrum partials (perceived as loudness), and dominance of the fundamental (perceived as type of voice production).

The perceived pitch corresponds to the frequency of vocal fold vibration. Thus when the pitch of A_4 is being sung, the vocal folds open and close the glottis 440 times per second ($A_4 = 440$ Hz). The main determinant of fundamental frequency is the length and vibrating mass of the vocal folds: the longer and thinner the folds, the higher the pitch (as mentioned earlier). These properties are controlled by the laryngeal musculature. The approximate ranges covered by the main singer classifications are as follows: bass singers, 80–330 Hz (pitch range E_2–E_4); tenors, 123–520 Hz (C_3–C_5); altos, 175–700 Hz (F_3–F_5); and sopranos, 260–1,300 Hz (C_4–E_6). Fundamental frequency is also influenced by subglottal pressure. So, to stay in tune while producing a *crescendo*, a singer needs to reduce the activation of the laryngeal muscles that regulate fundamental frequency as the subglottal pressure increases. This may partly explain why less-skilled singers find it difficult to sing high tones softly. Their laryngeal muscles are not yet skillfully coordinated enough to ensure that the vocal fold tension matches the low subglottal pressure. Instead, they rely on increased subglottal pressure to raise pitch, resulting in loud and sometimes mistuned singing. As with all human control systems, the key to success is an awareness of the target in relation to possible means of achieving that target.

The voice source is also influenced by the degree of glottal adduction. Weak adduction results in a leaky or breathy voice, as in a voiced whisper. Overly strong adduction produces pressed phonation, or a tense or strangled voice, as when we phonate while lifting a heavy burden. In between these extremes is a range of adduction variations, with classically trained singers tending to have more consistent adduction across their pitch range. This enables such singers to produce a more even vocal sound across wide pitch ranges, whether singing softly or loudly. Adolescent voices tend to be rather breathier, reflecting this period of instability in vocal coordination during voice change. Untrained females tend to have breathier voices than untrained males across the life span (Linville, 1996). This may be because the gap between the female arytenoids cartilages is generally wider and their closure requires a larger gesture (cf. Södersten, 1994) or because of some underlying gender patterning of the vocal mechanism during childhood (Welch & Howard, in press) or both.

Another type of variation in the voice source corresponds to different patterns of vocal fold oscillation. These patterns are called *vocal registers*. There are at least three registers, generally referred to as *vocal fry*, *chest* (or modal), and *falsetto*. The modal register is sometimes further subdivided in singing into lower and higher subregisters (also termed as *chest* and *head* by singers because of the physical sensations involved) to create four registers.

As stated earlier, greater shortener muscle activity increases the mass of the vocal folds and lowers vocal pitch, while greater lengthener muscle activity reduces the mass of the vocal folds and raises vocal pitch. In vocal fry (pulse register), which frequently occurs at phrase endings in conversational speech, the vocal folds are thick and lax and vibrate asymmetrically; as a result, fundamental frequency is low, generally well below 100 Hz for male voices. By contrast, in the two components of the modal register (lower and upper) the folds are less lax and vibrate symmetrically. If there is a predominance of the shortener laryngeal muscles, there is more vertical tissue mass, creating a larger bottom-to-top contact area and more horizontal depth in the oscillating vocal fold tissues. The vocal folds tend to remain in contact with each other for longer in each cycle (Titze, 1994). The resultant tone sounds richer and full-bodied (often termed *chest voice*). However, if there is greater lengthener activity, the vocal folds are longer and thinner and vocal fold contact is confined only to their superior (upper) portion and outer layers. This reduced vertical mass, smaller bottom-to-top contact area, and less horizontal depth produces a vocal quality that generally sounds lighter and thinner (also termed *head voice*). In falsetto, the folds are thin and stretched and rarely close the glottis completely, unless the voice has been trained in this register (such as that of the countertenor). The shortener muscles are assumed to relax completely, so that vocal fold length is determined by the action of the lengtheners. The vertical tissue mass and horizontal depth can still be varied such that, in a trained falsettist, it is still possible to produce a sung pitch range of approximately two octaves (E_3 to E_5).

Singers are trained to change registers gradually, so that no salient timbre differences occur, unless specifically chosen to add particular voice coloring in their performance. As much of singing principally involves the two elements of the modal register (lower and higher), register transitions (*passaggi*) may best be rehearsed by first practicing *descending* rather than ascending pitch patterns and utilizing quieter phonation. This reduces the potential overinvolvement of subglottal pressure that can occur when singing ascending pitch patterns. Descending pitches require a gradual increase in tension of the shorteners within the vocal folds and a concomitant relaxing of the lengtheners.

A voice source characteristic of the trained singing voice is *vibrato*. There seem to be at least two types of vibrato, which are produced and sound differently (Dejonckere, Hirano, & Sundberg, 1995; Titze, 1994, p. 290). The vibrato used in classical singing is normally produced by pulsations in the pitch-raising lengthener muscle (cricothyroid) and is a *frequency vibrato*. In various types of popular music, a different kind of vibrato is often used, which is generated by variations in subglottal pressure imposing an undulation of voice source amplitude. It corresponds to an amplitude modulation of the voice source and is really an *intensity vibrato* (Sundberg, 1987). Frequency vibrato corresponds to a slow, nearly sinusoidal fundamental frequency modulation. Typically, the rate is somewhere between 5.5 and 7 undulations per second, with the extent of the modulation varying from ±50 to as much as ±150 cents (where 100 cents = 1 semitone). Both rate and extent are important. If the rate goes below 5 undulations per second, which may occur in older or strained voices, no clear pitch can be perceived; it sounds as if the pitch is swaying around. If it is faster than 7 undulations per second, the tone sounds nervous. Also, the acceptable range of frequency modulation is limited. If the extent surpasses about ±100 cents, it tends to sound exaggerated. In choral and in pop singing, vibrato typically has a much smaller extent than in classical singing.

Formants

As mentioned at the beginning of this chapter, the spaces above the vocal folds are a series of connected resonating chambers that filter the sounds that emanate from the voice source. Voiced sounds are acoustically rich, having many harmonics above the fundamental frequency. The tract amplifies certain component harmonics but dampens others. Formants are vocal tract resonances that appear at certain frequencies, the *formant frequencies*. Because partials of various frequencies are transmitted through the vocal tract simultaneously, those that coincide with the formant frequencies are radiated from the lip opening with a greater strength than others. Therefore, formants appear as peaks in the spectrum of the radiated sound (see Figure 16.1).

There are generally five formants relevant to singing, and they are crucial in our perception and discrimination of voiced sound. In speech communication our perception and labeling of certain sounds as vowels depends on the relationship between the lowest two formants. The frequency of the first formant is particularly sensitive to the size and shape of the pharynx and mouth cavity, which is largely influenced by the width of the jaw opening. Likewise, the second formant is particularly sensitive to the shape of the tongue body. If, for example, the first and second formants are located at 600 Hz (around $D\#_5$) and 1,000 Hz (C_6: soprano top C) respectively, the perceived vowel quality is /a:/ (as in *hard*); if they are located at 300 Hz ($D\#_4$) and 2,000 Hz (C_7) the perceived vowel quality is /i:/ (as in *heed*). The formant frequencies depend on vocal tract length and shape, which are controlled by the positioning of the lips, jaw, larynx, velum (soft palate), tongue, and pharyngeal side walls, that is, by articulation. In speech, the coordination of the vocal tract is not conscious but is a product of basic anatomy and physiology interacting through socialization with a particular sociocultural linguistic soundscape. Formant frequencies are decisive for vocal timbre. As well as determining perceived vowel quality, formants are important (alongside temporal patterns) for the perception of personal *voice quality*, permitting us to identify individual voices, such as those of favorite singers on a CD recording or family members on the telephone.

There is a close relationship between vocal tract shape and formant constellation. For example, a shortening of the tract, caused by retracting the corners of the mouth or by raising the larynx, increases all formant frequencies more or less. Both a narrowing of the pharynx and a widening of the mouth cavity increase the frequency of the first formant. This will make the sound brighter. Conversely, expanding the pharynx, protruding the lips, and lowering the larynx will lower the first two formants and make the sound darker in timbre. Moreover, if the pharynx is lengthened by lowering the larynx, the second formant is also lowered in vowels produced by a forward position of the tongue, such as /i:/ (as in *heed*). However, vocal tract length (and hence the formant frequencies of a given vowel) varies somewhat both among and within men, women, and children. Such differences explain some of the voice timbre variations among individuals. For example, it has been shown that for a given vowel tenors tend to sing with higher formant frequencies than basses (Sundberg, 1987, p. 110).

In trained classical singers, a characteristic feature of bass, baritone, tenor, countertenor, and alto voices is an exceptionally high energy peak, normally occurring somewhere between about 2.5 and 3 kHz (i.e., over one octave above C_6). This peak has been called the *singer's formant* (Sundberg, 1974, 1987). The energy peak allows the trained singer's voice to be heard above the sound of a full orchestra in a large concert hall. It appears in all voiced sounds and is normally a consequence of a clustering of the third, fourth, and fifth formant frequencies in a frequency range where the ear is particularly sensitive. This effect can be produced without excessive vocal effort, even when the orchestra is loud. This distinctive ring to the voice, and the source of its carrying power, is generated by a particular configuration of the vocal tract; a wide pharynx is often combined with a lowered larynx (as compared to the rest position). The amplitude of the singer's formant varies among vowels and also with vocal loudness, since vocal loudness affects the slope of the voice source spectrum, as mentioned earlier.

The center frequency of the singer's formant seems significant to voice quality. In bass voices, the center frequency is near 2.4 kHz, in baritone voices near 2.6 kHz, in tenor voices near 2.8 kHz, and in alto voices (female) near 3.0 kHz. These variations can be assumed to reflect differences in vocal tract length and pharyngeal shape. In addition, the wide pharynx needed for clustering the higher formants to create the singer's formant also brings changes to the first two formants. For example, the second formant in front vowels such as /i/ is considerably lower in classical singing than in neutral speech.

Another phenomenon of formants relates to the perception of vowels in singing. The frequency of the first formant varies between about 250 and 1,000 Hz (roughly C_4–C_6) depending on the vowel. So many of the sung pitches produced by tenors, altos, and sopranos can have their fundamental frequency above the typical value of the first formant for a particular vowel. In order to remain (or attempt to remain) intelligible, singers tend to adjust the configuration of the vocal tract in order to raise the value of the first formant under these conditions. In the vowel /a/, this is achieved by a widening of the jaw opening. In other vowels, the lip opening and/or the tongue constriction of the vocal tract is first widened up to a certain point, and after this possibility has been exhausted the jaw opening is widened.

Once again, singers do not deliberately set out to tune the formants per se; rather, they learn (and self-monitor) a set of vocal tract coordinations that produces the desired perceptual effect, namely, a range of vocal pitches and vowels that sound cohesive (cf. Miller & Doing, 1998). In singing pedagogy, for example, much use has been made of the vowel /u:/ (as in too) in training both child and adult aspiring soloists. In normal phonation of this vowel, the third formant is low, so formant clustering does not normally occur. However, a rearticulation of the tongue shape, with an anterior placement of the tip of the tongue, filling out the cavity behind the lower incisors, will raise this formant and increase the perceptibility of a singer's formant.

At high pitches in the soprano range, all vowels share approximately the same formant frequencies. If the first formant is near that of the fundamental frequency (corresponding to the perceived pitch), it has the effect of making the fundamental much louder. For classical sopranos singing at pitches above 700 Hz (F#$_5$, top of the staff), for example, such loudness increases come with no increase in vocal effort. However, since vowel quality is determined mainly by the two lowest formant frequencies, vowel intelligibility at high pitches becomes problematic. Faced with a choice between inaudible tones with normal vowel quality and audible tones with modified vowel quality, singers generally choose the latter. The intelligibility of very high singing relies almost exclusively on consonants, not vowels.

Thus formants are the principal resonances of the vocal tract. Other resonances occur also in the subglottal airways and the nasal sinus system. From the audience's point of view, there appears to be little significant contribution to perceptual voice quality in classical singers from either the chest region (except at low pitches for basses) or the nasal cavities and sinuses. Other vocal genres, such as certain folk singing, may make greater use of nasal resonance. For the singers themselves, any kinesthetic sensations during singing from these bodily parts may assist in their self-monitoring of how they feel the voice is placed during performance.

Choral singers show less evidence of the singer's formant. This probably reflects the need to ensure that individual voices do not stand out in the creation of a choral blend (see also chapter 17). Similarly, *country* singing is more similar to normal speech than classical singing. Thus when one is singing loudly at higher pitches, there is often greater vocal fold adduction. Likewise, vocally untrained and inexperienced singers tend to use habitual speech coordinations when they sing. With increasing pitch, such singers tend to raise their larynxes and change their tone production toward pressed voice. This adds an edgy quality to the voice, corresponding to a weak fundamental and loud high partials, which is a characteristic also of some *folk music* styles.

Another popular singing style is the *belt voice* (Estill, 1988). This is a term that was used to describe singing in the American music theater in the 1940s and 1950s by Ethel Merman but is now also found outside the theater in the performance of other musical genres, such as gospel, spirituals, and jazz. Some popular singers (such as Whitney Houston, Gloria Estafan, Alanis Morissette, and Anita Baker) exploit this quality to create a particular emotional impact at certain moments in a song. The sound is loud and the vowel quality is more similar to that used in very loud speech than in operatic singing. It is produced with a narrow pharynx, a raised larynx, and high lung pressures.

One particularly striking use of formants in a musical genre is found in the throat singing (overtone singing) of Tuva (or Tyva), an autonomous republic within Russia on its border with Mongolia. This type of singing involves producing two distinct pitches simultaneously. One is low and sustained (such as in a bagpipe) and corresponds to the fundamental, while the other is much higher, with a flute- or whistle-type quality, and corresponds to one of the harmonics. There are different styles of throat singing, but each involves a particular voice source behavior (keeping the vocal folds closed for longer in each vibratory cycle) and shaping of the vocal tract (manipulating the tongue tip and root and its midpoint to cluster the second and third formants, with a protrusion of the jaw and a narrowing and rounding of the lips and, in some cases, using the false folds to vibrate an octave below at half the rate of the vocal folds). The result is a low sustained fundamental and a finely tuned formant peak. Depending on the pitch of the fundamental, up to 12 harmonics can be isolated individually. Enhanced in succession, they can create a melody (Levin & Edgerton, 1999). Throat singing is not taught formally but learned in the same way as language. It can be mastered also by non-native singers. This type of singing is also found in Tibet, Japan, and South America (Klingholz, 1993), and elements from such musics have been incorporated into modern Western music performance (Schaefer, 2000).

Performance and Pedagogy

Voice is an essential element of self-identity. It helps to define who we are and how other people experience us. It conveys our inner feeling states, both to ourselves and to others (Thurman & Welch, 2000). Emotion and mood are central characteristics of voice production and reception. This is because of the integrated networking of the body's nervous, endocrine, and immune systems. Whether we are feeling elated, relaxed, stressed, or threatened, each inner state is likely to be reflected in voice behavior and to be communicated to others and to ourselves (Welch, 2000b). Hence, the voice is exceedingly useful as a musical instrument.

Solo singers in training often have vocal habits that are potentially challenging for the voice teacher for five main reasons:

- Much voice behavior is not conscious. It is habitual and not readily accessible to conscious processes. It is also typically influenced (as well as being a reinforcement) by how we feel at the moment of voice use (Thurman & Welch, 2000).
- We cannot physically see the sound source (vocal folds) or tongue shape; we have to rely on our proprioception (from muscle receptors) and auditory feedback to sense what our voice is doing.
- Highly skilled musical performance requires consistent musical behaviors. The moment-to-moment changes in articulation that are characteristic of normal conversation are often inappropriate and inimical to culturally derived classical music performance (Sundberg, 2000, p. 235).
- Vocal music is a highly complex sociocultural artifact. The words and music each present separate challenges to the performer, as does their combination (Welch, 2000a). The text is often a narrative that has its own internal rules, whereas the music makes physical production demands on the vocal system that might be contrary to those expected in normal speech articulation (Welch, 1985a).
- The grouping of tones in musical motifs and phrases is an important aspect of music performance (Gabrielsson, 1999). Changes in voice timbre are often used for marking boundaries in musical structures. This makes the elimination of timbral differences between different pitch regions in a voice an essential aspect of vocal pedagogy.

One of the first tasks for the singing teacher is to bring elements of voice production to conscious awareness, such as an awareness of the underlying anatomical structures and their function in skilled voice production. Major professional associations for singing teachers (such as the National Association of Teachers of Singing in the United States and the Association of Teachers of Singing in the United Kingdom) now include scientific articles in their journals (*Journal of Singing* and *Singing*) in order to assist singing teachers and performers to understand better the data from voice science.

For many centuries, one pedagogical strategy has been to utilize small musical building blocks (*solfeggi* patterns of pitches, such as scales, motifs, arpeggios). Such simple musical exercises allow the singer to focus on and memorize isolated or simple combinations of elements from the dominant musical culture. Solfeggi may also help the singer to work toward a greater evenness of vocal timbre across the pitch range. In untrained voices, vocal timbre tends to automatically change with pitch. However, through the use of such exercises, a greater evenness of vocal timbre is likely, particularly if (1) consonants are reduced in time (although consonant duration is varied for expressive purposes in actual singing performance) and (2) vowels are modified from typical habitual speech patterns.

Although imagery plays an important traditional role in voice pedagogy, it has rarely been researched systematically. Callaghan's (1997) survey of Australian teachers of singing reported three different types of imagery evidenced in practice (visual, kinesthetic, and aural). However, such practices were based on teachers' craft knowledge rather than empirical data. The experiential evidence of the efficacy of imagery continues to need corroboration in terms of well-controlled formal experimentation.

The scientific study of vocal production in singing is a relatively modern phenomenon. The human voice's invisibility has required the application of new technologies to reveal its underlying activity. For example, MRI (Story, Titze, & Hoffman, 1996), X-ray photography, and high-speed imaging are just some of the more important techniques that have been adapted from clinical studies for the analysis of singing.

The basis for performance is a variety of practice and rehearsal strategies that allow the singer to shape the perceptual and physical systems toward the identified musical goal (cf. Welch, 1985b). The practice of constituent elements in isolation can facilitate conscious awareness and control of basic coordination, as well as permitting the conscious overlaying of musical stylistics according to the particular genre and narrative context. Furthermore, reaction time studies indicate that we need approximately 300 ms to make a conscious adjustment to our motor behavior (cf. Schmidt, 1975, p. 137; Welch, 1985a), yet this is rather slow in relation to the requirements of vocal musical performance (such as for rapid scalic passages or arpeggios).

Given the complexities of the voice production in (classical) singing, the implications of a sound knowledge of vocal structure and function for vocal pedagogy are that

- Feedback from the teacher should be related directly to shaping conscious awareness, such as in understanding the relationship between tongue shape and formant tuning.
- The more complex the vocal task, the greater the opportunity for the student to misinterpret teacher feedback (Welch, 1985a, 1985b). Simpler vocal tasks, therefore, are more accessible to focused change.
- The biological aging process changes structure and function, not withstanding the relative stability of voice production across four decades (ages 20 to 60: Titze, 1994, p. 182). For example, the laryngeal cartilages begin to ossify (become more bonelike) in the third decade of life, suggesting that younger voices are more suited to agile musical requirements, whereas older voices are more able to sustain vocally strenuous performance. Therefore, different musical demands are appropriate for different age groups.

In summary, successful solo singing across the life span is more likely if both teachers and performers have developed habitual singing behaviors that are underpinned by an understanding of their physical and psychological reality.

References

Callaghan, J. (1997). *Voice science and singing teaching in Australia.* Unpublished doctoral thesis, University of Western Sydney, Australia.

Dejonckere, P. H., Hirano, M., & Sundberg, J. (Eds.) (1995). *Vibrato.* London: Singular Press.

Estill, J. (1988). Belting and classic voice quality: Some physiological differences. *Medical Problems of Performing Artists, 3,* 37–43.

Gabrielsson, A. (1999). The performance of music. In D. Deutsch (Ed.), *The psychology of music* (2nd ed., pp. 501–602). London: Academic Press.

Harris, T., Harris, S., Rubin, J. S., & Howard, D. M. (1998). *The voice clinic handbook.* London: Whurr.

Klingholz, F. (1993). Overtone singing: Productive mechanisms and acoustic data. *Journal of Voice, 7*(2), 118–122.

Levin, T. C., & Edgerton, M. E. (1999). The throat singers of Tuva. *Scientific American, 281*(3), 70–77.

Linville, S. E. (1996). The sound of senescence. *Journal of Voice, 10*(2), 190–200.

Miller, D., & Doing, J. (1998). Male *passaggio* and the upper extension in the light of visual feedback. *Journal of Singing, 54*(1), 3–14.

Nordström, P.-E. (1977). Female and infant vocal tracts simulated from male area functions. *Journal of Phonetics, 5,* 81–92.

Schaefer, J. (2000). "Songlines": Vocal traditions in world music. In J. Potter (Ed.), *The Cambridge companion to singing* (pp. 9–27). Cambridge: Cambridge University Press.

Schmidt, R. A. (1975). *Motor skills.* New York: Harper & Row.

Södersten, M. (1994). *Vocal fold closure during phonation—physiological, perceptual, and acoustic studies.* Doctoral dissertation, Department of Logopedics and Phoniatrics, Huddinge University Hospital, Karolinska Institutet, Stockholm.

Story, B. H., Titze, I. R., & Hoffman, E. A. (1996). Vocal tract area functions from magnetic resonance imaging. *Journal of the Acoustical Society of America, 100,* 537–554.

Story, B. H., Titze, I. R., & Hoffman, E. A. (1997). Volumetric image-based comparison of male and female vocal tract shapes. *National Center for Voice and Speech Status and Progress Report, 11,* 153–161.

Sundberg, J. (1974). Articulatory interpretation of the "singing formant." *Journal of the Acoustical Society of America, 55,* 838–844.

Sundberg, J. (1987). *The science of the singing voice.* DeKalb, IL: Northern Illinois University Press.

Sundberg, J. (1996). The human voice. In R. Greger and U. Windhorst (Eds.), *Comprehensive human physiology,* Vol. 1 (pp. 1095–1104). Berlin: Springer.

Sundberg, J. (2000). Where does the sound come from? In J. Potter (Ed.), *The Cambridge companion to singing* (pp. 231–247). Cambridge: Cambridge University Press.

Thomasson, M., & Sundberg, J. (1999). Consistency of phonatory breathing patterns in professional operatic singers. *Journal of Voice, 13*(4), 529–541.

Thurman, L., & Welch, G. F. (2000). *Bodymind and voice: Foundations of voice education* (2nd ed.). Iowa City: National Center for Voice and Speech.

Titze, I. R. (1994). *Principles of voice production.* Englewood Cliffs, NJ: Prentice-Hall.

Welch, G. F. (1985a). A schema theory of how children learn to sing in-tune. *Psychology of Music, 13*(1), 3–18.

Welch, G. F. (1985b). Variability of practice and knowledge of results as factors in learning to sing in-tune. *Bulletin of the Council for Research in Music Education, 85,* 238–247.

Welch, G. F. (2000a). Singing development in early childhood: The effects of culture and education on the realisation of potential. In P. J. White. (Ed.), *Child voice* (pp. 27–44). Stockholm: Royal Institute of Technology.

Welch, G. F. (2000b). Voice management. In A. Thody, B. Gray, D. Bowden, and G. F. Welch, *The teacher's survival guide* (pp. 45–60). London: Continuum.

Welch, G. F., & Howard, D. M. (in press). Gendered voice in the cathedral choir. *Psychology of Music.*

17

Choir

STEN TERNSTRÖM & DUANE RICHARD KARNA

Choir singers and directors frequently find themselves grappling with acoustical issues that appear to affect their ability to perform well. Hearing one's own voice, for example, is crucial. It improves with increased singer spacing and depends also on the room acoustics. Singer preferences are diverse but on average one's own voice needs to be about 6 dB stronger than the rest of the choir. In most rooms this implies a fairly spread-out formation. Precise intonation may be jeopardized by pitch perception discrepancies and by mechanisms inherent to voice control but it can also be facilitated by acoustically informed measures such as articulatory enhancement of common partials. Researching such issues necessitates decomposition while remaining aware of the true complexity of the situation: that of many people singing together and hearing each other in a room.

Many people who choose to perform music as a satisfying pastime do so as choir singers. Singing in unison or in harmony with other people is a low-cost, enjoyable activity, which at the beginner's level demands little more than one's time and a certain dedication to the task.

During the past couple of decades, research into the acoustics of choir singing has uncovered numerous interesting effects that are of potential relevance to choral performance. Some concern voice production, others have to do with the acoustics of the stage and the auditorium, while still others are related to our sense of hearing. Many of them are rather subtle and, if taken in isolation, of minor importance. When the acoustical circumstances combine constructively, however, choral singing is certain to become easier; conversely, when they combine destructively, choral performance is likely to suffer. For this chapter, we have chosen to describe in detail some phenomena that we expect and hope to be particularly interesting and useful to choral directors and singers who are curious about acoustics.

Fundamentals of Room Acoustics

We note first that choirs are particularly dependent on the acoustics of the room, a subject that is not covered by other chapters in this volume.

Sound waves are a form of energy. One adult singer emits about three milliwatts (mW) of acoustic power in *forte*. Most of the energy emitted by the singer will bounce around in the room as reverberation until it is absorbed (into heat) by the walls and furnishings. The greater the absorption, the quicker the sound energy disappears, and the shorter the reverberation time will be. A minuscule proportion of the radiated sound energy eventually reaches the eardrums of listeners. The sound that reaches the listener from the source has three components: the direct sound, the early reflections, and the diffuse field (or reverberation). The *direct sound* travels in a straight line from source to receiver; it arrives first and reveals the distance and the direction to the source. The nearer the source, the stronger the direct sound. *Early reflections* are sounds that arrive at the listener after only one or two bounces against nearby walls. At delays less than about 40 ms we do not perceive these as separate echoes, but they are still very important for our impression of the acoustical liveness of a room. The *diffuse field* is the sum of the thousands of all later reflections that rapidly die down as a small amount of energy is lost into the wall at each bounce. The *reverberation time* is defined as the time it takes for the diffuse field to become 60 decibels (dB) weaker once the sound source has been turned off. After that time, the reverberation is essentially inaudible.

The diffuse field is so called because the many reflections tend to merge into a practically uniform sound field with no direction of its own. For a given source, the intensity of the diffuse field is much the same throughout the room. (Analogy: when you have been swimming in a pool for a while, the slosh of waves won't tell you where in the pool you have been.) There exists a distance from the source such that the intensities of the direct sound and the diffuse field are equal; this is called the *reverberation radius* of the room. If we move out farther from the source, the diffuse field dominates and the total sound intensity does not diminish appreciably with distance. If instead we approach the source, the direct sound will dominate and become louder the closer we are to the source. Considering the situation inside the choir, in rooms typical for choir performance only the one or two nearest circles of neighbors in the choir are within one reverberation radius of each other; the rest of the choir is outside.

Physical Versus Perceptual Sound Properties

The loudness, pitch, and timbre of a sound are *perceptual* entities that can be measured only by asking listeners what they hear. Fortunately, these three entities correspond closely—but not exactly—to three measurable *physical* entities of sound: pressure level (SPL), fundamental frequency (F_0), and distribution of energy over frequency. The physical properties are the main entry points of the acoustician, who can measure them, study their evolution over time and space, and subject them to statistical analysis.

All the physical parameters of a tone can to some degree influence any or all perceptual parameters (Fletcher, 1934). The study of these dependencies is the basis of psychoacoustics. For example, a tone that has a strong fundamental partial but weak overtones is perceived as dull. When presented at very different loudness levels, such a tone may also appear to change somewhat in pitch, even though its fundamental frequency remains the same. This so-called pitch-amplitude effect is not generally known to musicians, but it may influence choral intonation in certain circumstances.

Sound Properties and Mechanisms as an Organizing Principle

For any research project on choir acoustics it is convenient to constrain the issue to one or two of the measurable *properties*, usually adopting a perspective either of voice production, of room acoustics, or of hearing, which are all *mechanisms*. It must be stressed that such constraints are for practicality only, because the reality of choral performance is too complex to be studied all at once. In Table 17.1 we list some examples of topics related to choir acoustics, categorized along these lines.

The intricacy of possible topics means that there is no obvious, systematic path for us to follow in order to cover the subject of choir acoustics in this compact overview. Instead, we will state some acoustical problems commonly encountered by choirs and point to ways of understanding and negotiating these problems. In each case we will first list the relevant acoustical issues and provide some practical recommendations. This will be followed by an in-depth background discussion of the problem, with explanations of the recommendations and references to scientific research.

Balance of Loudness

Choral singers sometimes complain that they cannot hear their own voices. Why might this be, and what can be done about it?

Relevant Factors

1. The physical spacing between singers
2. The amount of reverberation in the room
3. The presence or absence of reflectors close to each singer
4. The vocal power of the complaining singers relative to that of their neighbors

Recommendations

1. Increase the spacing between singers, and/or have the choir stand in fewer rows. If this is not possible, mix the sections.

Table 17.1. A tentative categorization of topics in choir acoustics. Topics discussed in this chapter are indicated in italics.

	Loudness/ Balance	Intonation	Timbre	Multivoice Issues
Voice production	Diversity of singers' vocal power; directivity of the human voice	Breath support, vibrato in choirs; *articulatory perturbation of pitch*	Acoustic differences between S-A-T-B, between trained voice and untrained, singer's formant or not	*The role of flutter in ensemble sound*; placement of singers within the choir; does uniformity of vowels matter?
Room acoustics	Effects of choir size, formation, *singer spacing and room absorption on the self-to-other ratio (SOR)*; distances; risers, shells, and reflectors	Effect of the SOR on intonation ability; can the pitch of the reverberation seem to go flat?	Effects of room response on voice usage; effects of different types of absorbents; wall proximity for basses; where to hold the music folder	Choir placement relative to audience; trade-off between room reverberation and the number of singers; ensemble timing
Perception	*Reflection, occlusion and bone conduction of one's own voice; diversity of singer preferences as to the SOR*	The *pitch/ amplitude effect* as an intonation hazard; *the pitch can differ slightly in the left and right ears*	*Pitch is more salient with certain timbres; role of common partials*; why some voices fit together and not others	Blending ability of different voice types; differences between choirs and vocal groups; *combination tones and beats*; how close is unison?
Sound technology	Choir with instrumental combo; public-address systems; self-monitoring for the choir	*What devices are suitable for giving the starting pitch?*	Faithful reproduction or enhancement?	Placement of microphones and loudspeakers

2. Decrease the amount of reverberation in the room by introducing absorbents, closing curtains, admitting the audience, or opening several windows.
3. Encourage the singers to experiment with the sheet music and folder as a small personal reflector. There is a particular angle that noticeably improves the perception of one's own voice. Remove any shells or other large reflecting surfaces at close range, because these tend to exacerbate the problem.
4. Place the quieter voices near the ends of the choir and the louder ones near the center.

Scientific Background

Self and Other. Inside a choir we have a complex transmitters-receivers situation with many directional sound sources, all of whom are also listeners (Marshall & Meyer, 1985). Taking the perspective of an individual singer in the choir, we will refer to the sound of one's own voice as *Self* and to the sound of the rest of the choir as *Other*. The Self sound is dominated by *airborne* sound coming out through the mouth, but it also has a component of *bone-conducted* sound. The relative contribution of the bone-conducted sound is hard, however, to measure objectively (von Békésy, 1949). For example, it can vary dramatically with vowels: block your ears and sing to compare /u/ with /a/! An open mouth radiates more sound, leaving less energy to be coupled through the body's tissues.

The airborne part of Self is entirely dominated by the direct sound from the mouth. The room reflections of Self are typically 15 to 20 dBs weaker than the direct Self. This means that inside any choir they will be drowned out (*masked*) by Other.

The Self-to-Other Ratio. A choir singer hears the Self sound together with the Other sound; ideally these should both be discernible in some optimal proportion. The *Self-to-Other Ratio* (*SOR*) can be measured on location for any particular singer and can be expressed in decibels. When the ears of a singer are subjected to the sounds of Self and Other simultaneously, Self will usually be a certain number of decibels stronger, in which case the SOR is said to be positive. Clearly, the SOR is a predictor of how well a singer will hear his or her own voice. Typical SOR values in live choral performance range from +1 to +8 dB (Ternström, 1994).

The major factor to influence the SOR is the intersinger spacing (item 1 above). The farther apart the singers are standing (especially from their own section colleagues), the greater the SOR, and the easier it will be for them to hear their own voices—and, conversely, the harder it will be for them to hear the others. Daugherty (1996) found that both singers and auditors preferred the choral sound produced in spread formations over that produced in close formation.

The SOR is also inversely related to the amount of reverberation in the room: the less reverberation, the weaker the total sound will be, and so the easier it will be to make out the sound of one's own voice (B). For a given choir placement in a room with given physical properties, the SOR can be predicted with some accuracy. This is important because it gives the architect's acoustics consultant a tangible goal: to design for a SOR onstage in the vicinity of +6 dB (Ternström, 1999).

Singer Preferences. In a normal situation, the individual choir singer cannot do very much to change his or her hearing-of-self, other than to use the music folder as a personal reflector to increase SOR. The permissible loudness of one's own voice is constrained by the music's dynamics. Vocal artists who perform with adjustable amplification, however, can be very fussy about the exact amount of monitor feedback they require. Ternström (1999) did an experiment with 23 experienced singers to determine (1) whether choir singers are particular about their preferred SOR in a choral context and (2) how large the preferred SOR might be. The singers were indeed quite precise about their personal preferences: they reproduced their individual preferred SOR to within ±2 dB, which is a remarkably close tolerance. The overall average preferred SOR was +6 dB. However, tastes varied wildly, from +15 dB down to 0 dB. In other words, some of these singers wanted to hear their own voice a lot, while others preferred the rest of the choir to be just as loud. This large variation may be due to different habitual placement within the choir (see later), to individual voice timbres, and even to certain hearing losses so small as to be unknown by the singer.

Loudness Issues. The choir director should be aware that singer placement is not just a question of how well or poorly different voices sound together but also one of how comfortable each singer is with the balance of loudness of voices in his or her vicinity.

Having the choir stand in many rows will cause large differences in SOR between the center and the periphery of the choir, since some singers will have many neighbors and others will have few. In single-row formations, the SOR varies less with position in the choir. Furthermore, the SOR will be lowest in the bass section and highest in the soprano section when all sections are singing (Ternström, 1995). This is because sopranos are loudest: the human voice radiates acoustic power more efficiently at high fundamental frequencies. In terms of SPL, the Other sound will thus be dominated by sopranos, except in very close choir formations.

The ability to monitor one's own voice is crucial for accurate singing. As an example, have some volunteer singers carry small tape recorders to record their own voices (without headphones!) at very close range in various choral performance situations. Ask them to assess their own performances from the tape a few hours later. If the tape reveals unexpected errors, chances are that they could not hear themselves well enough.

Unison singing—all voices in synchrony on the same tones—is the worst case for monitoring one's own voice, since Other masks Self most efficiently when the frequencies overlap. If the SOR is too low, the singers may be able to hear their own voices only by making mistakes, and the scatter in intonation is likely to increase. In very large choirs, therefore, sectional formation is likely to be problematic.

Intonation

We are working on a piece that often tends to go out of tune at a particular point. Why might this be?

Relevant Factors

1. The *intrinsic pitch* of vowels and consonants is an acoustical and physiological phenomenon known from phonetics. In speech, some sounds tend to have a slightly raised or lowered F_0 because of the way the voice organ must be configured to produce them.

2. The *pitch-amplitude effect* is a perceptual phenomenon that makes it possible for the perceived pitch of a constant-frequency tone to change slightly with changes in loudness. Some people are more susceptible to this effect than others. The effect is most relevant to high and loud soprano singing.

3. *Breath support* has a direct bearing on intonation, particularly on long sustained tones in the upper pitch ranges. This is not really a choral issue but one of vocal training, although the problem is very common in choral singers.

4. *Complex modulations* between tonally distant keys is a music theory issue that many others have described, although little of predictive use has been reported; see any text on scales and temperament.

Recommendations

1. Analyze the text for intrinsic pitch effects (see later). Temporarily change the lyric to something completely different and see whether the intonation is affected.

2. If some sopranos tend to sing sharp on high, loud tones, chances are that their ears are fooling them. In this situation, conductors sometimes accuse the singers of a poor sense of pitch; however, most of the time they are doing their best and have no way of knowing they are sharp. Instead, try to ascertain whether the pitch-amplitude effect is in fact the culprit. An individual test for the pitch-amplitude effect is suggested later.

3. Have the singers learn vocal technique. The term *breath support* refers to a singer's proficiency in controlling the subglottal pressure. The fundamental frequency of vocal fold vibration is regulated mainly by the subglottal pressure (coarse, slow control issued by many large respiratory muscles) (Titze, 1989) and by the pull of the rather small *cricothyroid* muscle (fine, rapid control). If the subglottal pressure is too low, as with insufficient breath support, then the cricothyroid muscle must exert a much larger force to achieve a high target pitch, and so it tires quickly (chapter 16).

Acoustical and Psychoacoustical Background

In speech, there is rarely a need for precise intonation of sustained tones; rather, it is *gestures* or *inflections* in pitch that carry important information. Pitch in speech is also closely related to vocal effort. Increased subglottal pressure will normally raise the fundamental frequency, or F_0 (e.g., Titze, 1989). Hence, we expect in speech a strong covariation of loudness and pitch: the louder, the higher. Singers, however, must learn to control loudness and F_0 separately. This is a task that requires considerable coordination.

From an engineer's viewpoint, the voice organ is an unruly and entangled conglomerate of cartilage, muscle, and soft tissue. For such a device to produce sound at a stable F_0, it must be controlled by use of a host of auditory and neuromuscular mechanisms with compensatory action, or *servo systems*, that continuously monitor the voice output and apply corrective signals until the output is perceived to match the target. Voice research has shown that the servo-system paradigm is in fact a good model for F_0 control (Larson et al., 2000; Ternström & Friberg, 1989). Since the voice organ is driven mainly by lung pressure, is steered by minute muscular control in the larynx, and is monitored by hearing and other types of receptors in the body, there seem to be few aspects of vocal function and near-field acoustics that could *not* have some bearing on intonation.

Because the intonation precision needed for choral harmony is very high, even small disruptions to pitch can be significant. Here we will discuss two of these: *intrinsic pitch*, which is a voice production phenomenon; and the *pitch-amplitude effect* that was mentioned earlier, which is a pitch perception phenomenon.

Articulatory Perturbation of Pitch (Intrinsic Pitch). In a voice science context, the term *articulation* refers to the action of adjusting and positioning the jaw, tongue, and lips to produce a given sequence of sounds. To phoneticians it is well known that in running speech some vowels tend to be produced with a slightly lower or higher F_0 than the average for the speech as a whole (Ladd & Silverman, 1984). Front vowels such as /i:/ and /e:/ (with the tongue held forward) tend to receive a slightly higher F_0, and back vowels such as /a:/ and /e:/ tend to be lower, on the order of a semitone or two. Phoneticians call this *intrinsic pitch*. Despite its name (*pitch* normally refers to perception or experience), this is not a perceptual effect but rather a vowel-dependent bias on F_0 that is somehow exerted by the articulation. Several biomechanical and acoustic hypotheses have been advanced to explain these deviations, but the matter is not yet closed.

In addition, the articulation of consonants sometimes involves movements of the larynx or changes in the air pressure differential that drives the vibration of the vocal folds. This can cause the F_0 of voiced consonants to differ from that of the adjacent vowels. For example, say very slowly *ahdahdah* and notice how the pitch drops during the *d* consonants. In fact, this intrinsic drop in pitch is a strong cue for us to interpret the sound as the consonant *d*.

In singing, intrinsic pitch effects would presumably be compensated for, as the singer is striving to reach a target frequency for each note. But what happens if it is hard to hear one's own voice, as is often the case in a choir? Ternström, Sundberg, and Colldén (1988) asked choir singers to sustain tones over a change of vowel and measured the average F_0 before and after the vowel transition. The subjects wore closed headphones in which they alternately heard their own voice fed back and a masking noise that completely drowned out their own voice. Each vowel pair was sung in noise and was then immediately repeated without noise. Intrinsic pitch effects were found in *both* conditions, but they were larger in noise, as expected. On the average, the largest F_0 changes were observed between /i:/ (high) and /ɛ:/ (low). For this case the average effect was about thirty cents, larger in noise and smaller with normal feedback. Such a pitch change is certainly large enough to make a chord go out of tune. Figure 17.1 summarizes the *occurrence* of pitch changes for the different vowel pairs in this experiment. The vowel /a:/ was not included, but it is known to have an even lower intrinsic pitch than /ɛ:/.

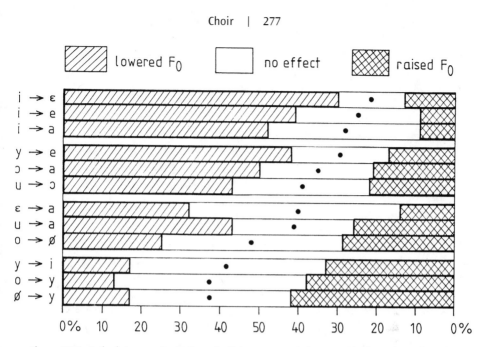

Figure 17.1. Articulatory perturbation of pitch over vowel changes. The bars show the relative occurrence of intrinsic pitch effects found when six subjects changed vowels on sustained tones (see text). The conditions with and without auditory feedback are pooled. For example, the top line is interpreted as follows: when the vowels /i:/ and /ɛ:/ were paired, /ɛ:/ was sung at a lower pitch in 70% of the cases and at a higher pitch in 13% of the cases, regardless of whether /i:/ or /ɛ:/ came first. (From Ternström, Sundberg & Colldén, 1988. Copyright American Speech-Language-Hearing Association, reprinted with permission.)

A practical consequence of this result is that intonation problems can sometimes be ascribed to a particular sequence of vowels and consonants (for example, *dies irae* or *kyrie eleison*) and that not hearing one's own voice will make things even worse.

The Pitch-Amplitude Effect.   To test yourself for the pitch-amplitude effect, you will need a sound source that can produce a pure or nearly pure sine wave with stable loudness and frequency. Such a wave is best produced with a tone generator or a synthesizer with a Sine program or a very dull flutelike sound. Failing that, you can use a high-quality microphone and tape recorder to record somebody whistling a pure tone or have a soprano sing on a closed vowel. Try three or four tones that range from middle C (262 Hz) and two octaves up. Connect a pair of headphones to the sound source. Place the headphones on a table in front of you and adjust the volume so that you easily can tell whether the tone is playing or not, but no louder. Listen to its pitch, then put the headphones on without adjusting the volume and listen again. Many people will perceive a lower pitch when the tone thus becomes louder. To some, the drop will be large (a semitone or more); to others, it will be small or inaudible.

The pitch-amplitude effect is well known to psychoacousticians (e.g., Verschuure & van Meeteren, 1975). It is typically at its strongest in the region of 300 to 500 Hz, becomes insignificant at 1 to 2 kHz, and reverses at very high frequencies, where the pitch instead seems to increase with level. This explains why dull tones with only a few low partials are the most susceptible. The more high-frequency overtones there are in the stimulus sound, the less their combined pitch is perturbed, and the weaker the pitch-amplitude effect becomes. Ternström and Sundberg (1988) found a pronounced pitch-amplitude effect in some but not all male subjects who were attempting to sing in unison with a synthesized stimulus vowel /u:/, which is poor in high partials, but not with /a:/, which is rich in high partials. Ternström has also demonstrated the pitch-amplitude effect for soprano tones in syntheses of ensemble sounds (not published). For the effect to occur, the reference tone and the tone produced by the subject must be very different in loudness and the louder tone must have strong low partials and weak high partials. This situation is quite rare in choirs, but it does occur for sopranos who are singing high and loud. The effect will probably be more pronounced in venues with little reverberation, because then the difference in loudness will be large between one's own voice and the rest of the choir (the SOR will be high).

A soprano whose sense of hearing happens to have a steep pitch-amplitude dependency is faced with this problem: when singing high and loud she is likely to perceive her own voice as a little flat, because it is stronger than the other sounds around her and because high soprano tones are necessarily dominated by the fundamental partial (chapter 16). To compensate, she will probably produce a tone that is perceived as sharp by everyone else. Not knowing about the pitch-amplitude effect, she will feel unjustly accused of singing sharp and having a poor sense of pitch. Unfortunately, there is not much she can do to determine exactly at what pitch she should really be singing, other than gradually to learn how flat she should hear herself for the others to stop complaining. We believe choral directors should be aware that the pitch-amplitude effect exists, that it is an innate property of our auditory system, and that it has nothing to do with musical ability or talent.

A related phenomenon is the relationship between *timbre* and *pitch salience*, that is, whether the perceived pitch is clear or unclear (Terhardt, 1975). Listeners tend to agree less on the pitch of a tone if its spectrum is not balanced. For example, it is probably a bad idea to give the starting tone to the choir using a low flute stop on the organ, which has strong low-frequency partials and weak high-frequency partials, because different singers may perceive its pitch slightly differently. It is also risky to use small electronic beeper devices, which are rich in high partials but completely lacking in low partials. A voice or a piano should serve most singers well.

Singers sometimes try to hear their own voice better by blocking one ear with a fingertip. Blocking the ear does make the Self sound louder, but it also becomes muffled, while the Other sound becomes a lot weaker. This jeopardizes intonation, because such conditions increase the risk of the pitch-amplitude effect. Of course, closing one's ear would also look silly on stage. But wearing an earphone or hearing aid, for example, would have much the same effect.

Finally, we cannot even trust our two ears to perceive the same pitch. It is not uncommon to hear slightly different pitches from a tone generator—or tuning fork—that is held first to one ear and then to the other. A choir director giving pitch might need to know if one of his or her ears is slightly out of tune.

Overtones

In some long chords I can hear a tone that is not being sung by anyone in the choir. The tone typically sounds like a high-pitched whistle and is sometimes musically appropriate, sometimes not. What is going on?

Relevant Factors

1. One or more of the following circumstances may combine to make a particular partial tone especially loud: (a) the partial tone is a component of many of the constituent tones of the chord, (b) the formant frequency configuration of the vowel happens to enhance it, (c) many of the singers happen to agree very closely on the formation of that vowel, (d) vibrato is small or nonexistent.
2. The so-called *chorus effect* makes it easier for the ear to pick out the individual partial tones in ensemble sounds than in solo sounds.
3. In loud and/or pressed voice, in which the high-frequency partials are more intense than in soft voice, this phenomenon becomes more likely. This is in fact a strategy adopted for example by the Tuva throat singers (Levin & Edgerton, 1999).

Recommendations

1. If the unsung tone is a problem, sing in a softer nuance or experiment with a different vowel to see if the problem goes away. Modify open vowels to closed or vice versa. If the unsung tone is a desired effect, modify the vowel very slowly and carefully until the effect is maximized. Decide and explain to the singers which section is to act as the intonation reference at various points in the piece.
2. If the singers are having difficulty tuning a particular harmony and if different sections have different lyrics, try making them sing the same text. Change closed vowels to open; in particular, let the basses sing on *ah* for a while. More often than not, rich overtones will facilitate accurate intonation.
3. In practice, independently audible overtones are rarely a problem but rather an interesting curiosity that often goes unnoticed by the audience, unless the composer and the performers have taken extra pains to make the effect come across. In some traditions overtones are even cultivated as an instrument in its own right. Singers often wonder about overtones and how to enhance them, and the choral director can sometimes exploit overtone enhancement in the service of intonation.

Background

Combination Tones, Beats, and Harmony.   When two stable unison tones of similar loudness are tuned slightly apart, they sound not like two tones but like one tone that *beats*. If the mistuning is gradually increased, the beating becomes too rapid to be perceived as such but rather invokes a roughness of timbre; at some point the ear will also start to resolve the two tones. Furthermore, for tones that are close in frequency to each other, distortion effects inside the ear can generate various audible *combination tones* whose frequencies are sums and differences of the frequencies of the two physical tones and their harmonics.

On instruments with stable pitch, so-called just or pure intonation sounds pure because it minimizes the beating and hides the combination tones by lining them up with the real partial tones. In choral sounds, however, things are rather different. Regular beats are never heard in a choir, for two reasons. The first and foremost is that the human voice is not stable enough in frequency for regular beats to occur. Even when singing an acceptably straight tone, most voices *flutter* up and down by 10 to 20 cents (Ternström & Friberg, 1989). This makes the beats irregular, and therefore they are not readily perceived. One interesting consequence of this is that there should be no inherent advantage of using just intonation in choir music (cf. Chapter 12). Ternström and Nordmark (1996) found that musically trained listeners who were asked to fine-tune major third intervals in synthesized sustained, nonvibrato ensemble sounds had diverse preferences but averaged between just intonation and equal temperament.

The second reason we do not hear the beats in the choir is that with more than two unison voices even the smallest F_0 differences between them will cause each voice to beat against each other voice, creating a great multitude of irregular beats. The beating is in fact so profuse and irregular that it sounds like something else. We might define the *chorus effect* or *ensemble effect* to be that character of sound that prevents us from hearing exactly how many voices are singing in unison. The minimum is three, which sounds distinctly different from both one and two voices (Ternström, Friberg, & Sundberg, 1988).

In vocal groups that perform close harmony with one voice to a part, the chorus effect is often intentionally avoided. Instead they strive to achieve harmonies that are so precisely tuned and so straight in pitch that the voices fuse together and we hear one instrumentlike chord rather than several part singers.

Reinforced Partials as an Aid to Intonation.   We assume here that the reader is already somewhat familiar with the harmonic series of partial tones (fundamental plus overtones) and its relation to the musical scale.

In any sound from a single tone source, some partials will be stronger than others, but if they all vary together, the auditory brain centers will assume that they all derive from the same source and report only one percept to the listener. Therefore, we do not hear individual partial tones, unless one of them is markedly reinforced (see discussion of overtone singing in chapter 16). In ensemble sounds, however, the partial tones do not vary strictly together, as they do in the sound of a single voice. Thus it can be easier to hear out individual partials in a sustained choral sound than in one voice.

Ternström and Sundberg (1988) did intonation experiments in which individual male singers sang fifths and major thirds together with both synthetic tones and with a prerecorded unison male choir. The experiment showed that when partial number three of the lower tone (which sounds like a fifth) was reinforced by the formant structure of the vowel, the subjects were more agreed on the intonation of fifths; similarly, when partial number five (which sounds like a major third) was strong, the subjects were more agreed on the intonation of major thirds. While the effect was not very large, it appeared even though the subjects were ignorant of the purpose of the experiment. The implication for choral directors is that accurate intonation of a particular chord can sometimes be facilitated by judiciously choosing a vowel that will emphasize (a partial tone at some octave of) the reference tone in the chord.

The formants of the vocal tract are only resonances and produce no sound of their own (chapter 16). Instead, they reinforce whatever frequencies are produced by phonation and frication. In most languages, the two lowest formants, F_1 and F_2, are sufficient to determine the identity of the vowel. The legend to Figure 17.2 discusses how this can be relevant to choral intonation. Read the words shown in Figure 17.2 in a loud whisper, without voicing, and you will probably hear the pitches of F_1 and/or F_2, albeit vaguely.

In the first example in Figure 17.2, with *who'd*, F_2 reinforces the tone B, which is common to the harmonic series of both the sung tones E and G; this is likely to facilitate intonation. In the *hood* example, F_1 emphasizes the G that is common to bass and tenor; again, this is probably good for intonation. In addition,

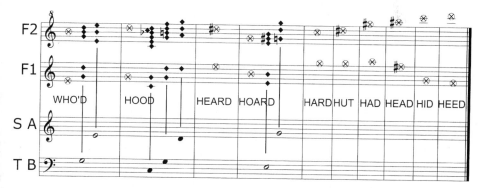

Figure 17.2. Some examples of possible interactions between formants and partials. The crossed circles indicate the approximate frequencies of the first and second formants (F_1 and F_2) for spoken English vowels as pronounced by adults (Peterson & Barney, 1952). These frequencies are vowel-specific and essentially independent of the sung pitch. Notice the *octava* on the clef for F_2; it needs to be notated an octave higher. The diamonds indicate the lowest few partial-tone frequencies of the corresponding sung tones on the S A and T B lines (soprano, alto, tenor, bass).

the F_2 of *hood* emphasizes the high D, which is common to all three voices; this is likely to reinforce the ninth of the chord. On *hoard*, however, F_2 might cause a problem by amplifying the clash between the $G_\sharp$ that is the fifth partial of the bass tone and the $G_\natural$ that signals the minor tonality.

A good place to learn more about intonation and overtones is at barbershop rehearsals and workshops. Because of their particular style requirements, barbershop singers usually take a keen interest in acoustical matters and often present lessons on the intricate relationship between the formant frequencies and the configuration of the common partials.

Conclusion

With this small sampler, we hope to have stirred the reader's interest in the field of choir acoustics, which of course encompasses many more topics, such as room and stage design, choral formations, the use of choral risers and reflecting shells, the deployment of sound equipment, and so on. More references to literature by others as well as ourselves can be found at www.speech.kth.se/~sten. While many issues are already addressed by the literature, there are still many more questions that remain to be answered. In anticipation of future research (Daugherty, 2000), let us close with some intriguing questions that have *not* been investigated at the time this chapter was written:

- Does a choral piece that tends to go flat generally stay in tune if it is sung a semitone higher, and if so, why?
- How is it that one or two key singers can seem to lead a whole section, while others seem to become expert at following the leader?
- How is it that some pairs of voices sound better together than others?

Acknowledgements.   Ternström's and Sundberg's work in choir acoustics has been funded by the Swedish Council for Research in the Humanities and Social Sciences (HSFR), the Swedish Natural Science Research Council (NFR), and the Bank of Sweden Tercentenary Foundation (RJ). Karna's work and travel was funded by the Swedish Information Service (Bicentennial Swedish-American Exchange Grant) and the Office of Sponsored Grants and Research, Salisbury State University, Salisbury, Maryland.

References

Daugherty, J. F. (1996). *Spacing, formation, and choral sound: Preferences and perceptions of auditors and choristers*. Doctoral thesis, Florida State University, Tallahassee.

Daugherty, J. F. (Ed.) (2000). *International Journal of Research in Choral Singing*, on-line publication at www.choralresearch.org.

Fletcher, H. (1934). Loudness, pitch, and timbre of musical tones and their relations to the intensity, the frequency, and the overtone structure. *Journal of the Acoustical Society of America, 6*, 59–69.

Ladd, D. R., & Silverman, K. E. A. (1984). Vowel intrinsic pitch in connected speech. *Phonetica*, *41*, 31–40.

Larson, C. R., Burnett, T. A., Kiran, S., & Hain, T. C. (2000). Effects of pitch-shift velocity on voice F_0 responses. *Journal of the Acoustical Society of America*, *107*(1), 559–564.

Levin, T. C., & Edgerton, M. E. (1999). The throat singers of Tuva. *Scientific American*, *281*(3), 80–87.

Marshall, A. H., & Meyer, J. (1985). The directivity and auditory impressions of singers. *Acustica*, *58*, 130–140.

Peterson G. E., & Barney, H. L. (1952). Control methods used in a study of the vowels. *Journal of the Acoustical Society of America*, *24*, 175–184.

Terhardt, E. (1975). Influence of intensity on the pitch of complex tones. *Acustica*, *33*, 344–348.

Ternström, S. (1994). Hearing myself with the others—sound levels in choral performance measured with separation of the own voice from the rest of the choir. *Journal of Voice*, *8*(4), 293–302.

Ternström, S. (1995). Self-to-other ratios measured in choral performance. In M. J. Newman (Ed.), *Proceedings of the Fifteenth International Conference on Acoustics* (pp. 681–684). Trondheim: Acoustical Society of Norway.

Ternström, S. (1999). Preferred self-to-other ratios in choir singing. *Journal of the Acoustical Society of America*, *105*(6), 3563–3574.

Ternström, S., & Friberg, A. (1989). Analysis and simulation of small variations in the fundamental frequency of sustained vowels. *Speech Transmission Laboratory Quarterly Progress and Status Report*, *3*, 1–14.

Ternström, S., Friberg, A., & Sundberg, J. (1988). Synthesizing choir singing. *Journal of Voice*, *1*(4), 332–335.

Ternström, S., & Nordmark, J. (1996). Intonation preferences for major thirds with non-beating ensemble sounds. Proceedings of NAM96 (Nordic Acoustical Meeting) (pp. 359–365). Helsinki: Acoustical Society of Finland.

Ternström, S., Sundberg, J., & Colldén, A. (1988). Articulatory F_0 perturbations and auditory feedback. *Journal of Speech and Hearing Research*, *31*, 187–192.

Titze, I. R. (1989). On the relationship between subglottal pressure and fundamental frequency in phonation. *Journal of the Acoustical Society of America*, *85*(2), 901–906.

Verschuure, J., & van Meeteren, A. A. (1975). The effect of intensity on pitch. *Acustica*, *32*, 33–44.

von Békésy, G. (1949). The structure of the middle ear and the hearing of one's own voice by bone conduction. *Journal of the Acoustical Society of America*, *21*, 217–232.

18

Piano

RICHARD PARNCUTT & MALCOLM TROUP

On the basis of research on the physics and physiology of the keystroke, the acoustics and perception of piano timbre, and the psychology of piano fingering, we explain observations such as the following, and investigate their practical implications. The timbre of an isolated tone cannot be varied independently of its loudness but depends on finger-key, key-keybed, hammer-key noise, and on the use of both pedals. The timbre of a chord further depends on the balance and onset timing of its tones, whereby louder tones tend to sound earlier (melody lead, velocity artifact). Both the sustaining pedal and *una corda* can enhance *sostenuto*. Leap trajectories are curved and asymmetrical. Optimal fingering is determined by physical, anatomic, motor, and cognitive constraints interacting with interpretive considerations, and depends on expertise.

Scientific thinking, methods, and results have influenced piano performance and piano teaching for well over a century, and innumerable piano-pedagogical publications have claimed scientific validity. On the one hand, artistic writers—often great pianists and piano teachers—have tended to fashion complex pseudo-scientific theories post hoc to match their beliefs, so that such theories can be controversial and unreliable. On the other hand, scientific writers tend to focus on simple hypotheses and assumptions that are easy to demonstrate and explain but are of limited interest to musicians. It is little wonder, therefore, that modern piano students are often unaware of the basic findings (Parncutt & Holming, 2000).

Ortmann (1929/1981) successfully challenged influential but unfounded assumptions on touch and relaxation. Like him, we begin with observations that are easy to demonstrate scientifically and move gradually toward more complex ideas that are more likely to be of interest to modern pianists and piano teachers. We attempt a fresh approach by combining old and new acoustical and psychological thinking and drawing upon our own performing and teaching experience.

Physics and Physiology of the Keystroke

Curved Versus Straight Fingers

The motor independence required to perform the complex sequences of finger movements that are typical of piano performance can only be acquired over many years of concentrated practice. Pianists must control not only the order and precise timing of keystrokes but also their force and the resultant key velocity (Parlitz, Peschel, & Altenmüller, 1998).

The force required to depress a key in the middle register varies by a factor of 100: to hold down the key requires about 0.5 newton (equivalent to 50 grams), and to play *fortissimo* requires about 50 newtons (5 kilograms) (Askenfelt & Jansson, 1991). One way to accommodate this wide range is to vary the curvature of the fingers (Ortmann, 1925).

Loud, scalelike passages are often better played with curved fingers. First, this allows force to be applied vertically and so most efficiently (Ortmann, 1929/ 1981; Gát, 1965). Second, this reduces the distance between the fingertip and the knuckle, increasing the available force at the fingertip for a given muscle force (lever principle).

Straight fingers are often preferred in softer, slower, single-line melodies, where the fleshy pads of flatter fingers allow a bigger skin area to touch the surface of the key, appropriate for *cantabile*. Extended fingers can also move through a larger horizontal arc than curved fingers and are appropriate when big stretches are required at a low to moderate dynamic level.

Fingers or Arms?

As a rule, *all* moving joints in the arms and fingers are involved to some extent in *all* piano playing; to try to prevent one joint from moving would cause unnecessary tension. Beyond that, basic physics predicts that small, lightweight limbs (e.g., the fingers) are suited for fast and/or quiet playing, while larger, heavier limbs (the upper and lower arm) are best for slow, loud playing (Ortmann, 1929/1981). According to this principle, movements of the hand (from the wrist) and forearm (from the elbow) are suitable for intermediate tempi and dynamic levels and for combinations like fast and loud (e.g., Liszt's Hungarian Rhapsody No. 6, with its right-hand presto octaves and left-hand chord leaps, all marked *sempre forte*). Similarly, scales in fast, lightweight octaves are best played from the wrist, moderately fast and loud octaves from the elbow, and loud, *bravura* octaves from the shoulder (cf. Gát, 1965), examples of all of which are also to be found in Liszt's Hungarian Rhapsody No. 6.

The underlying physical principle is Newton's second law of motion—force equals mass times acceleration (cf. Schultz, 1949)—which states that greater masses require more force to accelerate them and exert more force when they decelerate (inertia). Thus the fingers can move back and forth more quickly, but the arms can exert more force.

This principle is mirrored in the historical evolution of keyboard technique (Gerig, 1974; Kochevitsky, 1967). In keyboard music of the eighteenth century, the fingertips did most of the work and the arms were held to the sides. In the nineteenth century, a heavier keyboard action, larger concert halls and orchestras, the new mass public, the emergence of the solo recital, and more elaborate writing for the keyboard made wrists and forearms more important (Kalkbrenner, Leschetizky). This led to Deppe's (1885) and Breithaupt's (1905) concept of arm weight and Matthay's (1903) emphasis on relaxation. Their basic idea was to relax the arm in free fall, then introduce minimal muscle tension to control the movement.

A similar pathway is still traveled by most pianists during their development from beginners to professionals. But advanced technical concepts such as arm weight can also be introduced quite early. For example, György Kurtág's *Játékók*, a collection of children's pieces elaborated into a system of piano tuition by Kase (2001), introduces larger scale bodily movements from the start, delaying focused finger movements until later.

Leap Trajectories

Performers of pieces like Brahms's *Paganini Variations* and Second Piano Concerto are constantly confronted with high-speed leaps across the keyboard. Ortmann (1929/1981) observed that the optimal trajectory for a leap is not only *curved* but also *skewed* (asymmetrical): it departs close to horizontal and lands somewhere between horizontal and vertical. This minimizes the chance of missing the target and allows the force on the target key to be applied almost vertically.

During a leap, the hand and arm must accelerate from stationary to a maximum velocity and decelerate again before reaching the target. Since acceleration is a vector (with both magnitude and direction), leap trajectories cannot include sharp corners, which would require short bursts of high acceleration (Ortmann, 1929/1981). For similar reasons, it is widely held that rounded or curved movements are preferable in all areas of piano technique: "The shortest distance between two points is not a straight line but a curve" (Neuhaus, 1973).

In general, the likelihood of missing a target increases as the trajectory becomes longer, the time available becomes shorter, and the target becomes smaller (Fitts, 1954; Huron, 2001). For the piano, the margin of error at the target is the width of the key as seen from the approaching finger—greatest if the approach is vertical (from the air) and zero if horizontal (along the keyboard). When approached from the left or bass, the widest black-key targets are the tones C♯ and F♯; from the right or treble, B♭ and E♭. The optimal trajectory toward these keys is therefore flatter, and they can be reached more accurately. According to this logic, the falling leap at the start of Beethoven's Opus 111 (E♭ down to F♯ in left-hand octaves) may be more difficult than a slightly longer leap to a bigger target (e.g., D♭ to E♭).

While performing, pianists tend to be unaware of leap trajectories. The process seems highly automatic and intuitive, with the attention focusing aurally and visually on the target, not the trajectory, and relying on a combined tactile-auditory-visual memory of the keyboard. If unnecessary tension is avoided, an appropriately curved and skewed trajectory results automatically. The kinesthetic sense of joint, tendon, and muscle movements during the trajectory can be developed either by practicing leaps out of context without depressing the target tone (just preparing it) or by practicing leaps in the dark (without visual feedback). It is difficult to practice leaps at a slow tempo, just as high jumpers cannot practice in slow motion.

Tone Repetitions

High-speed repetitions are usually easier to perform by changing (alternating) fingers, because it is easier to move one finger horizontally off the key and drop another finger onto it, than to quickly move the same finger up and down. The latter requires more finger acceleration, which in turn requires more muscle force. Slow tone repetitions are often best performed *without* changing fingers, because at slower tempi the listener is more sensitive to the unevenness (variation in loudness) that can result from the differing strengths of the fingers. Moreover, at slow tempi there is less finger-key noise. Conversely, changing fingers can be useful if accentuation (i.e., *deliberate* unevenness) is required.

Fast repetitions were enabled by Sebastien Érard's *repeating action* of 1823 (Frey, 1933). The *let-off distance* (Askenfelt & Jannson, 1990) is the distance between the string and the top of the hammer after a key is slowly and silently depressed. Typically some one to three millimeters, it is also the distance traveled by the hammer in free flight after the jack is pushed away by the escapement dolly. The roughly corresponding *let-off point* of a piano key is found by slowly pressing the key until resistance is felt (as the jack escapes).

Depending on tempo and dynamics, fast repetitions may be best played *under the surface*, that is, by depressing the key to the keybed, lifting to the let-off point, and depressing again. The minimum time between repetitions is the time taken for the jack to return to its original position. A short setting of the let-off distance facilitates fast, quiet repetitions, as for example in the left-hand opening (*pp, très fondu, en trémolo*) of *Scarbo* from Ravel's *Gaspard de la nuit*. Playing from the let-off point also prevents the damper from reaching the string between keystrokes, so that a continuous sound can be obtained without pedaling.

Acoustics and Perception of Piano Timbre

Relationship Between Timbre and Loudness

We use the words *timbre* and *loudness* in the widely accepted psychoacoustical sense of how a sound is perceived or experienced by a listener (H. Fletcher, 1934). In general, the timbre of a sound–its perceived tone quality or color—depends on at least two physical variables: its *spectral envelope* (relative amplitude of spectral partials at a given moment) and its *temporal envelope* (which rises suddenly as the hammer hits the string and then decays gradually). The critical importance of temporal envelope for piano timbre becomes clear when a piano tone is recorded and played backward. If the amplitude gradually increases instead of decreasing, with the hammer noise at the end instead of the beginning, the result sounds strangely like an organ (Houtsma, Rossing, & Wagenaars, 1987).

The experience of loudness may be distinguished from the physical measurement of *SPL*, measured in decibels, and from *dynamic level*, which is an instruction, recommendation, or suggestion from a composer to a musician. For practical purposes, loudness, SPL, and dynamic level are often the same, but they do diverge in everyday musical situations. Consider for example a thick bass chord marked *ppp*. The physics of the piano do not allow such a chord to be played with a very low SPL (as measured with an SPL meter). But a pianist playing as softly as the piano allows can manipulate other contextual variables such as timbre (pedaling, relative key velocity) and timing (tempo, delay) to enhance the impression of *ppp*.

Against the backdrop of these definitions, we may assert that the spectral and temporal envelope of an isolated piano tone cannot be changed independently of its SPL; hence, timbre cannot be changed independently of loudness (Baron & Hollo, 1935; Gát, 1965; Gerig, 1974; Hart, Fuller, & Lusby, 1934; Ortmann, 1937; Seashore, 1937). In a simple physical model of the piano action (Fletcher & Rossing, 1998, Figure 12.1), both the SPL and the spectral and temporal envelopes of a piano tone are determined uniquely by *hammer velocity*—the speed with which the hammer hits the string, which is determined in turn by key velocity (cf. Palmer and Brown, 1991). The crucial point is that the hammer hits the string in *free flight*: at (and just before) impact, there is no physical contact between the key and the hammer. Thus—apart from some interesting possibilities described later—the pianist cannot influence *how* the hammer hits the string, only the *speed* with which it does so.

Acousticians and psychologists have often wondered why, in spite of this evidence, so many pianists still believe that the timbre of a piano tone depends on *touch*—not only how fast but also *how* the key is depressed. A possible reason is that movements of a pianist's body and arms (smooth and round versus jagged and tense) seem to both performers and audiences to result in different timbres. But we cannot necessarily rely on this impression for the following reasons:

- Pianists almost never perform isolated tones without pedal, and the timbre of more complex textures clearly depends on a range of factors other than the way each individual key is depressed (see later).
- Movements that directly affect *control* may indirectly affect timbre. Consider the difference between *percussive* (or *staccato*) *touch* (when keys are hit from a distance above the surface) and *nonpercussive* or *legato touch* (when the key is depressed from the surface). Ortmann (1925) found that nonpercussive touch permits finer key control.
- Listeners can easily perceive timbral differences between piano performances but are not necessarily able to explain the origin of those differences (Heinlein, 1929b).

- Listeners cannot necessarily separate timbre from other perceptual variables. Timbre is often confused with pitch in ratings of performed intonation (chapter 12) and in other psychoacoustic experiments (Singh & Hirsh, 1992). Listeners regularly use the interdependence of timbre and loudness to deduce dynamic level in situations where sound intensity cues are lacking or unreliable, such as recordings. In most instruments (including the voice), louder tones have more jagged waveforms and hence relatively more high-frequency energy. In the piano, a sharper hammer blow produces sharper waveform peaks (Hall, 1991). The strongest perceptual cue to the original dynamic level of a piano recording is its timbre—regardless of how loudly the recording is played back.
- In general, auditory perception is influenced by visual perception (intermodal interference). Visual processing can affect the appraisal of piano performances (Behne, 1990; Shimosako & Oghushi, 1996), and an important part of the emotional and interpretive message sent from a performer to an audience is visual (chapter 15 in this volume; Rosen, 1995). For example, if an audience sees a pianist brutally hitting the keys, they may get an impression of a hard or brittle tone—beyond what the music actually sounds like.
- Pianists' perceptions of their own performances are multimodal (Galembo, Askenfelt, & Cuddy, 1998): the pianist's perception of timbre can be influenced by kinesthetic feedback from finger contact with the keys.

Askenfelt and Jansson (1991) suggested the possibility that *hammer-shank vibrations* at around 50 Hz might be greater in percussive touch and could theoretically affect piano string vibration—either by changing the angle of impact and thus shifting the striking point (only significant in the extreme treble: Galembo et al., 1998) or by allowing the hammer to rub along the string during contact. But Hart, Fuller, and Lusby (1934) and others (see Galembo et al., 1988) had already concluded that the influence of the hammer shank on the physical string motion is negligible, and when the matter was tested empirically Askenfelt and Jansson (1991) were unable to observe any rubbing motion between hammer and string. Even if effects of this kind are possible, the pianist can hardly manipulate them independently of finger-key noise (see later), so they cannot contribute *independently* to piano timbre.

Tone quality in piano performance is determined not only by the physics of individual keystrokes but also involves a complex and largely intuitive interaction among body movements, technical finesse, and musical interpretation (Kochevitsky, 1967). For example, it is possible that the exact timing of a *rubato* melodic phrase affects the global perception of timbre. The ability to produce a variety of timbres and to apply them appropriately to the interpretation of repertoire can only develop gradually over years of concentrated practice and careful listening.

Timbre of a Chord

The timbre of a piano chord depends on the timing and relative loudness of the tones (Baron & Hollo, 1935), because these affect both the temporal and the spectral envelope. The attack portion of the temporal envelope can be manipulated by adjusting the timing of the tone onsets. An extreme case is an arpeggiated chord, whose timbre depends on the speed and direction of the arpeggiation—an expressive strategy employed by both performers (e.g., Glenn Gould's interpretations of Bach) and composers (e.g., Boulez's Sonate No. 3, *Constellations*). The spectral envelope can be manipulated by playing some tones louder and some softer. If the louder tone takes on a singing quality, it is either because its pitch becomes more *salient* (clear, prominent, audible, able to attract attention: Terhardt, Stoll, & Seewann, 1982) and/or because the timbre of the whole sonority becomes less rough (the roughness of a beating pair of pure tones falls rapidly as the difference between their amplitudes increases; cf. Terhardt, 1974). The technique of bringing out a tone is addressed later under "Melody Lead and the Velocity Artifact."

Sources of Percussive Noise

Percussive onset noise is as characteristic and integral to piano timbre as is the scraping of the bow of a stringed instrument or the breath activation of a wind instrument. This is clearly demonstrated when onset noise is electronically excluded from the tone, creating a drastic change in timbre. Normally, we hear holistically—we do not, and perhaps cannot, hear the onset noise separately. If the amount of noise increases, we hear the sound as increasingly harsh, dry, ugly, or forced and may be unaware of the physical source of the timbral change.

The three main sources of noise in piano timbre are *finger-key*, *key-keybed*, and *hammer-string*. Finger-key noise can be varied independently of string amplitude, but the biggest contributor to the noisy onset, hammer-string noise, cannot (Baron, 1958; Baron & Hollo, 1935; Hill, 1940), and, for practical purposes, neither can key-keybed noise.

Hammer-String Noise.   The physical intensity of the hammer blow depends directly on its velocity, being most intense in *fortissimo*. For this reason, *cantabile* can sometimes be enhanced by limiting loudness. Perceptually, the situation is more complex, because the tone's partials mask the onset noise, so louder tones do not always *seem* more percussive. If higher tones seem more percussive than lower tones, it is because their noise component is more intense by comparison to the partials—not because the noise is more intense in an absolute sense.

Finger-Key Noise.   This can contribute to the percussiveness of piano sound (appropriate, e.g., in many of Bartók's *Mikrokosmos*). It can also enhance an impression of *staccato* (Gát, 1965). Its audibility can be demonstrated by holding down a cluster of keys with one hand hitting them with the fingertips of the other hand. In practice, finger-key noise is not completely independent of hammer-string noise, because pianists tend to play louder when using percussive touch (Ortmann, 1925).

The impact between finger and key causes a sudden high acceleration and associated shock excitation (or thump) dominated by two flexing resonances of the key at about 290 and 445 Hz (Steinway); this is transmitted through various structural parts of the piano to the soundboard (Askenfelt & Jansson, 1990, 1991). It is called *touch precursor* because it precedes the hammer blow by about twenty to forty milliseconds, depending on dynamic level (Askenfelt, 1993). Like early reflections in a concert hall (Hall, 1991; chapter 17 in this volume), the touch precursor can contribute to timbre but cannot be heard separately.

In a musical context, the tonal part of the piano sound may partially or completely mask finger-key noise, depending on dynamic level, texture, register, room acoustics, and position of the listener. Finger-key noise is more audible in higher registers, because it is less masked by the tone.

Finger-key noise may seem important to the performer but be irrelevant to the listener. Preliminary experiments suggest that listeners can discriminate percussive from nonpercussive touch, but only within some twenty centimeters of the string (Galembo et al., 1998; Koornhof & van der Walt, 1993). Pianists' perceptions of their own finger-key noise may also be influenced by the kinesthetic sensation of the finger hitting the key.

Key-Keybed Noise.   This may be separately heard by holding the hammer against the string while pressing the key. In a musical context, key-keybed noise occurs almost simultaneously with hammer-string noise and so blends easily with it. Its low frequency gives it a deep timbre.

Theoretically, pianists can indirectly control key-keybed noise (Askenfelt & Jansson, 1991, Figures 4 and 5). In nonpercussive touch, the key velocity increases steadily during the key depression, reaching a maximum at the keybed. In percussive touch, the key velocity first increases, then decreases (as the energy is transferred to potential energy in parts of the action and kinetic energy in vibrations of the hammer shank), then increases again. So for a given dynamic level, key-keybed noise is greater in percussive than nonpercussive touch. In practice, due to limitations of sensory feedback to motor control, it is virtually impossible to vary key-keybed noise independently of the percussiveness of touch and dynamic level.

Cantabile and the Pedals

Cantabile means "singable" or "songlike." The sustaining pedal enhances the singing quality of a piano melody by improving the legato and enriching the timbre. The *una corda* pedal can also enhance *cantabile*, by increasing the effective tone duration.

The Sustaining Pedal

Banowetz (1985) regarded the sustaining pedal as "equivalent to the vibrato of the singer or the string player" (p. 13). Pianists do not simply depress and release the pedal but take advantage of a quasi-continuous series of intermediate positions that allow for more or fewer dampers to clear the strings in different registers—part-pedaling (half, quarter, three-quarter, etc.), pedal squeezing, and flutter (or vibrating) pedal (K. U. Schnabel, 1950). The effectiveness of these techniques depends on a variety of physical factors (the instrument's make; wear and tear of the hammer heads; pre- and postrelease duration of tones in a given register; room acoustics), technical considerations (how many fingers are held down at a given instant), and interpretation (phrasing, tempo, dynamic and timbral shading, tonal relationships) and is controlled by highly intuitive auditory reflexes and responses (Heinlein, 1930; Repp, 1999)—which may explain the considerable differences in pedal usage observed even among expert pianists (Heinlein, 1929a).

Walter Gieseking considered that "just as one learns correct finger technique from the head and not the fingers, so one learns correct pedaling from the dictates of the ear and not the foot" (Banowetz, 1985, p. 231). The independent manipulation of pedal and fingers, as well as the ability to adjust to a variety of instruments and acoustic conditions, is one of the most difficult and important pianistic techniques to learn. This complexity makes pedaling hard to investigate scientifically.

Decay Time and Melody

Is the piano a suitable instrument for the performance of melody? Two of the perceptual factors that encourage a sense of melody (across cultures) are *sustain* (slow decay) and *pitch salience* (Huron, 2001). The piano best satisfies both conditions in the middle registers: high tones decay quickly, and both very high and very low tones have low pitch salience (cf. Terhardt et al., 1982).

By convention, the decay time of a sound is the time taken for its SPL to fall by 60 dB. This corresponds roughly to its perceived or effective duration. The decay of a piano tone before the finger is lifted is called *prerelease decay*, and varies from some 15 seconds in the deep bass to 0.5 second in the highest register (Hall, 1991; Repp, 1997; Martin, 1947). *Postrelease* decay times are roughly half a second in both treble and bass (Repp 1997, Figure 4), but they vary unpredictably from tone to tone, depending on the state of the dampers and their pressure on the string. The timbral effect of damping the string is more audible in the lower registers where the strings are heavier.

A sense of melody may be created in high registers by use of the sustaining pedal and by *legatissimo*, the overlapping of successive keystrokes (Repp, 1997). Legatissimo can be acoustically effective in all but the extreme high register where there are no dampers. Finger legato is important not only where the pedal is being changed frequently but also where part- or flutter pedaling is being used, which tends to damp the upper strings more than the lower.

Another way to create an impression of melody is suggested by Bregman's (1990) theory of *auditory streaming*. Successive tones are more likely to hang together as melody if they are close in pitch and time and similar in loudness and timbre. Thus a pianist can optimize *cantabile* by holding key velocity relatively constant, compensating for the piano's acoustic discontinuity in the higher registers. If a passage calls for metrical or structural accentuation (chapter 13), other means may be used, such as agogic accents in the melody or dynamic accents in the accompaniment.

The Sustaining Effect of Una Corda

Casella (1936) considered that the *una corda* (soft) pedal "allows the executant to interpret a *cantabile* melody with greater depth of touch while never overstepping the mark" (our translation). Rubinstein (1980) remarked that he often produced his best *cantabile* by playing the melody *ff* with soft pedal.

The underlying physics was explained by Weinreich (1977; see also Hall, 1991; Fletcher & Rossing, 1998). The *una corda* pedal reduces the decay rate of the tone and so increases the effective duration. On a grand piano, the pedal shifts the mechanism sideways so that the hammer strikes only two (not one, as the Italian name suggests) of three unison strings. This reduces loudness, mellows the timbre, and modifies the hammer-string noise, because a different part of the hammer—the ridges between the grooves formed during normal playing— strikes the strings.

When the *una corda* pedal is *not* depressed, the three unison strings initially vibrate in phase, allowing them to transmit energy efficiently to the bridge and causing the sound level to fall rapidly. But the strings are never tuned to exactly the same frequency—and good tuners sometimes deliberately slightly mistune unison strings, for timbral reasons (Wead, 1921; Weinreich, 1977). So they soon get out of phase with one another, reducing the efficiency of sound transmission to the bridge. Once the phase relationship between the strings is effectively random, a second, slower decay phase—the *aftersound*—begins. With the *una corda* pedal depressed, one string begins almost at rest. Over the next few seconds, energy is transferred from the struck to the unstruck strings via the bridge. The overall decay rate is slower, because the struck and unstruck strings are out of phase from the start; the aftersound begins sooner and lasts longer (Hall, 1991, Figure 10.9).

We recommend experimenting with the sustaining effect of *una corda* in relatively quiet passages whose timbre is not adversely affected by the soft pedal. Melodic tones should be relatively long (say, a full second or more), to give the unstruck string time to start vibrating. The audibility of the effect will of course vary according to the instrument, chosen register, and room acoustics.

Melody Lead and the Velocity Artifact

Integral to piano technique is *polyphonic touch*, or the differentiation of dynamic levels within a chord, which enables melodies to be brought out of a contrapuntal context. Pianists have been doing this since the earliest clavichords and fortepianos allowed key velocity to determine dynamic level, allowing for example the entries of Bach fugal subjects to be projected. Sophisticated exercises and studies that addressed this technique appeared in the late nineteenth century. For a later generation, Artur Schnabel suggested that students play the cluster CDEFG repeatedly with fingering 1-2-3-4-5, each time bringing out a different tone to create a melody, for example, 5–3–3, 4–2–2, 1–2–3–4–5–5–5 ("Hänschen klein," a German nursery tune) (Wolff, 1972, p. 177). In the eighth measure of his Klavierstück Nr. 2 (1) of 1954 (London: Universal), Stockhausen notated a widely spaced five-note chord for the right hand and labeled the individual tones *ff*, *fff*, *f*, *mf*, and *f*—a tall order for a human performer but something that the piano is at least physically capable of.

Vladimir Horowitz recommended that "in striking a chord, in which a single note is to be accented, the effect can be produced by holding the finger which is to play the melody note a trifle lower and much firmer than the fingers which are to play the unaccented notes. The reason for holding the finger a trifle lower is only psychological in effect; in actual practice, it isn't altogether necessary" (Eisenberg, 1928). Along similar lines, Schultz (1949, p. 176) suggested that "to accent the *C* in the chord *E-G-C* . . . fingered 1-2-5, the thumb and second finger show more joint-movement than the fifth, the muscles of which contract relatively strongly. The accented tone is actually played a fraction of a second before the unaccented ones, but the difference in time is too small to be readily observable."

The asynchrony referred to by Schultz is known in modern music-psychological literature as *melody lead*. In the piano, the time taken for a single key to fall from the surface to the keybed ranges from about 25 ms in *forte* to 160 ms in *piano* (Askenfelt & Jansson, 1991). When fingers strike the key surface simultaneously but descend at different velocities, the maximum possible asynchrony is around 100 ms (remembering that, in quiet percussive touch, the hammer reaches the string up to 35 ms before the key reaches the keybed but only 2 to 5 ms in *forte*: Askenfelt & Jansson, 1990, Figure 8). In practice, melody leads are typically in the range of 20 to 40 ms, which is short enough to be inaudible (again, like early reflections in a concert hall). They are observed in performances at all levels of expertise (Palmer, 1989, 1996; Repp, 1996).

Goebl (2001) found that melody lead times could be predicted accurately by calculating key and hammer travel times on the basis of their measured velocities, confirming that in one-hand chords his pianists were striking the key surfaces almost simultaneously, regardless of emphasis. This was consistent with the pianists' apparent lack of awareness of melody lead in interviews. Melody lead may thus be regarded primarily as an *artifact* of keyboard construction.

Melody leads of similar duration also occur in ensemble performance (Rasch, 1979). This could be an artifact of a different kind: those that lead an ensemble tend to do just that and play infinitesimally earlier than the others who follow— just as less-experienced piano accompanists sometimes tend to drag. Alternatively, the effect may be a deliberate or intuitive expressive device to help bring out the melody. Pianists, too, may *deliberately* anticipate melody tones by different degrees, depending on the expressive intention (Rasch, 1978; Henderson, 1936; Palmer, 1989, 1996). But this is difficult to confirm experimentally, as one must first subtract out the effect of the velocity artifact.

Melody lead (or lag) can render a tone more salient than other tones in a chord, independent of the associated intensity differences. The anticipated tone is initially not masked by the other tones; and according to Bregman's (1990) theory and experiments, a slightly asynchronous tone is more easily heard as part of a melody. Thus, from a perceptual point of view, it may be unnecessary or even inappropriate to develop a deliberate strategy to compensate for the velocity artifact—that is, to attempt to control the relationship between key velocity and synchrony.

A pianist who wishes to do this consciously and thereby widen the range of available interpretive possibilities is faced with a technical problem. Due to intrinsic motor and physiological limitations, it is extremely difficult to directly manipulate the timing of almost-simultaneous finger movements, because the time required by sensorimotor and aural-neurophysiological feedback between the fingers and the brain would be similar to the typical duration of melody lead times (some tens of ms). The first author of this chapter gets around this by raising the finger whose onset is to be delayed and setting all fingers in motion at about the same time, applying more force and velocity to the raised finger. That finger then hits the key surface slightly later than the others—not earlier, as suggested by Horowitz, and perhaps corresponding to the "diametrically opposed" method referred to by Eisenberg (1928). By adjusting the height of the raised finger and listening carefully, the asynchrony at the keyboard can be reduced. The technical and artistic effectiveness of this technique, which follows logically from the psychological findings but seems to contradicts much pianistic practice, is yet to be systematically investigated.

We have not addressed the tendency of some pianists—especially pianists from the early days of recording—to deliberately *delay* the melody (sometimes called bass lead: Goebl, in press; Repp, 1996; Vernon, 1936). This is technically relatively easy, since the asynchrony is between rather than within hands and may be regarded as a kind of agogic accent (chapter 13).

Psychology of Piano Fingering

> To impose a fingering cannot logically meet the different
> conformations of hands . . . the absence of fingerings is an
> excellent exercise, suppresses the spirit of contradiction
> which induces us to choose to ignore the fingerings of the
> composer, and proves those eternal words: "One is never
> better served than by oneself." Let us seek our fingerings!
>
> Debussy, *Douze Etudes*

How do pianists determine fingerings? What are the underlying criteria? How do fingerings differ among pianists? Only recently have questions such as these been regarded as amenable to psychological research methods.

In the following, we limit ourselves to psychological aspects of fingering and assume that pianists are free to choose their own. The question of whether fingerings prescribed by composers such as Schubert, Chopin, Brahms, Liszt, Rachmaninoff, and Bartók should be followed (as, for example, Claudio Arrau has insisted) is a cultural, historical, and perhaps even ethical one and beyond our scope here.

Optimal Fingering

Optimal fingering emerges from a trade-off or compromise among various physical, anatomic, motor, and cognitive constraints, in conjunction with interpretive considerations. It depends on the relative importance of these different aspects for a given pianist or musical context. The complex interaction among these various constraints and their dependence on pianist and style mean that one can rarely speak of a single best fingering for a given passage.

Physical constraints on fingering include the horizontal and vertical arrangement of the black and white keys. In the determination of fingerings, these interact with *anatomic* constraints and associated individual differences: hand size and shape (measured by Wagner, 1988; see photos of pianists' hands in Gát, 1965) or the maximum comfortable stretches between pairs of fingers (included in the model of Parncutt et al., 1997; see also Jacobs, 2001).

Motor constraints can apply either within a single hand or between hands. Within a hand, they limit finger independence. According to Ortmann (1929/1981), such motor constraints can be reduced by practice but never eliminated. Between hands, motor constraints are involved in the coordination of tremolos, two-hand trills, and shakes; the execution of seamless transitions from one hand to another within Thalberg-style thumb melodies or accompanying figures; and the sharing of technically difficult figurations between the hands.

Cognitive constraints determine how well we can encode and retrieve complex finger patterns and their context dependencies. Fingerings that stay the same in different keys may reduce cognitive demands but are physically and anatomically more difficult. A change of fingering at a key change may be worthwhile if the anatomic and physical advantages balance the added cognitive load. To master these difficulties, many piano pedagogues, including Liszt (and, e.g., Frey, 1933), have recommended transposing difficult passages to all keys without changing the fingering.

Interactions between the two hands are primarily limited by cognitive constraints. In sight-reading unison passages (hands an octave apart), for example, two different fingerings must be planned and executed simultaneously (Parncutt, Sloboda, & Clarke, 1999). The cognitive load is reduced in mirror-image patterns in contrary motion, where fingerings can be identical in both hands—for example, in Messiaen's *Vingt regards sur l'enfant Jésus* (Troup, 1983, 1995).

By *interpretive* considerations we mean both communication of musical *structure* (chapter 13) and *emotion* (chapter 14). Fingering choices are often determined by matching a constraint to a given interpretive intention, for example, thumb on black at the start of a measure or phrase (Clarke et al., 1997) or second (index) finger at the end of a phrase. A more general interpretive consideration is flexibility: pianists need a fingering that allows for changes of interpretation without changes of fingering that would increase the rate of errors (Sloboda et al., 1998).

Procedural Versus Declarative Knowledge

The knowledge (or memory) that underlies fingering choices may be described as episodic or semantic, or as procedural or declarative. These terms are defined in psychology (see, e.g., introductory texts) as follows. *Episodic* knowledge refers to a specific event: a pianist may finger a passage in a certain way because the passage resembles a previously encountered and fingered passage. *Semantic* knowledge is more generalized: here it includes rules and principles of fingering. Both episodic and semantic knowledge can be either declarative or procedural. *Declarative* knowledge can be verbalized (knowing *that*), but *procedural* knowledge (knowing *how*) typically refers to *automated* movements that underlie a skill, such as riding a bicycle or producing grammatically correct sentences: a five-year-old may be able to do both but is unable to describe the underlying physical or grammatical rules or principles.

All four aspects are important at all levels. Even the most experienced pianists try out fingerings at the keyboard (procedural) but can also explain their fingering choices (declarative: Clarke et al., 1997). Procedural knowledge of fingering may be acquired either by applying declarative knowledge (rules) to repertoire excerpts (episodic: see, e.g., technical methods of the 1920s and 1930s) or by improvising exercises to address specific fingering issues (semantic: e.g., Cortot, 1958; Gellrich & Parncutt, 1998).

Dependence on Task

Optimal fingering depends on whether a passage of music is improvised, sight-read, played from the score after rehearsal, or performed from memory. For example, marked differences were observed between fingerings spontaneously used by pianists in the sight-reading task of Sloboda et al. (1998) and fingerings written on scores of the same music by the same participants several months previously (Parncutt et al., 1997). Standard fingerings for scales and arpeggios are of course more useful in sight-reading (where they reduce the cognitive load) than in memorized performance, where the pianist has time to automate new fingerings (Clarke et al., 1997)—although this does not necessarily apply to professional sight-readers, who have usually seen the score in advance (chapter 9).

Differences between written and sight-read (or improvised) fingerings may be explained if we assume that writing primarily taps declarative knowledge and sight-reading (or improvisation) primarily taps procedural knowledge. Only during rehearsal does a pianist have the chance to allow declarative and procedural knowledge to interact, as new fingering patterns are deliberately learned and automated. Teachers and performers may therefore develop different fingering approaches and strategies for sight-reading as apart from rehearsed performance, beyond merely learning standard fingerings for scales and arpeggios (cf. Deutsch, 1959).

Dependence on Expertise

Fingering depends on expertise (Clarke et al., 1997; Sloboda et al., 1998), because technique (finger independence, coordination of finger, arm, and hand movements, and so on) typically matures before interpretive ability and personal style. Beginners focus almost entirely on anatomic and physiological constraints but may not yet have the experience and knowledge necessary to choose the easiest variant. Young professional pianists (e.g., conservatory graduates) tend to use a fingering that is anatomically and physiologically optimal. Seasoned artists with consummate techniques usually focus on interpretive considerations; for example, Schnabel was famous for sacrificing digital expediency for interpretive integrity, regarding hand position ("handing") as more important than fingering (Wolff, 1972). Thus a teacher's best fingering is not necessarily best for a student, and while it is always advisable to extend the student's awareness of available fingerings, it may be unwise to expect rigorous imitation.

Acknowledgments.   The first author of this chapter thanks Diana Weekes, his piano teacher from the University of Melbourne, for her copious, insightful, and challenging comments on this chapter, and another pianist and piano teacher, Patrick Holming, for ideas, discussions, and literature sources. For technical comments, we thank Anders Askenfelt, Alexander Galembo, Werner Goebl, Hans Christian Jabusch, and authors of other chapters. The second author acknowledges Alberto Guerrero, with whom he studied in Canada alongside Glenn Gould, and Walter Gieseking, with whom he studied in Germany.

References

Askenfelt, A. (1993). Observations on the transient components of the piano tone. In A. Friberg, J. Iwarsson, E. Jansson, & J. Sundberg (Eds.), *Proceedings of the Stockholm Music Acoustics Conference* (pp. 297–301). Stockholm: Royal Swedish Academy of Music.

Askenfelt, A., & Jansson, E. V. (1990). From touch to string vibrations. I . Timing in the grand piano action. *Journal of the Acoustical Society of America, 88,* 52–63.

Askenfelt, A., & Jansson, E. V. (1991). From touch to string vibrations. II: The motion of the key and hammer. *Journal of the Acoustical Society of America, 90,* 2383–2393.

Banowetz, J. (Ed.) (1985). *The pianist's guide to pedaling.* Bloomington: Indiana University Press.

Baron, J. G. (1958). Physical basis of piano touch. *Journal of the Acoustical Society of America, 30,* 151–152.

Baron, J., & Hollo, J. (1935). Kann die Klangfarbe des Klaviers durch die Art des Anschlages beeinflusst werden? *Zeitschrift für Sinnesphysiologie, 66,* 23–32.

Behne, K.-E. (1990). "Blicken Sie auf die Pianisten?!": Zur bildbeeinflussten Beurteilung von Klaviermusik im Fernsehen. *Medienpsychologie, 2,* 115–131.

Bregman, A. S. (1990). *Auditory scene analysis.* Cambridge, MA: MIT.

Breithaupt, R. M. (1905). *Die natürliche Klaviertechnik.* Leipzig: Kahnt.

Casella, A. (1936). *Il pianoforte.* Rome: Ricordi.

Clarke, E. F., Parncutt, R., Raekallio, M., & Sloboda, J. A. (1997). Talking fingers: An interview study of pianists' views on fingering. *Musicae Scientiae, 1,* 87–107.

Cortot, A. (1958). *Principes rationnels de la technique pianistique.* Paris: Salabert.

Deppe, L. (1885). Armleiden des Klavierspielers. *Deutsche Musiker Zeitung,* p. 325.

Deutsch, L. (1959). *Piano sight-reading.* Chicago: Nelson-Hall.

Eisenberg, J. (1928, June). Noted Russian pianist urges students to simplify mechanical problems so that thought and energy may be directed to artistic interpretation. *Musician,* p. 11. http://users.bigpond.net.au/nettheim.

Fitts, P. M. (1954). The information capacity of the human motor system in controlling the amplitude of movement. *Journal of Experimental Psychology, 47,* 381–391.

Fletcher, H. (1934). Loudness, pitch, and timbre of musical tones and their relations to the intensity, the frequency, and the overtone structure. *Journal of the Acoustical Society of America, 6,* 59–69.

Fletcher, N. H., & Rossing, T. D. (1998). *The physics of musical instruments* (2nd ed.). New York: Springer.

Frey, E. (1933). *Bewusst gewordenes Klavierspiel und seine technischen Grundlagen.* Zurich: Hug.

Galembo, A., Askenfelt, A., & Cuddy, L. L. (1998). *On the acoustics and psychology of piano touch and tone.* Paper presented at Sixteenth International Congress on Acoustics, Seattle. Abstract: *Journal of the Acoustical Society of America, 103,* 2873.

Gát, J. (1965). *The technique of piano playing* (3rd ed.). Budapest: Corvina.

Gellrich, M., & Parncutt, R. (1998). Piano technique and fingering in the eighteenth and nineteenth centuries: Bringing a forgotten method back to life. *British Journal of Music Education, 15*(1), 5–24.

Gerig, R. R. (1974). *Famous pianists and their technique.* Washington, DC: Luce.

Goebl, W. (2001). Melody lead in piano performance: Expressive device or artifact? *Journal of the Acoustical Society of America, 110,* 563–572.

Hall, D. E. (1991). *Musical acoustics.* Pacific Grove, CA: Brooks/Cole.

Hart, H. C., Fuller, M. W., & Lusby, W. S. (1934). A precision study of piano touch and tone. *Journal of the Acoustical Society of America, 6,* 80–94.

Heinlein, C. P. (1929a). A discussion of the nature of pianoforte damper-pedalling together with an experimental study of some individual differences in pedal performance. *Journal of General Psychology, 2,* 489–508.

Heinlein, C. P. (1929b). The functional role of finger touch and damper-pedalling in the appreciation of pianoforte music. *Journal of General Psychology, 2,* 462–469.

Heinlein, C. P. (1930). Pianoforte damper-pedalling under ten different experimental conditions. *Journal of General Psychology, 3,* 511–528.

Henderson, M. T. (1936). Rhythmic organization in artistic piano performance. In C. E. Seashore (Ed.), *Objective analysis of musical performance, University of Iowa Studies in the Psychology of Music,* Vol. 4 (pp. 281–305). Iowa City: University of Iowa Press.

Hill, W. G. (1940). Noise in piano tone. *Musical Quarterly, 26*, 244–259.

Houtsma, A. J. M., Rossing, T. D., & Wagenaars, W. M. (1987). *Auditory demonstrations on compact disc.* New York: Acoustical Society of America. http://asa.aip.org/discs.html.

Huron, D. (2001). Tone and voice: A derivation of the rules of voice-leading from perceptual principles. *Music Perception, 19*, 1–64.

Jacobs, J. P. (2001). Refinements to the ergonomic model for keyboard fingering of Parncutt, Sloboda, Clarke, Raekallio, and Desain. *Music Perception, 18*, 505–511.

Kase, S. (2001). Clusters: The essence of musicality and technique. *Piano Journal, 22*(64), 13–18.

Kochevitschy, G. (1967). *The art of piano playing: A scientific approach.* Evanston, IL: Summy-Burchard.

Koornhof G. W., & van der Walt, A. J. (1993). The influence of touch on piano sound. In A. Friberg, J. Iwarsson, E. Jansson, & J. Sundberg (Eds.), *Proceedings of the Stockholm Music Acoustics Conference* (pp. 318–324). Stockholm: Royal Swedish Academy of Music

Martin, D. W. (1947). Decay rates of piano tones. *Journal of the Acoustical Society of America, 19*, 535–541.

Matthay, T. (1903). *The act of touch.* London: Longmans.

Neuhaus, H. (1973). *The art of the piano* (K. A. Leibovitch, Trans.). London: Barrie & Jenkins.

Ortmann, O. (1925). *The physical basis of piano touch and tone.* New York: E. Dutton.

Ortmann, O. (1929/1981). *The physiological mechanics of piano technique.* New York: Da Capo.

Ortmann, O. (1937). Tone quality and the pianist's touch. *Proceedings of the Music Teachers National Association*, 127–132.

Palmer, C. (1989). Mapping musical thought to musical performance. *Journal of Experimental Psychology: Human Perception and Performance, 15*, 331–346.

Palmer, C. (1996). On the assignment of structure in music performance. *Music Perception, 14*, 21–54.

Palmer, C., & Brown, J. C. (1991). Investigations in the amplitude of sounded piano tones. *Journal of the Acoustical Society of America, 90*, 60–66.

Parlitz, D., Peschel, T., & Altenmüller, E. (1998). Assessment of dynamic finger forces in pianists: Effects of training and expertise. *Journal of Biomechanics, 31*, 1063–1067.

Parncutt, R., & Holming, P. (2000, August). Is scientific research on piano performance useful for pianists? Poster presented at the Sixth International Conference on Music Perception and Cognition, Keele University, UK.

Parncutt, R., Sloboda, J. A., & Clarke, E. F. (1999). Interdependence of right and left hands in sight-read, written, and rehearsed fingerings of parallel melodic piano music. *Australian Journal of Psychology, 51*, Special Issue: Music as a Brain and Behavioural System, 204–210.

Parncutt, R., Sloboda, J. A., Clarke, E. F., Raekallio, M., & Desain, P. (1997). An ergonomic model of keyboard fingering for melodic fragments. *Music Perception, 14*, 341–382.

Rasch, R. A. (1978). The perception of simultaneous notes such as in polyphonic music. *Acustica, 40*, 21–33.

Rasch, R. A. (1979). Synchronization in performed ensemble music. *Acustica,* *43,* 121–131.

Repp, B. H. (1996). Patterns of note onset asynchronies in expressive piano performance. *Journal of the Acoustical Society of America, 100,* 3917–3932.

Repp, B. H. (1997). Acoustics, perception, and production of legato articulation on a computer-controlled grand piano. *Journal of the Acoustical Society of America, 102*(3), 1878–1890.

Repp. B. H. (1999). Effects of auditory feedback deprivation on expressive piano performance. *Music Perception, 16,* 409–438.

Rosen, C. (1995). *The romantic generation.* Cambridge, MA: Harvard University Press.

Rubinstein, A. (1980). *My many years.* New York: Knopf.

Schnabel, K. U. (1950). *Modern technique of the pedal.* London: Mills Music.

Schultz, A. (1949). *The riddle of the pianist's finger.* New York: Fischer.

Seashore, C. E. (1937). Piano touch. *Scientific Monthly* (New York), *45,* 360–365.

Shimosako, H., & Oghushi K. (1996). Interaction between auditory and visual processing in impressional evaluation of a piano performance. *Journal of the Acoustical Society of America, 100*(4), pt. 2, 2779.

Singh, P. G., & Hirsh, I. J. (1992). Influence of spectral locus and F_0 changes on the pitch and timbre of complex tones. *Journal of the Acoustical Society of America, 92,* 2650–2661.

Sloboda, J. A., Clarke, E. F., Parncutt, R., & Raekallio, M. (1998). Determinants of fingering choice in piano sight-reading. *Journal of Experimental Psychology: Human Perception and Performance, 24*(3), 185–203.

Terhardt, E. (1974). On the perception of periodic sound fluctuations (roughness). *Acustica, 30,* 201–213.

Terhardt, E., Stoll, G., & Seewann, M. (1982). Pitch of complex tonal signals according to virtual pitch theory: Tests, examples and predictions. *Journal of the Acoustical Society of America, 71,* 671–678.

Troup, M. (1983). Regard sur Olivier Messiaen. *Piano Journal, 4*(11), 11–13.

Troup, M. (1995). Orchestral music of the 1950s and 1960s. In P. Hill (Ed.), *The Messiaen companion* (pp. 392–447). London: Faber & Faber.

Vernon, L. N. (1936). Synchronization of chords in artistic piano music. In C. E. Seashore (Ed.), *Objective analysis of musical performance, University of Iowa Studies in the Psychology of Music,* Vol. 4 (pp. 306–345). Iowa City: University of Iowa Press.

Wagner, C. (1988). The pianist's hand: Anthropometry and biomechanics. *Ergonomics, 31,* 97–132.

Wead, C. K. (1921). Acoustical notes. *Science, 54,* 467–469.

Weinreich, G. (1977). Coupled piano strings. *Journal of the Acoustical Society of America, 62,* 1474–1484.

Wolff, K. (1972). *The teaching of Artur Schnabel.* London: Faber.

19

String Instruments

KNUT GUETTLER & SUSAN HALLAM

Research on the physics of bowed stringed instruments can help the string teacher to explain the underlying acoustical phenomena and to develop corresponding pedagogical strategies. The first part of this chapter surveys current and historical acoustical research, focusing on information that can be related to technique. This section discusses not only the bowed attack with specific exercises to improve performance, but also other topics such as harmonics, rosin, timbre, and aspects of room acoustics during performance. An overview of psychological research relating to the distinctive aspects of playing a bowed stringed instrument and the characteristics of string players follows. This considers the importance of well developed aural skills, practice, and conscientiousness on the part of the player to develop high levels of expertise. The need for the teacher to demonstrate and provide opportunities to develop aural schemata, and give detailed constructive feedback is also discussed.

The first serious acoustical research on the violin can be dated back to the first half of the nineteenth century, when the French physicist Felix Savart borrowed from violin maker Jean Baptiste Vuillaume free top and back plates of violins crafted by Stradivari, Guarneri, and others, to examine how they vibrated at different frequencies (Savart, 1819, 1840). Contrary to popular belief, Savart discovered that the sound post does not function primarily to transmit the vibrations from the top to the back of the violin. Rather, its main function is to impose a nearly stationary point about which the top plate can rock.

The next major step toward an understanding of the acoustics of the violin was taken by Hermann von Helmholtz (1862/1954). Through acoustical filtering he was able to break tones down into pure tone components or partials (i.e., fundamental plus overtones), whose relative amplitudes influence timbre. In this way, he could study each partial separately. Using a microscope, vibrating with nearly the same frequency as the string, he could watch the string in slow motion and show that bowing and plucking the string produced quite different patterns of vibration. With this method, he discovered the *slip-stick* action between the bow and the string, now called *Helmholtz motion*, which underlies the sawtooth-shaped force waveform acting on the bridge.

In the first part of the twentieth century, scientists from many countries contributed to research on the violin. While most of these focused on the instrument body and its vibrations, varnish, and wood, an Indian, Chandrasekara V. Raman, was particularly interested in the parameters of bowing technique: bow speed, bowing pressure (the correct physical term being *force*), and the bow-to-bridge distance, which together control the string wave form. Raman (1920) constructed a mechanical bowing machine that enabled him to measure the minimum required bowing pressure for any given pitch on the instrument, a value he found to be inversely proportional to the square of the bow-to-bridge distance. Interestingly, Raman found that particularly resonant tones required higher bowing pressure than less resonant ones. For resonant tones, more low-frequency wave energy is drained from the string through the bridge to the instrument's body, so the string will not maintain its fundamental-frequency oscillation with the same ease as for less resonant tones. In most cases, increasing the bow pressure can compensate for this energy loss. (String players normally adjust these bowing parameters intuitively, but if the sound is unsatisfactory, intuition does not always provide guidance as to what is wrong.) When the energy loss surpasses a certain magnitude, a steady-state oscillation is impossible at any bow pressure. Such tones are commonly termed *wolf tones* due to their (sometimes) howling character.

In the early 1950s, four Americans formed a group, jokingly calling themselves the Catgut Acoustical Society. Their ambition was "to increase and diffuse the knowledge of musical acoustics and to promote construction of fine stringed instruments" (currently used as their journal's cover-page motto). The organization now has worldwide membership comprised of scientists, luthiers, and musicians, who communicate through semiannual journals. Their publications provide a wealth of information for anyone interested in learning about string-instrument acoustics.

Research in the 1970s returned to the bow-string interaction. McIntyre and Woodhouse (1979) and Schumacher (1979) made the first computer simulations of the bowed string. This led to the discovery of the important role of *string torsion* (twisting or rolling under the bow) during the *attack phase* (defined as the first part of the tone, before it has settled into a steady vibration, or the transitional state between rest and the sustained tone). Without some torsion, strings would be much harder to bow. Computer simulations also increased the demand for quantification of physical string properties (Pickering, 1985) and knowledge about different string materials' effect on tone quality (Pickering, 1990). The results contributed to the design and manufacture of modern, well-responding strings.

Fundamentals of the Bow-String Contact

Helmholtz Motion

In a typical bowed tone, the string alternatively *sticks* to and *slips* against the bow hair. There is one *sticking interval* and one *slipping interval* per period of the tone (i.e., 440 times per second on an open violin A string). After the attack phase, the string takes the shape of two almost straight lines joined in a kink or corner, which follows a lens-shaped path (see Figure 19.1). On a violin A string, the corner travels along the string at a speed of approximately 290 meters per second. As the corner passes the bow in the direction of the bridge, the bow loses its grip (stick) on the string and begins to fly back (slip) along the bow hair. During the slipping interval, the corner reaches the bridge and is reflected back in the direction of the bow. At the instant the bow is passed again, the string portion under the bow starts moving much slower relative to the hair, allowing the string to stick again and stay stuck for the remaining, longest part of the cycle period (provided no other disturbance occurs). This particular string movement is called the Helmholtz motion.

In a violin upbow, the rotation along the string (relative to the player) is counterclockwise; in a downbow, clockwise. Thus a new rotational orientation has to be developed after each bow change. Bowing technique is primarily concerned with the creation and maintenance of Helmholtz motion.

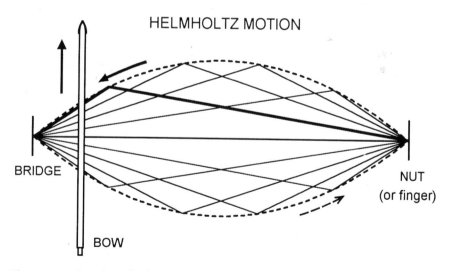

Figure 19.1. When the string is bowed in a steady state, the (idealized) string takes the form of two straight lines connected by a rotating corner. When the corner is traveling from the bow to the bridge and back, the string slips on the bow hair. In the remaining interval, the string sticks to the hair, if bowed properly.

Figure 19.2 (a) shows, in somewhat idealized form, the force exerted by the string on the bridge as a function of time. This force tries to move the bridge sideways and, as a result of the bridge's downward force shifting from leg to leg, causes the instrument body to vibrate, thereby creating sound.

Other Cyclic String Patterns

The Helmholtz mode is only one of several possible modes of vibration, and the one that produces the clearest pitch and the smoothest, fullest timbre. When more than one slipping interval occurs per cycle (producing more than one corner on the string at a given moment in time), the lower partials are weakened, and the sound becomes scratchy, with increased slipping noise (see "Hiss (Rosin Noise)" later). Figure 19.2 (b) shows the force wave with one extra slip per cycle. An easy way to recognize this mode is to look at the midpoint of the string, where its amplitude appears constricted during the attack phase. In most cases, a multislip pattern soon dies out as the corners are softened by string stiffness and the following energy absorbers:

- The compliant, not-totally-reflecting bridge (transferring energy to the instrument body)
- Damping by the soft finger pad
- The internal friction of the string (e.g., friction between windings, molecular friction)
- The drag of surrounding air

The faster some high-frequency wave energy is lost in these ways, the sooner the Helmholtz motion will form, provided that the bowing speed and pressure are in the right range. The concept of energy loss can explain why open strings, strings not yet broken in (having less internal friction), and strings with great ability to sustain *pizzicato* (ditto) are more susceptible to whistling and onset noise when bowed.

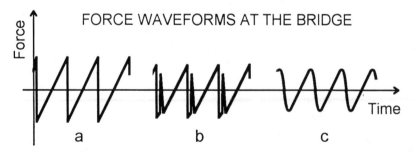

Figure 19.2. Different force waveforms acting sideways on the bridge in the plane of bowing (about three periods shown of each): (a) brilliant sound, (b) scratchy tone, (c) soft timbre that results from low bowing pressure and a rounded corner.

Rounding off the Helmholtz Corner

In practice, the string can never make a perfectly sharp corner. String stiffness and the losses mentioned earlier round it off. However, the bow will, to some degree, sharpen the corner every time it passes, depending on the bowing pressure. So as long as the player does not choke the string, a higher bowing pressure means a sharper corner and thus—according to the basic mathematical theory of Fourier analysis—a higher energy content of high partials. Correspondingly, lower bowing pressure encourages rounding and a softer tone color (see Figure 19.2 c).

Hiss (Rosin Noise)

During the slipping interval, an audible hiss or buzz is produced when the string slides on the rosined bow hair. Physically this consists of short bursts of noise (one per period of the fundamental frequency) and so is referred to as pulsed noise. This is an important contributor to the characteristic timbre of stringed instruments. In the scientific literature, the bow-to-bridge distance divided by the length of the vibrating string is termed β. (For example, if the bow is midway between the finger and the bridge, $\beta = 0.5$.) This ratio determines the duration of the hiss pulse relative to the cycle period. By bringing the bow nearer to the fingerboard (*sul tasto*), one increases β and the time proportion of hiss. Very low bowing pressure (as in *flautando*) lengthens the slipping period even further, adding even more breathiness to the sound.

Noise may also be generated during the sticking interval, especially on the violin, when bowed near the bridge. This largely undesirable spiky quality is particularly audible at high bowing pressure and is caused by minor local string slips across the hair-ribbon width (McIntyre, Schumacher, & Woodhouse, 1981; Pitteroff, 1995). Tilting the bow reduces the width and minimizes the effect.

Getting the String into Helmholtz Motion

So far, only the steady-state (postattack) oscillation of the string has been discussed. To get the string into Helmholtz motion quickly, a good strategy is to aim for a regular stick-slip pattern from the very onset. The violin body has a *response time* of the order of 5–15 ms, but the bowed string normally needs considerably longer to reach full amplitude (Melka, 1970). (Response time is here defined as the time required to reach 90% of full amplitude if a steady-state input signal is abruptly switched on.) The attack of bowed instruments is relatively slower than that of most wind instruments, making the string sound appear later than the wind, even when they start simultaneously. This delay is most noticeable at lower pitches (e.g., in the double basses), because transient duration varies inversely with fundamental frequency (so, for example, a tone an octave lower takes twice as long to sound fully). The string buildup time is, however, partly habitual (having to do with wrist action, etc.) and may, if desirable, be shortened through practice. We will return to this point later. First we will consider of the production of clean tone onsets.

During the attack phase, the motion of the string, for a given fundamental frequency and bow-to-bridge distance, is primarily determined by bowing *pressure* and *acceleration*. After the attack, when full amplitude has been reached, string motion is determined primarily by bowing *pressure* and *speed*. Based on computer simulations (Askenfelt & Guettler, 1998), Figure 19.3 shows schematically how the cleanness of the attack is influenced by bowing pressure and acceleration. For each relative bow-to-bridge distance (β), the noise-free region forms a (white) triangle in the figure, from which the following conclusions can be drawn:

- A certain minimum bowing pressure is required to start the proper slip-stick triggering directly (typically in the order of 0.1–0.2 Newton, comparable to 10–20 grams, for a violin).
- The required bow *acceleration* increases with the bow-to-bridge distance if the bowing pressure is kept unchanged (compare the positions of the rectangles drawn in the two panels of Figure 19.3).
- Near the minimum bowing pressure, the acceleration *tolerance* (i.e., the range of acceleration values that will produce noise-free attacks) is very small, but it increases with bow pressure, and with the bow-to-bridge distance (compare the widths of the rectangles drawn in the two panels of Figure 19.3).

In addition:

- For noise-free attacks with a given string, the required bow acceleration increases proportionally with the fundamental frequency and so does the acceleration tolerance.

The latter means that bowing can be varied more freely for high-pitched in-

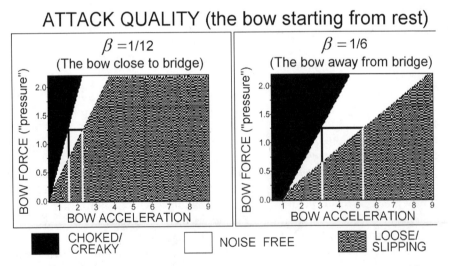

ATTACK QUALITY (the bow starting from rest)

$\beta = 1/12$
(The bow close to bridge)

$\beta = 1/6$
(The bow away from bridge)

BOW FORCE ("pressure")
BOW ACCELERATION

■ CHOKED/CREAKY   □ NOISE FREE   ▦ LOOSE/SLIPPING

Figure 19.3. The combination of bowing pressure and acceleration (both scaled in arbitrary units) determines the quality of the attack. NOISE FREE means regular slip-stick triggering from the very onset. Within this (white) area, high acceleration gives the quickest tone buildup. Rectangle widths show the acceleration tolerances for a given bowing pressure.

struments than for their low-pitched counterparts. In order to make a quick tone buildup for a given bow pressure and position (i.e., reaching full amplitude as quickly as possible), the player must try to find the maximum (farthest to the right in the figure) acceleration within the noise-free (white) area. Only through practice and trial and error can this limit be found. The lower limit (i.e., the *lowest* noise-free acceleration) might also be practiced, as preparation for smooth bow changes.

If non-Helmholtzian waveforms are created, these will prevail for a number of *periods* before expiring, implying a longer lasting onset noise for low-pitched strings than for high-pitched ones (Guettler & Askenfelt, 1997).

How to Control Bow Acceleration in the Attack Phase

The generalizations outlined earlier need only be considered when the player is trying to account for problems in attack. For deciding what sounds best, the ear is always superior.

Many players prefer to start the stroke from the air, deliberately producing an onset with a certain airy or slippy sound. However, for low-pitched strings such an airy introduction may be too persistent, especially in *forte*.

In practice, acceleration is not an easy concept to grasp or to teach. Newton's second law, force equals mass times acceleration, suggests the following approach: When one is playing near the bridge, an almost constant acceleration can be achieved by adding mass to the bow, so that small deviations in the frictional force will have less effect on the bowing speed. This can be achieved by temporarily reducing the suppleness of one or more joints in order to add the mass of the fingers, hand, forearm, upper arm, and torso to the mass of the bow itself. (When one is doing this, bowing pressure should not be influenced!) For low-pitched tones and/or playing close to the bridge, this technique effectively reduces the influence of a rapidly fluctuating frictional force, which could otherwise make the acceleration uneven. The technique works best on heavier strings, where the magnitude of frictional fluctuations is greatest. A posture that allows for flexibility of the upper body is essential for a consistent and well-controlled bow-arm movement on any string instrument. For a double-bass player, it is particularly important not to let the instrument's body lock the chest in a fixed position.

Practice Suggestion: The student should learn the arm/finger action that produces noise-free attacks when making repeated attacks close to the bridge. The following should be varied: (1) the suppleness of the arm/finger joints, (2) the dynamic level, (3) the bow's starting point (frog-middle-tip), and (4) the pitch.

Control of String Vibration during the Steady-State Phase

As soon as a correct Helmholtz pattern is established, the player has a wide palette of timbres to choose from. For a given bow speed, different bow pressures may subsequently produce anything from "harmonics" and *flautando*, via "loose," "firm," and "pressed" timbres, to "raucous" and "creaky" sounds (Schelleng, 1970). As long as some kind of Helmholtz motion is present, the fundamental frequency will be well defined, so the pitch will be clear. When bowing pressure is far too high or the speed far too low, the sound may best be described as raucous or creaky. However, before raucousness appears, there is a point where the sound is pressed and the fundamental frequency is slightly reduced (flat), because the sticking rosin delays the string release (i.e., the transition from sticking to slipping phase) at excess bowing pressure. The effect is more pronounced for softer rosins, larger distances of the bow from the bridge, and shorter lengths of the vibrating strings, which increases the effective string stiffness (e.g., high positions on a violin G string). Moving the bow closer to the bridge hence reduces the flattening. As the bow-to-bridge distance becomes smaller, the palette of different timbres shrinks. Near the bridge, the bowing pressure must be held close to a single theoretically defined value (which depends on the chosen bow speed) if Helmholtz motion is to result. This means that when one is playing near the bridge fluctuations in bowing speed and pressure must be kept to a minimum.

Implications for Performance

When one is performing a *diminuendo*, both pressure and speed of bowing must be reduced simultaneously if a consistent tone quality is to be achieved—regardless of bow-to-bridge distance. Simplified, the ideal situation occurs when bowing speed is balanced against the combination of bowing pressure, relative bow-to-bridge distance (β), and fundamental frequency. Whenever one element is changed, compensation by one or more of the remaining three is normally required.

Example 1.   If one keeps the bow pressure and distance to the bridge fixed, playing the same pitch on alternative strings will require a higher bow speed on the lowest tuned string. This is because the relative bow-to-bridge distance is greater for the string fingered in the highest position. (In some cases, this rule of thumb will not apply to a crossing between the third and the fourth string, because the lowest string is often disproportionately heavier in order to allow for a bigger sound in the instrument's lowest register. Such strings require lower bow speed and acceleration than others.)

Example 2.   In double-stops that span large intervals, the highest sounding string should be given a relatively lower bowing pressure to prevent it from sounding pressed or flattened. (In these cases, both β and the fundamental frequency are higher for the upper tone, regardless of which string it is played on.)

Practice Suggestion: (1) Play several strokes, keeping two elements (e.g., speed and pressure) fixed while varying the third one (e.g., bow-to-bridge distance). After doing so, try to repeat the combination that gave the best sound, directly. Practice on different strings and at different pitches. (2) Play pairs of tones, two low and two high, in intervals of an octave or larger. Notice the difference required in bow speed.

It is the bow speed that controls the string amplitude for a given bow-to-bridge distance and hence largely the physical loudness of a tone, which is mainly determined by the (loudest-sounding) lower partials. Increasing the bow pressure moderately may produce a slightly brighter sound but rarely increases the total sound level more than one or two decibels before the sound becomes pressed. However, bright sounds are usually *perceived* as loud. For example, when listening to the radio we are never in doubt of an orchestra's dynamic level, regardless of the listening volume. A change of bowing position toward the bridge increases the brilliance and may give the impression of a louder sound, even when compensated for by a lower bow speed.

The Smooth Bow Change

The rotational orientation of the Helmholtz corner is determined by the stroke direction. So when one starts a new stroke in the opposite direction, the whole transient process needs to begin again. Any release of the bow pressure during this phase implies a slower buildup of the new tone, as well as reduced brilliance. This type of temporary change in timbre is less noticeable in the violin than the double bass, due to the longer transient of the latter. If a brilliant, noise-free sound is to be maintained during the entire bow change, a stable bow pressure, combined with suitable bow acceleration, must be observed.

It is important to minimize the remains of the old corner rotation before developing a reversed one to avoid slipping noise caused by interference between two opposing corners. The bow *deceleration* that precedes the change of direction can be of considerably greater magnitude than the acceleration that follows. This has been confirmed by measuring the smooth bow changes of skilled players (Williams, 1985).

Practice Suggestion: Play bow changes at different dynamic levels and different bow-to-bridge distances. Experiment to find the wrist action, or suppleness, that works best in each case.

Spiccato *and* Ricochet

Computer simulations show that the requirements of bowing pressure and acceleration (as described in Figure 19.3) are met during clean *spiccato* attacks and that the bow quickly dampens the string prior to each new attack (Guettler & Askenfelt, 1998). If one places a small mark at the bow-stick midpoint, a horizontal figure of eight (∞) should be seen when one watches the mark during rapid *spiccato*. Any other figure is likely to produce some onset noise. In *ricochet*, where several strokes are performed in the same direction, the remains of the old Helmholtz pattern can easily be picked up and refreshed without any predamping, minimizing the buildup time. The same goes for other linked strokes like *slurred staccato* and *portato*. This is why such attacks often sound cleaner than normal *spiccato* and *détaché*.

"Harmonics" (Flageolet Tones)

"Harmonics" are played by placing the finger at certain points of the string, thus filtering out the fundamental and some of its partials and allowing only some selected partials (overtones) to vibrate. (In physics, however, a *harmonic* means a frequency that is an integer multiple of the fundamental.) When harmonics are played, the string is almost motionless at certain points called nodes. Between these, the string behaves like several short strings, each of which exhibits Helmholtz motion (see Figure 19.4). The nodes are equally spaced along the string. This implies that on a string the stretch between the pressing and the touching finger in an "artificial harmonic" will remain the same whether it is performed as an octave, fifth, fourth, or major-third "harmonic" (see lower part of Figure 19.4). However, the highest position will give the shortest transient, due to earlier reflections between the bridge and the touching finger. A harmonic cannot be excited at the node and requires bowing pressure, speed, and acceleration comparable to that of a fingered tone of the same frequency. This is easily forgotten when combining harmonics with lower-pitched tones on the same string.

Rosins

Rosin temporarily melts in the near vicinity of a sliding string, increasing the difference in frictional force between stick at maximum hold, and slip. It is this difference (its span often referred to as the friction delta)—not the absolute friction values—that uniquely defines the harmonic spectrum for a given bow speed and position on a mounted string. Statements such as "You should be playing with the scales," ". . . barbs," or even ". . . teeth of good-quality hair, not the rosin"

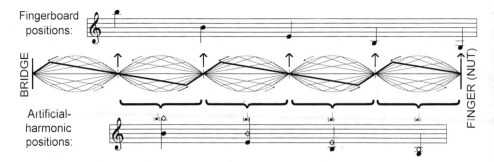

Figure 19.4. When one is playing harmonics, the string forms a series of Helmholtz figures separated by nodes. The distance between adjacent nodes equals one-half the wavelength of the harmonic frequency (here B_5).

are therefore scientifically unjustified. However, as advice to *limit the amount* of rosin such statements make some sense, since a thick layer of rosin tends to cause uneven friction characteristics. The hair should be judged from its ability to hold rosin evenly, rather than from its ability to cause mere friction, to which scale thickness of no more than 1/200 mm will not contribute much anyway (Rocaboy, 1990). The friction delta increases with the bowing pressure and with the softness of the rosin and decreases with increasing string weight (physical term: *wave resistance*). Because of this, soft rosins are often preferred for low-pitched instruments with heavier strings.

Pizzicato

Pizzicato and *arco* produce completely different string movements, as *pizzicato* involves no corner rotation, only a simple side-to-side movement, symmetrical over the string's midpoint. Although different, their spectra are both functions of the relative bow- (or finger-) to-bridge distance, with a large distance giving the highest proportion of fundamental-frequency amplitude and hence the longest sound-buildup time, while a small distance gives the brightest and most direct sound. High overtones tend to fade quickly. This depends, however, on both frequency and plucking *angle*, as the mobility, thus the individual overtone absorption, of the bridge varies with both. Test it!

Sound Radiation

The vibrating string does not produce any audible sound if not coupled to a body of adequate size. In fact, even the bodies of the violin family do not properly radiate the fundamental frequencies of their lowest tones. For the double bass and cello, a compliant floor sometimes comes to the rescue, as low-pitched vibrations are transmitted through their spikes much like tuning forks on a tabletop. Each string instrument has two groups of resonances: one dominated by the enclosed air and one by the wooden body parts. The main air resonance is for violin about 270 Hz $\approx C_4$–$C\sharp_4$, viola: 240 Hz $\approx B\flat_3$–B_3, cello: 115 Hz $\approx B\flat_2$, and double bass: 65 Hz $\approx C_2$, with their main body resonances a good fifth higher (Hutchins, 1962). (A wolf tone would most likely be situated near the latter, by which the top, and hence the bridge, moves considerably.)

The number of resonances per octave rapidly increases with frequency. In *vibrato*, many string partials temporarily coincide with body resonances and are thus well transmitted—while others fall between the resonances. This continuously varying timbre brings out a harmonic totality that is otherwise imperceptible. (One may compare it to viewing a landscape through a picket fence: unless moving, one cannot see it all.) Another interesting feature is the *directional dispersion* of high tones, by which a good instrument may produce an illusion of multiple sound sources in a reflecting room (Weinreich, 1997). In general, different-frequency bands have different radiation characteristics, which are important to bear in mind when positioning the instrument with respect to microphones or even an audience (Meyer, 1972).

When one is performing a solo in a large hall, an early first reflection increases definition and clarity. Instead of approaching the very front edge of a wide stage, stepping back might be better, because it will help to mirror the instrument for the audience in the acoustically reflective stage floor. Brilliance is crucial for perceptibility of rapid passages and should be slightly boosted, for example by bowing closer to the bridge in dark-sounding or reverberant halls. In addition, any view-obstructing music stand will also obstruct high frequencies.

Psychology of String Instrument Performance

Playing a Stringed Instrument

So far we have considered evidence that relates to how sound is produced on bowed stringed instruments and the relationship between this and acoustics. We now consider research evidence that relates to string players and what is distinctive about playing a stringed instrument. To date, research in the psychology of music has tended to neglect these issues, assuming that musicians are a relatively homogeneous group and that what applies to one musician will apply to all. Increasingly researchers are recognizing that there may be important differences between musicians, but as yet there is little research evidence.

What Is Distinctive about Playing a Bowed Stringed Instrument?

As the previous section infers, the technical requirements of the string repertoire are varied and demanding, requiring the acquisition of many skills that must become automated to enable fluent professional performance. To play a bowed stringed instrument requires sensitive motor control to enable secure intonation, clear articulation of bowing, and the coordination of two very different kinds of movements being undertaken by left and right hands. In addition, well-developed aural skills are required to monitor accuracy, as any finger can be used to play almost any note. The demands of the repertoire and professional work schedules also require high-level cognitive processing skills in relation to reading music, as the demands made on string players, particularly the first violins, tend to be greater than those made on other orchestral players. So what does the research evidence tell us about string players and the way they acquire their skills?

The Characteristics of String Players

Using psychometric techniques, Kemp (1995) found that orchestral string players tended to demonstrate more aloofness, conscientiousness, and considerable willpower than other instrumentalists. He suggested that these characteristics were necessary to maintain the level of practice required to master the complexity of playing a stringed instrument. In a further breakdown of the personality profiles into specific instruments, at the school and student level, Kemp found that secondary school violinists emerged as having a tendency to be easily upset and emotional. In contrast, cellists emerged as both self-sufficient, shrewd, and aloof, demonstrating a greater social awareness not apparent in the other instrumentalists. The viola players at student level were more emotionally stable than their fellow string players, while the double-bass players presented a profile that was typical of the overall string profile. These findings must be viewed with some caution, as the number in each group was relatively small, but they are relevant to pedagogy to the extent that those who are learning to play stringed instruments may need a higher level of commitment to practice than those who are learning other orchestral instruments (see also chapter 1 in this volume).

Personality and Practice

How does the research on the personality of string players relate to what we know about their practice? Although there has been little research, such as there is supports the notion that string players, especially the violinists, undertake more practice than their orchestral peers (Jørgensen, 1997). This supports the findings outlined earlier. The reasons for the violinists' undertaking more practice may relate to the larger and more demanding repertoire. We know that there is a strong, if not perfect, relationship between the amount of time spent practicing and the level of expertise attained (Ericsson, Krampe, & Tesch-Römer, 1993; Hallam, 1998; Williamon & Valentine, 2000). Similarly, differences in practice patterns across instruments seem to reflect the demands of particular instruments. As practice draws on limited physical and mental resources, the amount of practice sustainable daily is limited by the individual's ability to recover. Four hours daily seems to be the maximum sustainable over long periods without burnout occurring (Ericsson et al., 1993; Hallam, 1995; Jørgensen, 1997). To accrue the additional hours of practice to achieve professional entry to a music conservatory, string players would need to start playing at a younger age than their wind- and brass-playing colleagues and violinists at an earlier age than other string players. While there is no formal evidence to support this, pianists (who undertake the most practice) and violinists who attain status as international soloists do tend to start playing at very early ages.

Learning to Play a Bowed Stringed Instrument

Given the lack of other cues to inform feedback, it is crucial for string players to develop accurate aural *schemata* (mental representations) against which to evaluate their performance. The evidence suggests that this does not occur until they have developed considerable expertise (Hallam, 2001). Teachers can provide aural representations through modeling, but they tend to spend little time in demonstration, although a large proportion of the variance in performance can be accounted for by their willingness to model aspects of their playing (Sang, 1987).

Feedback has an important role in learning to play any instrument. To be effective, it needs to be appropriate and relevant to the task. Conditions of restricted and unrestricted vision, for instance, had no differential effect on string players' intonation, while verbal feedback produced more accurate intonation than recorded or model performance feedback in university-level string players (Salzberg, 1980). Violin posture can be improved through the teacher providing corrective feedback (Salzberg & Salzberg, 1981), and biofeedback techniques, where musicians receive through electronic monitoring direct feedback that regards muscular activity, have proved very useful in enabling string players to learn to relax specific muscles as they are playing (Irvine & LeVine, 1981; LeVine & Irvine, 1984; Morasky, Reynolds, & Clarke, 1981). These techniques can be used while students perform passages from the repertoire they are learning (Cutietta, 1986).

Practical Applications

What can we learn from the research findings in this chapter that will offer specific help to string players? Playing a stringed instrument is distinctive because of its relative difficulty and its particular reliance on well-developed aural skills. String players need to start playing young, undertake a considerable amount of practice, and be given numerous opportunities for listening to music and developing aural skills. Modeling and the provision of detailed verbal feedback are very important in teaching.

References

Askenfelt, A., & Guettler, K. (1998). The bouncing bow: An experimental study. *Catgut Acoustical Society Journal, 3*(6), Ser. 2, 3–8.

Cutietta, R. (1986). Biofeedback training in music: From experimental to clinical applications. *Bulletin of the Council for Research in Music Education, 87*, 35–42.

Ericsson, K. A., Krampe, R. T., & Tesch-Römer, C. (1993). The role of deliberate practice in the acquisition of expert performance. *Psychological Review, 100*(3), 363–406.

Guettler, K., & Askenfelt, A. (1997). Acceptance limits for the duration of pre-Helmoltz transients in bowed string attacks. *Journal of the Acoustical Society of America, 101*(5), pt. 1, 2903–2913.

Guettler, K., & Askenfelt, A. (1998). On the kinematics of spiccato and ricochet bowing. *Catgut Acoustical Society Journal, 3*(6), Ser. 2, 9–15.

Hallam, S. (1995). Professional musicians' orientations to practice: Implications for teaching. *British Journal of Music Education, 12*(1), 3–19.

Hallam, S. (1998). The predictors of achievement and drop out in instrumental tuition. *Psychology of Music, 26*(2), 116–132.

Hallam, S. (2001). The development of expertise in young musicians: Strategy use, knowledge acquisition and individual diversity. *Music Education Research, 3*(1), 7–23.

Helmholtz, H. von (1862/1954). *Lehre von den Tonempfindungen (On the sensations of tone)*. New York: Dover.

Hutchins, C. M. (1962). The physics of violins. *Scientific American, 207*, 78–93.

Irvine, J. K., & LeVine, W. R. (1981). The use of biofeedback to reduce the left hand tension for string players. *American String Teacher, 31*, 10–12.

Jørgensen, H. (1997). Time for practicing? Higher level music students' use of time for instrumental practicing. In. H. Jørgensen and A. C. Lehmann (Eds.), *Does practice make perfect? Current theory and research on instrumental music practice* (pp. 123–140). Oslo: Norges Musikhøgskole.

Kemp, A. E. (1995). Aspects of upbringing as revealed through the personalities of musicians. *Quarterly Journal of Music Teaching and Learning, 5*(4), 34–41.

LeVine, W. R., & Irvine, J. K. (1984). In vivo EMG biofeedback in violin and viola pedagogy. *Biofeedback and Self-Regulation, 9,* 161–168.

McIntyre, M. E., Schumacher, R. T., & Woodhouse, J. (1981). Aperiodicity in bowed-string motion. *Acustica, 49*(1), 13–32.

McIntyre, M. E., & Woodhouse, J. (1979). On the fundamentals of bowed-string dynamics. *Acustica, 43*(2), 93–108.

Melka, A. (1970). Klangeinsatz bei Musikinstrumenten. *Acustica, 23,* 108–117.

Meyer, J. (1972). Directivity of the bowed string instruments and its effect on sound in concert halls. *Journal of the Acoustical Society of America, 51,* 1994–2009.

Morasky, R. L., Reynolds, C., & Clark, G. (1981). Using biofeedback to reduce left arm extensor EMG of string players during musical performance. *Biofeedback and Self-Regulation, 6,* 565–572.

Pickering, N. C. (1985). Physical properties of violin strings. *Catgut Acoustical Society Journal, 44,* 6–8.

Pickering, N. C. (1990). String tone related to core material. *Catgut Acoustical Society Journal, 1*(5), Ser. 2, 23–28.

Pitteroff, R. (1995). *Contact mechanics of the bowed string.* Unpublished doctoral dissertation, University of Cambridge.

Raman, C. V. (1920). Experiments with mechanically played violins, Vol. 6, parts 1 and 2. *Proceedings of Indian Association of Cultivation of Science,* 19–36.

Rocaboy, F. (1990). The structure of bow-hair fibres. *Catgut Acoustical Society Journal, 2d, 1*(6), 34–36.

Salzberg, R. S. (1980). The effects of visual stimulus and instruction on intonation accuracy of string instrumentalists. *Psychology of Music, 8*(2), 42–49.

Salzberg, R. S., & Salzberg, C. L. (1981). Praise and corrective feedback in the remediation of incorrect left-hand positions of elementary string players. *Journal of Research in Music Education, 29*(2), 125–133.

Sang, R. C. (1987). A study of the relationship between instrumental music teachers' modelling skills and pupil performance behaviors. *Bulletin of the Council for Research in Music Education, 91,* 155–159.

Savart, F. (1819). *Mémoire sur la construction des instruments à cordes et à archet.* Paris: Deterville.

Savart, F. (1840). Cours de physique expérimentale, professé au College de France pendant l'année scolaire 1838–1839. *L'Institut.*

Schelleng, J. C. (1970). Pressure on the bowed string. *Catgut Acoustical Society Newsletter, 13,* 24–27.

Schumacher, R. T. (1979). Self-sustained oscillations of the bowed string. *Acustica, 43*(2), 109–120.

Weinreich, G. (1997). Directional tone color. *Journal of the Acoustical Society of America, 101*(4), 2338–2346.

Williamon, A., & Valentine, E. (2000). Quantity and quality of musical practice as predictors of performance quality. *British Journal of Psychology, 91*(3), 353–376.

Williams, C. E. (1985). *Violin bowing skill analysis: The mechanics and acoustics of the change in direction.* Unpublished doctoral dissertation, University of Melbourne, Australia.

20

Wind Instruments

LEONARDO FUKS & HEINZ FADLE

In mouth-blown wind instruments, the energy provided by the respiratory system is converted directly into sound. In all cases a primary vibrating element, generically called *reed*, controls the airstream. The reed may be a piece of bamboo, the lips, a metallic tongue, or even the air jet (in flutes and recorders). Players control loudness, attack, intonation, and timbre by means of embouchure settings, blowing pressure, airflow, and length of the air column. The respiratory muscles perform complex and systematic movements, generating wide ranges of pressures, and coordinated oscillations that produce the vibrato effect. Intonation may be affected by the characteristics of the lung air. We address the associated sensory, physiological, and acoustical phenomena. Common controversial or misleading concepts among wind players are discussed and some simple experiments are proposed for pedagogical applications.

Mouth-blown wind instruments convert pneumatic energy, in the form of air pressure and velocity, into sound waves. They belong to the category that Sachs (1940) describes as *aerophones*. Other aerophones include the human voice, the pipe organ, and the accordion.

Wind players use their respiratory apparatus as an air compressor to supply energy to the instrument. At the mouth, air is delivered through a sophisticated interface with the instrument, which musicians refer to as their *embouchure*. Each subtle action from muscles of expiration and embouchure imprints the sound, forming part of the musical expression. The arms, hands, and fingers skillfully control a complex of tone holes, slides, rotating valves, levers, and other mechanisms. Inside the instrument, several phenomena take place, including reflection, diffraction, resonance, shock waves, damping, vortex generation, and chaotic oscillations. Body posture, respiratory techniques, and a psychological strategy to deal with stressful situations are additional key aspects of performance. This rich environment challenges the abilities of players and educators to deal with a number of principles that are associated with performance on wind instruments. Some of the most important are described in this chapter.

The Reed

Every wind instrument has some mechanism that cyclically disturbs or interrupts the air stream. This mechanism can be generically called a *reed*. Therefore, rather than a component of bamboo or other elastic material, *reed* in this context stands for a valve that controls the air passing through the instrument, as shown in Figure 20.1. This concept has been consistently adopted by several authors in music acoustics (Campbell & Greated, 1987; Sundberg, 1991; Strong & Plitnik, 1992). The tongue, the lips, and the moving structures of the respiratory system may also be used to regulate the airflow, serving as additional valves.

Winds may incorporate a *mechanical reed* (reed woodwinds), *free reed* (mouth harmonicas), *lip reed* (brass instruments), or *air reed* (flutes and recorders), where one side is in contact with the player's mouth and the other attached to the instrument. Figure 20.1 shows four simplified models of reeds, each one representing a different type of oscillation. Because instruments such as the flute involve an air reed with no solid vibrating part, they are discussed separately.

As the air stream encounters resistance in passing the reed, a difference of pressure will be created between both sides. The pressure in the upstream (before the reed) is in principle higher than that of the downstream side due to friction losses. As the reed is flexible, it will tend to bend or move due to this pressure difference. In much the same way as a spring, a reed's elasticity will allow it to return to its original position and shape. The reed also contains mass that is distributed along its body. This defines a *spring-mass* system that has its own resonance frequencies.

In a similar manner to a tuning fork, a reed can be excited to oscillate at its own frequencies. This is the case in free reeds and, exceptionally, in clarinets

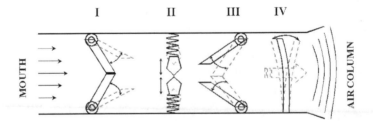

Figure 20.1. Oscillation types found in lip, mechanical, and free reeds: rest position of the reed (solid line) and extreme position during vibration (broken line). (I) outward-striking and (II) sideways- or upward-striking oscillations as found in brass instruments; (III) inward-striking oscillation, typical of reed woodwinds; and (IV) free-striking oscillations, which occur in free reeds.

that produce the so-called *squeak sounds* (Bouasse, 1929/1986). However, the tissue of the lips, forming a cushion pressed against the reeds, absorbs most of the reed energy in every cycle, with the oscillations being damped more than those of a tuning fork.

Another factor is the so-called *Bernoulli force*. When air passes through a narrow passage, the particles' velocity must increase in order to maintain a constant flow. This results in a drop in pressure past the narrow passage and a subsequent partial vacuum between air molecules. This negative pressure tends to suck the reed toward the closing position. If the closing reed blocks the air, this suction is immediately interrupted, releasing the reed to return to its original state.

In spite of being easily explained in general terms, the Bernoulli force is not important in all cases. It is certainly relevant in double reeds, especially the oboe, and for the higher range of brass instruments (Fletcher & Rossing, 1998). However, in the case of the clarinet its role is in most cases negligible, because it is not strong enough to make this instrument's reed vibrate (Worman, 1971).

The Air Column

The *air column* is the length of vibrating air in the instrument during sound production. The airflow that crosses the reed creates pressure waves that travel along the air column toward its end and are then reflected back to the reed. In lip and mechanical reeds, if the reflected wave pressure is strong enough it will make the reed reverse its direction. At this point, the system is ready for a new cycle, as it establishes a chain of *self-sustained oscillations*. In an air reed, the air jet flows alternately into the column and out into the ambient, as a result of the waves set up in the air column (Benade & Gans, 1968).

The connection between the air column and the reed, technically referred to as acoustical coupling, forces the reed to vibrate at certain frequencies. When producing a steady tone, the reed vibrates with a frequency close to one particular mode of the air column, so that reflected waves arrive precisely when the reed, depending on the oscillation type, closes or opens. Benade (1990) described this situation as the reed being "enslaved" by the air column. Each configuration of tone holes, keys, pistons, valves, or slide in a wind instrument determines the length and shape of the air column.

A given air column resonates at a set of frequencies that are possible inside it. Each of these frequencies corresponds to a resonance mode. The set of tones obtained with a fixed air column should ideally coincide with those of a harmonic series. However, instruments usually deviate from the perfect geometry of a cylinder or a cone, so that the real modes also deviate from the exact harmonics. Wind players must develop the skill of matching the embouchure and blowing controls to select the desired mode of the air column, which will result in particular tones. Whenever the reed and the air column achieve a pattern of self-sustained oscillations, a *playing mode* is defined. *Overblowing* happens when the instrument jumps from a mode to a higher one.

The four models in Figure 20.1 are *pressure-controlled valves*, as pressure is the main controller of the reed movement. Only air reeds such as the flute are directly controlled by airflow (Benade & Gans, 1968).

While the instrument is being played, the sound waves generated in the reed propagate both to the tube and to the mouth cavity, toward the player's airways. However, most of this energy propagated into the mouth is lost by absorption through the multiple branches and soft walls of the respiratory apparatus. Nevertheless, the vocal tract may respond to some frequencies, as it does for the formation of the vowel sounds. In such cases, the vocal tract can be considered as an internal air column that interacts with the reed and the instrument's air column.

Some skilled players attempt to master the control of the vocal tract to improve their sound quality and stability and to help in the transition between playing modes. While some authors consider that a player's vocal tract has a negligible influence on an instrument's tone (e.g., Backus, 1985, in reed woodwinds), others (Benade, 1986; Johnston, 1987; Fletcher & Rossing, 1998) claim a considerable influence of the vocal tract in instruments such as the clarinet, saxophone, harmonica, and brass.

Types of Reed Oscillation

Lip, mechanical, and free reeds perform characteristic types of oscillations according to their mechanical configuration, as shown in Figure 20.1. The airflow from the lungs crosses the reed, which is subject to forces provided by the embouchure. Helmholtz (1863/1954) referred to type I as an outward-striking and to type III as an inward-striking oscillation. Similarly, type II can be called upward- or sideways-striking and type IV a free-striking oscillation (Fletcher & Rossing, 1998).

In general, the playing frequencies in types II and III are lower than the resonant frequencies of the air column and of the reed itself, while in type I oscillations the playing frequency is higher than those of the air column and the reed alone (Fletcher & Rossing, 1998). Free reeds, corresponding to type IV, are not strongly coupled to an air column and essentially vibrate at their resonance frequencies.

The Embouchure

The *embouchure* can be defined as the constellation of forces and positions in the lips, mouth region, and face that act on the wind instrument (Porter, 1967). It consists of the muscles that form and surround the mouth, the teeth, the upper jaw and mandible, and muscles responsible for mastication. The embouchure controls the reed behavior, thus affecting tone color, articulation, dynamics, and other parameters. In defining the embouchure, it is possible to include the internal mouth configuration, such as the positioning of jaw and tongue. In this sense, the mouth cavity can be regarded as a secondary air column.

In reed woodwinds, the embouchure regulates the reed parameters, such as the stiffness, the aperture for the airflow, the degree of absorption, and, to some extent, its effective mass (Nederveen, 1969). The embouchure also provides an airtight attachment of the lips to the instrument. In brass instruments, the lips obviously serve both as a reed and as an embouchure component and include the same functions cited earlier. In the flute, the embouchure must be skillfully shaped and managed to ensure proper generation and control of the sound. In spite of the importance of the embouchure in performance and sound production, these latter aspects seem to have been unexplored and therefore deserve more research interest.

Wind Instrument Families

Brass

Stroboscopic observations of the lip vibrations in a professional trombone player indicate that the upper lip vibrates with greater amplitudes than the lower lip in all frequencies and dynamic levels (Copley & Strong, 1996). This study also showed that on average, two-thirds of the mouthpiece diameter is covered by the upper lip and one-third by the lower lip. However, considerable variations of this proportion can be observed in the general playing population, which suggests that players tend to optimize their embouchure during the process of learning.

Lip reeds correspond to types I or II in Figure 20.1. In both cases air pressure tends to open the lips, but in type II the Bernoulli forces act alone to close the lips back. Usually, the type I occurs in the lowest playing modes, with type II being more frequent in the higher modes (Yoshikawa, 1995). It is also possible that both types of motion take place in combination, as observed across the whole compass in a trombone study (Copley & Strong, 1996). Not all studies, however, found the same behavior, probably due to differences in the measurement methods that were employed and particular techniques that were adopted by individual players (Chen & Weinreich, 1996).

A common warm-up practice among brass players consists of buzzing on the mouthpiece or with lips only. This exercise is also claimed to develop flexibility and control of lip vibrations. However, according to Yoshikawa (1995), the isolated mouthpiece represents a completely different acoustical system from the full instrument bore, supporting only type I oscillations but not type II. This finding suggests that exercises of this type do not develop lip flexibility in the way often assumed by brass teachers.

The vibration frequency of the lips increases with a combination of higher muscular tension and lower mass. This *mass* refers to the section of the lip that effectively vibrates. Also, raising the pitch requires higher blowing pressure (Bouhuys, 1964). Therefore, it could be expected that the player would tend to press the lips more firmly against the mouthpiece when playing higher tones. This was corroborated by Barbenal, Davies, and Kenny (1986), who observed that the compressive forces between lips and mouthpiece increase systematically with increasing pitch in professional players. Once again, this finding contradicts some performers' claim that it is possible to develop a rather "loose" and "fixed" embouchure, regardless of pitch and dynamic level. However, the idea of a loose embouchure may work as a mental image that helps to achieve the goal of minimizing the effort and strain of the embouchure muscles in order to preserve the necessary sensory response of the tissues.

Reed Woodwinds

Mechanical reeds correspond to type III oscillations in Figure 20.1, where the airflow tends to blow them closed. In the oboe and in the bassoon, the reeds beat against each other almost all the time, completely interrupting the airflow in every oscillation. Similarly, in the saxophone, the reed tends to repeatedly beat against the mouthpiece. This occurs because the conical shape of those instruments creates comparatively high pressures where the reeds are located. In the clarinet, however, with its cylindrical shape, the reed does not necessarily beat against the mouthpiece for the relatively soft tones (Worman, 1971). This explains why softer tones of the clarinet have comparatively much stronger fundamentals than louder tones.

One major distinctive characteristic among mechanical reeds is their *hardness*, also referred to as heaviness or strength. Many players agree that harder reeds need higher blowing pressure and greater lip tension. Also, harder reeds are supposed to produce darker tones with less prominent high frequencies. In a study with oboe, bassoon, clarinet, and alto saxophone (Fuks, 1998a), two contrasting reeds were used in each, one rated as hard (heavy) and another as soft (light). In all reeds and instruments, louder tones required more airflow and higher blowing pressure. Among hard and soft reeds, the harder reeds always produced louder tones, needed more airflow, and involved higher blowing pressure.

Harmonicas and Similar Instruments

Free reeds correspond to type IV oscillations in Figure 20.1. The air tends to close the free reed until it reaches the vertical line and then starts to open it. The harmonica is the most typical instrument in this category. As mentioned earlier, its usual blown frequency is about the same as if it were plucked and left to vibrate alone.

As mentioned previously, the vocal tract acts as an additional air column. The effect of the vocal tract on the sound of a diatonic harmonica can be demonstrated just by moving the tongue back and forth inside the mouth while blowing, which produces clear changes in the relative intensity of the overtones.

Air Reeds: Flutes and Recorders

Air reeds contain a jet that is directed toward an air column, which generates airflow fluctuations inside the tube. In flutelike instruments, the airflow is guided through the player's lips toward a mouth hole. In recorderlike instruments, the flow is conducted through a *flue* channel that is directed toward a sharp edge called the labium.

Two different kinds of tone can be produced in such instruments: a *pipe tone* and an *edge tone*. A pipe tone results when the jet and the air column are acoustically coupled. All pipe tones coincide with the tube's modes, which roughly belong to a harmonic series and can be shifted by overblowing. However, when the jet is relatively distant from the resonant tube acoustical coupling to the pipe is poor and the jet interacts mainly with the labium. This produces edge tones with high frequencies that are proportional to the jet velocity. Therefore, they are not discrete as pipe tones but continuously varying. Edge tones may be important during the attack of a new tone. For example, if a flute player is starting a low C_4 (247 Hz), it takes a moment before the tone is actually initiated. During this period, the edge tones sound alone, contributing to the onset of the tone and to its sound quality. Edge tones are also generated when the pipe is damped (filled with cotton) and when the pipe is simply removed (Verge, 1995).

Air reeds are *flow-controlled* systems in which the pressure at both ends of the air column is close to the ambient pressure. For that reason, the air particles reach higher velocity close to these ends, so that they are directly affected by the airflow. Consequently, the player's vocal tract is usually weakly coupled to the flute and therefore has only a limited influence on the sound (Coltman, 1973; Fletcher & Rossing, 1998).

Boehm (1871/1964), the inventor of the modern flute, explains that the air stream strikes the sharp edge of the mouth hole and is broken (or divided) so that one part goes over or beyond the hole while the other part produces the tone. This is not a perfect description of what really happens, but it is still to be found in many textbooks. A flute can even produce a pipe tone when the edge of the mouth hole is dull. This can be demonstrated by applying a thin layer of wax or chewing gum to the edge of the mouth hole. If the wax or gum is placed in the right position, sound production might still be possible. In this case, however, the edge tones may be hampered, thus affecting the attack and overall sound quality.

Techniques

Using the Respiratory Muscles

The diaphragm is a large and thin muscle group located at the base of the lungs. It separates the thorax from the abdomen. Contrary to common belief, the diaphragm is solely an inspiratory agent that contracts when one breathes in by descending its central part, drawing the lungs downward, increasing the longitudinal dimension of the chest, and elevating the lower ribs (Roussos, 1995). These actions produce negative pressure around the lungs. During wind playing, blowing pressures range from almost 0 (e.g., *piano* low tones in the flute) to values that exceed 120 cm H_2O in *fortissimo* high-pitched trumpet tones (Bouhuys, 1968; Pawłowski & Zołtowski, 1987; Fletcher & Tornapolsky, 1999). If a player completely fills the lungs and closes the airways, without any expiratory effort, a pressure between 30 and 50 cm H_2O will be achieved. This is called relaxation pressure and is generated by the elasticity of the respiratory system.

Similarly, if the lungs are only partially filled—to 70% of their capacity, for example—the relaxation pressure will not exceed 20 cm H_2O (Agostoni & Mead, 1964).

Whenever pressures higher then the relaxation pressure are needed, the expiratory muscles (abdominal and internal intercostal muscles) will be used. However, if pressures lower than the relaxation values are necessary, the inspiratory muscles (external intercostal muscles and the diaphragm) will be used (Bouhuys, 1968). An example of the latter is playing the recorder at high lung volume, when the relaxation pressure is relatively higher than the required blowing pressure. This may also happen at some ranges of the flute and other instruments. Diaphragm activity in skilled flutists has been assessed in at least three studies (Gärtner, 1973; Cossette, 1993; Cossette, Sliwinski, & Macklem, 2000), and all of them indicate that some players make systematic use of the diaphragm, while others do not use it most of the time. These findings suggest that excessive emphasis has been given to the diaphragm in the description of wind performance.

Blowing Pressures

The pressure measured inside the player's mouth during performance is a major input parameter that has been documented in a number of studies. In reed woodwinds, blowing pressure is intimately related to airflow. Acoustical and aerodynamical considerations show that in reed woodwinds the oscillations initiate at a minimal pressure of approximately one-third of the pressure that completely closes the reed. In clarinets, for a fixed embouchure, the airflow and the sound power radiated by the instrument tend to decrease with increasing blowing pressure (Worman, 1971). If the player keeps a constant embouchure while increasing blowing pressure, the tone gets softer until eventually the reed simply closes. This apparent discrepancy explains why players must reduce the embouchure tightness when playing a *crescendo*.

Fuks and Sundberg (1999a) found that blowing pressures in the oboe, bassoon, clarinet, and alto saxophone are systematic in professional players. These authors measured the variation of blowing pressure with loudness and fundamental frequency at four dynamic levels: in isolated tones and musical arpeggios performed by two players of each instrument. Figure 20.2 displays part of the results, where each instrument presents characteristic curves, differing only slightly between players.

Vivona (1968) observed that nonprofessional trombone players use blowing pressures that increase with pitch and dynamic level. For tones Bb_2, Bb_3, and Bb_4, the average pressures were 11, 16, and 39 cm H_2O in "soft volume level" and 24, 39, and 67 cm H_2O for "loud levels." This behavior is similar to reed woodwinds and should also apply to other brass instruments at different ranges.

A study of experienced trumpet players (Fletcher & Tornapolsky, 1999) showed that the minimal blowing pressure (i.e., threshold pressure) increased proportionally with the frequency of the tone played. In the first range, starting from threshold pressure, each doubling of blowing pressure caused the sound pres-

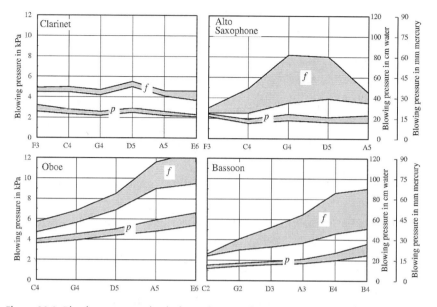

Figure 20.2. Blowing pressures in clarinet, alto saxophone, oboe, and bassoon tones, played at different dynamic levels by two professionals on each instrument. Pressure values are marked in kilopascal on the vertical axis on the left and in cm H₂0 and mm of mercury on the right. In all instruments, blowing pressures increased from *piano* to *forte*. In the oboe and bassoon, the pressure systematically increased with fundamental frequency. In the clarinet, there was a slight decrease of pressure with fundamental frequency. In the saxophone, the pressure tended to increase with pitch in the first octave and followed the clarinet in the second octave. (From Fletcher & Rossing, 1998, after data from Fuks & Sundberg, 1999a. Copyright Springer-Verlag 1998, used by permission.)

sure level to increase by about fifteen decibels, whereas in a second and higher range, called the saturation region, doubling of blowing pressure increased the sound level by only three decibels. In some players, extreme pressures as high as 25 kPa (250 cm H₂O) were measured.

In reed woodwinds, there is also an important relationship between blowing pressures and intonation. As a rule, as the blowing pressure is increased, the fundamental frequency rises. This can be explained by an increase in the reed's natural frequency. Some clarinet players believe that playing tones louder makes the pitch go flat, because a player automatically reduces the embouchure tension to increase loudness (as discussed earlier) and thus decreases the reed's natural frequency (Bak & Doemler, 1987). In other words, the effect of lip relaxation on fundamental frequency is greater than the effect of pressure.

A rather linear relationship between blowing pressures and fundamental frequency has been found for flutes and recorders (Herman, 1959; Coltman, 1968; Fletcher & Rossing, 1998). This means that an octave leap by overblowing will require approximately twice the pressure.

In flutes, blowing pressure varies between 2 cm H_2O for C_4 and 20 cm H_2O for C_7, with little increase between soft and loud tones (Cossette et al., 2000). A crescendo is obtained by airflow velocity increase via the reduction of the oval lip opening, in both height and width. Interestingly, professional flutists tend to use the maximal blowing pressure that a given mode can take without overblowing. They do this to ensure steadiness and quality of tone. To control the dynamic level, a player needs to change the shape and dimension of the lip opening and also move the lips forward and backward. These maneuvers affect the embouchure, the jet length, and the proportion of mouth-hole covering (Fletcher & Rossing, 1998; Cossette et al., 2000).

Perception of Pressure

The results cited earlier suggest that the sensory functions in the abdominal, thoracic, and lung regions are important to effective wind instrument playing. Also, the ability of players to reach the required pressures quickly and systematically, to produce the target values with limited feedback from aural and other bodily senses, indicates that they have intuitively memorized the relevant parameters of their instrument. This assumption was confirmed by Smith et. al., (1990), who investigated the sensation of inspiratory volume and inspiratory pressure in wind instrument players. Their findings show that wind musicians have a considerably higher sensation for both inspiratory volume and pressure than nonmusical subjects. Fuks (1998b) applied a psychophysical production method to assess the sensation of blowing pressures in eight professional reed wind players. He found a proportional relationship between the measured blowing pressure and the estimated pressure level that expresses the players' perception. This approach showed that the subjects could judge quite accurately the multiplication of internal lung pressure, which seems to be a highly relevant sensory skill in wind performance. This particular ability may be trained by means of special exercises, for instance with the help of mechanical devices or a system controlled by a computer.

Lung Air Composition and Intonation

The temperature inside the instrument is related to intonation, so that an increase of 10°C (18°F) will raise the pitch by about a third of a semitone, or 31 cents (a semitone contains 100 cents).

Other factors may also affect intonation. Considerable variations in the concentration of carbon dioxide (CO_2) and oxygen (O_2) can be expected during playing. Fuks (1997) measured variations in the proportion of carbon dioxide in the air exhaled by players. This typically started at 2.5% and reached 8.5% at the end of long phrases. Meanwhile, the percentage of oxygen dropped from 21% to 12%.

The speed of sound depends on the gas properties and so proportionally affects the fundamental frequency of a wind instrument (excluding the free reeds). This can be demonstrated by having a wind player take a full breath of helium before playing: the tones may be transposed by an interval that exceeds nine semitones.

Under more realistic atmospheric conditions, the effect of the changes in gas composition, together with the change in air humidity, can produce a frequency decrease of up to 15 cents (15% of a semitone) during a long phrase. Trained players tend to compensate for this tendency for the pitch to fall by adjusting their embouchure and blowing pressure during their performance.

Vibrato

Vibrato consists of pulsations of pitch, usually accompanied by simultaneous pulsations of loudness and sound quality (Seashore, 1938/1967). Vibrato in winds can be produced by isolated or combined variations in blowing pressure or air-flow, restrictions in the airways caused by the movement of the larynx and tongue, and movement and tension of the lips and jaw (affecting the reed vibrations). In the case of the trombone, mainly in jazz but also in some classical players, vibrato may be obtained by the variation of the instrument's length. On the trumpet, a common type of vibrato consists of a gentle shaking of the instrument, which affects the embouchure. This technique is called hand vibrato.

In general, vibrato seems to include blowing pressure oscillation, be it in flutes (Fletcher, 1975; Gärtner, 1973), reed woodwinds (Brown, 1973; Weait & Shea, 1977; Fuks, 1998a; Secan, 1997), or brass. Some studies have observed oscillations of the vocal folds during vibrato, suggesting that they play a role as a control mechanism. For intense vibrato tones produced on oboe, bassoon, and saxophone, wide pressure oscillations have been observed, on average 10 cm H_2O for the oboe and bassoon and reaching values of 20 cm H_2O in some cases (Fuks, 1998a). These wide undulations cannot be produced merely by the laryngeal mechanism, which otherwise would produce vocal sounds simultaneously, but require a great deal of expiratory force.

Vibrato is seldom taught, in spite of its ability to enhance the player's sonority and expressivity. Many educators consider that vibrato should be discovered by the student. Some others prescribe a series of respiratory maneuvers, most of which involve pulsation in the respiratory flow, thought to facilitate the acquisition of vibrato. A possible reason for this pedagogical attitude is that vibrato involves such a complex neuromuscular coordination that a simplified or step-by-step method for its production might produce an unsatisfactory, artificial effect.

Respiratory Movements

Much attention has been given in the teaching of wind playing to respiratory techniques. Instructions on how to breathe in and out during sound production are usually given by the teacher, often while he or she is examining the student's body posture.

A few physiological methods are available to assess respiratory movement during wind performance. The technique called body plethysmography involves confining the player in a closed box, with only the head outside. Any variation in the body volume is detected and registered by the equipment. In spite of the rather clumsy setup, this technique has been successfully applied to both singing and trombone experiments (Bouhuys, 1968). Another technique employs magnets and sensors connected to the player's thorax. These accurately record the respiratory movements. Magnetometers have been used during the playing of sustained tones in the flute (Cossette, 1993; Cossette et al., 2000). The latter study with three professional flutists found that they used similar movements when inhaling but quite different patterns of expiratory movements during expiration and that these differences did not result in perceptible differences in sound quality.

Respiratory Inductive Plethysmography (*RIP*) is a technique that also employs electromagnetic technology. Elastic bands that contain electrical coils are wrapped around the chest and abdomen of the player. These bands permit indirect measurement of cross-sectional areas (Strömberg, 1996). The variations of chest and abdominal areas reflect the variations in lung volume and significant changes in body position. In a study with eight professional players of the bassoon, clarinet, oboe, and saxophone, all performing different musical and respiratory tasks, the musical phrases were initiated at 55 to 87% and terminated at between 14 and 52% of the players' vital capacity, depending on instrument, piece, and phrase length (Fuks & Sundberg, 1999b). Vital capacity is the maximal air volume that a person can exhale from full lungs. The players generally showed simultaneous and in many cases equally important contributions from rib cage and abdominal wall during playing. These findings often contradicted the players' own idea of how they used their respiratory apparatus. Some of the players even claimed that their rib cage was not moving at all during inhalations and playing, while the technical equipment demonstrated quite conclusively that their rib cage was responsible for more air displacement than the abdominal wall.

The studies mentioned earlier, undertaken with professional players of the flute and reed woodwinds, show that there is no single correct way to make expiratory movements in wind playing. We nevertheless recommend a relatively constant, systematic, and automatic expiratory pattern, as this allows the player to focus on other aspects of performance, such as blowing pressure and embouchure control.

Pedagogy and Winds

Wind playing imposes high demands in terms of learning and handling respiratory techniques, arm/hand/finger movement, tongue articulation, body posture, and embouchure control. Physiological aspects are therefore extremely important. However, it is also important for players to understand something of the acoustical behavior of the instrument they play, in terms of the function of the mechanisms and practical factors that produce the sound. In addition, psychological issues are involved, such as the aesthetic dimension of music and the emotional stress induced by intensive practice and public performance. Therefore, it is not uncommon that wind players inherit and develop an informal investigative attitude toward the physical, physiological, and psychological phenomena that they experience and try to apply these principles in teaching and reasoning on the art. In some cases, these ideas are grounded in scientific knowledge but also include a combination of empirical conception and mental images. These images are supposed to represent an ensemble of complex tasks and sensations, which can hardly be expressed objectively (Kohut, 1985).

Physical, physiological, and psychophysical variables are continuously coordinated during performance and must be trained through systematic and repeated exercises, usually with the support of method books and under the supervision of an experienced teacher. The usual approach of most teaching methods is to combine the performance of musically significant studies with scales, arpeggios, and other drills that are used to hone the playing of complete works. Modern teaching tends to emphasize musical expression, even in studies that are relatively mechanical.

Many pedagogical methods briefly consider techniques for respiration and breathing for sound production and sometimes the underlying acoustical principles. In some cases, these methods review some basic anatomy of the respiratory apparatus, sometimes complemented by descriptions of the inspiratory and expiratory muscles, recommendations on posture during playing and on optimal inhalation strategy, and instructions on how to achieve "support" and "use the diaphragm." Some educators suggest that these terms may evoke an image of stressful playing that has led to a number of breathing and embouchure problems, even with experienced performers (Fadle & Kohut, 1999; Kohut, 1985).

Arnold Jacobs (1915–1998), a brilliant tuba player and teacher, spent his entire professional life studying respiratory and psychological aspects of winds. Jacobs was probably the most influential wind instrument teacher in the United States and other countries, particularly among brass players (Stewart, 1987; Frederiksen, 1996; Kohut, 1985). In his lessons and workshops, Jacobs used an ensemble of devices, developed for respiratory clinical purposes, to provide visual feedback to his pupils that regarded pulmonary pressure, airflow, and lung volume. Interestingly, Jacobs used a terminology that was more pedagogically oriented than based on physical facts. For instance, he emphasized *flow* as a key word for playing control, as opposed to *pressure*, which he deemed as a somewhat negative term. Because of their psychological effect, different terms tend to trigger different behaviors in players. There is another reason that Jacobs used the term *flow*. In brass instruments, a wide range of combinations of mouth pressure and lip resistance produce the same output level (Weast, 1965). If the player is able to use configurations that require lower pressures, such as lower embouchure resistance and/or stiffness, then the airflow should be maximized and the playing effort reduced (Nederveen, 1969/1998). These general principles are likely to apply also to other winds.

Final Remarks

Knowledge acquired through scientific research cannot replace, and should not challenge, the rich imagery that inspires and guides the artist. But it may help to question, consolidate, and fill the gaps left by individual observation, thus providing an objective background for education in wind playing. Without doubt, some research results conflict with common practice and concepts among the profession, which are often based on obsolete hypotheses that have gained credibility among musicians over many generations.

However, because measurement methods and experimental procedures are still coarser than the musical subtleties involved in performance, it is important for researchers to understand the artists' reality and to take advantage of their skills and long-term experience when designing musically relevant investigations. Collaboration among areas such as physiology, acoustics, psychology, engineering, and musicology will help to enhance knowledge of music performance in winds. As a first step, there is a need to develop some consensus concerning the meaning of technical terms, in ways that promote a better understanding and effectiveness of their application to music teaching and learning.

References

Agostoni, E., & Mead, J. (1964). Statics of the respiratory system. In W. O. Fenn and H. Rahn (Eds.), *Handbook of physiology*, section 3: "Respiration," Vol. 1 (pp. 387–409). Washington, DC: American Physiological Society.

Backus, J. (1985). The effect of the player's vocal tract on woodwind instrument tone, *Journal of the Acoustical Society of America*, *63*, 17–20.

Bak, N., & Doemler, P. (1987). The relation between blowing pressure and blowing frequency in clarinet playing. *Acustica*, *63*, 238–241.

Barbenal, J., Davies, J. B., & Kenny, P. (1986). Science proves musical myths wrong. *New Scientist*, *1502*, 29–32.

Benade, A. H. (1986). Interactions between the player's windway and the air column of a musical instrument. *Cleveland Clinic Quarterly*, *53*, 27–32.

Benade, A. H. (1990). *Fundamentals of musical acoustics* (2nd ed.). New York: Dover.

Benade, A. H., & Gans, D. J. (1968). Sound production in wind instruments. *Sound Production in Man: Annals of the New York Academy of Sciences*, *155*(1), 247–263.

Boehm, T. (1871/1964). *The flute and flute playing*. New York: Dover.

Bouasse, H. P. M. (1929/1986). *Instruments à vent*. Paris: Blanchard.

Bouhuys, A. (1964). Lung volumes and breathing patterns in wind instrument players. *Journal of Applied Physiology*, *19*(5), 967–975.

Bouhuys, A. (1968). Pressure-flow events during wind instrument playing. *Sound Production in Man: Annals of the New York Academy of Sciences*, *155*(1), 264–275.

Brown, A. F. D. (1973). *A comprehensive performance project in oboe literature with a cinefluorographic pilot study of the throat while vibrato tones are played on flute and oboe*. Unpublished doctoral dissertation, University of Iowa.

Campbell, M., & Greated, C. (1987). *The musician's guide to acoustics*. New York: Schirmer.

Chen, F. C., & Wienreich, G. (1996). Nature of the lip reed. *Journal of the Acoustical Society of America*, *99*(2), 1227–1233.

Coltman, J. W. (1968). Sounding mechanism of the flute and the organ pipe. *Journal of the Acoustical Society of America*, *44*, 983–992.

Coltman, J. W. (1973). Mouth resonance effects in the flute. *Journal of the Acoustical Society of America, 54*, 417–420.

Copley, D. C., & Strong, W.J. (1996). A stroboscopic study of lip vibrations in a trombone, *Journal of the Acoustical Society of America, 99*(2), 1219–1226.

Cossette, I. (1993). *Étude de la méchanique respiratoire chez les flûtistes.* Unpublished doctoral dissertation, Université de Montréal, Canada.

Cossette I., Sliwinski, P., & Macklem, P. (2000). Respiratory parameters during professional flute playing. *Respiration Physiology, 121*, 33–44.

Fadle, H., & Kohut D. (1999). *Musizieren.* Essen: Die Blaue Eule.

Fletcher, N. H. (1975). Acoustical correlates of flute performance technique, *Journal of the Acoustical Society of America, 57*, 233–237.

Fletcher, N. H., & Rossing, T. D. (1998). *The physics of musical instruments* (2nd ed.). New York: Springer.

Fletcher, N. H., & Tornapolsky, A. (1999). Blowing pressure, power, and spectrum in trumpet playing. *Journal of the Acoustical Society of America, 105*(2), 874–881.

Frederiksen, B. (1996). *Arnold Jacobs: Song and wind.* Gurnee, IL: Windsong.

Fuks, L. (1997). Prediction and measurements of exhaled air effects in the pitch of wind instruments, *Proceedings of the Institute of Acoustics, 19*(5/2), 373–378.

Fuks, L. (1998a). Aerodynamic input parameters and sounding properties in naturally blown reed woodwinds. *KTH Speech, Music, and Hearing Quarterly Progress Status Report, 4*, 1–11.

Fuks, L. (1998b). Assessment of blowing pressure perception in reed wind instrument players. *KTH Speech, Music, and Hearing Quarterly Progress Status Report, 3*, 35–48.

Fuks, L., & Sundberg, J. (1999a). Blowing pressures in bassoon, clarinet, oboe and saxophone. *Acustica / Acta Acustica, 85*(2), 267–277.

Fuks, L., & Sundberg, J. (1999b, March). Using respiratory inductive plethysmography for monitoring professional reed instrument performance. *Medical Problems of Performing Artists, 14*(1), 30–42.

Gärtner, J. (1973). *Das Vibrato unter besonderer Berücksichtigung der Verhältnisse bei Flötisten.* Regensburg: Bosse.

Helmholtz, H. von (1862/1954). *On the sensations of tone as a physiological basis for the theory of music.* New York: Dover.

Herman, R. (1959). Observations on the acoustical characteristics of the English flute. *American Journal of Physics, 27*, 22–29.

Johnston, R. B. (1987). Pitch control in harmonica playing. *Acoustics of Australia, 15*(3), 69–75.

Kohut, D. (1985). *Musical performance: Learning theory and pedagogy.* Englewood Cliffs, NJ: Prentice-Hall.

Nederveen, C. J. (1969/1998). *Acoustical aspects of woodwind instruments.* DeKalb: Northern Illinois University Press.

Pawłowski S., & Zołtowski, M. (1987). A physiological evaluation of the efficiency of playing the wind instruments—an aerodynamic study. *Archives of Acoustics of Poland, 12*(3–4), 291–299.

Porter, M. (1967). *The embouchure.* London: Boosey & Hawkes.

Roussos, C. (Ed.) (1995). *The thorax* (2nd ed.). New York: Marcel Dekker.

Sachs, C. (1940). *The history of musical instruments.* New York: Norton.

Seashore, C. E. (1938/1967). *The psychology of music.* New York: Dover.

Secan, S. (1997). *Frequency and amplitude modulation in oboe vibrato.* Master's thesis, Ohio State University.

Smith, J., Kreisman, H., Colacone, A., Fox, J., & Wolkove, N. (1990). Sensation of inspired volumes and pressures in professional wind instrument players. *Journal of Applied Physiology, 68*(6), 2380–2383.

Stewart, D. (Ed.) (1987). *Arnold Jacobs: The legacy of a master.* Northfield, IL: Instrumentalist.

Strömberg, N .O. T. (1996). *Respiratory Inductive Plethysmography (RIP): Calibration, breathing pattern analysis and external CO_2 dead space measurement.* Doctoral thesis, Linköping University.

Strong, W. J., & Plitnik, G. R. (1992). *Music speech audio.* Provo: Soundprint.

Sundberg, J. (1991). *The science of musical sounds*, San Diego, CA: Academic Press.

Verge, M. P. (1995). *Aeroacoustics of confined jets, with applications to the physical modelling of recorder-like instruments.* Doctoral thesis, Technical University of Eindhoven, the Netherlands.

Vivona, P. M. (1968). Mouth pressures in trombone players. *Sound Production in Man: Annals of the New York Academy of Sciences, 155,* 290–302.

Weait, C., & Shea, J. B. (1977, January/February). Vibrato: An audio-video-fluorographic investigation of a bassoonist. *Applied Radiology.* http://www.applied radiology.com. January/February.

Weast, R. D. (1965). *Brass Performance.* New York: McGinnis & Marx Publishers.

Worman, W. (1971*). Self-sustained nonlinear oscillations of medium amplitude in clarinet-like systems.* Doctoral thesis, Department of Physics, Case Western Reserve University.

Yoshikawa, S. (1995). Acoustical behavior of brass players lips. *Journal of the Acoustical Society of America, 97*(3), 1929–1939.

21

Rehearsing and Conducting

HARRY E. PRICE & JAMES L. BYO

Conducting and rehearsal behaviors play a role in establishing an appropriate and effective rehearsal atmosphere. Situations in which conductors provide predominantly positive feedback result in better attitudes, attention, and performance. Fast paced rehearsals are usually the most effective, and comprise frequent and generally brief episodes of teacher talk and ensemble performance. Enthusiastic or dynamic rehearsing features stark contrasts of behavior at optimal times—loud and soft talk, expressive and neutral conducting, group and individual eye contact. Rehearsals should be structured to include processes of diagnosis, prescription, presentation, monitoring, and feedback, with brisk paced and clear directions. Essentially, a conductor should focus on making verbalizations efficient and keeping them to a minimum, while enhancing nonverbal behaviors to include large amounts of eye contact and clear and unambiguous conducting gestures.

"From the moment a conductor steps on the podium a special world is in the process of being constructed" (Faulkner, 1973, p. 149). By definition, conductors are leaders. Leadership requires competence, credibility, and charisma, and these qualities can influence musicians' attitudes and performances (Parasuraman & Nachman, 1987).

The current role of the conductor dates back to the late eighteenth century. Not until the mid-twentieth century, though, did a traditional focus on gesture or baton technique evolve to include issues of rehearsal technique. The application of scientific inquiry to rehearsing and conducting is a recent phenomenon, and the psychology of large ensemble leadership, even in a popular sense, remains insubstantially addressed.

One might consider conducting and rehearsing as distinctly separate acts, conducting being a nonverbal physical act, and rehearsing being conductor-led ensemble preparation (largely verbalizations) for musical performance. It is our view that conducting and rehearsing are inextricably linked. When done well, they are complementary, even indistinguishable. In the school music environment, where the focus is on the nature of the rehearsal process with the concert serving to set a context (Reimer, 2000), rehearsing and teaching are analogous. One might argue that everything involved in rehearsing and conducting can be characterized via a teaching paradigm, even in a professional ensemble environment.

The Rehearsal

Rehearsal Atmosphere

Even actions that occur before the first words are uttered or downbeat given influence ensemble members' perceptions of a conductor's abilities. A hesitant approach to the podium, fumbling of materials, low levels of eye contact, and poor posture and hand position have a negative effect on perception of conductor competence, while the converse of these behaviors has a positive effect (Fredrickson, Johnson, & Robinson, 1998).

Conductor behaviors play a role in establishing authority. The likelihood that authority figures are persuasive is in part dependent on the extent to which they are viewed as decisive. Conductors who are inspiring and persuasive can be said to be exercising a form of domination over the performers (Faulkner, 1973). This domination, however, does not preclude the necessity of collaboration between conductor and ensemble. The rehearsal atmosphere must be such that the combination of conductor persuasiveness and collaboration results in an ensemble that is responsive and receptive to the conductor's verbal and nonverbal behaviors. Indeed, performances appear to benefit when ensemble members feel a part of the learning process rather than functioning as passive recipients of information (Hamann et al., 1990).

Feedback

Another aspect of conductor behavior that is relevant to rehearsal atmosphere is conductor feedback. Feedback is necessary in order to achieve the ultimate performance envisioned. Situations in which conductors provide predominantly positive feedback result in better attitudes, attention, and performance than ones in which conductors provide instruction without feedback (see Price, 1983). Indeed, positive rehearsal environments tend to result in better ensemble attentiveness and attitudes than do negative ones (e.g., Madsen & Yarbrough, 1985; Price, 1992). In contrast, there are accomplished conductors and teachers in instrumental music who use more negative than positive feedback, which results in successful performances and positive student attitudes (Cavitt, 1998; Duke & Henninger, 1998). It is important to consider that negative feedback delivered constructively is likely to function quite differently from that delivered angrily. Negative feedback is necessary and can function well if the combination of instruction and feedback, both negative *and* positive, leads to accomplishment of musical goals. If, however, the rehearsal is characterized by inordinate amounts of ensemble failures, the potential for negative feedback to be detrimental to attitude and attentiveness is increased.

Pacing

In general education, fast pacing of instruction has been linked to effective teaching, though it is recognized that in seeking an optimal pace one must consider the nature and complexity of the subject matter being taught as well as the sophistication of those being taught (e.g., Brophy & Good, 1986). Slow pacing is not necessarily an indication of ineffective teaching.

There is no unequivocal definition of rehearsal pacing nor of an optimal pace of activity. However, frequency and duration of ensemble performance episodes, conductor talk, lag time between cutoff and conductor talk, and conductor rate of speech are thought to be components of pacing. Experienced observers have been asked to view videotaped rehearsal examples and rate conductor pacing on a scale from very slow to very fast, and the responses correlated fast pace to fast rate of conductor speech (Single, 1990). This association is reinforced by findings in rehearsal settings, including a professional orchestra with Bruno Walter conducting that found most teacher/conductor verbal behaviors occurred in short bursts (Yarbrough, 1988).

In an attempt to describe pacing empirically, Duke, Prickett, and Jellison (1998) selected fast- and slow-paced videotaped examples of rehearsal conducting and music teaching, based on observers' personal perceptions of pacing, not on one prescribed definition. Fast and slow paces were then described according to the frequency and duration of conductor versus ensemble activities. They found that fast paced rehearsals comprised frequent and generally brief episodes of teacher talk and student performance.

In one of the few longitudinal studies of the rehearsal process, pacing was defined as change of focus of activity between director and ensemble (Yarbrough, Dunn, & Baird, 1996). An examination of rehearsals with the lowest and highest performance ratings found that the lowest performance rated rehearsal, which was the first rehearsal of a work, had a considerably slower pace than the higher rated and later rehearsal. These findings suggest that pacing should be examined as a change in activity and a function of the relative familiarity and difficulty of the literature being rehearsed.

A conductor might endeavor to quicken the rehearsal pace by speaking more succinctly, thus reducing the duration of talk episodes. While less-accomplished conductors stop and restart ensembles frequently, as is suggested by the preceding description of fast pace, they tend to do so without providing instruction (Goolsby, 1999). In addition, expert band conductors vary the rate of alternation between conductor talk and student performance episodes according to the issue being addressed (Cavitt, 1998). Thus advising a novice conductor to quicken the pace by working faster fails to acknowledge the fact that some performance errors and rehearsal conditions simply require more time to correct than others do.

Performance Error Detection

Related to conductor feedback and rehearsal pacing is the conductor's response to performance errors. How best to prepare prospective conductors to cope effectively with a "great confusion of sound" (Bruno Walter in Chesterman, 1976, p. 22) in rehearsal has been the object of study in performance error detection. There is no definitive hierarchy, by difficulty, across the different types of errors (pitch, rhythm, articulation, etc.) that may occur in rehearsals (Byo, 1997). A performance error is more or less audible depending on its type, its timbre, the texture and tempo of the music, whether the listener is conducting, and whether the listener opts for a focused or unfocused approach to the listening task (Byo & Sheldon, 2000). It may be advantageous for conductors to be aware of musicians' performance tendencies, such as rushing rather than dragging tempi and playing sharp rather than flat.

Conductors may improve their abilities to detect performance errors by practicing error detection (Byo, 1997). It is tempting to assume that tasks such as sight singing and harmonic dictation enhance skill in error detection. Research, however, shows that this may not be the case (Brand & Burnsed, 1981). It is likely that skill in error detection is most affected by practicing it directly. There seems to be pedagogical potential in structuring personal error detection practice experiences to begin with one line of music only. If one line of music is approached as the musically rich, comprehensive entity it can be (involving issues of tempo, pitch, rhythm, articulation, intonation, dynamics, and interpretation), it can present a formidable challenge to the intellect and ear of the conductor. The ability to detect errors effectively, in any context, begins with the ability to hear and evaluate one line of music completely and precisely. Further, there are indications that error detection skill increases when conductors go to rehearsal with a well-developed internal sound image of the score (Byo & Sheldon, 2000). This sound-based knowledge of the score can reduce or override aural distractions in rehearsal. Conductors should study scores in such a way that they are able to ask to what extent they hear from their ensemble what they expect to hear. Then, when the ensemble's performance fails to match their internalized images of the ideal sound, they will be able to begin the process of error detection.

Conductor Demeanor

In examining the effects of conductor enthusiasm on ensemble performance, attentiveness, and attitude, one might expect an enthusiastic conductor to be more interesting, if not more effective, than a dull one. However, the musicians in Yarbrough's (1975) study, in a statistical sense, did not perform better for, or pay more attention to, the enthusiastic conductor. This result caused the investigator to look more deeply at precisely what enthusiastic conductors do. A novice conductor who is not naturally dynamic might have the same concern. Yarbrough hypothesized that the enthusiastic rehearsal conductor is one who makes high levels of eye contact with the ensemble and varies it from group to individual, frequently approaches the ensemble by moving or leaning forward, manipulates speech across a wide range of volumes, and gestures expressively with hands/arms and face (i.e., using a variety of movements and contrasts of facial expression).

Notice a recurring theme—that is, the behaviors of an enthusiastic conductor are not static; rather, they vary. Results of a detailed analysis that used an observation form designed to isolate these behaviors made apparent what was not readily seen through more casual observation—that *variation* in conductor behavior is perhaps more salient than doing *more* of a behavior (e.g., talking louder without contrast or conducting expressively without contrast). It appears that enthusiastic conducting (dynamic conducting, if you prefer) might best be described in terms of the conductor's ability to exhibit stark contrasts of behavior at optimal times—loud and soft talk, expressive and neutral conducting, group and individual eye contact (Byo, 1990). Much as music without appropriate variety and contrast is typically uninteresting, so is a rehearsal. By analyzing one's own conducting via videotape in combination with a conductor observation form, the aspiring conductor can apply a tested research procedure in order to see more clearly the behaviors related to enthusiastic rehearsing and conducting (Madsen & Yarbrough, 1985).

Of course, effective rehearsing and conducting extend beyond the mere delivery of information to include the accuracy of information conveyed by the conductor, both verbally and nonverbally, and the quality of the interaction between conductor and ensemble (Standley & Madsen, 1987). Conductors' abilities to create and sustain an intense rehearsal atmosphere hinge on their abilities to handle the subject matters of music, rehearsal, teaching, and group psychology accurately, appropriately, and in an engaging manner. This intensity can be reduced or lost by a conductor's mistake, slow or dull delivery, or casual demeanor (Madsen, 1990). For a conductor who lacks rehearsal intensity (or whose passion is not apparent to ensemble members), observation from analysis combined with videotape review can offer specific diagnosis of the problem and suggest corrective action (e.g., Cassidy, 1990; Kaiser, 1998).

Rehearsal Structure

Although originally it referred to the interaction of child with environment, Vygotsky's *Zone of Proximal Development* (ZPD) construct is pertinent to structuring rehearsals. ZPD, in the context of the rehearsal, can be thought of as the difference between what an ensemble can achieve without and with the direction of a conductor. It is the distance between what problems individuals can fix independently and the possible solutions that can be achieved in collaboration with peers or under the guidance of an authority (Vygotsky, 1978). As ensemble members become more sophisticated, they are increasingly independent of the conductor in their abilities to make appropriate decisions about the music and its performance. A group of students in a secondary school would require more basic direction about phrasing, articulation, and intonation tendencies than would a professional ensemble. It may be said that the conductor's task is to move the ZPD forward toward independence. Here the metaphor of scaffolding may be useful. It refers to establishing a situation in which musicians can achieve at a higher level when provided external support. For example, a conductor might structure rehearsals and organize appropriate tasks so that an ensemble is better able to interpret and perform the music than if it were unaided. Studio teachers employ scaffolding strategies to help student progress across the zone by assisting students in moving from what they can accomplish dependently to reaching their potential to function independently (Kennell, 1989). With increased sophistication (independence), ensembles approach what may be comparable to self-regulation in individuals; thus less scaffolding is necessary to achieve a performance goal.

Rehearsing music is typically a process of successive approximations or small steps toward performance objectives. A rehearsal consists of any number of units or rehearsal frames in which the conductor identifies a problem in need of rehearsing, extracts it from the music, divides the problem into parts, rehearses the parts (by providing information, giving directions, asking questions, modeling, modifying a part for rehearsal purposes, providing feedback), and finishes with the problem being performed in context before the conductor moves on to other material (Duke, 1999/2000). "Accurate finger technique in the woodwind ostinato leading to letter D" might be considered a performance objective. A rehearsal frame would comprise all conductor and ensemble interactions as they relate to the development of accurate finger technique. A conductor's ability to clearly articulate and order instructional steps such that there is fairly constant improvement in the performance of this passage would likely be a major factor in an ensemble's perception of success—and perception of success by the ensemble is no trivial matter.

By viewing a videotaped rehearsal in these small units rather than as one complex whole, developing conductors are likely to see more clearly and with fewer distractions the elements involved in their decision-making processes. Knowledge of one's own sequencing of rehearsal instruction is possible through the use of formal observation tools designed to illuminate forward, failed, and repeated approximations of objectives (Duke & Madsen, 1991). Without structured videotape review of the rehearsal, it is difficult to obtain a precise evaluation of the conductor's ability to organize primarily in a forward or positive direction.

Basic to effective teaching in general education is a three-step sequence of instruction that involves (1) teacher task presentation, (2) student response, and (3) teacher feedback (Becker, Englemann, & Thomas, 1971). In music education, a parallel instructional model (conductor presentation of a task, ensemble interaction with the task, and conductor feedback) has been applied to and studied across many levels of ensemble sophistication (e.g., Arnold, 1995; Price, 1983; Tipton, 1996). Though many interaction patterns can be found in any rehearsal, the preferred complete sequential pattern is one that begins with the conductor providing a musical task for the performers, followed by the ensemble attempting to perform the task, and ending with descriptive, positive feedback from the conductor. In fact, experienced band conductors tend to use complete patterns more so than do less-experienced conductors (Goolsby, 1997). This three-step model holds promise for providing conductors with a scaffold on which to develop rehearsal structure. Again, videotape combined with relevant observation techniques helps one to see rehearsals in the context of these smaller units of instruction.

Rehearsing should be a process of diagnosis, prescription, presentation, monitoring, and feedback, with brisk-paced and clear directions. It can be characterized by frequent use of nonverbal communication, prioritization of rehearsal materials, task-related and contingent feedback, clear statement of rehearsal objectives, encouragement of ensemble-generated ideas, and, depending on the level of the ensemble, the teaching of musical in addition to performance skills (McCoy, 1985). Model secondary school choral conductors exhibit thorough preparation and maintain an appropriate atmosphere. Nonverbal communication tends to be positive. There is little sarcasm and a businesslike image is projected. Ensemble members talk little and disciplinary action is generally unnecessary (Fiocca, 1989).

Verbal Communication

Content

Verbal communication accounts for approximately 40 to 60% of ensemble rehearsal time (e.g., Single, 1990; Watkins, 1996; Yarbrough, 1988; Yarbrough & Price, 1989). While this is a large proportion of the rehearsal, it may be understandable, given some research evidence that indicates that ensemble members respond more accurately to verbal instruction than to conducting gestures (Skadsem, 1996, 1997).

In instrumental ensembles, conductors tend to focus on rhythm and tempo, although the sophistication of the conductor appears to have an impact on rehearsal emphasis. Experts tend to work more with overall ensemble sound, including more demonstrations, instruction on intonation, and guided listening, than do inexperienced conductors. Experienced conductors also address balance, style, and tone more than do novices (Goolsby, 1997, 1999).

Regardless of the content, less-experienced conductors tend to spend more time talking in rehearsals. They stop and restart ensembles more frequently without providing instruction and are less efficient, thus taking longer to prepare a piece for performance (Goolsby, 1999). Therefore, when conductors stop ensembles, they should make concise and substantive suggestions.

Experienced teachers not only talk less, but they provide more breaks between musical selections, spend more than half the rehearsal time performing, use more nonverbal modeling, and use less time getting started. They appear to be more proactive in that they use similar amounts of rehearsal time across pieces rehearsed, while less experienced conductors tend to spend more time on the first piece rehearsed, indicating that they are in a reactive mode. Evidently, inexperienced conductors get distracted from their rehearsal plans when responding to ensemble performance (Goolsby, 1996).

There is an evolution of focus over time as performance approaches, from fundamental issues of accuracy and precision to more general concerns of nuance and interpretation. As the quality of performance increases or as a concert approaches, conductors tend to talk less and focus more on ensemble performing in rehearsals (Davis, 1998).

Aural Modeling

Aural modeling alone and in combination with language is among the most frequent verbal modes in rehearsals. It generally consists of a conductor providing a demonstration—vocal, acoustical or MIDI instrument, recording—followed by ensemble kinesthetic, vocal, or instrumental response. Models can be effective in demonstrating both appropriate and inappropriate performances and can be used to minimize verbalizations. Conductors pervasively use sung or quasi-sung sounds or other means of demonstration (e.g., clapping, tapping), both imitating salient features of what was previously performed and presenting examples of what they would like to hear (Weeks, 1996).

Ensemble directors' abilities to model have a strong relationship to the quality of instrumental music student performance, and strong modelers tend to spend more rehearsal time modeling than do less skillful modelers (Sang, 1987). Modeling is critical to a rehearsal, and experienced ensemble directors use more nonverbal instruction (e.g., modeling and demonstration) and talk less than do novices (Goolsby, 1996).

Conceptual Teaching

While considerable proportions of rehearsals are spent in verbal activity and modeling, principally on the part of the conductor, little of it elicits higher order or conceptual thinking on the part of the performers. General music and ensemble classes generally involve students in lower cognitive processes, emphasizing mechanics of performance almost to the exclusion of the application and accumulation of musical knowledge and the abilities to think about music (Goodlad, 1983). Conductors' efforts appear to be weighted toward providing guidance on how to make corrections or presenting exact solutions, by saying things such as "you need more air" or "the percussion need to play softer." This limits opportunities for self-correction on the part of the ensemble through slight hints or scaffolding (Weeks, 1996). In these situations, ensemble members function much like simple machinery, rendering only specific responses to specific instructions about a specific point in a specific piece of music.

Conversely, conceptual rehearsing reinforces or introduces concepts in ways that encourage the transfer of concepts from one passage to another passage or work. Statements can be as simple as "whenever you see a terraced dynamic, take care not to anticipate it with a slight crescendo or decrescendo" or as sophisticated as "this section is the recapitulation; what does that mean?" In secondary school choral settings, approximately 1% of rehearsal time is spent attempting to evoke higher order thinking, such as analysis, synthesis, or evaluation (e.g., Watkins, 1996). This same automatonlike approach to rehearsing has also been found in secondary school instrumental rehearsals, where less than 3% of rehearsal time is spent in attempts to improve the grasp of musical concepts (Blocher, Greenwood, & Shellahamer, 1997). The literature, the bulk of which comes from the United States, is quite clear with regard to learning: unless one teaches for the transfer of ideas, there is no transfer.

Even though it appears that there is little encouragement of higher order thinking and the development of concepts in rehearsals, it would seem that planning and employing strategies to promote these throughout the rehearsal would be most effective in the long-term growth of performers and ensembles. Without these attributes, a conductor is condemned to reteach an idea every time a similar passage or concept is encountered, as opposed to musicians making connections cognitively and transferring knowledge and skills to new situations. More sophisticated performers have likely attained higher order music skills through inductive reasoning as a result of synthesis of many experiences; thus conductors of highly skilled ensembles are better able to attend to the performance nuances that help make music rapturous.

Nonverbal Issues

Facial Expression

The research in interpersonal communication indicates that the face is the primary nonverbal means of conveying six emotions—happiness, sadness, anger, fear, surprise, and disgust (Bull, 1983; Ekman & Friesen, 1975; Izard, 1997). Though it is tempting to assume that a conductor must somehow look like the music facially in order to achieve maximum effect, there is not a research base in music to support this notion. Research that isolates the conductor's face has only focused on approving, disapproving, and neutral expressions (e.g., Byo & Austin, 1994; Madsen & Yarbrough, 1985; Price & Winter, 1991). The face has been viewed as a means for conductors to respond approvingly (e.g., smile or nod) to appropriate ensemble performance or disapprovingly (e.g., furrowed brow) to inappropriate performance.

Seldom has the face been examined as a means to convey musical information (Berz, 1983; Mayne, 1993). In fact, one conductor-training technique involves mask work (covering the face) to prompt the conductor to focus on the expressive potential of the trunk and shoulders (Tait, 1985). This focus away from the face and toward the communicative power of the torso and breath in conductor training is a concept borrowed from theater and mime (Oertle, 1999). It appears that novice conductors should first develop a varied repertoire of nonverbal skills in gesture and body (see Conductor demeanor earlier). The area of greatest concern facially is eye contact.

Eye contact

The communicative advantages of eye contact are well documented in several research literatures (Burgoon et al. 1984; Fredrickson, 1992). Greater conductor eye contact with an ensemble is associated with increased attentiveness by ensemble members (Yarbrough & Price, 1981). There is evidence, however, that directors of school ensembles look at the score more than the ensemble (Fredrickson, 1992; Sherrill, 1986).

Given the potential for conductor eye contact to interact with other nonverbal behaviors to result in an intensified message (e.g., Burgoon et al., 1984; Price & Winter, 1991), it is clear that conductors should look at the ensemble more often than not. One of the variables that separates accomplished and novice conductors is the tendency of accomplished conductors to combine expressive nonverbal behaviors (eyes, arm/hands, body movement) for optimal effect (Byo & Austin, 1994). By analyzing their own conducting via videotape and in combination with research-based observation techniques, conductors can formulate a clear picture of their eye contact tendencies and, if change is desired, create a plan of action (Byo & Austin, 1994; Madsen & Yarbrough, 1985).

While there is little research that examines ensemble member eye contact with the conductor, it is likely that the extent to which ensemble members are aware of their rehearsal and performance surroundings bears heavily on whether they are in a position to receive the full impact of nonverbal messages. Byo and Lethco (2001) examined musical events and conductor-related conditions during which student musicians tend to look at the conductor. High school band musicians looked up with much greater frequency during slow music than fast music where the demands of the music superseded effects of eye contact and expressive gesture. School-based conductors might promote watching the conductor by teaching ensemble members to look up for specific reasons at predetermined places in the music, for example, at entrances, releases, rehearsal numbers or letters, changes in meter, tempo, and dynamics, and the beginning and end of the piece or movement.

Conductors should be aware of two research findings that bear on issues of eye contact by ensemble members: (1) eye contact by ensemble members increases with musical sophistication, a result that is consistent with research findings in the recognition of specific conducting gestures (Mayne, 1993; Sousa, 1988), and (2) singers performed a dynamic change most successfully following concise verbal instructions from the conductor, despite having predicted that they would respond best by watching the conductor (Skadsem, 1997).

Gesture

Conductors must possess a large repertoire of nonverbal behaviors from which to choose in order to impart expressivity within the context of the structure and style of any composition. They must interpret and shape the elements that contribute to musical expression. Expressiveness/musicianship or musical effect is one of the primary factors in assessing performances (Bergee, 1995; Burnsed & King, 1987). The often-quoted statement by Seashore "beauty in music largely lies in the artistic deviation from the exact or rigid" (1938/1967, p. 249) would relate to both a conductor's interpretation and ability to demonstrate these "deviations." Otherwise, a metronome at varying tempi would serve as well as a person to lead an ensemble.

Employment of movement techniques by Rudolf von Laban, among the most influential figures in dance and movement education in the twentieth century, can result in superior performance than that achieved by typical verbal ensemble instruction (Holt, 1992). Laban characterized effort as having eight basic motions—thrusting, slashing, floating, gliding, wringing, pressing, flicking, and dabbing (Preston-Dunlop, 1980). Each of these and their permutations have analogues in conducting gestures and music performance. A conductor who has a physical command and understanding of these could draw upon them as needed; for instance, the appropriate employment of flicking, pressing, and thrusting may yield the exact representation desired of a specific *marcato* style within a passage. Given a lack of body movement coverage in conducting textbooks and traditional conducting courses, the application of principles of Laban to the pedagogy of conducting has been advocated. Laban Movement Analysis (Laban, 1975) is a framework within which conducting movement has been viewed and analyzed (Benge, 1996) and through which expressive gestures may be enhanced (Miller, 1988). A better understanding of movements and their possible interpretive meanings might well strengthen the communication between conductors and ensembles.

Whether individuals interpret other nonverbal behaviors consistently has been the focus of research on conducting emblems. Sousa (1988), adopting language from Ekman and Friesen (1969), applied the term *emblems* to conducting gestures whose meanings were interpreted reliably by musicians (e.g., changed conducting pattern size to indicate *piano, subito forte,* or *crescendo*; lowering of the left hand for *decrescendo*; or reboundless pattern for *staccato*). Among secondary school and college musicians, the ability to identify emblems on a paper-and-pencil test increases with years of instrumental music experience. With inexperienced musicians, even brief instruction in the recognition of emblems that reflect expressive musical characteristics such as *crescendo, staccato, legato,* and *tenuto* results in increased ability to derive meaning from gestures and perform accurately in response to them (Cofer, 1998; Kelly, 1997).

In studies that have examined the effects of conducting gestures on performance quality of high school musicians, investigators have found expressive gestures to elicit better performance quality than unexpressive ones (Grechesky, 1985; Laib, 1993; Sidoti, 1990). In research that involved young band students, however, expressive gestures did not result in better performance quality (Price & Winter, 1991). These results taken together are consistent with the positive relationship between performance experience and emblem recognition. It may be expeditious to specifically teach emblems of conducting to less-experienced musicians so they can better interpret them.

While conducting, a form of nonverbal communication, is a complex task, it can be learned outside the traditional apprenticeship and course modes. Basic conducting skills have been enhanced in research that focused on systematic self-observation of behavior—precise definitions of conducting skills, opportunities to practice, reinforcement through videotape feedback, and self-analysis (e.g., Madsen & Yarbrough, 1985; Price, 1985).

Conclusion

Everything conductors and ensemble members do in rehearsals should be of consequence, from the moment when everyone is assembled before the first passage is rehearsed to the concert performance. Conductors therefore need to establish their authority and expertise immediately and willfully decide on the rehearsal atmosphere to be created.

A conductor must engage the ensemble in such a way that an intense rehearsal atmosphere is established and then maintained. This will not happen if conductors fail to control the nature of their interactions with ensembles, lack overt enthusiasm for the task at hand, provide inaccurate information either verbally or nonverbally, or allow the pace of the rehearsal to be slow. It is the conductor's responsibility to bridge the gap between what the ensemble can do independently and what it could do with carefully crafted rehearsals under the guidance of an expert who uses well-ordered instruction. The rehearsal must be proactive, structuring scaffolding that will allow for successive approximations in which every effort will likely result in progress.

Rehearsal models must be accurate and need to address all learning styles and modalities by providing visual, aural, and kinesthetic experiences. Providing information in a multimodal (sensory) fashion is most effective, for example, conducting (visual) while providing a singing (auditory) model or having ensemble members move (kinesthetic) while singing their parts.

The conductor must have an arsenal of verbal and nonverbal skills. Instruction is most effective when it is substantive and delivered concisely, clearly, and without sarcasm. It should help move ensemble members beyond their current knowledge and conceptions to higher order musical thinking. Conductors need to maintain and elicit eye contact and have command of a large repertoire of facial expressions, conducting emblems and movements, and other means of communicating musical expression and precision.

In short, capable conductors must be remarkably prepared and have complete knowledge of the score and how to realize it. They need to know what they should be hearing, how it differs from the current rehearsal performance, and how to get to the level needed for concert performance. All aspects of the rehearsal should be planned. Components such as teaching conceptually and giving feedback are not done in isolation; the rehearsal should be imbued with these and other activities continuously.

Not only do aspects of conducting and rehearsing develop through experience and practice, but rehearsals also need to be audio- and videotaped and reviewed by conductors. There is a consistent theme in the literature that regards the benefits of systematic self-observation and feedback in enhancing podium skills. This helps us to see ourselves objectively or as others do.

It is an extremist perspective to suggest that either conducting or verbalization is unnecessary in an ensemble setting. There are those who hold the view that if a conductor could manage to present gestures that are perfect models, lacking in any ambiguity, there would be no need for talk. Conversely, there are those who suggest that most of the productive work in a rehearsal is done when the conductor verbally and directly tells performers what is wanted. It is true that nonverbal and verbal forms of communication must be done exceptionally well; however, both are necessary.

Visual communication (nonverbal, inaudible, symbolic, or demonstrative behavior) alone is significantly less effective in improving ensemble performance than visual communication in combination with verbalization (oral use of meaningful words to convey information) and modeling (demonstration of behaviors). The combination of verbal and modeling communication is also more effective than visual communication alone. However, the combination of verbal, modeling, and visual communication is the most effective approach (Francisco, 1994). All must be done effectively, skillfully, and efficiently to have optimal rehearsals for excellent performances.

References

Arnold, J. A. (1995). Effect of competency-based methods of instruction and self-observation on ensemble director's use of sequential patterns. *Journal of Research in Music Education, 43*(2), 127–138.

Becker, W. C., Englemann, S., & Thomas, D. R. (1971). *Teaching: A course in applied psychology.* Chicago: Science Research Associates.

Benge, T. J. (1996). Movements utilized by conductors in the stimulation of expression and musicianship. (Doctoral dissertation, University of Southern California). *Dissertation Abstracts International, 58*(01), 18A (University Microfilms No. 9720183)

Bergee, M. J. (1995). Primary and higher-order factors in a scale assessing concert band performance. *Bulletin of the Council for Research in Music Education, 126,* 1–14.

Berz, W. L. (1983). The development of an observation instrument designed to classify specific nonverbal communication techniques employed by conductors of musical ensembles (Doctoral dissertation, Michigan State University). *Dissertation Abstracts International, 44*(09), 2702A (University Microfilms No. 8400532)

Blocher, L., Greenwood, R., & Shellahamer, B. (1997). Teaching behaviors of middle school and high school band directors in the rehearsal setting. *Journal of Research in Music Education, 45*(3), 457–469.

Brand, M., & Burnsed, V. (1981). Music abilities and experiences as predictors of error-detection skill. *Journal of Research in Music Education, 29*(2), 91–96.

Brophy, J. E., & Good, T. L. (1986). Teaching behavior and student achievement. In M. Wittrock (Ed.), *Handbook of research on teaching* (3rd ed.) (pp. 328–375). New York: Macmillan.

Bull, P. (1983). *Body movement and interpersonal communication.* New York: Wiley.

Burgoon, J. K., Buller, D. B., Hale, J. L., & deTurck, M. A. (1984). Relational messages associated with nonverbal behaviors. *Human Communication Research, 10*(3), 351–378.

Burnsed, V., & King, S. (1987). How reliable is your festival rating?. *Update: Applications of Research in Music Education, 5,* 12–13.

Byo, J. L. (1990). Recognition of intensity contrasts in the gestures of beginning conductors. *Journal of Research in Music Education, 38*(3), 157–163.

Byo, J. L. (1997). The effects of texture and number of parts on the ability of music majors to detect performance errors. *Journal of Research in Music Education, 45*(1), 51–66.

Byo, J. L., & Austin, K. R. (1994). Comparison of expert and novice conductors: An approach to the analysis of nonverbal behaviors. *Journal of Band Research, 30*(1), 11–34.

Byo, J. L., & Lethco, L. (2001). Student musicians' eye contact with the conductor: An exploratory investigation. *Contributions to Music Education, 28*(2), 21–35.

Byo, J. L., & Sheldon, D. A. (2000). The effect of singing while listening on undergraduate music majors' ability to detect pitch and rhythm errors. *Journal of Band Research, 36*(1), 26–46.

Cassidy, J. W. (1990). Effect of intensity training on preservice teachers' instruction, accuracy, and delivery effectiveness. *Journal of Research in Music Education, 38*(3), 164–174.

Cavitt, M. E. (1998). A descriptive analysis of error correction in expert teachers' instrumental music rehearsals. (Doctoral dissertation, University of Texas–Austin). *Dissertation Abstracts International,* 59(06), 1958A (University Microfilms No. 9837917)

Chesterman, R. (Ed.) (1976). *Conversations with conductors.* London: Robson.

Cofer, R. S. (1998). Effects of conducting-gesture instruction on seventh-grade band students' performance response to conducting emblems. *Journal of Research in Music Education, 46*(5), 360–373.

Davis, A. P. (1998). Performance achievement and analysis of teaching during choral rehearsals. *Journal of Research in Music Education, 46*(4), 496–509.

Duke, R. A. (1999/2000). Measure of instructional effectiveness in music. *Bulletin of the Council for Research in Music Education, 143,* 1–48.

Duke, R. A., & Henninger, J. C. (1998). Effects of verbal corrections on student attitude and performance. *Journal of Research in Music Education, 46*(4), 482–495.

Duke, R. A., & Madsen, C. K. (1991). Proactive versus reactive teaching: Focusing observation on specific aspects of instruction. *Bulletin of the Council for Research in Music Education, 108,* 1–14.

Duke, R. A., Prickett, C. A., & Jellison, J. A. (1998). Empirical description of the pace of music instruction. *Journal of Research in Music Education, 46*(2), 265–280.

Ekman, P., & Friesen, W. V. (1969). The repertoire of nonverbal behavior: Categories, origins, usage, and coding. *Semiotica, 1*(3), 49–98.

Ekman, P., & Friesen, W. V. (1975). *Unmasking the face.* Englewood Cliffs, NJ: Prentice-Hall.

Faulkner, R. A. (1973). Orchestra interactions: Some features of communication and authority in an artistic organization. *Sociological Quarterly, 14,* 147–157.

Fiocca, P. D. H. (1989). A descriptive analysis of the rehearsal behaviors of exemplary junior high and middle school choir directors. *Contributions to Music Education, 16,* 19–33.

Francisco, J. M. (1994). Conductor communication in the ensemble rehearsal: The relative effects of verbal communication, visual communication, and modeling on performance improvement of high school bands. *Dissertation*

Abstracts International, 56(08), 3045A (University Microfilm No. AAC 95-42638).

Fredrickson, W. E. (1992). Research on eye contact with implications for the conductor: A review of literature. *Update: Applications of Research in Music Education*, 11(1), 25–31.

Fredrickson, W. E., Johnson, C. M., & Robinson, C. R. (1998). The effect of pre-conducting and conducting behaviors on the evaluation of conductor competence. *Journal of Band Research*, 33(2), 1–13.

Goodlad, J. I. (1983). *A place called school.* New York: McGraw-Hill.

Goolsby, T. W. (1996). Time use in instrumental rehearsals: A comparison of experienced, novice, and student teachers. *Journal of Research in Music Education*, 44(4), 286–303.

Goolsby, T. W. (1997). Verbal instruction in instrumental rehearsals: A comparison of three career levels and preservice teachers. *Journal of Research in Music Education*, 45(1), 21–40.

Goolsby, T. W. (1999). A comparison of expert and novice music teachers' preparing identical band compositions: An operational replication. *Journal of Research in Music Education*, 47(2), 174–187.

Grechesky, R. N. (1985). An analysis of nonverbal and verbal conducting behaviors and their relationship to expressive musical performance (Doctoral dissertation, University of Wisconsin-Madison, 1985). *Dissertation Abstracts International*, 46(10), 2956A (University Microfilms No. 8513459)

Hamann, D. L., Mills, C., Bell, J., Daugherty, E, & Koozer, R. (1990). Classroom environment as related to contest ratings among high school performing ensembles. *Journal of Research in Music Education*, 38(3), 215–224.

Holt, M. E. (1992). The application of conducting and choral rehearsal pedagogy of Laban effort/shape and its comparative effect upon style in choral performance. *Dissertation Abstracts International*, 53 (02), 437A. (University Microfilm No. AAC92–14439).

Izard, C. E. (1997). Emotions and facial expressions: A perspective from differential emotions theory. In J. A. Russel and J. M. Fernandez-Dols (Eds.), *The psychology of facial expression.* (pp. 57–77). Cambridge: Cambridge University Press.

Kaiser, K. A. (1998). The effect of differentiated high- versus low-intensity teaching on band musicians' evaluation of teaching effectiveness. *Dissertation Abstracts International*, 59(03), 764A. (University Microfilms No. 9827669)

Kelly, S. N. (1997). Effects of conducting instruction on the musical performance of beginning band students. *Journal of Research in Music Education*, 45(2), 295–305.

Kennell, R. P. (1989). *Three teacher scaffolding strategies in college instrumental applied instruction.* Unpublished doctoral dissertation, University of Wisconsin.

Laban, R. (1975). *Laban's principles of dance and movement notation.* Boston: Plays.

Laib, J. R. (1993). The effect of expressive conducting on band performance (Doctoral dissertation, University of Georgia, 1993). *Dissertation Abstracts International*, 54(02), 3258A. (University Microfilms No. 9404667)

Madsen, C. K. (1990). Teacher intensity in relationship to music education. *Bulletin of the Council for Research in Music Education*, 104, 38–46.

Madsen, C. K. and Yarbrough, C. (1985). *Competency-based music education.* Raleigh, NC: Contemporary Publishing.

Mayne, R. G. (1993). An investigation of the use of facial expression in conjunction with musical conducting gestures and their interpretations by instrumental performers (Doctoral dissertation, Ohio State University, 1992). *Dissertation Abstracts International*, 53(08), 2729A (University Microfilms No. 9238229)

McCoy, C. W. (1985). The ensemble director as effective teacher. *Update: Applications of Research in Music Education*, 3(3), 9–12.

Miller, S. (1988). The effect of Laban Movement Theory on the ability of student conductors to communicate musical interpretation through gesture (Doctoral dissertation, University of Wisconsin-Madison, 1988). *Dissertation Abstracts International*, 49(05), 1087A. (University Microfilms No. 8809040)

Oertle, E. (1999). Bud Beyer: Bodyspeak. *Journal of the World Association for Symphonic Band and Ensembles*, 6, 19–21.

Parasuraman, S., and Nachman, S. A. (1987). Correlates of organizational and professional commitment: The case of musicians in a symphony orchestra. *Group and Organization Studies*, 12(3), 287–303.

Preston-Dunlop, V. (1980). *A handbook for modern educational dance* (new rev. ed.). Boston: Plays.

Price, H. E. (1983). The effect of conductor academic task presentation, conductor reinforcement, and ensemble practice on performers' musical achievement, attentiveness, and attitude. *Journal of Research in Music Education*, 31(4), 245–257.

Price, H. E. (1985). A competency-based course in basic conducting techniques: A replication. *Journal of Band Research*, 21(1), 61–69.

Price, H. E. (1992). Sequential patterns of music instruction and learning to use them. *Journal of Research in Music Education*, 40(1), 14–29.

Price, H. E., & Winter, S. (1991). Effect of strict and expressive conducting on performances and opinions of eighth-grade band students. *Journal of Band Research*, 27(1), 30–43.

Reimer, B. (2000). Why do humans value music? In C. K. Madsen (Ed.), *Vision 2020: The Housewright symposium on the future of music education* (pp. 25–48). Reston, VA: MENC: The National Association for Music Education.

Sang, R. C. (1987). A study of the relationship between instrumental music teachers' modeling skills and pupil performance behaviors. *Bulletin of the Council for Research in Music Education*, 91, 155–159.

Seashore, C. E. (1938/1967). *The psychology of music*. New York: Dover.

Sherrill, M. H. (1986). An analytical study of videotaped rehearsal and conducting techniques of selected junior high and senior high school band conductors (Doctoral dissertation, University of Rochester, Eastman School of Music, 1986). *Dissertation Abstracts International*, 47(04), 1231A. (University Microfilms No. 8614150)

Sidoti, V. J. (1990). The effects of expressive and nonexpressive conducting on the performance accuracy of selected expressive markings by individual high school instrumentalists (Doctoral dissertation, Ohio State University). *Dissertation Abstracts International*, 51(10), 3270A. (University Microfilms No. 9105212)

Single, N. A. (1990). An exploratory study of pacing in instrumental music rehearsals. *Contributions to Music Education*, 17, 32–43.

Skadsem, J. A. (1996). The effect of verbal, written, gestural, and choral stimuli on singers' performance responses to dynamic changes in music. *Missouri Journal of Research in Music Education*, 33, 28–44.

Skadsem, J. A. (1997). Effect of conductor verbalization, dynamic markings, conductor gesture, and choir dynamic level on singers' dynamic responses. *Journal of Research in Music Education, 45*(4) 509–520.

Sousa, G. (1988). Musical conducting emblems: An investigation of the use of specific conducting gestures and their interpretation by instrumental performers (Doctoral dissertation, Ohio State University, 1988). *Dissertation Abstracts International, 49*(08), 2143A. (University Microfilms No. 8820356)

Standley, J. M., & Madsen, C. K. (1987, Summer). Intensity as an attribute of effective teaching. *Quodlibet,* 15–20.

Tait, M. (1985). Striving to become a creative artist. *CBDNA Journal, 2*(1), 25–28.

Tipton, D. G. (1996). *The use of sequential patterns in select children's, youth, and adult Southern Baptist choir rehearsals.* (Doctoral dissertation, University of Alabama).

Vygotsky, L. S. (1978). *Mind in society: The development of higher psychological processes* (Michael Cole, Vera John-Steiner, Sylvia Scribner, and Ellen Souberman (Eds.). Cambridge, MA: Harvard University Press.

Watkins, R. E. (1996). Nonperformance time use in high school choral rehearsals: A follow-up study. *Update: Applications of Research in Music Education, 14*(1), 4–8.

Weeks, P. (1996). A rehearsal of a Beethoven passage: An analysis of correction talk. *Research on Language and Social Interaction, 29*(3), 247–290.

Yarbrough, C. (1975). Effect of magnitude of conductor on students in selected choruses. *Journal of Research in Music Education, 23*(2), 134–146.

Yarbrough, C. (1988). Content and pacing in music teaching. *Proceedings of Symposium on Current Issues in Music Education, 13,* 9–28.

Yarbrough, C., Dunn, D. E., & Baird, S. L. (1996). A longitudinal study of teaching in a choral rehearsal. *Southeastern Journal of Music Education, 8,* 7–31.

Yarbrough, C., and Price, H. E. (1981). Prediction of performer attentiveness based upon rehearsal activity and teacher behavior. *Journal of Research in Music Education, 29*(3), 209–217.

Yarbrough, C., and Price, H. E. (1989). Sequential patterns of instruction in music. *Journal of Research in Music Education, 37*(3), 179–187.

Contributors

RITA AIELLO is a visiting scholar in the psychology department of New York University. She is the editor of *Musical Perceptions* (Oxford University Press, 1994). Her research addresses the mental representation of music, the effect of musical training on the perception and cognition of music, and parallels between music and language. She has taught courses on the perception of music at the Juilliard School, the Manhattan School of Music, New York University, and Queens College of the City University of New York and has been a visiting honorary adjunct professor at Teachers College, Columbia University. She was trained as a classical pianist and has extensive teaching experience.

ECKART ALTENMÜLLER is professor at the Hannover University of Music and Drama and director of its Institute of Music Physiology and Performing Arts Medicine. He graduated in medicine (1983) and music (1985) and trained as a neurologist and neurophysiologist (Habilitation 1992). Since 1985 he has been researching brain processing of music and motor learning in musicians. He has published 46 scientific articles in peer-reviewed journals and 60 book contributions. Major awards include the Young Scientists Award of the German Physiological Society (1984), the Kornmüller-Award of the German Society for Clinical Electrophysiology (1992), and the Richard Lederman Lecture, Aspen (1999).

NANCY H. BARRY holds a Ph.D. in music education and certificates in computers in music and electronic music from Florida State University. She is currently professor and coordinator of graduate music education at the School of Music of the University of Oklahoma. She serves on the editoral boards of *Update: Applications of Research in Musical Education, Professional Educator*, and *Journal of Technology in Music Learning*. She has published numerous articles in journals such as *Psychology of Music, Update, Arts and Learning*, and *Journal of Music Teacher Education*. She has given over 40 presentations at conferences and seminars in the United States, Puerto Rico, Brazil, Germany, and Australia.

She is also an experienced studio teacher and frequent adjudicator of woodwinds and piano.

GIOVANNI UMBERTO BATTEL is director of the Conservatory of Music "B. Marcello" in Venice. He holds a degree and a postgraduate diploma from the Tartini Conservatory in Trieste and the Accademia di Santa Cecilia in Rome and a degree in musicology from Bologna University. His published articles address new methodologies of performance analysis. As a pianist, he has won six Italian national competitions and prizes at seven international competitions, including first prizes in Stresa and Enna and other prizes at the Viotti and Busoni competitions. He has given concerts throughout Europe and the United States, playing with chamber and symphony orchestras conducted by De Bernant, Gavazzeni, and Steinberg. Battel has also recorded for Italian radio and television (RAI).

ALICE G. BRANDFONBRENER received her undergraduate education at Wellesley College and her doctor of medicine from Columbia University. She is assistant professor of medicine at the Northwestern University Medical School and adjunct professor of performance studies at the Northwestern University School of Music. She directs the Medical Program for Performing Artists in Chicago and is editor of the journal *Medical Problems of Performing Artists*. She founded the Aspen symposium on medical problems of musicians and dancers in 1983 and was first president of the Performing Arts Medicine Association. A frequent lecturer to medical and musical audiences, she has written many articles for music education as well as medical journals on musicians' medical problems.

JAMES L BYO is professor of music education at Louisiana State University and editor of *Update: Applications of Research in Music Education* (published by MENC: National Association for Music Education). In 1997, he completed a six-year term as chair of the International Wind Band Education Committee of the World Association for Symphonic Bands and Ensembles. In this capacity, he presented research and presided over sessions in England, Spain, Japan, and Austria. His articles on issues relevant to music teacher/conductor effectiveness appear in all major U.S. research journals in music education. He is the recipient of two distinguished professor awards at LSU.

JORGE SALGADO CORREIA is lecturer at the University of Aveiro and a professional flute soloist. He graduated in philosophy from the University of Porto and studied flute performance at Porto Conservatoire and at the University of Amsterdam. His areas of research include the investigation of teaching and learning of performance skills from historical, analytical, psychological, sociological, and philosophical perspectives and reflexivity in musical performance: defining and developing practical music making as research. His specialist performance area is contemporary music, and he has given many world premieres and has had works specially commissioned for him. His publications include a recent article in *Psychology of Music* and a number of articles written in collaboration with Jane Davidson.

JANE W. DAVIDSON studied music, dance, and education at Newcastle-upon-Tyne and London before undertaking advanced vocal studies in Canada. She completed her M.A. in performance studies at City University (London) and after a period of time teaching in schools gained her Ph.D. in the psychology of music. She worked in the psychology department at Keele University and the music department at City University before taking up her current post as senior lecturer in music at the University of Sheffield. She is a former editor of the international journal *Psychology of Music*. Besides her teaching and research work, she performs as a vocal soloist and has appeared at the Queen Elizabeth Hall, St. Paul's Cathedral, and the London International Opera Festival.

HEINZ FADLE is professor of trombone at the Hochschule für Musik, Detmold, Germany. His publications include *Looking for the Natural Way* (Piccolo-Verlag, 1996) and *Musizieren* (Die Blaue Eule, 1999). He served as president of the International Trombone Association from 1996 until 1998. Invitations to teach and lecture have led him to the United States, Russia, Kazakhstan, Britain, and Hungary. He hosted the 21st International Trombone Workshop in Detmold (1992) and also served as a jury member at international competitions. For 22 years he was first chair of the Philharmonic State Orchestra Hamburg, also performing as a member of the Bayreuth Festival Orchestra, the Berliner Philharmoniker, Radio Sinfonie Hamburg, Münchner Staatsoper, and Deutsches Sinfonieorchester Berlin.

ANDERS FRIBERG is a research assistant in music acoustics at the Royal Institute of Technology (KTH), Stockholm. He holds a master's degree in applied physics from KTH. His doctoral thesis, *A Quantitative Rule System for Musical Performance* (1995), developed the computer-based music performance simulator *Director Musices*. His published research on the technology of music performance addresses phrasing, punctuation, intonation, synchronization, swing, and links with human motion and emotion and has appeared in *Computer Music Journal*, *Journal of the Acoustical Society of America*, and *Journal of New Music Research*. He plays piano in salsa and jazz groups and holds a piano performance diploma from Berklee College of Music, Boston.

LEONARDO FUKS is associate professor of music acoustics and voice physiology at Universidade do Brasil/UFRJ in Rio de Janeiro. His musical studies were undertaken at the Villa-Lobos Music School and Uni-Rio University. He has been a professional oboist in several Brazilian orchestras and chamber music groups and holds a degree in mechanical engineering, a master of science degree in design engineering, and a doctor of philosophy in music acoustics from the Royal Institute of Technology (KTH), Stockholm. His main research topics include wind instrument performance and vocal techniques in ethnic and contemporary music. He has created a number of low-cost wind instruments for music education and is the founder and director of a bicycle orchestra, the Cyclophonica.

JANINA FYK holds a master of arts in music education from the Paderewski Academy of Music in Poznan (Poland), a doctoral degree in music theory from the

Chopin Academy of Music in Warsaw, and a habilitation in musicology from the Institute of Arts of the Polish Academy of Sciences in Warsaw. She is now professor of musical arts at the Academy of Music in Krakow. Her areas of research interests include psychoacoustics, music psychology, and music education. She is involved in research that concerns the perception of pitch, vocal, and instrumental intonation as well as absolute pitch. She is author and coauthor of numerous articles and the monographic book *Melodic Intonation, Psychoacoustics, and the Violin.*

ALF GABRIELSSON graduated from Uppsala University and the Royal University College of Music in Stockholm. His Ph.D. thesis was titled *Studies in Rhythm*, and he has subsequently published numerous research articles on music performance and music experience. He teaches general psychology and music psychology and is the head of a research group on expressive performance in music, dance, speech, and body language. He is a member of the Swedish Royal Academy of Music and the Acoustical Society of America and a vice president of the International Association for Empirical Studies of the Arts (IAEA) and was president of the European Society for the Cognitive Sciences of Music (ESCOM) from 1997 to 2000.

MARTIN GELLRICH studied piano, violoncello, secondary teaching, psychology, and musicology and holds a Ph.D. from the Hochschule der Künste und the Technische Universität Berlin in music education and psychology. His research addresses instrumental teaching, developmental psychology of music, instrumental practice, group teaching methods, relative sol-fa, improvisation, history of music education, piano technique, and musical interpretation. His publications include *Üben mit Lis(z)t* (Frauenfeld, 1992), *Impulse zu einer Veränderung der Instrumentalpädagogik* (Regensburg, 2002), and articles in the *British Journal of Music Education*, *Üben and Musizieren*, and *Bulletin of the Council for Research in Music Education*. As a freelance piano teacher he has given over 200 presentations on instrumental teaching, particularly on improvisation.

HEINER GEMBRIS studied music education at the Music Academy of Detmold and musicology at the Technical University of Berlin. From 1991 to 2001 he was professor of musicology at the universities of Münster and Halle. Since 2001 he has been professor of music and music education at the University of Paderborn and director of the Institut für Begabungsforschung und Begabtenförderung in der Musik. He is author of *Grundlagen musikalischer Begabung und Entwicklung* (Wissner, 1998) and coeditor of the series *Musikpädagogische Forschungsberichte* (Wissner, 1992ff). He has published numerous research articles on musical development and music listening. Currently he is the president of the Deutsche Gesellschaft für Musikpsychologie.

WILFRIED GRUHN is professor and head of the music education department at the Freiburg Academy of Music. He has published several books and many articles on the history of music education, on music perception and cognition, on teaching methods, and on neurobiological learning theory. He was coeditor of *Musik und Unterricht* (1980–1998) and founded the first Internet *European Music Journal* (in 1999). He has participated as clinician and presenter at various international conferences and functions as national representative of ISME in Germany. A past president of the International Research Alliance of Institutes for Music Education (RAIME), he is currently a member of the editorial board of *Research Studies in Music Education* and of *Music Education Research*.

KNUT GUETTLER is professor of double bass at the Norwegian Academy of Music and also teaches at the Royal Conservatory of the Hague, the Netherlands. His main research focus is the computer modeling of the bow–string interaction. Another area is the physical properties of bows, in collaboration with the Royal Institute of Technology, Stockholm, He has published in the *Catgut Acoustical Society Journal* (*CAS Journal*), *Journal of the Acoustical Society of America*, and *Music Perception* and is a contributing editor for the *CAS Journal*. He is a former principal player of the Oslo Philharmonic, with international experience as a lecturer on string performance. He has solo recordings on Camerata (Japan) and Musica Viva (Germany), among others.

SUSAN HALLAM trained as a violinist at the Royal Academy of Music, after which she spent 10 years as a full-time professional musician working for the BBC. After completing a B.A. in psychology externally with London University and an M.Sc. and Ph.D. in the psychology of education at the Institute of Education, London University, she took a post in the department of psychology there. After a year at Oxford Brookes University as professor of teaching and learning, she returned to London Unviersity in 2001. She is chair of the education section of the British Psychological Society, and has acted as coeditor of the *BPS Education Section Review*, and editor of *Psychology of Music*.

PATRIK N. JUSLIN holds a Ph.D. in psychology from the Department of Psychology, Uppsala University, Sweden, and currently holds a position there as researcher. He has published extensively on music and emotion, and his research is concerned with developing and testing a new theoretical framework for studies of communication of emotion via musical performance, as well as methodological developments for the field of music education. He is a member of the International Society for Research on Emotions and received ESCOM'' Young Researcher Award in 1996. He has edited a book on music and emotion for Oxford University Press together with John Sloboda. In addition to Juslin's work as a researcher, he has worked professionally as a guitar player and toured internationally with blues/jazz bands.

DUANE RICHARD KARNA is director of music ministry at the First Congregational Church in Eugene, Oregon. He was director of choral activities and associate professor of music at Salisbury State University (Maryland) from 1988 to 1996 and a member of the music faculty (voice/choral) at Central Washington from 1996 to 1999. He holds a bachelor's degree in vocal performance from the University of Puget Sound in Tacoma, Washington; master's degrees in vocal performance and in choral conducting from Southern Methodist University in Dallas, Texas; and a doctor of musical arts in choral conducting from the University of Arizona in Tucson. He is a member of the American Choral Directors Association, the International Federation of Choral Music, and the National Association of Teachers of Singing.

ANTHONY E. KEMP is emeritus professor at the University of Reading, where he supervises research students. Originally trained as a musician and teacher, he later studied at Sussex University, gaining his D.Phil. in psychology. He is a chartered psychologist and fellow of the British Psychological Society and also senior research fellow at the University of Surrey Roehampton. He is visiting professor at the Sibelius Academy, Helsinki, where he supervises doctoral students. He was chairman of the research commission and member of the board of directors of the International Society for Music Education and has written several books and articles on music psychology, and education. His book *The Musical Temperament: The Psychology and Personality of Musicians* was published by Oxford University Press in 1996.

BARRY J. KENNY studied music at Sydney University and the University of New South Wales and holds undergraduate degrees in English literature (Sydney University) and music (University of New South Wales). He has lectured and tutored in the School of Music and Music Education, University of New South Wales, in musical analysis and jazz history and is in the process of completing his doctoral studies. Barry's published work addresses the cognitive mechanisms involved in jazz improvisation and also discuss sociocultural issues that surround the interpretation and analysis of musical forms. His work has been published in *Research Studies in Music Education* and *Annual Review of Jazz Studies*. As a professional musician, he has been actively involved as a jazz pianist, teacher, and accompanist.

JAMES M. KJELLAND holds a bachelor's degree in music education, a master of music degree from the University of Wisconsin, Madison, and a doctorate in music education from the University of Texas at Austin. He is associate professor of music education and coordinator of string pedagogy at Northwestern University. He has also presented at numerous conferences in string and orchestra pedagogy throughout the United States and is a frequent guest conductor, adjudicator, and clinician for school orchestras. His publications include his coauthored *Strictly Strings: A Comprehensive String Class Method* (Highland/Etling) and numerous articles in journals such as: *American String Teacher, Instrumentalist*, and *Bulletin of the Council for Research in Music Education*.

ANDREAS C. LEHMANN researches and teaches music psychology at the School of Music in Würzburg, Germany. He holds a degree in music education and a Ph.D. in musicology from the Hochschule für Musik und Theater, Hannover, and worked as a researcher in the psychology department at Florida State University, Tallahassee, and in the musicology department of the University of Halle, Germany. His research addresses the structure and acquisition of high-level instrumental music performance skills (sight-reading, memory, improvisation, practice). In 1997, he received the Young Researcher Merit Award from the European Society for the Cognitive Sciences of Music (ESCOM). With Harald Jørgensen, he is coeditor of *Does Practice Make Perfect? Current Theory and Research on Instrumental Music Practice* (Norges Musikkhøgskole).

VICTORIA MCARTHUR is program director of piano pedagogy and coordinator of group piano at Florida State University. She has published in *Psychology of Music* and *Bulletin of the Council for Research in Music Education*. She is a member of the editorial board of *Piano and Keyboard*, former senior editor for FJH Music Company, Miami, and currently keyboard editor for Alfred Publishing Company, Los Angeles. She has lectured extensively and authored and edited instructional books on sight-reading. Her other research areas are practice and motor memory. Her background in piano performance, piano pedagogy, music education research methods, cognitive and motor psychology, and biomechanics has formed her ideas and approach to the teaching of piano sight-reading.

GARY E. MCPHERSON studied music education at the Sydney Conservatorium of Music before completing a master of music education at Indiana University and a doctorate of philosophy at the University of Sydney. He is an associate professor of music education at the University of New South Wales and former treasurer for the International Society for Music Education and national president of the Australian Society for Music Education. His published research addresses visual, aural, and creative aspects of musical performance in young developing musicians. McPherson is currently on the editorial boards of all flagship journals in music education, as well as being editor for *Research Studies in Music Education*. As a trumpeter, he has performed with several of Australia's leading ensembles.

JANET MILLS gained her B.A. in music and mathematics from York University and her D.Phil. at Oxford University. She began her career as a secondary music teacher and then taught in higher education before becoming an H.M. Inspector of Schools in 1990. Currently she is a research fellow at the Royal College of Music in London.

STEVEN J. MORRISON is assistant professor of music education at the University of Washington, where he teaches courses in instructional methods and research. He is an instrumental music specialist whose research includes perceptual and performance aspects of intonation and the relationship of cultural context to music preference. He is currently investigating neural aspects of cross-cultural music comprehension in a joint research project with the University of Washington medical center. His articles have appeared in the *Journal of Research in Music Education, Bulletin for the Council of Research in Music Education, Up-*

date: Applications of Research in Music Education, and *Music Educators Journal*. He is chair of the Perception and Cognition Special Research Interest Group of the Society for Research in Music Education.

SUSAN A. O'NEILL is senior lecturer in psychology and Associate Director of the Unit for the Study of Musical Skill and Development at Keele University. Her research interests include motivation, identity, and gender issues associated with children's and adolescents' development of musical performance skills. She has published widely in the fields of psychology and music education. As a consultant for the Associated Board of the Royal Schools of Music she has presented seminars and workshops for professional development and teacher training courses throughout the United Kingdom. She is currently project leader for the Young People and Music Participation Project, which involves a longitudinal study of young people's motivation, identity, and engagement in music. She has taught flute and has performed extensively as a soloist and chamber musician in Canada and Europe.

RICHARD PARNCUTT holds undergraduate degress in in physics and music from the University of Melbourne and a Ph.D. in physics, psychology, and music from the University of New England, Australia. He is now professor of systematic musicology at the University of Graz, Austria. He is author of *Harmony: A Psychoacoustical Approach* (Springer, 1989) and research articles on the perception of harmony, tonality, rhythm, and piano performance, including psychoacoustic and cognitive theories and models. He is a member of the editorial advisory boards of *Psychology of Music*, *Music Perception*, *Musicae Scientiae*, *Journal of New Music Research*, *Jahrbuch Musikpsychologie*, *Systematische Musikwissenschaft*, *Contemporary Music Review*, and *Research Studies in Music Education*. He is an internationally experienced pianist, piano teacher, and accompanist.

ROLAND S. PERSSON holds a master of arts in music education from Ingesund College of Music (Sweden) and a Ph.D. in psychology from Huddersfield University (England). He is currently associate professor of psychology at Jönköping University and director of its center for psychology. He is editor in chief of *High Ability Studies* (Taylor & Francis) and a former piano performer, organist, and music educator. His research interests fall within the domain of social psychology, particularly talent and giftedness, gender issues, and psychometrics, where he has written numerous scholarly articles on the training of musical performers and their psychological health and education.

HARRY E. PRICE is professor and head of music education at the University of Alabama. In addition to his current research and teaching, he was a classical and jazz performer and secondary school and university band conductor and clinician. He is the former editor of the *Journal of Research in Music Education* and is on the editorial board of *Research Studies in Music Education* and the *International Journal of Music Education*. He edited *Music Education Research: An*

Anthology from the *Journal of Research in Music Education* and has over 50 research articles in publications such as *Journal of Research in Music Education*, *Bulletin of the Council for Research in Music Education*, *Research Studies in Music Education*, and *Boletín de Investigación Educativo-Musica*.

DAVID ROLAND is a consultant clinical psychologist and a classical guitarist. He completed an honors degree at the University of Sydney and a Ph.D. in clinical psychology at the University of Wollongong. His area of research interest is the management of performance anxiety and the application of mental skills to performing. He is the author of *The Confident Performer* (Currency Press, 1997) and has published in *Research Studies in Music Education*. He has presented his research to the International Society of Music Education (ISME Korea, 1992). He has been on the staff of the Canberra School of Music (Australian National University); guest-lectured for many universities and conservatories, and worked with a number of performing arts groups.

JOHAN SUNDBERG is a professor of music acoustics at the Royal Institute of Technology in Stockholm, where he led its music acoustics research group from 1970 to 2001. A prolific author of peer-reviewed journal articles, his main research interests are the singing voice and music performance. As president of the Music Acoustics Committee of the Royal Swedish Academy of Music, he edited 10 volumes of proceedings of public seminars. He is a member of the Royal Swedish Academy of Music and the Swedish Acoustical Society (President 1976–1981) and a fellow of the Acoustical Society of America. He has sung in the Stockholm Bach Choir (nine years as its president) and made his public solo debut with a lieder recital on his fiftieth birthday.

STEN TERNSTRÖM holds a doctoral degree from the Royal Institute of Technology (KTH), Stockholm, and is currently senior researcher and university lecturer there. He is the author of numerous research articles on the acoustics of choir singing and other topics in music acoustics and voice, often collaborating with Johan Sundberg. Ternström is associate editor of *Logopedics Phoniatrics Vocology*, board member of the Swedish Voice Society, and member of the scientific advisory board of the Voice Foundation in Philadelphia. A choir singer and arranger, he has performed extensively with leading a cappella vocal groups in Sweden.

MALCOLM TROUP is the founding (and now emeritus) professor of the music department of City University, London. He holds a D.Phil. in music from the University of York and honorary doctorates from City University, the Memorial University of Newfoundland, and the University of Chile. He is currently the European chair of the European Piano Teachers' Association and edits its *Piano Journal*. He is also chair of the Beethoven Society of Europe, president of the annual Oxford Philomusica Piano Festival, and vice president of the World Piano Competition, London. His research addresses performance practice, history of ideas, and aesthetics. As a solo pianist he has toured five continents, received the 1998 Liszt medal, and recorded for RCA Victor and the Continuum label.

GRAHAM F. WELCH (Ph.D.) is professor of music education at the University of London Institute of Education. He is a trained singer and semiprofessional performer for over 20 years whose research and associated publications include singing development across the life span, particularly in childhood and adolescence and including the trained chorister voice. Recent publications include *Bodymind and Voice: Foundations of Voice Education*, coedited and coauthored with Leon Thurman for the National Centre for Voice and Speech, and chapters on voice management, musical development and learning in the United Kingdom, and the teaching profession. He is currently chair of the Society for Research in the Psychology of Music and Music Education and cochair of the ISME Research Commission.

AARON WILLIAMON is a research fellow in psychology of music at the Royal College of Music. He completed his Ph.D. in cognitive psychology at the University of London (Royal Holloway), where his research centered on how skilled musicians learn, rehearse, and recall information when practicing and performing. In 1998, he was awarded the Hickman Prize by the Society for Research in Psychology of Music and Music Education (SRPMME) for his work on how audiences evaluate memorized performances. In addition to his continued interest in music cognition (particularly memorization and practice), he is currently researching the nature and effects of performance anxiety and how skilled musicians work together when learning and rehearsing compositions.

GLENN D. WILSON is reader in personality at the University of London Institute of Psychiatry and adjunct professor at the University of Nevada, Reno. He is author of some 200 scientific papers and 25 books, including *Psychology for Performing Artists* (Whurr, 2002) and (with Andrew Evans) *Fame: The Psychology of Stardom* (Vision, 1999). He makes frequent radio and TV appearances and has lectured widely abroad, for example, as guest of the Italian Cultural Association and as visiting professor at several U.S. institutions, including Stanford and California State University, Los Angeles. He is also a trained opera singer with an international freelance career.

Author Index

Subject Index

Printed in the USA/Agawam, MA
December 5, 2013

582669.095